Praise for Bettany Hughes's

THE SEVEN WONDERS OF THE ANCIENT WORLD

"This is an entrancing book, at once a love letter to the ancient world and a learned introduction to some of the most astonishing feats of imagination and engineering in human history. It is a pleasure to wander lost realms and inspect (mostly) vanished marvels through Bettany Hughes's bright and erudite writing."
—Dan Jones, author of *Powers and Thrones: A New History of the Middle Ages*

"The beginning of wisdom is wonder, so readers of Bettany Hughes's new book are due to be wondrously wised up as they follow in the footsteps of their Herodotean-style guide from Africa to Asia to Europe, in search of deeper appreciation of some of humanity's greatest creations."
—Paul Cartledge, author of *Thebes: The Forgotten City of Ancient Greece*

"A thrilling armchair journey from a very wise woman. Bettany Hughes is the eighth wonder of the world."
—Lucy Worsley, author of *Jane Austen at Home: A Biography*

"So vividly written that it is as if the reader is there, discovering the Seven Wonders firsthand. The stories behind them are endlessly fascinating, often surprising, and stay in the memory long after the last page has been turned. A dazzling achievement." —Tracy Borman, author of *Thomas Cromwell: The Untold Story of Henry VIII's Most Faithful Servant*

Bettany Hughes

THE SEVEN WONDERS OF
THE ANCIENT WORLD

Bettany Hughes is an award-winning historian, author and broadcaster. Her previous books include *Venus and Aphrodite: A Biography of Desire* (shortlisted for the Runciman Award); *Istanbul: A Tale of Three Cities* (a *Sunday Times* bestseller and shortlisted for the Runciman Award); *The Hemlock Cup: Socrates, Athens and the Search for the Good Life* (a *New York Times* bestseller and shortlisted for the Writers Guild Award); and *Helen of Troy: The Story Behind the Most Beautiful Woman in the World*. All her books have been translated into multiple languages. She has made many documentaries for the BBC, Channel 4, PBS, National Geographic, ABC, and the Discovery and History channels. Hughes has been a Professor at the New College of Humanities and Research Fellow at King's College London. She has been honored with numerous awards, including the Medlicott Medal for History, the EU Prize for Cultural Heritage and an OBE for services to history.

Also by Bettany Hughes

*Helen of Troy: The Story Behind the Most
Beautiful Woman in the World*

*The Hemlock Cup: Socrates, Athens
and the Search for the Good Life*

Istanbul: A Tale of Three Cities

Venus and Aphrodite: A Biography of Desire

THE SEVEN WONDERS OF
THE ANCIENT WORLD

THE SEVEN
WONDERS OF
THE ANCIENT
WORLD

An Extraordinary New Journey
Through History's Greatest Treasures

BETTANY
HUGHES

VINTAGE BOOKS
A DIVISION OF PENGUIN RANDOM HOUSE LLC
NEW YORK

Library of Congress Cataloging-in-Publication Data
Names: Hughes, Bettany, author.
Title: The Seven Wonders of the ancient world : an extraordinary
new journey through history's greatest treasures / Bettany Hughes.
Description: New York : Vintage Books, 2024. | "A Vintage Books original." |
Includes bibliographical references and index.
Identifiers: LCCN 2023057360 (print) | LCCN 2023057361 (ebook) |
Subjects: LCSH: Seven Wonders of the World.
Classification: LCC N5333.H84 2024 (print) | LCC N5333 (ebook) |
DDC 709.01—dc23/eng/20231215
LC record available at https://lccn.loc.gov/2023057360
LC ebook record available at https://lccn.loc.gov/2023057361

Vintage Paperback ISBN: 978-0-593-68615-7
eBook ISBN: 978-509-368616-4

In loving memory of my father, Peter, who showed me the value of wonder, and who died the day I entered Khufu's pyramid-tomb.

And of my mother, Erica, who passed one night while I was in Illyria's mountains searching for Artemis and so who never knew this book was completed, but who taught me never, ever to stop wondering.

You were my guiding lights. I miss you both terribly. My journeys are in honour of you.

CONTENTS

✦

For beauty, like the sun, makes it impossible to see other things when it is itself radiant.

PHILO OF BYZANTIUM, *ON THE SEVEN WONDERS OF THE WORLD*,
ALMOST CERTAINLY WRITTEN IN ALEXANDRIA,
EGYPT, SECOND CENTURY BCE

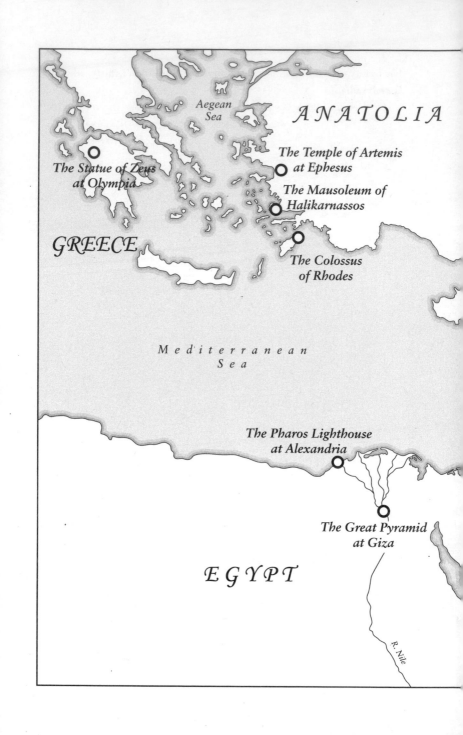

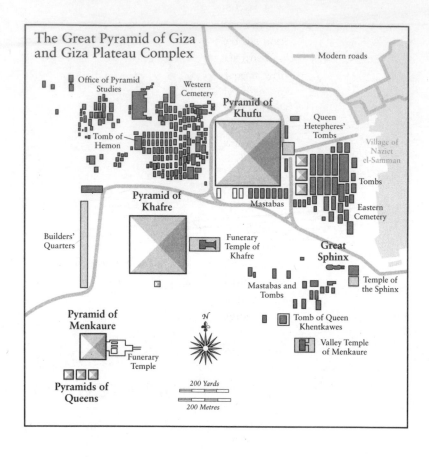

The Great Pyramid of Giza and Giza Plateau Complex

Modern roads

Office of Pyramid Studies

Western Cemetery

Pyramid of Khufu

Queen Hetepheres' Tombs

Village of Naziet el-Samman

Tomb of Hemon

Tombs

Pyramid of Khafre

Eastern Cemetery

Mastabas

Builders' Quarters

Funerary Temple of Khafre

Great Sphinx

Temple of the Sphinx

Mastabas and Tombs

Pyramid of Menkaure

N

Tomb of Queen Khentkawes

Funerary Temple

Valley Temple of Menkaure

Pyramids of Queens

200 Yards

200 Metres

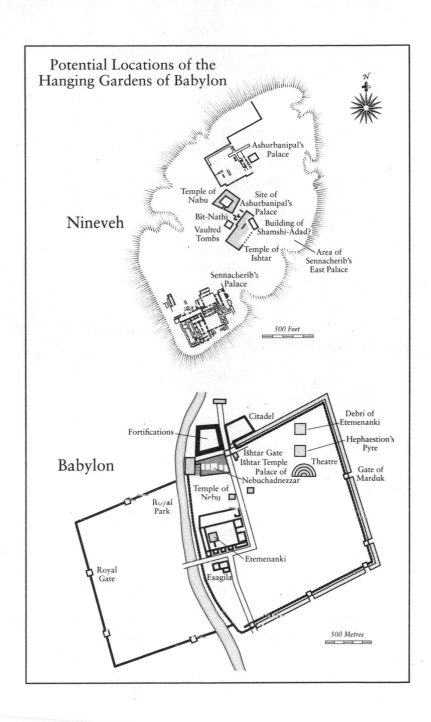

Potential Locations of the Hanging Gardens of Babylon

N

Nineveh

Ashurbanipal's Palace

Temple of Nabu

Site of Ashurbanipal's Palace

Bit-Nathi

Building of Shamshi-Adad?

Vaulted Tombs

Temple of Ishtar

Area of Sennacherib's East Palace

Sennacherib's Palace

500 Feet

Babylon

Citadel

Fortifications

Debri of Etemenanki

Hephaestion's Pyre

Ishtar Gate

Ishtar Temple

Palace of Nebuchadnezzar

Theatre

Gate of Marduk

Temple of Nebu

Royal Park

Etemenanki

Royal Gate

Esagila

500 Metres

The Temple of Artemis at Ephesus

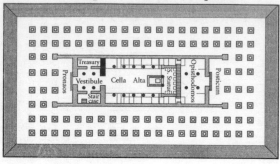

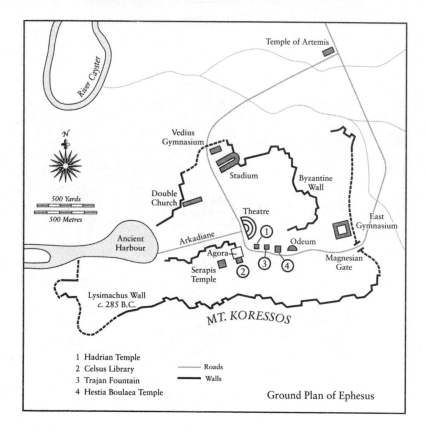

Ground Plan of Ephesus

The Statue of Zeus at Olympia

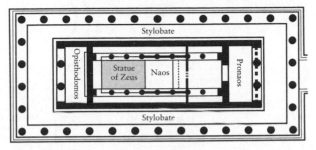

Stylobate

Opisthodomos

Statue of Zeus

Naos

Pronaos

Stylobate

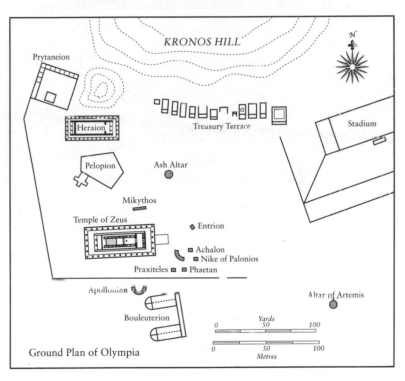

KRONOS HILL

Prytaneion

N

Heraion

Treasury Terrace

Stadium

Pelopion

Ash Altar

Mikythos

Temple of Zeus

Entrion

Achalon

Nike of Palonios

Praxiteles

Phaetan

Apollonion

Altar of Artemis

Bouleuterion

Yards
0   50   100

0   50   100
Metres

Ground Plan of Olympia

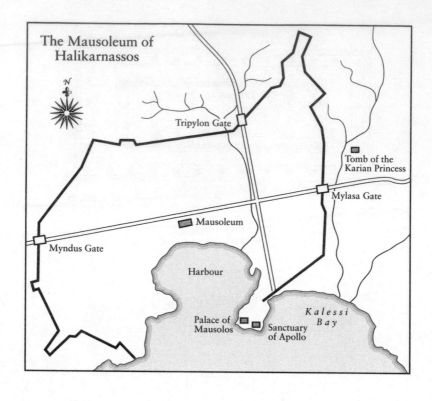

The Mausoleum of Halikarnassos

Tripylon Gate

Tomb of the Karian Princess

Mylasa Gate

Mausoleum

Myndus Gate

Harbour

Kalessi Bay

Palace of Mausolos

Sanctuary of Apollo

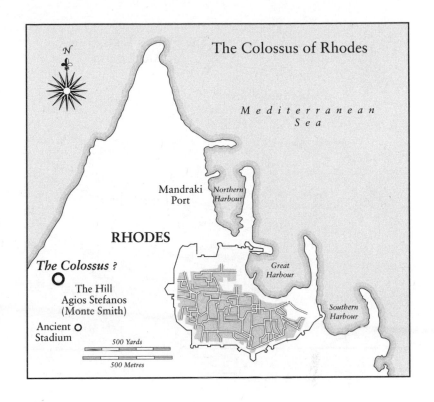

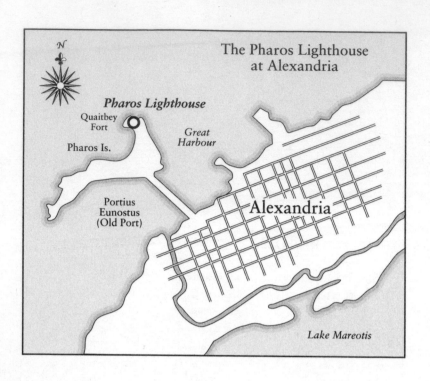

The Pharos Lighthouse
at Alexandria

N

Pharos Lighthouse

Quaitbey
Fort

Pharos Is.

*Great
Harbour*

Portius
Eunostus
(Old Port)

Alexandria

Lake Mareotis

LIST OF ILLUSTRATIONS

❖

PLATE SECTION CREDITS

✦

4 The Statue of Zeus at Olympia imagined by A.-C. Quatremère de Quincy in
      1814 (*History and Art Collection / Alamy Stock Photo*).

   A panorama view of the archaeological site of Olympia in Greece (*Pavel
      Dudek / Alamy Stock Photo*).

5 One of the many imagined representations of the Mausoleum of
      Halikarnassos, crucially missing the brightly coloured paint we know
      decorated the marble (*DeAgostini / Getty Images*).

   A lion statue and horse's head from the Mausoleum at Halikarnassos, c. 350
      BCE, both currently in the British Museum. (Horse: *Art Media/Print
      Collector / Getty Images;* Lion: *Universal Images / Getty Images*).

   Mausolos' name carved in stone at Labraunda, photo taken by the author.

6 'Dutch Ships Entering the Port of the Island of Rhodes', c. 1818/30 by Japanese
      artist Utagawa Kunitora (*Heritage Images / Getty Images*).

   One of the men thought to be responsible for the design of the Colossus was
      Chares of Lindos, himself a student of the renowned sculptor Lysippus.
      A number of works by Lysippus survive, including this statue of an
      Hellenistic hero in bronze (*Shutterstock.com*).

   The Colossus of Rhodes, 1760, imagined by an unknown artist (*Heritage
      Images / Getty Images*).

7 A 3D rendering of the Pharos Lighthouse at Alexandria (*Shutterstock.com*).

   The female Pharaoh Hatshepsut's Punt expedition – to collect precious
      minerals and trees – on the walls of her funerary temple at Deir-el-Bahri
      (*Mauricio Abreu / Alamy Stock Photo*).

8 Two of the stained-glass panels commissioned for the Empire State Building
      in New York and installed in the north lobby in 1963 – the Great
      Pyramid and the Hanging Gardens of Babylon (*Keith Stanley*).

   Modern 3D reproductions of all Seven Wonders supplied by the press
      department of Australian Insurance company Budget Direct (*Image
      courtesy of Budget Direct Insurance*).

TIMELINE

✤

All dates up until 700 BCE are accurate approximations.

BCE

3100 Egyptian royalty are buried at a site in Abydos.

2800 Egyptian royal burial grounds are moved to Saqqara.

2589–2566 reign of King Khufu. (Alternative new dates 2633–2605.)

2580–2540 the Great Pyramid at Giza (Khufu's Pyramid) is built.

2520 Khafre's Pyramid is built at Giza.

2490 Menkaure's Pyramid is built at Giza.

2120 waning of the religious cult of Khufu as Great King.

2000 eunuchs become part of Assyrian culture.

1700 stories are first told about the Great Walls of Babylon

1680–1120 Hittites rule over modern-day Turkey, Northern Iran and Iraq.

1600 enormous heron-like creatures become extinct in Egypt.

1500 Egyptian rulers begin to be called 'Pharaoh'.

1300 eunuchs in Assyria begin to hold positions of high status.

1250 Bronze Age mansion in Kydonia in Crete felled by earthquake.

900 Hekate is simultaneously worshipped with Artemis at the Sanctuary at Ephesus.

900–800 walnuts and olives appear in the Peloponnese.

900–500 Iron Age Greece.

776 first Olympic Games; Zeus is worshipped at Olympia.

732–626 Neo-Assyrian Empire rules Babylon.

722 Chaldean dynast Marduk-apla-iddina II seizes Babylon from the Assyrian king Shalmaneser V.

710 Neo-Assyrian King Sargon II reconquers Babylonia from the Chaldeans.

705–703 first reign of Assyrian King Sennacherib.

703 Chaldean dynast Marduk-zakir-shumi II incites revolts among the Elamites and Babylonians, overthrowing Sennacherib's rule in South Babylonia.

Chaldean dynast Marduk-apla-iddina II deposes Marduk-zakir-shumi II.

Sennacherib marches on Babylon to defeat the rebels. Babylon surrenders. As a mark of victory, Sennacherib appoints Bel-ibni as his vassal king in Babylon.

700 archaic Temple of Artemis at Ephesus is built.

The Sanctuary of Zeus at Olympia experiences growth as people donate personal items, and temporary wells are sunk to provide water for pilgrims and visitors to the Olympic Games.

Sennacherib deposes Bel-ibni and appoints his son Ashur-nadin-shumi as vassal king of Babylon.

694 description of the palace and gardens of Babylon written on the prism cylinder of Sennacherib.

Sennacherib's son Ashur-nadin-shumi is captured and executed by Elamites.

The Babylonian Nergal-ushezib is installed as king by the Babylonians.

693–689 Chaldean dynast Mushezib-Marduk rules Babylon.

690–550 the Hanging Gardens of Babylon are probably created and adapted.

689 King Sennacherib attacks and destroys Babylon, partly as revenge for the death of his son, partly as punishment for many years of rebellions.

689–681 second reign of Sennacherib in Babylonia.

681–669 rule of Esarhaddon.

669 the walls of Babylon are described as a Wonder by the Assyrian King Ashurbanipal.

668–648 Ashurbanipal appoints vassal king Shamash-shum-ukin to reign in Babylon.

648–646 Second reign of Ashurbanipal, following a retaking of Babylon.

653 King Tennemu is defeated in the battle of Ulai.

626 Babylonian rebel Nabopolassar defeats the Neo-Assyrian king Sinsharishkun, beginning the rule of a Neo-Babylonian dynasty in Babylonia.

612 Nineveh is attacked by a combined force of Babylonians, Medes and other allies.

609 Nebuchadnezzar I participates in the campaign to decisively defeat the Assyrians, winning out against Ashur-uballit at Harran.

605–562 reign of King Nebuchadnezzar II.

605 King Nebuchadnezzar II triumphs at the Battle of Carchemish.

604–562 according to Berossus, the Hanging Gardens are commissioned by Babylonian King Nebuchadnezzar II for his wife Amytis.

597 Nebuchadnezzar II brings the King of Judah and other Jewish prisoners to Babylon.

593 Ancient Greek graffiti scrawled on the statue of Pharaoh Ramesses II at Abu Simbel.

586 Nebuchadnezzar II deports the entire Jewish population to Babylon.

585 King Croesus attacks Ephesus.

585–546 reign of King Croesus.

580–570 building of a new version of the Temple of Artemis at Ephesus commences.

557 King Servius Tullius builds a temple to Diana in Rome, based on the Wonder at Ephesus.

550 the archaic temple of Artemis at Ephesus is largely completed.

539 Babylon is taken by Persian forces.

530 Zeus widely recognised as patriarch of the Olympian pantheon.

500–450 Persian Wars between Greeks and Persians.

500–400 'Golden Age' of Athens; development of Athenian democracy.

474 Pindar composes Olympic Ode 10, featuring the word 'idea'.

471–456 building of the Temple of Zeus at Olympia.

463 *The Suppliant Women* by Aeschylus is performed at the Dionysia in Athens.

456 the Temple of Zeus at Olympia is completed.

449 peace treaty between Athenians and Persians.

447 building of the Parthenon begins.

438 Athens dedicates the statue of Athena by Pheidias on the Acropolis.

438–430 construction of the Statue of Zeus at Olympia.

436 eighty-sixth Olympiad.

432 the Parthenon is completed in Athens; Pheidias returns to Athens.

431–404 the Peloponnesian War.

430 the Statue of Zeus at Olympia is completed.
The classical Temple of Artemis at Ephesus is completed.

430–428 plague in Athens.

425 Herodotus' *Histories* completed

420 birth of Karian King Hekatomnos; Sparta attacks the city of Lepreum during the Olympics.

416 Alcibiades triumphs in the chariot race at the Olympic Games.

408 the city of Rhodes is established.

400 Xenophon visits Babylon.
The female artist Timarete paints a panel of the statue of Artemis at Ephesus.
Thucydides' *History of the Peloponnesian War* completed.

377 Mausolos comes to the throne in Karia.
The Second Athenian League is founded, with Rhodes as a founding member.

377–353 reign of Karian King Mausolos.

370 Mausolos relocates his capital from Mylasa to Halikarnassos.

361–351 the Mausoleum of Halikarnassos is built.

360 Mausolos takes Lycian territory along the coast of modern-day Turkey.

356 20–21 July, Alexander the Great is born. Herostratus burns down the Temple of Artemis at Ephesus.

353 Mausolos dies.

351 the Mausoleum of Halikarnassos is completed; Artemisia, wife of Mausolos, dies and is buried in the Mausoleum alongside her husband.

340 the new Temple of Artemis at Ephesus is under construction.
Persian ambassadors visit the court of Philip II of Macedon in Pella.

338 Battle of Chaeronea; Chryselephantine statue of Alexander the Great is placed in the sanctuary at Olympia.

336–323 reign of Alexander the Great; conquest of land as far as India.

335 Alexander the Great dismantles the ziggurat temple tower in Babylon.

334 Alexander the Great comes to Ephesus, claiming that he should be named as a benefactor of the new Temple of Artemis.

Alexander the Great visits Karia and the Mausoleum of Halikarnassos.

332 Rhodes surrenders to Alexander the Great with a delegation of ten ships at Tyre.

331 7 April, Alexandria in North Egypt is officially founded.

323 11 June, death of Alexander the Great in Babylon.

Reconstruction of the Temple of Artemis at Ephesus begins.

310 Antigonid Prince Demetrius Poliorcetes, later Demetrius I, invades and ravages Babylon.

306 Rome begins to show political and military interest in the Hellenic world.

305–304 siege of Rhodes by Antigonus I and Demetrius Poliorcetes.

304 weapons are sold which later finance the building of the Colossus of Rhodes.

297 construction of the Pharos Lighthouse at Alexandria begins.

297-282 building of the Pharos Lighthouse at Alexandria.

292 the Colossus of Rhodes is raised.

290 Berossus claims the Hanging Gardens of Babylon exist within Babylon's palace walls.

283–246 reign of Ptolemy II over Alexandria and the kingdom of Egypt.

283–282 Eusebius, Bishop of Caesarea, claims that the construction of the Pharos Lighthouse begins.

280 construction of the Colossus of Rhodes is completed.

The Library of Alexandria is founded.

250 Callimachus composes his *Aetia* in Alexandria.

228 Rhodes devastated by earthquake; the Colossus is destroyed.

200 Rhodes is allied to the Romans.

167 Antiochus IV sacks the Temple of Solomon in Jerusalem, renaming it as the Temple of Olympian Zeus, and erects a statue of Zeus. Rhodes distances itself from Rome. Rome retaliates and makes Delos a free port as punishment.

150 the *Laterculi Alexandrini* Seven Wonders list is compiled, almost certainly in Alexandria.

146 sack of Corinth by Lucius Mummius bringing Greece under Roman rule; Mummius places war spoils on the walls of the Temple of Zeus at Olympia.

140–100 Antipater of Sidon composes a Wonders poem in Rome.

133–129 Ephesus is incorporated into the Roman province of Asia and becomes the capital.

84 Ephesus is deprived of its freedom.

71 Lucullus reports *venationes* (fights between humans and animals) taking place in Ephesus.

60 Diodorus Siculus composes his *Bibliotheca Historica*.

48–47 the Alexandrian War; fire set by Caesar's troops destroys the Library of Alexandria.

46 Cleopatra VII's half-sister Arsinoe is paraded in Rome as a captive in Caesar's triumph.

42 Cleopatra VII's half-sister Arsinoe shelters in Ephesus, having been banished there by Cleopatra.

41 Mark Antony arrives in Ephesus dressed as Dionysos-Bacchus.

33–32 Cleopatra and Antony winter in Ephesus.

30 death of Ptolemaic Pharaoh Cleopatra VII in Alexandria. Rome conquers Alexandria.

29 Strabo witnesses the rites of Artemis at Ephesus

25 Strabo comes to Alexandria.

CE

1 a Greek named Antipater, serving L. Calpurnius Piso, writes an eyewitness account of the Seven Wonders.

23 sections of the Temple of Artemis are destroyed by an earthquake.

41 Emperor Caligula orders the head of Zeus at Olympia to be replaced by his own. Caligula is assassinated.

50 Zenodorus' giant statue of Mercury is built.

52 Paul the apostle comes to Ephesus.

55 Paul visits to Ephesus for the second time.

67 Emperor Nero competes in the Olympic Games.

68 Nero commits suicide.

75 Nero's Colossus is erected; it is then re-styled as a sculpture of the sun god, as Nero himself has been disgraced.

79 Tiberius Claudius Balbillus is honoured at Ephesus with the Balbillean Games.
Eruption of Mount Vesuvius in the Bay of Naples, which kills Pliny the Elder.

81–96 reign of Domitian.

95 John the apostle returns to Ephesus, dies and is buried overlooking the Temple of Artemis.

96–8 reign of the Roman Emperor Nerva.

104 Rites of Artemis start to become more complex, attracting more pilgrims to Ephesus.

112–13 the historian Tacitus is governor of the province of Asia.

120 the Library of Celsus at Ephesus is completed and opens to the public.

126–8 Emperor Hadrian moves the Sol-Colossus statue to his own temple just outside the Flavian amphitheatre, subsequently called The Colosseum.

153 Anatolian Peregrinus Proteus attacks the popular philanthropist Herodes Atticus and has to take sanctuary from an angry mob in the Temple of Zeus at Olympia.

160 Pausanias writes his *Guidebook to Greece*.

162 the Romans extend Artemis's festival in Ephesus as recompense for the affront of a Roman doing business on her holy days.

190 First Council of Ephesus.

192 end of reign of Roman Emperor Commodus.

200 oldest surviving complete Greek musical inscription at Aydin, near Ephesus, belonging to Seikilos is created.

250 Roman Emperor Decius initiates a period of persecution of Christians.

262 a second fire at the Temple of Artemis at Ephesus, caused by an earthquake shaking the roof beams, which fall onto altar fires.

267 the Heruli tribes from North Germany invade Olympia, turning the Temple of Zeus into a fortress.

272 the Roman Emperor Aurelian sets fire to the quarter of Alexandria where the remnants of the Library of Alexandria remain.

280 an earthquake damages the Temple of Zeus at Olympia.

300 Christian author Epiphanius of Salamis writes about the Pharos Lighthouse.

320 a series of earthquakes shake the Pharos Lighthouse.

393 the Olympic Games are banned by the Christian East Roman Emperor Theodosius I.

394 last description of Rome's Colossus as standing.

401 end of Artemis's cult in the ruins of the Artemision at Ephesus. Emperor Constantius II orders an empire-wide removal of all pagan statues. Demeas pulls down the statue of Artemis in Ephesus' town centre.

420 Statue of Olympian Zeus displayed next to a water cistern in Constantinople.

424 Theodosius II orders the vandalisation of the Sanctuary of Zeus at Olympia.

426 fire in the settlement of Olympia.

431 Second Council of Ephesus takes place.

435–51 the Temple of Zeus at Olympia is converted into a Byzantine church.

449 Third Council of Ephesus takes place.

475/6 fire at the Palace of Lausos in Constantinople.
Statue of Olympian Zeus destroyed by fire.

531 images of the Pharos Lighthouse appear on the mosaics of the Church of St John the Baptist in Jerash, Jordan.

532 series of riots and fires in Constantinople.

535–50 images of the Pharos Lighthouse appear on the mosaics of the Church of Saints Peter and Paul in Jerash, Jordan.

539 local mosaic-makers add the lighthouse into a panel of fifty images in a church built by Bishop Makarios in the Calansho Desert in Central Libya.

551 the Temple of Zeus at Olympia is destroyed by a violent tsunami.

614 earthquake and Sassanian attack destroy the Temple of Artemis.

646 Arabs arrive in Alexandria.

653 the remnants of the Colossus of Rhodes are reportedly sold off by a Jewish scrap-metal merchant.

700 the first recorded Western tourist, the Anglo-Saxon daredevil Willibald, visits Ephesus.
The Nomos Rhodion Nautikos is developed in Constantinople.

832 Abbasid Caliph al-Ma'mun forces an entrance to Khufu's Pyramid.

944 Al-Masudi describes 'jewels' on the seabed around the Pharos as 'thrown in by Alexander the Great'.

956 earthquake shakes the Pharos Lighthouse.

1110–17 Abu Hamid al-Gharnati visits Alexandria.

1154 Al-Idrisi visits Alexandria.

1166 el-Balawi explores the Pharos.

1200 St Mark's Basilica in Venice includes the Pharos on the ceiling of Zeno's Chapel.

1204 sack of Constantinople in Fourth Crusade by Western forces.

1244 Ephesus' harbour is silted up.

1303 8 August, earthquake in the Eastern Mediterranean destroys the Pharos Lighthouse at Alexandria and loosens the stones of the Great Pyramid at Giza.

1311 spire of Lincoln Cathedral raised in England.

1326 Abu Abd Allah Mohammed Ibn Battuta visits the Pharos and reportedly is still able to reach its main door.

1394–5 Niccolo di Martoni fancifully describes the Colossus of Rhodes straddling the harbour entrance.

1400 the Mausoleum of Halikarnassos is largely in ruins after a series of earthquakes.

1402 Crusader knights from Rhodes arrive in Halikarnassos to begin the construction of St Peter's Castle on the site of Mausolos's palace.

1437 completion of the walls of St Peter's Castle using materials from the Mausoleum of Halikarnassos.

1477 Qait Bey builds a stocky fortress on the footprint of the Pharos, Alexandria.

1494–1522 stones from the ruins of the Mausoleum of Halikarnassos are used to strengthen Bodrum Castle against Ottoman attack.

1522 Bodrum Castle is surrendered; Commandeur de la Tourette visits the Mausoleum site.

1624 England's Earl of Arundel sends Revd William Petty on a mission to seize antiquities from Asia Minor, especially from Ephesus.

1639 John Greaves completes the first systematic survey of the Great Pyramid by a European.

1699 Colley Cibber writes about Herostratus setting fire to the Temple of Artemis.

1748–9 Earl James Caulfield has drawings made of the Amazonomachy reliefs taken from the Mausoleum of Halikarnassos in St Peter's Castle.

1765 Nathaniel Davison crawls up inside Khufu's Pyramid to the stone attic above the King's chamber.

1766 site of Olympia re-discovered.

1818 Percy Bysshe Shelley publishes his poem 'Ozymandias'.

1820 Giovanni Battista Caviglia excavates in Khufu's Pyramid, firing the European trend of pyramid exploration.

1830 Temple of Zeus at Olympia re-discovered.

1830–57 Muhammad Ali Pasha's Alabaster Mosque is built in Cairo, using blocks of casing stone from the Great Pyramid.

1840 the Temple of Artemis at Ephesus is excavated.

1844 Sir Stratford Canning sets up excavation scheme in Bodrum.

1858 the first photographic coffee-table book about Egypt is produced.

1863–75 John Turtle Wood begins to excavate on the site of the Temple of Artemis.

1877 Wood publishes *Discoveries in Ephesos*. Sections of the Mausoleum of Halikarnassos are shipped out to Britain.

1885–1909 sustained removal of sculpted stone from the Temple of Artemis to Europe.

1886 the Statue of Liberty is unveiled.

1935 Hitler's architect Speer uses the Seven Wonders as architectural inspiration.

1958 Pheidias' workshop is identified at the site of Olympia.

1961 The *Colossus of Rhodes* film is released.

1994 Excavations underwater on the seabed below the Pharos Lighthouse take place.

2007 fire at the site of Olympia.

2013 discovery of over 1,000 papyri fragments in a man-made cave at Wadi al Jarf.

2019 archaeological excavation of the tomb Mausolos built for his father Hekatomnos.

2020–22 Covid 19 global pandemic halts archaeological excavations in Giza and Alexandria in Egypt, in Babylon and Nineveh in Iraq, in Ephesus and Bodrum in Turkey, and in Olympia and Rhodes in Greece. The fascination with Wonders sites continues.

PREFACE

✢

Wunder – Old English
'a marvellous thing, miracle, object of astonishment'

In 1303 CE a monstrous earthquake ripped through the Eastern Mediterranean. The trauma shook glittering casing stones loose from the Great Pyramid at Giza in Egypt – the most ancient of our Seven Wonders – and brought the remains of the youngest, the towering Pharos Lighthouse of Alexandria, crashing to the ground.[1] The Great Pyramid embodied enormous effort for the sake of one, virtually omnipotent man. Alexandria's Pharos Lighthouse had been a public beacon to keep travellers from four continents safe, and to announce a repository of all the knowledge that was possible for humankind to know. But across that complex arc of experience, spanning nearly 4,000 years, from the vision of a single, almighty human to a network of human minds, no human-made Wonder could prove a match for the might of Mother Earth.

The Seven Wonders of the Ancient World were staggeringly audacious impositions on our planet. Incarnations of the beautiful, mournful, axiomatic truth of our species that we are compelled to make the world in our image and to modify it to our will. They were also brilliant adventures of the mind, test cases of the reaches of human imagination. This book walks through the landscapes of both ancient and modern time; a journey whose purpose is to ask why we wonder, why we create, why we choose to remember the wonder of others. I have travelled as the ancients did across continents to explore traces of the Wonders themselves, and the traces they have left in history. My aim has been to discover what the

Seven Wonders of the ancient world meant to 'them' – to our relatives across time – and what they do and can mean to us.

The word *wonder* is pliable: wonder is both a phenomenon and a process. Wonders are potent because wondering helps us to realise that the world is bigger than ourselves. The wonderful generates interest, and frequently empathy, and that interest and empathy nourishes connection. We process and internalise these connections. Intellectually and emotionally, via the physical process of thought, we realise we are, truly, one world. So we seek wonders – natural, man-made, philosophical, scientific, whether they are near or far – as a socialising act.

How then do we collectively decide what is wonderful?

One time-honoured way is to create Wonder-lists. There have been many wonders at many times. There are wonders of the ancient, the modern, the engineered and the natural worlds. At the last count, seventy monuments have been officially claimed as catalogued wonders of history.[2] There is now a vogue for the nationalism of wonders – the Seven Wonders of Everywhere, from Azerbaijan to Zimbabwe, from Canada to Colombia. Spiritual too, the Seven Wonders of the Buddhist, Islamic, Hindu and Christian faiths have all been eagerly gathered together.[3]

But there was one international wonder-selection which seems to have formed a blueprint for all others. The discovery, and indeed survival, of this fragmentary alpha-to-omega inventory is close to miraculous. Compiled in the second century BCE, the earliest extant recording of a Seven Wonders of the World compendium was found on a scrap of papyrus used to wrap an ancient Egyptian mummified body. This mummification wrapping – cartonnage – was itself discovered in an excavation at Abusir el-Melek in Central Egypt. Close to modern-day Beni Suef, Abusir el-Melek is a Nile river-city which was once an ancient capital of Upper Egypt, and which has endured as a stolid commercial centre, manufacturing linen and carpets. If one sails down the Nile today, the flourishing settlement announces its presence via a cement factory. From afar, clouds of cement-dust, somewhat ironically, reveal the Nile waters and desert all around with the appearance of a romantic late-eighteenth-century watercolour.

The ancient city, called se Hut nen nesut by the Egyptians (known as Hnes in Coptic, and renamed Heracleopolis Magna by Greeks and Romans), enjoyed its own prosperity – a place that was rich in both lives and afterlives. The many burials on the Nile's sandbank-shores here privileged a cult of the Ancient Egyptian god of life and death, of fertility and immortality – the god named Osiris. The hero-gods Herishef ('Ruler of the Riverbanks') and Herysfyt ('He who is over strength') were also adored here – the latter a figure associated by Egypt's Greek rulers of the Hellenistic Age with their own hero Herakles.[4] And wrapping up one of the thousands of entombed humans found at Abusir el-Malek, in the form of mummification material, inked onto flat-reed paper – was that earliest, extant Wonder-list. Now known as the Berlin Papyrus 13044, the *Laterculi Alexandrini* was created 2,200 years ago.[5]

The *Laterculi Alexandrini* (the name *laterculus* was used from late antiquity onwards to denote an inscribed tablet or a stone publishing information in a list or calendar form) is a fragmentary list of many lists – not just of the Seven Wonders of the World, but a cornucopia of sevens: the seven most important islands, the seven most beautiful rivers, the seven highest mountains, the seven best artists (the catalogue continues) – a kind of vital, ancient *Who's Who,* if you like, or antiquity's Buzzfeed.[6]

Almost certainly written in the city of Alexandria, the *Laterculi Alexandrini* papyrus comes from a time and place with immense confidence. The warrior-king Alexander the Great, the ultimate coloniser who rose up from Macedonia to seize lands from Egypt to India (desiring an empire that stretched further – from the edge of the Atlantic to China) had prematurely died while effecting his world takeover, and his vast territories were being divvied up by his generals – once loyal, but now bickering amongst themselves.[7]

The original Seven Wonders list was therefore a product of the Hellenistic Age, that baggy epoch spanning the death of Alexander the Great (Alexander III of Macedon) in 323 BCE and the death of Cleopatra of Egypt (Cleopatra VII of the Ptolemies) in Alexandria itself in 30 BCE. This was a time when Greek culture had seeped around the edges of the world, and was also being actively forced upon it. So we find prototypes of the palaces, temples and tombs from Alexander's birthplace at Pella in Northern Greece also turning up in exact, mathematical replicas from Sudan in Africa to Sogdia (an ancient civilisation ranging across modern-day Uzbekistan, Turkmenistan, Tajikistan, Kazakhstan and Kyrgyzstan).[8] The great Buddhist kings of what is now Nepal and Northern India, such as Aśoka, left inscriptions of Buddhist philosophy outside towns like

Kandahar (named for Alexander) in modern-day Afghanistan, in a Greek script and language.[9] Homer was quoted in Pakistan, and the tragedies of Sophocles, Aeschylus and Euripides played to audiences in Susa in modern-day Iran, on the shores of the Caspian Sea and in Babylon – close to Baghdad, in what is now Iraq.[10]

Alexander the Great, responsible for this fervour for Hellenic culture, thought nothing was impossible. His famed exclamation, 'The world is not enough!' only goes part of the way to encapsulate his appetite and his drive.[11] Insisting on literary, athletic and cultural contests wherever he went, carrying a copy of Homer's *Iliad* annotated by Aristotle,[12] one of his inspirations was the legendary hero Perseus (a mythological character claimed by Alexander's family as an ancestor), whose life-story taught that our greatest fear is of fear itself.[13] In a remarkable Hellenistic tomb at Derveni in Northern Greece, uncovered by accident during modern-day road-widening, a coin minted by Alexander has been unearthed with an image of Herakles' club on one side and the goddess of wisdom, Athena, on the other.[14] Alexander saturated his campaigns with a kind of pugilistic optimism and belief in the power of the pen and the sword. The Hellenistic world followed suit, sponsoring a worldview that was at once aggressive and aspirational, appetitive and erudite. Belief in astrology – that pseudo-science which could allow all things to be a possibility – escalated,[15] and the worship of the goddess of Tyche – Good Fortune – was fostered in the majority of Hellenistic cities.[16] Travel through many sites of the Hellenistic Age, from King Antiochus I's tomb-burial on the top of Mount Nemrut in Eastern Turkey to incense-trading cities in Oman, and you find stubborn, weathered representations of Tyche, the good luck goddess.

Just as neuroscientists now tell us we invent our memories to match a narrative of ourselves, so Hellenistic mythmakers re-wrote global history to match their self-belief (declaring, for example, that Buddha was in fact a descendant of a Greek soldier who invaded India with the god of wine and ecstasy, Bacchus-Dionysos – a deity whose trail Alexander the Great would endeavour to follow).[17] The Hellenistic Age gaslit contemporaries and future generations into experiencing the world through an Hellenic lens. It is an influence to be both feared and admired.

Alexander gave his name to at least fifty cities across Asia, Africa and Europe. Scholars and scientists in Alexandria invented extraordinary things: the first known steam-engine, the first computer, geometry, longitude and latitude – a calculation that divided the earth into the climate zones we still use today, as well as a means to accurately measure the circumference of the earth.[18] And in the other Alexandrias around the world they took note, took interest, and took their cue to explore and draw inspiration from the wonders of the world that felt relevant and cogent. The Seven Wonders concept reinforced an exciting, and nourishing, notion that humans could make the impossible happen.

The *Laterculi Alexandrini* opens with an imagined conversation between Alexander the Great and the *gumnosophists* – literally, the naked-sapience-speakers – of the Indian sub-continent about the nature of rule. Surely referring to the Sadu, to Brahmin peripatetics, and to the Buddhist monks of Bactria (men described as being vegetarian and living naked), these *gumnosophists* from the East were considered by the Hellenistic world to be primordial wisdom-makers, men who understood the broadest possible sweep of human experience (and who, interestingly, advised Alexander the Great that the most powerful man on earth is the man whose power is not feared).[19] The Greek biographer Plutarch also tells us that Alexander met these wise men, the exacting ruler being counselled, 'hard questions have hard answers'.[20] Their presence at the top of this fragmentary list of our ancient Wonders is significant: the Seven Wonders compilation was a catalogue not just of arcane or passing interest, it was being flagged as an exercise in understanding.

The Seven Wonders list was therefore conceived as an interrogation of the nature of power, and as an advertorial, a boastful guidebook to the 'known world' – that is, the world known, and colonised, by the Hellenistic Greeks and their allies. All the Wonders had connections one to the other, and all the locations could be physically visited, with relative ease. The Seven Wonders of the Ancient World – a list which varies but is most typically the Great Pyramids at Giza, the Hanging Gardens of Babylon, the Statue of Zeus at Olympia, the Temple of Artemis at Ephesus, the Mausoleum of Halikarnassus, the Colossus of Rhodes, and the Pharos Lighthouse of Alexandria, the majority of which had a direct connection to Alexander the Great and to his family and followers – immortalised a celebration of Hellenism as well as of native inspiration, and the reach of Greek culture in the star-stream wake of Alexander.

So who arbitrated this protean, impactful inventory of seven? Callimachus of Cyrene (born in Libya but also based in Alexandria) compiled
A Collection of Sights in Lands throughout the World at the time that one
Wonder, the Pharos Lighthouse, was being raised, but this work has
been lost to time. The oldest entire seven-strong list that we know of was
almost certainly compiled by a poet born on the bright, wide coastline of
Lebanon, a man called Antipater of Sidon. Antipater travelled to Rome,
and he composed his wonder-verse sometime between 140 and 100 BCE.
The poem features both the walls of Babylon and the Hanging Gardens
of Babylon but ignores the lighthouse at Alexandria. This might seem odd
given that Alexandria was the epicentre of the Hellenistic world and that
the Pharos Lighthouse was such an extraordinary existing construction.
Perhaps, though, the Pharos was just too obvious. The Seven Wonders list
came from the vantage point of the lighthouse – a beam seeking out and
illuminating Wonders that could be reached by a journey. It is almost as
if the Pharos Lighthouse was, as it were, base camp for Wonder quests,
so familiar to authors, many of whom were based in Alexandria, that it
was simply a given.[21]

Other Wonder-list versions followed. Diodorus Siculus, a Greek historian of the first century CE who wrote a vast *History of the World*, added an
obelisk in Babylon to the list.[22] Pseudo-Hyginus, another Roman-period
author, in his *Fabulae* omits the Hanging Gardens of Babylon.[23] The
geographer Strabo, the military leader Josephus, and historian Quintus
Curtius Rufus published their own lists in an age when Roman generals,
from Julius Caesar onwards, had moved into Egyptian and Eastern territories.[24] Rather like the British Empire's scouts or Napoleon's savants,
the Romans were scoping out and aligning themselves with the treasures of territories that they desired to call their own. A slightly shadowy
figure, another Greek called Antipater, in the service of the globe-trotting
Roman senator Lucius Calpurnius Piso, who flourished around the year
1 CE, a hundred years or so after the first Antipater (of Sidon), could quite
possibly be one of the earliest known eyewitnesses to all Seven Wonders:
'I have seen the walls of rock-like Babylon that chariots can run upon,
and the Zeus on the Alpheios; and the Hanging Gardens, and the great
statue (Colossus) of the Sun, and the huge labour of the steep pyramids,
and the mighty tomb of Mausolos . . . I wonder too at the statue of Artemis at Ephesus.'[25] (This second Antipater also neglects to mention the

lighthouse at Alexandria.) In the fifth century CE, in Constantinople, another enigmatic author, the Pseudo-Philon of Byzantium, seems to have written a short travel guide-book on the subject of antiquity's wonderful seven – copies of which made their way to Mount Athos in Greece, and to the Vatican, where one manuscript was stolen by Napoleon's forces, and which has now ended up in the Palatine Library, Heidelberg.* All surviving copies of this text are incomplete, stopping halfway through Chapter Six of seven. A fourteenth-century version of Pseudo-Philon's work has been digitised by the British Library and is freely accessible. The tightly written charcoal-brown ink with carmine additions dashes across the page, emphasising the (rewarding) effort it would take to visit each Wonder within a lifetime, and the power of holding images of these great works of mankind in the mind's eye.[26]

Across time the very Wonder-lists themselves became objects of desire. The Greek word used in many of the original documents for the Wonders was *theamata* – a 'sight', a thing that was 'seen', a 'spectacle'. The word 'theme' in Greek evolved into a site, or a thing that was placed. The notion *theamata* then morphed into something new: *thaumata* – a physical phenomenon that generated amazement and wonder. Wonders were positioned, set down; Wonders were, and still are, things both on earth and in our minds, touchstones in every sense of the word.

And these touchstones ended up as a catalogue, in that Hellenistic culture which was driven by the rational, empirical, taxonomic approach of thinkers such as Aristotle (personal tutor to Alexander the Great).[27] For the inhabitants of Alexandria, the formulation of categorising lists was paramount. Alexandria was the Hellenistic and Roman world's search-engine – and the Seven Wonders were the marvels that those living in the city, or in the wider Eastern Mediterranean, could physically travel out to visit. Indeed, although the great lighthouse of Alexandria first appears in an extant Wonder-list in the fifth century CE (originally in an

---

* The earliest extant manuscript dates to the ninth century CE and clearly carries the author's name at the top: 'Philo of Byzantium'. Now Philo of Byzantium, also known as Philo Mechanicus, was an engineer who lived most of his life in Alexandria in the second century BCE. Whether it was this Hellenistic Philo, or the Pseudo-Philo who lived in the New Rome, Constantinople in the Byzantine Empire, 500-odd years later, who wrote this guidebook to the Seven Wonders is a scholarly bit of detective work still to be convincingly resolved.

anthology of Greek epigrams, it is also described as the 'first' Wonder in and a Christian science text of c. 300 CE, and is then listed in the work of the monk-scholar from Gaul, Gregory of Tours), it is essential to include it here because the Pharos Lighthouse protected the very city that housed the scholars, poets and scientists – supported by a library packed floor to ceiling with papyri – who ensured not only that the story of the world was marked out by its wonders, but that knowledge of them was essential for a fully functioning world.[28]

As I have discovered, though, in the writing of this book, the fundamental truth of the Seven Wonders is more nuanced, more capacious, more about internationalism than pure patriotism. Because the original Seven Wonders are as much about the East as they are about the West, and as much to do with human psychology as with physical triumph. Hellenistic Greeks might have colonised the notion of Wonders in Alexandria in the third or second century BCE (the Greek culture that invented the word-idea *history* was famously adept at writing itself into it*),[29] yet the taxonomy of 'wonders' – especially when grouped together seven at a time – was, in fact, a Middle Eastern tradition. The word in a written script originally used to describe wonders is *tabrati* – a Babylonian notion dating back 5,000 years.[30] We hear of *tabrati* first, and most consistently, applied to the Great Walls of Babylon – those walls that were set to come tumbling down and which appear as one of the Seven Wonders in many ancient lists.[31]

Wonder, in its original application, seems to mean something monumental. Something to fear. The walls of Babylon, for instance, and the ziggurats of Babylonia were wonders because they were, literally, sights to behold, to take the breath away, to intimidate. *Tabrati* is a sight, a thing made to be seen. We still understand the power of raw awe. 'Look on my Works, ye Mighty, and despair', the King of Kings Ozymandias (the Egyptian Pharaoh Ramesses II) is imagined by the poet Shelley to have thundered.[32]

For many cultures in the Middle East, seven was also a number which started and ended all things – there were Seven Heavens, Seven Hells, Seven Gates to Hell (through which the almighty love goddess Inanna

---

* *Historie* is an Ancient Greek word meaning rational enquiry, and the 'Father of History' was the Greek investigative journalist and memorialist Herodotus from Halikarnassos.

proceeded, shedding an item of clothing at each opening – a precursor of Salome's apocryphal dance of the Seven Veils), Seven Ages of Man, Seven Ages of Creation in the Qu'ran.[33]

There were Seven Celestial Bodies and eventually Seven Sages of Greece; the Assyrian word for the world, *kissatu*, equates with seven. The number seven had a natural, symbolic and associative power. Seven was a potent sum because it connected the four elements of the earth (earth, air, fire and water) and the three of the heavens (the sun, the moon and the stars). Seven was magical, it was all that mattered; neither a product nor a factor of the first ten numbers, it was indivisible. Pythagoras, the mathematician from the island of Samos, a short bird-flight away from all but one of our Seven Wonders, named the number seven the Athena – the Virgin. A virgin who has enjoyed many lovers.[34]

The power of seven could be malign as well as benign. In an Akkadian text of the ninth or eighth century BCE – written a hundred years or so before the Hanging Gardens in Babylonia were probably constructed – seven sons of heaven on earth call on Irra, the god of plague, to destroy mankind. Irra, also known as Erra, pulls back just before annihilation, retreating with these seven personified weapons, these terrifying 'peerless champions' – who reappear in other texts and contexts as the evil of disease.[35] The incantations of seven heroic saviours – the Mesopotamian *bit meseri* ritual – were believed to neutralise the maleficent seven.[36] Greek interaction with the East from around this time, as adventuring Greeks pushed towards the rising sun from the eighth century BCE onwards, seems to have brought seven-themed stories into the Greek canon – the Seven Against Thebes, the seven-headed hydra *et al*. So although we might be led to think of the Seven Wonders as emerging from the Hellenistic world, the concept has far deeper Middle Eastern and Asian roots.

Collectively and individually, the impact of the Seven Wonders of the Ancient World was not just the shock and awe that was their original aim, but a yeast for ideas. The very act of connecting disparate expressions of culture gives us hope as a species – it is an act of communion. Listing them is also a political one. Collective intelligence is the hallmark of our species.[37]

Wonders have currency because we can wonder with them. Thinking of them, we can imagine the human effort to create, we witness our strange, sometimes constructive, sometimes destructive, urge to engage with the rest of the world on the front foot. It was the selection of seven that made the subjects of this work and the compilation of those Wonder-lists extra-wonderful, that gave them a quasi-mystical aura; the Wonders themselves were very much accumulations of human wit and will, human endeavour and imagination marked out in cubits and cuts.

So why write this book? Why choose to read it? Perhaps because we are driven to want some select affairs in our shared lives to have significance – what has been called symbolic inheritance – a significance which we pass down in memory and therefore in the molecular.[38] We still feel a connection to these distant Wonders of antiquity, Wonders that range from the Early Bronze Age to the apogee of the Hellenistic experience, partly because our ancestors did too. Let us not forget that fascinating new research demonstrates that each and every one of us is the direct descendant of either a pharaoh who ordered the construction of the pyramids, or a worker who built them.[39] Does this help to explain the allure of the golden ages that raised ancient Wonders, the notion that if we achieved 'greatness' once, we can do so again? Certainly it is curious, if we pause to think about it, that many of us know what at least some of these Wonders are, that we have a sense of them, even if we can only name one or two, out of the many hundreds of thousands of ancient monuments that exist across the earth (UNESCO alone currently has 1,154 World Heritage Sites listed, a tiny fraction of the total created).[40] But we feel a connection to the Seven Wonders because we want to, because our distant ancestors did. We want to follow in the tradition of the many generations who have told themselves (and therefore us) that these places matter. We want to feel that these wonderful works could be connected to us, that somehow, we have taken on the privilege of their guardianship, and therefore of their domains. So from illuminated panels depicting the Seven Ancient Wonders in the lobby of the Empire State Building (installed in the 1960s and removed in 2007) to the Flemish painter Bruegel's vision of Babylon, brushed in oil on ivory and wood; from the decorative schemes of Nero's Golden House in Rome's imperial capital, to references in *Game of Thrones*,[41] generation after generation have felt themselves custodians of the fact and fantasy of these Wonders – real and imagined. Just listen to the great Roman historian Tacitus describing the continuum of guardians at the Temple of Artemis at Ephesus:

The victorious Father of ecstasy, the god Bacchus, pardoned suppliant Amazons who had gathered round Artemis's shrine. Then, with the permission of Hercules, when the hero was subduing Lydia, the temple's grand ceremonies were augmented, and during Persian rule its privileges were not curtailed. After that its rites and customs were maintained by the Macedonians *and finally by ourselves* [i.e. by the might of Rome].[42]

Just as the philosopher asks: if a tree falls in a forest with no one to hear it, does it make a sound? – so for the Wonders: without those willing to wonder, are they nothing? Wonders are the incarnation of a concept that spans at least 5,000 years of the human experience, *KLEWS NDGEWITHOM* – 'immortal fame' – an early Proto-Indo European phrase which becomes *kleos* in ancient Greek and means the value of being talked about, of being remembered. Travelling on the trail of those people, ancient and modern, who sought to see these Wonders with their own eyes or in their minds, and have been inspired, moved or dismayed by this experience, this book attempts not just to catalogue the Seven Wonders, but to comprehend them, to appreciate them as they were first experienced and remembered; to ask why things in general, and these in particular, are wonderful, why they are worthy of wondering.

Rather than pick over these Wonders with the detachment of the clinician, I want to try to imagine them as they would have been seen by their original makers, and by the men (and occasionally women) who travelled thousands of miles to wonder at them, or who devoted whole nights'-worth of precious ink, or breath to describe them, and to pass on their story, keeping the Seven Wonders concept alive. Because these were never husks, they were living monuments with an immediate purpose. It has been a fabulously rewarding experience to research and imagine each in its heyday and to unpick and investigate the close and intriguing connections between them all. It has been a stimulating (if sometimes perilous) adventure to follow the trails of those who have pilgrimaged to each by land and sea, from Roman authors to Arab merchants, from Ottoman officials (at one point all of the Seven Ancient Wonders were contained within the Ottoman Empire) to fervid mediaeval nuns, braving what has been labelled the Dark Ages in order to pay homage to these ancient Wonder attractions.

In that original papyrus list, the *Laterculi Alexandrini*, scratched onto flattened reeds in Alexandria from dried pellets of ink – which recent analysis shows was made with a mixture of soot, ochre, vegetable oil, water, vinegar and gum arabic (dried sap derived from acacia trees often grown in Somalia)[43] – the Temple of Artemis at Ephesus is entered first. In this book I have chosen to list the Wonders chronologically. The creation of each one tells us something salient about history and about a historical moment; its impact speaks of the passage of time, and of the evolution of the human experience. After the Temple of Artemis, the Wonder that then follows is both the oldest, and, counter-intuitively, the only Wonder from the original, ancient seven which still survives pretty much intact. It is, indeed, still a thing of wonderment: it is the family of 4,500-year-old pyramids on the Giza Plateau in Egypt, and in particular, Giza's Great Pyramid.[44]

CHAPTER 1

❖

THE GREAT PYRAMID AT GIZA

c. 2580/2540 BCE

Man fears Time, yet Time fears the pyramids.

TRADITIONAL ARABIC PROVERB[1]

'The Pyramids of Giza' engraving produced by Philips Galle after designs by Maarten van Heemskerck in 1572.

The Great Pyramid is still a wonderful thing. Built over 4,500 years ago, at the height of Egypt's Old Kingdom, it is the only one of the Seven Wonders which survives virtually intact, and is the very summation of our compulsion to design, to create, to construct.[2] Also called Khufu's Pyramid, for its patron King Khufu, this man-made mountain is a statement about human attachment to the beauty of life, to power on earth, and about our relationship to the cosmos both within and beyond our lifetimes. Pyramids – towering, ancient tombs – tell us a great deal about our need to understand the world by telling stories about it. I challenge all who stand at the base of the Great Pyramid not to be amazed and awed.

To experience the land of the Great Pyramid first hand, around 10 million visitors a year travel to Egypt.[3] Waking up to the dusty, dun Giza Plateau, pierced by the Great Pyramid's 2.3 million limestone blocks, raised 480 feet high at the edge of the Western (once the Libyan) desert, the splendid isolation of Akhet Khufu – Khufu's Horizon as it was called by the ancient Egyptians – still fulfils romantic notions (and stereotypes) of ancient might, and of remote Eastern adventures.[4] Together with two other pyramids, one erected for King Khufu's son, Kahfre, another for his grandson Menkaure, along with their gargantuan guardian, the Sphinx, this constellation of monuments in North Africa has attracted tourists and wonder-seekers across four millennia. The Great Pyramid, Khufu's Pyramid, is one of the most famous sites in the world.

But immediately we have to wipe from our mind's eye almost everything we think we know about this oldest Wonder.

First, the pyramids were not a landmark in nothingness. The Giza Plateau was, forty-five centuries ago, a heaving complex. Akhet Khufu and its family of pyramids, temples, shrines and processional highways was Egypt's most vital political and religious expression. Where we see desertion, imagine an abundance of clover and thousands of homes; where there are sands, waterways; where there is emptiness, tens of thousands of workers in loincloths and linen kilts. Where there are now neutral horizons, there was once hectic colour; where piles of collapsed stone, dwarf-pyramids and sloping, mudbrick mastaba tombs. Where desert, gravid green. At night a thousand flames from lamps with linen wicks and castor-oil fuel would have been here, and bonfires of acacia charcoal with their tang and smoke covering the sap-bright planets in a star-saturated sky – a sky, at the beginning of the Bronze Age, only just beginning to be polluted by the drive of civilisation.

The creation of the pyramids, and the Great Pyramid in particular, was a state-busting project, with an intense psychological purpose.[5] Each pyramid was conceived to be a space for the eternal world, a tomb which could act as a resurrection machine – the very mechanism by which the king (the Egyptian ruler only comes to be called Pharaoh from the New Kingdom onwards, around 1500 BCE) could eternally exist to give Egypt sustained and sustainable life.* In some Wonder-lists it is the pyramids plural that are catalogued.[6] Built high on the Giza Plateau across a frenzy of sixty years (Khufu's Pyramid in c. 2550, Khafre's in c. 2520, and Menkaure's in c. 2490 BCE respectively), each giant displays heart-stoppingly perfect geometry.† Yet, as a species, we are compelled by narratives of 'first', and 'greatest' – so it is the Great Pyramid which has proved a word-of-mouth success. It is Khufu's Pyramid, the first and tallest on the Giza Plateau, which dominates history's collective imagination.

Gleaming out, still seeming to touch the sky, originally faced in sparkling, polished limestone slabs, Khufu's Pyramid became legendary before it became history. It turns up in the branding of other Egyptian dynasties – immortalised on a New Kingdom stele (an inscribed stone) discovered in 1937 – and in the literature of the Ancient Greeks, the Romans, the Byzantines, the Arabs and Ottomans.[7] It dominates the accounts of Napoleon's savants in the nineteenth century and of Nazi spies in the twentieth.[8] Weighing in at approximately 6.5 million tonnes, this Wonder is the heaviest structure built on earth. The intimidatingly monstrous Palace of the Parliament in Bucharest, Romania, dragged up by the megalomaniac communist leader Nicolae Ceaușescu – the heaviest modern building, at 4.52 million tonnes – does not get close.[9] When I first saw Ceaușescu's Palace in the aftermath of revolution in 1989, the Leviathan was hated by the ashen Romanians who had built it; the Palace of the Parliament looms as a reminder of obsession and oppression.‡

As with all of our Seven Wonders, we should never forget that the

---

* Ancient Egypt – Upper and Lower Egypt (Upper reaching into what is now Sudan, and Lower, down to the Mediterranean) had been consolidated around 3000 BCE. Much of the Egyptian leaders' energy was designed to maintain Egypt's unity, and the unity of Egypt's people.

† Mass mudbrick building programmes to bury high-net, high-status individuals had begun around 2900 BCE, and stone pyramids appear a hundred years after that; the pyramids on the Giza Plateau were, however, in a class of their own.

‡ It is surely no coincidence that Enver Hoxha, the Communist dictator of Albania who ruled for fifty years, was honoured after his death with the construction of a pyramidical Enver Hoxha Museum to celebrate his legacy. Built in 1988, the Pyramid of Tirana has since been used as a NATO base and, at the time or writing, is being refurbished as a centre for robotics and IT.

Great Pyramid, wildly ambitious, treasure-filled, exquisitely exacting, incarnates both the ecstatic possibilities of wonder, and the stringently harsh demands of making our dreams flesh.

Today, pyramid-pilgrims from scores of nations have the chance to penetrate Khufu's Wonder. From dawn we all race to enter, through a gape in the northern side – almost certainly gouged open by the Abbasid Caliph al-Ma'mun in 832 CE. The grandson of Harun al Rashid of *1001 Arabian Nights* fame, al-Ma'mun used trebuchets and fire to break open a structure whispered to be a repository of gold, and of ancient wisdom.[10] Today there is a febrile atmosphere in the public passageway which the Caliph's men first smashed through. After negotiating what was originally a robber's entry shaft, the sweat and breath of over 5 million visitors every year has already started to dull and darken the Pyramid's red interior, tinted in the Bronze Age with a fleshy ochre wash. Many panic in the close atmosphere. Some pray. Long-suffering local guardians chase out those who try to light candles, or, worse, scratch off flaky mementoes of the monument. But although al-Ma'mun and his colleague the Christian archbishop of Antioch, Dionysius Tell Mahre (Dionysius came from a town near Raqqa in what is now Syria),[11] journeyed here to 'expose the secrets concealed by the pyramids'[12] with a genuine interest in rational enquiry, in fact, the Great Pyramid's intimidating structure was almost certainly designed to represent something that lay beyond reason and rational comprehension.

This Wonder was probably planned to mirror a creation myth, mimicking as it did the great, mystical pyramid of earth (a combination of Egypt's fertile soil and the moistening waters of Nun, the watery chaos that created the River Nile), from which the glorious sun god, Ra or Atum, the father of all life and of all Egyptian kings, was believed to have been generated.[13] The pyramid form could also have been conceived as a solid version of shafts of light (sunlight was thought to be the sun god's sweat)[14] which punch through Egyptian clouds – fingers of God, as we still call them. The sun's rays above Cairo, Africa's largest city, still touch the western desert around Giza as perfect pyramid-shaped shafts at sunset, inverted-pyramid-shafts at dawn – an awe-inspiring feature of the wide, flat landscape. When the pyramids were built, the sun's bright power was honoured as a divine force at Heliopolis ('Sun City', as the Greeks called it), one of Egypt's first cities, now partially submerged

49–66 feet in Matariya under the suburbs of Ain Shams (Eye of the Sun in Arabic) in the Egyptian capital.[15] This Wonder surely had cosmic purpose – built by a people who did not see themselves as distinct from the rest of nature, but as a critical part of a precariously balanced system of the universe, and in particular of the power of the planets.

So to try to understand the truth of the Great Pyramid, as well as thinking about its physical construction, we have to appreciate that in Ancient Egypt the membrane between reality and imagination, between fact and fantasy, between the natural and the supernatural, was porous. For its creators, Khufu's Pyramid was far more than just a wonder of engineering. It was the summation of humankind's journeys of life and death through time and space.

The pyramid design also echoes squat obelisks that turn up in Egyptian legend as perches on which the giant, mythical Bennu birds (often imagined either as an outsize kingfisher or a heron) sat – these obelisks again representing the earth-reaching rays of the sun god Ra.[16] Recent discoveries in the United Arab Emirates of the remains of an enormous, well-beyond-human-size heron, up to 6-and-a-half feet tall, with a wing span of almost 9 feet, which only became extinct in c. 1600 BCE, suggest that this 'mythical' monster actually inhabited the earth at the time the Great Pyramid was being built.[17] Just as birds fly from the peak of their perches into the sky, so the pyramid was thought to be a foundation from which humans could rise to the skies. The Ancient Egyptian word for pyramid is indeed *MER* – a place of ascension.*

And Khufu's Great Pyramid, built to shield and transform the body of King Khufu – his name a shortening of *Khnum-kuefuit/khufu*, 'Khnum protect me' (Khufu's divine protector Khnum was one of the very oldest of all the Ancient Egyptian gods) – was not only a sacred, magic tomb. It was an engine for divine rule; a container for an idea of universal power and possibility unconfined by time, and also an incarnation of the temporal ambition and hubris of men. It was, too, a staggeringly audacious and sophisticated act of construction.

*

---

* *Pyramis* in Ancient Greek means a bun or wheat-cake – a phrase used as an insult. Thus the name 'pyramid' is Greek and means either a confection, or is a Hellenisation of the Egyptian pr-m-wa, 'height of a pyramid'.

The angle of the Great Pyramid's sides, less than 8 inches out of absolute mathematical perfection, and just one twentieth of a degree off true north, is a consistent 54 degrees and 54 minutes – the archetype for all future pyramids.[18] Each of its limestone blocks (recall, well over two million) weighs between 2 and 15 tonnes. At 481 feet high, the memorial of the dead is now missing a 30-foot peak and has lost its glittering capstone. The capacity of its 13.1-acre space is huge – St Paul's Cathedral and Westminster Abbey in London, St Peter's in the Vatican, and the cathedrals of Milan and Florence would each have fitted inside.[19] With sides that are arrow-straight, to date this is still the most accurate stone building ever made.

Symbolically too, the Great Pyramid was saturated with meaning. Its entrance faces north – the domain of the constellation Orion and Sirius where, Egyptians believed, the Great King's journey after death climaxed.[20] The Pyramid's internal burial chambers and one shaft are aligned almost exactly to the circumpolar 'indestructible' stars. Originally protected by a surrounding fortress wall – up to 33 feet high and 33 feet thick at the base[21] – this giant grave was the nuclear fission core within an industrial-scale, sacred power plant. The Giza Plateau is on the western side of the Nile, and its elevation ensures the Pyramid dominates the horizon along with the setting sun (in particular during the summer solstice). The Great Pyramid was a wonder in a time and a place where a kind of material mystery was thought to connect everything – a spun-sugar web of the cosmos that was constantly in danger of being cracked.

The Great Pyramid was also the tomb for a man who was considered by his people, and by himself, to be a god. King Khufu seems to have been the first Egyptian leader to explicitly style himself as an incarnation of the divine – Khufu's son would go on to call himself the son of the sun god Ra. Just as, at dawn, river-raptors still rise in darting clouds from the east to follow the course of the Nile, so the God-King was thought to be a manifestation of the Sky-God-Falcon Horus, or Re, travelling through the sky every morning when he appeared as the solar deity Ra and then as Re-Horakhty.[22] And after his death, it was accepted that those journeys continued through the night-sky. King Khufu's divinity and physical connection to the divine universe would keep his people safe: a gossamer-net of security that emanated from their ruler's person during his mortal life and after his death. The building of the Great Pyramid, more than just a hubristic, megalomaniac fever-dream, was an organ of state, a project at the outset of the Egyptian Old Kingdom's power which proved its might and reach.

What kind of man sponsored our first Wonder? King Khufu was the second sovereign of the Fourth Dynasty of the Old Kingdom, ruling Upper and Lower Egypt for at least twenty-three years between 2589 and 2566 BCE. To try to come face to face with the person his people called the Great King – Khayafwi(y) – we might travel to the Brooklyn Museum, in the United States of America, where a pink granite head has been identified by some as the imposing king, or to Munich, where a limestone version of the same face is on display in the State Museum of Egyptian Art. The only undisputed surviving 3D image of Khufu the man is still in Cairo, in the old, pink-washed Egyptian Museum – a diminutive ivory statuette from the ambitious, confident temple of Khentimentiu at Abydos, 330 miles from the Giza Plateau, upstream along the Nile. The tiny potentate sits wearing the red crown of Lower Egypt, holding a flail (added much later, in the twenty-sixth dynasty) in his right hand. Although Lilliputian, the form is intricately carved. And, as is usual for the period, a calm smile plays about Khufu's lips. This mini-King sits modestly in a Victorian-built glass display case – a far cry from the out-size statues of pure copper and gold that would once have been raised to the Great King.[23]

Much of the other figurative evidence for Khufu's reign has been lost, although he does appear as a character in a wonderful document known as the Westcar Papyrus,* a fascinating collection of morality tales and myth, miracle and magic stories – all set in Khufu's court. The tightly written lines, inscribed in the court-hand, hieratic Egyptian – inked across lines of flattened papyri reeds – offer a window into the mindset of the Egyptians, and into perceptions of Khufu.† In the Westcar Papyrus Khufu is portrayed both as a relentless ruler, and as a pioneering character, a man interested in new experiments in the realm of pseudo-science. Tellingly, Westcar also includes the world's first recorded saucy-fantasy-tale, telling of how Khufu's father Sneferu arranged a fishing party, while bored, with

---

* Named after the Victorian adventurer and collector Henry Westcar, more accurately catalogued as P. Berlin 3033.
† One caveat: this extant iteration of the work dates to generations after Khufu's death.

twenty ladies of his court, dressing them up in fishing nets; in another, an adulterous woman is lured to a watery grave by an enchanted wax crocodile.[24]

So robust sources for the truth of Khufu are scant. But now, thrillingly, on-going excavations on the shores of the Red Sea are helping us to understand more about the real world of this enigmatic leader and his audacious wonder. This stunning site, called Wadi al-Jarf, is the oldest and largest man-made harbour-complex ever identified, dating back to the reign of Khufu's father Sneferu – and its recent discoveries are genuinely remarkable. At last we can start to understand more logistical facts about the Pyramid, and to meet the man who ordered its creation and those too who did his bidding.

Archaeologists are uncovering many treasures at Wadi al-Jarf, including a number of mentions of Khufu's name.[25] Since 2011–12, finds have been pouring out of the sands and from under the sea. It seems that the harbour at Wadi al-Jarf was a facility developed specifically to feed the Great Pyramid's construction. The archaeologists working here, on a site that stretches over 3 miles, animatedly describe the level of tight Bronze Age organisation the finds reveal: limestone walls inscribed with the name of the head royal-scribe who oversaw import and export here 4,500 years ago. Storage jars, some with red hieroglyphic daubs describing the sailors who worked for King Khufu: 'Those who are known to Horus Two Falcons of Gold' and 'The Crew of the Followers of Khufu'. Lists of the rations given to labourers as payment – barley, dates, beer – fuel for ambitious sea and river journeys. Khufu's reign is no longer recondite; there are inscriptions everywhere, on the hundred-plus anchors discovered on the seabed, on metal tools, on pottery fragments, on the massive limestones used to block the entrances of giant storerooms – man-made caves carved above the shoreline. In these magazines (a word that comes from the Arabic *makhazin*, a depot or storehouse), huge clay storage jars have just been discovered. The contents of these jars once nourished those Egyptian crews as they embarked on state-sponsored long-distance voyages of trade and exploration across the Red Sea and then on by beast of burden beyond, collecting cedars of Lebanon from the north, frankincense from Southern Arabia, bitumen for waterproofing and caulking from the Dead Sea, and minerals from Sinai. All to help realise a Wonder.

Khufu is also present in splendid relief on rock-carvings at Wadi Maghareh in Sinai, known to ancient Egyptians as 'the Terraces of Turquoise'. Here the king is shown triumphantly smiting enemies and searching for copper and for the precious blue turquoise stone so adored in ancient Egyptian culture. Travelling through these vivid, mineral-rich crags today, and their corresponding mountains in what is now Saudi Arabia, helps us to understand the expanding worldview of the Ancient Egyptians. These dappled mountain ranges – a visible kaleidoscope of colour, running with seams of green, copper-bearing ore, red iron and creamy limestone – are natural pyramids veined with treasure. By leaching mountains to garnish his creations, Khufu was not just building himself into the story of nature; he was trying to better it.

We also hear about Khufu obliquely, in a rock-inscription in the Dakhla Oasis in the Western Desert, describing activity in the thirteenth cattle-count – a form of census and tax-collection, dating to the same year as much of the Wadi al-Jarf evidence.[26] He is there too in carvings at Elephantine Island close to Aswan on the Nile, and on two lovely terracotta figurines of the cat-headed goddess, Bastet, left in the giant human and animal necropolis at Saqqara, and only discovered in excavations that ran from 2001 to 2003.[27]

The Wonder-sponsor Khufu had at least two wives (Meritites I and Henutsen) and, clearly, singular, burning resolve. A man in charge of a population of 1.5 million and territories ranging from the Mediterranean and Heliopolis (on the outskirts of Cairo today) in the north and beyond Elephantine Island (opposite modern-day Aswan) to Sinai in the south. All territorial power in Egypt was within his grasp. Khufu would have looked out at the Giza Plateau, naturally raised so any building on it would have a monumental impact, visible for miles, and declared his will. In the stretching-of-the-cord ceremony called *Petshes*, with a priestess dressed as the goddess Seshat leading the ritual, Khufu ran a rope 755 feet long across the limestone of the Giza Plateau, to mark out the scale and orientation of his pyramid on the virgin land. King Khufu's refulgent, monstrous project – which would generate the oldest of the Seven Wonders – had begun.

King Khufu's efforts came at the end of what was already a 500-year-old tradition. Grand royal burials start to appear in the desert above the Nile at the settlement of Abydos (Abdju in Ancient Egyptian), where that figurine of Khufu was found, from c. 3100 BCE. And here, where the modern town peters out and the sands are thick with dark pottery fragments from the offerings left to the dead, where dogs roam hungrily, there has recently been a gruesome discovery. Predynastic kings – rulers apparently with vivid names such as King Scorpion, King Killer and King Cobra – are buried here in mudbrick structures. In one burial of the First Dynasty at Abydos, a horrible archaeological find was made: dozens of animals and hundreds of royal retainers – close on 400 people – who seem to have been sacrificed, strangled and then sent to the afterlife with their king.[28] A pernicious, divisive tradition was gathering momentum – total submission to the single most powerful man in Egypt.

Around 2800 BCE the principal royal burial grounds were moved over 300 miles north, downriver, to the deep deserts of Saqqara. Here, as would be the case with the Great Pyramid at Giza, the Saqqara pyramids had a root system – submerged channels and corridors carved for many miles underground into the bedrock itself. Exploring Saqqara today, 25 miles north of Giza, peering down into this subterranean world is stomach-churning. I have been at the opening of catacombs and nearly experienced a tragedy when a colleague, who took one wrong turning in the pitch-black maze, vanished for a long two hours. The absorption of kinetic energy by the limestone means sound is diminished, so the tunnels swallow up any cries for help. Many adventurers have lost their lives tumbling in by chance or exploring with the purpose of tomb-raiding – skeletons, ancient and modern, still turn up in these underworlds of the pyramids above.

It was here at Saqqara that Khufu's predecessors experimented with the pyramid form, a design concept that forced a sense of progression from below to above. First came the Step Pyramid, a series of mastaba tombs one on top of the other, raised by King Djoser of the Third Dynasty. Then in the 'Golden Age' of the Fourth Dynasty, Khufu's father Sneferu (his name means 'to make perfect, to make beautiful'), after experimenting with his Meidum Pyramid – a tall, thin affair, still partially standing but which suffered a debilitating collapse in antiquity – built his 'Bent' Pyramid – an attempt to reach the sky more directly. The so-called Red Pyramid followed (the red limestone visible today was originally covered in white); it now squats above palm trees and farmland at Dahshur. But the Bent Pyramid was a distressing failure, with an ugly kink where the pyramid's smooth tip should be. In the Fifth Dynasty that followed Khufu's, the tightly inscribed walls of Pharaoh Unas's tomb at Saqqara – at the end of a dark, 98-foot-long corridor underneath Unas's collapsed pyramid – repeat the prayer: 'The earth is made into steps for him towards heaven, so that he may ascend them to heaven.'[29] The Pharaohs truly believed that giant, man-made monuments, if perfectly composed, could help them ascend to the sky.

The imperfection of Sneferu's resurrection machine troubled the Egyptians. Perhaps though that ugly tip of the Bent Pyramid was a fillip to Khufu – an irritant in his eye and heart: his father had failed once, now he had to do better. And so the Great Pyramid became an embodiment of the tenacious trait of the human species that wants to advance that which has gone before, to raven for more. There would have been a personal urgency to the work at Giza too. The average age of death around Khufu's lifetime after the milestone of infancy had been passed, was thirty-four for men (thirty for women – who often died in childbirth).[30] The pyramids must climb their way up to the sky, fast, before King Khufu died without a finished tomb, without the equipment necessary to live forever. The wonder of the Great Pyramid reveals the curious ways humans choose to use their life's energy, in pursuit of an idea that appreciates its own logic and authority, despite being, in truth, illogical. It reveals how we create a map of meaning for ourselves.

So how was this Wonder raised? We have acute – and brilliant – evidence for the precise rhythm and nature of the precipitous work on the Great Pyramid project from another incredible find at that Red Sea site of Wadi al-Jarf. The discoveries come from a scorpion-rich, man-made cave above the flat, deceptively calm coastline here, where Egyptian boats had been hauled and stored along with copper and stone tools, food and water urns. Coping with seasonal winds, the storage rooms were packed with practical tools and the 'back-office' of the Pyramid's creation, all kept carefully while work was delayed by the cycles of Mother Nature. And here, in 2013, archaeologists uncovered a dry flutter of no fewer than 1,000 papyri fragments. It is an incredible stash which rewrites history. Because here for the first time we hear of the detail of labourers' lives, and one of the earliest day-by-day accounts ever of a worker's life-experience. One of these remarkable documents has been named the Merer Papyrus after a civil servant responsible for the Pyramid's construction. Merer was leader of a group of forty sailors and labourers, a *Saa*, who toiled in the punishing months between July and November to ship stone up the Nile on two or three round trips every ten days. The sometimes daily account of Merer's works comes from the twenty-sixth or twenty-seventh year of Khufu's reign when those radiant-bright casing stones were being added on top of the pyramid's interior skin, made of darker, local rock. Not only are these the oldest papyri inscribed with writing ever found, but the harbour here at Wadi al-Jarf is the oldest artificial harbour. And it is huge, with the site so far excavated stretching over 3 miles.

These unique, delicate, straw-yellow texts are more than worth their weight in gold for an historian, documenting as they do the ten-day-week missions to supply raw materials for the Great Pyramid's construction. The level of detail is sensational. Line by careful line, we hear of workers collecting limestone from Tura (Ro Aura in Ancient Egyptian, later Troyu), 9 miles south of Giza, docking, casting off, sailing down and across the Nile, turning back to repeat the process. The names of the different *Saa* – 'The Vigorous Team', 'The Big', 'The Prosperous', 'The Small', 'The Asian', 'The Enduring Team' – suggest there was competition between each group of workers to complete their tasks. There is evidence too of an administrative centre for the pyramid project up the Nile, very close to Giza, 'at the entry to the lake of Khufu', controlled by Khufu's half-brother Ankhhaf, who seems to have supervised the works here; a stretch of water easy to dock where labourers could rest at night – when the dark waters of the Nile are filled with the sounds of bullfrogs, water-rats, and the black-crowned night heron.

The trip from the Red Sea to the Nile Valley took about four days. Continuing excavations in the cave-complexes here, totalling thirty-one, are turning up finds that will teach us huge amounts about Khufu's massive engineering project. Along with raw ebony wood, frankincense and myrrh (incense was used for the first time in Egypt by the Fourth Dynasty) transported from the Gulf and the Arabian edges of the Indian Ocean, fragments of ropes, sails and sailors' boots are being discovered – under banks of sand inside the caves which stretch almost 100 feet deep. A fort at el-Makha on the Asian side of the Red Sea has been identified recently and is currently being excavated, built to protect the Egyptian state-workers from attack. An artificial jetty, running more than 650 feet east to west and 650 feet north to south, still visible on the seabed, would have been the start and end point of international adventures to collect the raw materials used in the pyramid's decoration, as, forty-five centuries ago, elegant boats nudged their way out through channels in the rich, luminous coral reef edging Wadi al-Jarf to the glittering open sea.

Along with this new evidence from the sun-bright shores of the Red Sea, the construction techniques of the Great Pyramid prove that Khufu's was an Egypt-wide enterprise. The core blocks of the Pyramid, carved from the Giza Plateau itself (the quarries are still visible a stone's throw south from the pyramids as somewhat treacherous, 100-feet-deep pits), might be local limestone, but other raw materials had to be brought in from across North Africa and the Near East – such as dolerite from the western desert, that hard volcanic rock used to form massive round hammers which, back-breakingly, just a centimetre and a half over a twelve-hour day, scraped stone from hills and valleys to make obelisks, temples, tombs and features both within and without the Pyramid. Rock inscriptions at turquoise and copper mines at Wadi Maghara in the Sinai Peninsula show that Khufu sent material-grabbing missions here too. Just as fortresses were set up to guard the trade in and out of Wadi al-Jarf at Serabit el-Khadim across the Red Sea, fortresses are also currently under excavation at Wadi Maghara. The teams working for Khufu there have left their names carved in the stone alongside commemorations of their vanquishing of the Bedouin people who attacked their supply chains. There was Yebu granite from the quarries on the charismatic, enigmatic Elephantine Island to the south by the First Cataract on the Nile (the island is still filled with ancient ruins and underground chambers). Black dolerite for fine sculptures and inscriptions was imported from the Hajar Mountains in what is now Oman. At 'Khafre's quarries' in the Nubian desert 40 miles north-west of Abu Simbel, Khufu's name was spotted in the 1980s in a cartouche (a cartridge-shaped inscription) protecting the supply of dark-green gneiss diorite used to form so many of the statues of Egyptian gods, royal women and men that would have sentinelled the pyramid complex.

Cedar, juniper, pine and oak were brought from Lebanon and the Eastern Mediterranean; copper ore, malachite, and mineral pigments for decoration.[31] The earth's gaudiest materials were used to decorate the mesmerically precise artwork on the fronts of temples in the Giza complex. For statues, the dark, coarse sandstone graywacke was chosen;

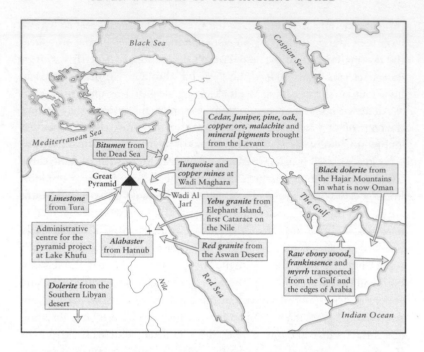

shot through with mica minerals, the sculptures' stone-skin would have gleamed in both lamp- and sunlight. Green malachite was used under the eyes of these stone-beings (just as powdered malachite is still used as eyeliner in the region today). Red granite columns would have been reflected in alabaster floors. Egyptian alabaster (also known as calcite or travertine) came from Hatnub, close to 186 miles south of Cairo – where miners today still follow the paths of ancient, millennia-old quarry roads.

In fact, startling new evidence from Hatnub may give us more precise clues as to exactly how the pyramids of Giza were built. While hieroglyphic graffiti in one of the ancient quarries here were being read in 2018, a series of holes and a ramp were discovered. The ramp, the team of archaeologists swiftly realised, dates to the time of Khufu, and leads to an ancient road-system which makes its way down to the Nile. Either side of the ramp are staircases, with holes for wooden posts. These would be used to attach ropes, which meant huge alabaster/travertine blocks could be dragged up slopes of 20 degrees, and across to the boats waiting at the Nile's edge. Evidence from the Middle Kingdom suggests each and every block was dated, marked-up with provenance, mason, transport and storage plan. Workers' huts, even simple religious structures, can be seen flanking the road at Hatnub, especially visible by drone.[32]

As a chief architect, Khufu's half-brother, Ankhaf, employed a super-high-ranking project manager named Hemiunu – a vizier – whose job it would have been to ensure completion of the Great Pyramid before the end of Khufu's reign. The pressure would have been immense. Remember, Khufu's father Sneferu had experimented with at least three different kinds of pyramids in his lifetime – following the example of the first ever pyramid, the Step Pyramid at Saqqara. First Sneferu built his seven-, then eight-stepped 'Pseudo Step Pyramid' (that steep-sloped pyramid deep in the country at Meidum, 62 miles south of Cairo). Only the second-ever pyramid, itself possibly begun by Huni, who was probably Khufu's grandfather, this Pseudo-Pyramid was then converted into a true pyramid – the Bent Pyramid at Northern Dahshur, with a dramatic reduction from a 54-degree slope to 43 degrees. As we know, it still failed in engineering terms and had to be finished with an ugly compromise. Finally, the true Red Pyramid was raised. Khufu's Pyramid had to stand, to stand proud, and it had to stand out from what had gone before.

The Great Pyramid project would be a staggeringly expensive undertaking. But with centralised control of all of Egypt's resources and an increasingly sophisticated taxation system in place, King Khufu had plenty to play with. International trade networks were burgeoning. Egypt had access to raw resources – gold, copper, precious stones – and to the agricultural gifts of the Nile as well as to the fine, luxury artworks that Egypt was famed for then as well as now ('made in Egypt' was a stamp of quality of which all self-respecting rulers of the Bronze Age wanted a piece). These desirable commodities would be bartered rather than sold, as the cash economy was still to be invented. The rulers of the region indulged in theatricalised, glorified 'gift-giving' – the exchange of precious goods under their own name to vaunt status and reputation and generate a healthy import/export economy. Khufu had the resources, and the technologies to hand. Egyptians had invented a base-number-10 system of mathematics, they applied complex geometry to their projects (one stone fragment from Saqqara, covered in red ochre jottings, shows the geometric workings to construct an arch feature), and all Egypt worked off a standardised system of measurements. So stone carved hundreds of miles away from Giza could match, down to the last millimetre, quarried limestone from the Giza Plateau itself. The conditions for success were set.

The Great Pyramid was built 130 feet higher than any other and was clad in that bright white Tura limestone from the Muqattam Hills, in whose southern reaches today Cairo's garbage collectors, many of whom are Zabballeen Coptic Christians, live and carve their cave-churches next to disused quarries. The purity of this particular stone gives it an almost silver gleam. Recent work on a surviving casing stone from the peak of the Pyramid has shown that these slim blocks were precision-carved with proportions relating to a circle – an apotropaic act.[33] It is interesting that the other two pyramids which followed on the plateau, Khafre's and Menkaure's, were dressed at the bottom with red granite. What was it about the Great Pyramid's gleaming whiteness that Khufu's sons thought they could improve upon? The Great Pyramid would have shimmered with a pure, futuristic other-worldliness. And at its peak was the *pyramidion*, or *benben*, the pyramid capping stone, covered in gold or electrum so that it powered the sun's rays back out into the sky, itself representing the earth mound of the original creator god.

A slither-line of Khufu's Pyramid's original limestone casing still exists at the base of the Great Pyramid's northern face. Today tourists use it as a convenient resting place for plastic bottles of water and camel keyrings, bought under some duress from determined teenage hawkers. A strange fate for a project as complex and sophisticated as this one, whose logistics and organisation are a window into the outlook and statecraft of Ancient Egypt.

So much effort, by many, for the benefit of one man. But, miraculously, we can now get even closer to those tens of thousands of other nameless humans who – at Khufu's will – raised on the Giza Plateau one limestone block every two to three minutes, ten hours a day, every day of a ten-day week, fifty-two weeks a year for at least twenty-four years, to realise his ambition. And although the jury is still out on the exact construction method – a combination of rollers, ramps, and hydraulic lifts is still the most likely – wonderfully, the details of the lives of Hemiunu's builders, and their masterpiece, are slowly coming to light. A short walk from the

Great Pyramid itself is the Pandora's box that is the field-lab and finds-house of the Giza Plateau – a glorious multi-storey shed which contains a truly extraordinary wealth of emerging evidence for both the building of this Bronze Age Wonder and its builders.

The finds-house is, frankly, for those who love history, beyond fantasy. It holds unique clues to the lives of the women and men who made Giza's Wonder possible. Away from the relentless glare of the sun in cardboard boxes and plastic crates and bags, all carefully labelled with felt-tip pen, and under layers of fine tissue paper and wadding, there are bone fragments, botanical remains, dinner services of plates, cups and tureens – all wedged on floor-to-ceiling shelves. There are turquoise-bright simple tubular beads – dropped in the sand and originally either worn by the workers or used by them in barter. There are mobile hot-bread and broth stands, made of singed, blackened terracotta; quartzite whetstones to sharpen copper tools, marbles for games, knives made of chert flint, giant pestles and mortars.

Around corners there are yet more intimate details of the lives of the individual people who built Khufu's towering Wonder. Traces of the knuckle-bone soup they spooned from a wide, standard-issue bowl with an anti-spill lip – meat seems to have been eaten here in much higher quantities than elsewhere in Egypt. There are terracotta pots of thick, sludgy grain beer that would have been drunk with a straw. Giant terracotta bread moulds too – designed to feed many at a time, on an industrial scale. Holding these outsize cooking accessories, feeling the crack of the charred pottery where the bread was baked, day in, day out, and the chafe where the loaves were scooped out to distribute to the women and men imported to build the pyramid-tomb, is immediately moving. The evidence of everyday lives feels as weighty as the pyramid stones. Because these utensils tell us both of the scale of a plan realised, and the binding reality of an entire generation of Egyptian poor.

Painstakingly, over the last forty years, the evidence of all of these lives has been brought out of the earth. Because now it is clear that a 12-acre city of workers, just south of the gated Wall of the Crow (itself monumental and in large part still standing), stretching down to the banks of the Nile, was established on the Giza Plateau to make the Pyramid a possibility.

Antipater of Sidon, one of those early compilers of a Seven Wonders list, speaks of the Pyramid and its 'great toil'.[34] A few of these workers may have volunteered, and employment did offer stability and food, but many would have been press-ganged from the villages of both Upper and Lower Egypt and forced to labour on Khufu's masterplan. All operating within what was, in effect, a feudal system. At least a full month of service as thanks for the king's protection. The Pyramid might have been an attempt to perpetuate the beautiful possibilities of life through to the afterlife, but we cannot help imagining how this vision, this desire, impacted all individual lives around the centrifugal point of power, the women and men whose existences were casualties of the Great King's dreams.

Cheek-by-jowl dwellings on the plateau for the Pyramid's builders contrast with the 'Royal Enclosure' – an administrative centre where rations were distributed and grains were ground to make flour to bake that state-standard-issue bread and brew that beer. Scribes and higher officials, with far roomier quarters, many decorated in a stylish red pigment, can be traced in a segregated area to the west. The majority of the workers slept like sardines in barracks, groups of ten under the grip of an overseer. Some of their simple mudbrick graves and grander rock-cut tombs have been discovered; many more are currently being excavated.

But for those who were not captives, this service to a divine-leader must surely have felt as though it had point and purpose – because without a safe tomb for the king, we must remember, there was a chance, in Egyptian rationale, that the world could end.

Egypt had a plan. A system that fed and buttressed the Egyptian world-view. In a land ultimately owned by one overlord, the king-pharaoh, all Egyptians had the right to farm, but under strict conditions. Egyptians had to yield a tithe, a proportion of their produce to their monarch, and they had to do royal service – a month spent building giant state projects – the Great Pyramid an extreme example of this system of biased, un-equable cooperation. In return, state officials would store buffer supplies for national crises – famine, pandemic, outside attack or civil strife. The Great Pyramid might not have been built without casualty, but it was built by Egyptians who were nominally 'free'. Belonging was of para-mount value in the prehistoric and early ancient worlds. Anarchy was rarely something to crave.

The logistics are certainly impressive – the latest estimates put a number of 20,000 labourers on the plateau at any one time. So how did these workers (and the worker-donkeys, the other mammal that helped to build Egyptian civilisation) manage to shift the 6.5 million tonnes' worth of material, and to form it into a structure of almost absolute mathematical perfection?[35]

The engineering and construction of the Pyramid – the way these blocks were shaped, lifted and set in place – has confounded researchers for centuries, triggering miles' worth of parchment and paper, and now volumes of iCloud storage. It is a conundrum that obsesses the modern world – taxing the minds of engineers, architects, archaeologists, surveyors, even mediums. There are some things we do know, such as that Ancient Egyptians had drills – these are represented in decorations within tombs at Saqqara, and the grooves in the antechamber of the Great Pyramid seem to show Egyptians also understood the use of rollers for force intensification. It is likely that the inner core was constructed to minimise earthquake damage, and that material was raised with a series of steep ramps, and the rising flood waters of the Nile. Sand or water was used as a counterbalance to lever the stones – including granite blocks weighing in at over 50 tonnes each. I have spent days with modern Egyptian stonemasons and stone-shifters, specialists in dragging huge carved stelae out of the earth and in moving tumbled Egyptian columns from one part of an archaeological site to another. There is enormous camaraderie. Singing, chanting and rhythm are essential to keep the project on track. Instructions are sung or called out by the group leader. Sweat and dust move from one man to another; there is joshing, joking, hardcore back-slapping. Try to imagine it – if those giant blocks were put in place every two minutes, every day of every week, the Great Pyramid would have taken twenty one to twenty-four years to build, plus more than two to plan. The work of a lifetime.[36]

Scanning has shown that the inner pyramid is built as those original step pyramids had been, constructed upwards as a series of horizontal layers of decreasing size, so the king inside could still walk to heaven. Casing stones were then added and shaped and smoothed in situ. Acute mathematics, using measurements based on cubits (the measurement from the tip of your longest finger to the bottom of your elbow), digits (the width of a finger) and palms (the span of a palm), and founded on a decimal basis, resulted in minute precision. The 'royal cubit' employed by the Old Kingdom in the construction of the pyramids measured 7 palms, each of 4 digits – so around 1-and-a-half feet. In the limestone bedrock all around the base of the Pyramid one can still see round and square pit-holes, which must have been used as holds for posts and ropes employed in complex measurements. But despite modelling, investigation and imagination, the truth is we still don't know whether it was ramps or internal stairways, or another method yet to be identified, that allowed men to make this mountain.[37]

There are many crackpot theories as to how the Pyramid was raised. Aliens are cited worryingly often. As is the notion that Noah built the Great Pyramid instead of the Ark. The KGB identified an electro-magnetic field on the Giza Plateau which they thought might explain the Pyramid's cultural magnetism.[38] For centuries it was asserted that the Pyramid was built by Jewish slaves. But now that modest evidence from Wadi al-Jarf, the lines of ink and ochre on papyrus strips and clay-pot sherds, ghost-trails of movement in nearby quarries, even those giant casseroles with lids and stands and terracotta bread-tins – can put paid to all this romantic creativity. The Great Pyramid pounds with human ambition. It was built for Khufu, by the men, women, children and captives of Egypt.

So the Pyramid is a work of dubious morality, and magisterial ingenuity: it is also a Wonder because it tells us not just of the efforts made to extend the life of one man, but the drive of humans to try to understand the point of living.

This Wonder, built soon after the end of the Stone Age, would not have been created without what, in truth, is a notion that sits somewhere between wild fantasy and chemical fact. In many ways, the Ancient Egyptian concept of humankind's connection to the universe is only now being scientifically realised. The people of Ancient Egypt recognised, before the Greeks had identified the concept of the atom, that we are not distinct from nature, but part of it, part too of the molecular chemistry of the wider cosmos, and subject to its planetary revolutions. They observed that matter never disappears; it becomes part of a bigger matrix, taking on other forms. So the passage of a human through death to the underworld and eternal life (with the rebirth of one's soul) was not a possibility, but a certainty – even if those perceived journeys varied somewhat depending on your rank and status. For Egyptians the cosmos was as ensouled and alive as they were.

This was also an age where death was ever-present, not only witnessed day by day, but actively remembered and celebrated in festivals and in mortuary temples and in house shrines. Egyptian life was an experience that was consistently juvenile; when 257 skeletons from Ancient Egypt (dating from 1500 BCE) were recently analysed, it was clear that the average age at death was 19. Death was a more common experience of youth than old age.[39] For Egyptians the afterlife was fast approaching, another dimension to be fully embraced, not ignored or denied. There was too an acute investment in aesthetic and sensuous beauty, an investment that continued into the second existence beyond the afterworld. The short, gilded lifespan of wealthy Egyptians had such possibilities, and they wanted a form of that life to last forever. The Great Pyramid was a good thing for the king; it was also a prophylactic to chaos in society.[40]

So the point of all this 'great toil' was to ensure that the omnipotent ruler enjoyed a glorious afterlife, in order that the people of Egypt could live safely in their land. The creation of the Pyramid as a giant ascension machine was vital; this project was simply the most important thing that could happen in heaven and earth. Everything had to be done perfectly.

When Khufu died (our best guess is age fifty-four in around 2556 BCE), having ordered up his exponential tomb, his advance into the Pyramid itself was designed to generate awe. Because this dead king would be making his journey as the revered, semi-divine dead, a temporary corpse, mummified, ready to breathe again. Over a seventy-day period of mummification magic, prayers, lake salt (hydrated soda ash) harvested from dry lake beds in both Upper and Lower Egypt, and a combination of oils and resins all aimed to allow the king to travel from life to death and back to life again. The dead in Ancient Egypt commanded the same respect as the living. Just as the theatrical, globally televised removal of the royal mummies from the charming, creaking old archaeological museum, the Egyptian Museum, in Cairo to the new National Museum of Egyptian Civilisation (NMEC) in 2020 – complete with armed guard, marching bands, costumed dancers and a reception by heads of state – caused quite the international stir and was watched by millions during lockdown, so, in the Bronze Age, the world of Giza would have stopped to allow the dead king to process.

To prepare the corpse for his pyramid-tomb, first there was the ritual mummification. Old Kingdom mummified remains would have been embalmed with natron (*ntrj* for the Ancient Egyptians), typically harvested from the Wadi El Natrun valley, which dried out flesh and acted as an antibacterial. (The chemical symbol for sodium today, Na, comes from the New Latin *natrium*.) The exact recipe for embalming has been hard to identify. But recent brilliant work by a team in Denmark has pieced together two strips of 3,500-year-old Egyptian papyrus, giving the recipe for eighteenth-century dynastic mummification.[41] Originally 26 feet long, possibly buried in an elite tomb, three entire columns of the papyrus deal with embalming, and a full half-column with the embalming of the face. Over twenty ingredients or pharmaceuticals were used in the process. Some of the ingredients listed also appear in records of mummification at the time of Khufu – oil of Byblos, oil of Lebanon. The organs were removed and amulets were left inside the body to ward off evil spirits, the skin was pasted with hot resin, limbs and the body's core were then tightly wrapped with linen bandages, and sometimes covered with a plaster, into which facial features were carved.

It was Khufu's death that would give the Pyramid purpose. Everything depended on the precise preservation of his body. This massive engineering project, all those responsible for its creation, all those sweated, broken-backed lives waiting on the Giza Plateau for the royal corpse. The physical handling of the dead – and, of course, in particular, of the most powerful human in the Egyptian empire – was paramount. If these temporarily dead humans were mistreated, they could come back to haunt the living. The miracle of this afterlife of the body shaped the Egyptian psyche.

Just as Christians would take comfort from the notion that their man-god, Jesus, suffered and was born again, so Egyptians knew that Osiris, a young, living king, had been unjustly killed by his brother Seth and was then resurrected – as a mummified body – to rule the world of the dead. In other words, in the Egyptian worldview, mummification worked. And the desert sands of North Africa told Ancient Egyptians that humans did not necessarily disappear when they died. The oldest naturally mummified Egyptian – an individual who lived a thousand years before the construction of the Great Pyramid – was discovered just 18.6 miles south of Luxor along the Nile. This man, aged somewhere between nineteen and twenty-three, was preserved by a natural desiccation process, not by embalming, yet his burial had clearly been ritualised. The mummified male remains are now on display in the British Museum and named

'Gebelin Man'.[42] Gebelin Man has a companion, the so-called 'Gebelin Woman', who sports the oldest known tattoos on a female body – a blue 'SS' shape on her upper arms – which are revealed particularly well under infra-red light.[43] The teenage boy's upper arm is also marked with a bull and a sheep tattoo. Lying on their left sides, rather as though waiting to be reborn like babies, the degree of preservation is extraordinary – it is easy to see the young man's beard-stubble, the woman's filed fingernails, and, gruesomely, the dagger attack to the young man's right shoulder-blade – an attack that punctured his lung and killed him.

The Egyptians knew the desert could mummify without intervention, but they did not want to leave this kind of preservation to chance. Khufu's mummy (probably also laid on his side with his head pointing south) would have been protected both physically and with magic; contained in one, two, sometimes three nested coffins, then a stone sarcophagus, and all around the spells or incantations which later become visualised as the Pyramid Texts. The interiors of the burial chambers in Giza are plain (an interesting style choice, as those that come after are highly decorated), but for the generations that followed, these Pyramid Texts would be inscribed on the walls of the pharaoh-King's tomb. Studying the earliest and one of the best preserved at Saqqara, after a crawl through the pitch-black, in the tomb of King Unas, who died three generations after Khufu, the exquisitely carved incantations are mesmeric. The name of the king pounds out of the perfectly regular incised walls in 238 spells – all written to ensure Unas's successful journey to the afterlife and survival in the other world, even if his funerary cult on earth, by any terrible chance or vicissitude, waned. Pyramid Text 508 reveals the physical plan for the king's ascension to the skies: 'I have trodden those thy rays as a ramp under my feet, whereon I mount up to that my mother, the living Uraeus [the rearing image of a cobra on royal headdresses as a symbol of divine sovereignty], on the brow of Ra!'[44] Khufu's ascent would have been imagined in a similar way; the Great Pyramid had to be so robustly built because it was the springboard for a phenomenally important physical journey.

Once mummified, the Great King's embalmed body would have been transported along the Nile to a building called the Valley Temple. Khufu's Valley Temple still lies unexcavated under Giza's streets, where boys ride horses and smoke, and pots and pans are mended and babies doze on balconies. Khufu's mummified remains would then have moved closer in, into the sanctuary whose perimeter is currently protected by camel-mounted police, and inquisitive dogs – here now in a fraction of the numbers that would have made their homes in this giant sacred necropolis back in the Bronze Age. Khufu was then processed up a grand ceremonial causeway to the Mortuary Temple (also called the Pyramid Temple) – a commemorative monument, similar to a cenotaph – and from there into the Pyramid itself. The causeway – built on a steep incline and stretching almost half a mile, once walled and roofed over – is now a ghost in the desert. The Mortuary Temple is also a ruin, dismissively surveyed by the rangy camels who wait, crossly, for their tourist burdens. Only a section of the foundation of tough black basalt remains – the stone brought from the Gebel Qatrani quarries to the north of Fayum, 50 miles up the River Nile, and which was perhaps used to represent the fertility of the black earth around the Nile after the inundation. This oil slick of colour, like a black stone moat right around the Great Pyramid's base, must have seemed astonishing, especially in contrast to the pillars and portals made of red granite, and the ceiling stones of white limestone.

Both the causeway and the Pyramid Temple would have been highly decorated. Fragments of the finely carved stele that lined them, which portray Khufu's warriors drawing back their bows, his fat, flower-draped cows preparing for sacrifice, and the king himself wearing a double-crown while impaling a hippopotamus, along with his cartouche describing Khufu 'Building the sanctuaries of the gods', have turned up reused in other sites – some as far away as the city of Tanis (San el-Hagar today) in the Delta of the Nile to the north (the settlement in which it was rumoured the Ark of the Covenant lay buried and which features in the Indiana Jones film *Raiders of the Lost Ark*).[45] Although the grand Giza causeway has been wilfully destroyed over time – including, shockingly, by developers in the twentieth century – we should imagine its monumental function. Huge blocks of stone are left, tumbled disrespectfully to the side. This course would have hosted a massive, pomp-filled burial parade – hidden within its protected passageway. If you can, to help envisage all this, travel to nearby Saqqara, where sections of just such a royal road still exist on the way to Unas's pyramid-tomb. The 4,000-year-old road is a line of human will in the sand. Originally covered and lit by a slit in the roof, the paving slabs that remain still offer a hint of cool and structure in the barren heat. Desert dogs play by their side, pouncing on the insects that also seek out their rare shade.

Passing through the Mortuary Temple, the funeral cortege would then have progressed to the huge enclosure wall which stood 33 feet from the Great Pyramid itself.

We have plenty of evidence about funerary practice from the New Kingdom – less detail for the Old, in which Khufu lived and died. But it would be unimaginable and unprecedented for any funerary procession to involve no singing, keening or music of any kind. Paintings on tomb walls indicate finger cymbals and rattling metal sistra were used. Rather brilliantly, the pulsing sound of Ancient Egyptian percussion can still be heard at certain times of the year in the Coptic Orthodox Church. On Good Friday – commemorating the death of Jesus Christ – a funerary chant is sung, whose melody comes from the pharaonic period in Egypt. The rhythmically complex clashing cymbals that accompany the singers are precisely those shown on wall paintings in tombs – for a brief moment, in a Coptic service, it feels possible to hear the haunting sound of Ancient Egyptian death-rituals.

Outside the pyramid-tomb itself the mouth of the mummified king (along with all his senses) would be opened so his *KA* – his soul – could breathe and he could consume ritual offerings. The actual flat flint knife, the *peseshfek*, decorated with Khufu's cartouche, was discovered in Menkaure's Valley Temple and can now be seen in the Museum of Fine Arts in Boston. This 'opening of the mouth' ceremony also allowed the king's *ANKH* – his life spirit – to escape. The ritual, it was believed, even gave him back his voice in the afterlife. Images of pharaohs in later tombs also have their mouths opened so the potentate's spirit could re-enter and inhabit his mummified body. Initially it seems Egyptians believed that the body itself would be immediately reborn, then it was agreed it was in fact predominantly the *KA*. Life was not simply given back to the dead, it was given back to the universe. Our own universe finishes where human imagination ends. Ancient Egyptians inhabited a universe that was imagination – full of eternal possibilities. So we should never underestimate the symbolic significance of the Great Pyramid in a visceral, vital, vivifying ritual.

Khufu's journey to the afterlife was thought to begin as the sun set, with rebirth coming at dawn. The final journey of the king's body inside the pyramid-tomb itself commenced through an entrance reached by a ramp originally 55 feet above ground level. This was a more select procession, accompanied only by the Great King's priests, very closest servants and companions.

And now, as a researcher of the Great Pyramid, one has the opportunity to follow the exact progress of the royal funeral and the king's mummified body. An intimate exploration of the Pyramid's secret chambers and passageways gives a sense of the mind-saturating, careful complexity of this Wonder, as well as the remarkable efforts and logistics to effect it; and the weight of custom it was designed to host.

A few yards into the Pyramid's initial entrance, through the enlarged tomb-raider hole, there are two passageways to choose from. Ahead, one travels steeply upward; but concealed on the left there is a second passage which drops and veers down into the bedrock itself. This narrow corridor is not normally open to the public, for good reason. Once one starts to move forwards, there is no turning back; this is a 236-foot descent through a tiny shaft. The passageway is unfinished. If willing to continue to explore, as you reach the final few feet, you have to crawl on hands and knees through chafing sand. Needless to say, down here it is pitch black. Unexpectedly, one sense that noticeably comes into play is taste – because here in the dark, you might not be able to see, but what you can do is taste the limestone substrate of the Pyramid. Crumbling ceilings and walls carved from the bedrock (still occupying around 7.75 per cent of the Pyramid's core) are thick with seashells, the crustacea that once formed a shell-bank, surmounted by a coral reef – because 50 million years ago, this was all sea.

On the left-hand side of a chambered room at the end of the hidden passage is a blind shaft. If this was indeed Khufu's original burial chamber, it would have been deeply unsuitable; bulges of bedrock still loom out, the slash and gash of tools made of bone and bronze score the surface. After just two hours inside, the air has a stultifying heaviness to it; all one's instincts are to try to break back out to the light. Early tombs do all descend into the earth. Was this original tunnelling route abandoned? Were builders shaken by a worrying earthquake? Was this pit, under 50,000 tonnes of stone with 460 feet of pyramid above, designed as an empty ritual chamber, made in order to propitiate the chthonic gods of this underworld kingdom?

Others have explored here before. Greeks and Romans have left their messages in soot-black. And the subterranean chamber is itself a catalogue of wonder-seekers. The travelling chronicler Herodotus, a man from Asia, enchanted by Egypt's African wonders, insisted Khufu was buried in the Pyramid in just such a subterranean chamber on an underground island washed by the waters of the Nile. The flamboyant European pyramid explorer-showman Giovanni Battista Caviglia, who also entered this lower cavern, forced his way through the sand in 1820 and excavated a 5-foot-deep pit in the corner, a pointless space which was then extended down to 36 feet deep by the English adventurer and tomb-raider Major General Howard Vyse in 1855.

In fact, throughout the Pyramid there are shafts and tunnels, hacked out as access routes by ancient engineers and by tomb-raiders of every era – all seeking the Pyramid's truth and a pharaoh's treasure. The conditions in these raids on ancient wealth are decidedly unpleasant. I have spent a day scrambling through just such an ancient robber tunnel at the underground tomb of Senwosret III in Abydos. After just 165 feet into the bedrock, the exercise is a petrifying one: the air quality is low, humidity constantly at 90 or so per cent, and snakes, scorpions and concealed trap-drops are a real issue. Accidental death was commonplace. Witness Thutmose III's tomb in the Valley of the Kings, where 20-foot-deep pits, false walls camouflaged by paint and concealed staircases all aim to thwart theft. And while mere explorers could escape, buoyed by the kudos of achievement, ancient tomb-raiders knew they risked the penalty of death, by impalement, even if they made it out of the robber shafts alive.

Deep and inaccessible as the Great Pyramid's lower corridor is, this enigmatic narrow passageway could just about accommodate a corpse and a wooden coffin, but never a sarcophagus. So we have to look elsewhere for the likely destination of the king's body itself.

The next passageway creeps upwards, and leads to what is now confusingly described as the 'Queen's Chamber'. This high-ceilinged interior space was almost certainly a room intended to hold a statue of the Great King, to which offerings would be donated. When I was last there, it was protected by anxious signs reading DO NOT TOUCH OR MOVE; NEGATIVE FILM; DON'T X-RAY; KEEP OUT, because inside was muon tomography equipment currently used by a Japanese–Egyptian team to scan enigmatic spaces within the Pyramid. (Thrillingly, it has now been announced that a new corridor has indeed been discovered within the Pyramid itself. One hundred feet long, gabled, close to the main entrance, this unfinished passageway was perhaps conceived to help redistribute some of the Pyramid's enormous weight. It was photographed by the scanning scientists in 2023 with a 6-millimetre-thick endoscope fed through a tiny gap where two stones joined.) The 'Queen's Chamber' (with a pointed inner gabled roof) is one of at least three key chambers within the Great Pyramid, sitting one on top of the other, with 40-tonne superior stones. Like the 'King's Chamber', the 'Queen's Chamber' boasts two channels high in the stonework, each nearly 8 inches wide. These two channels run upwards towards the stars (although in the Queen's case, they are blocked by a slab of stone). This Queen's Chamber may possibly have been an optional choice as the key burial room by the pyramid builders; but then the process moved on closer to the heavens and the King's Chamber was created.[46]

So, to reach Khufu's most likely burial place, we have to stoop back out of the Queen's Chamber, close the modern metal gates with their

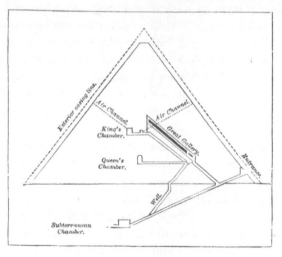

SECTION OF GREAT PYRAMID OF GHIZEH.

A schematic showing the arrangement of the chambers and tunnels within the Great Pyramid of Giza from Stanley in Africa *by James Penny Boyd, published in 1889.*

NO ENTRY signs, and start to climb the steep, appropriately named Ascending Corridor, which develops into what is now the Grand Gallery, 28 feet high – originally a shaft for transporting stone blocks. At the culmination of this 154-foot-long, cathedral-like staircase is a stunning corbelled vault, a unique piece of architecture, and then our goal – the King's Chamber itself.

Ducking, it is possible to make a stooped entrance into the booming burial room, made of polished granite, orientated east–west in the proportions of the Golden Mean. Originally this chamber was protected by a portcullis of red granite – a huge solid-grate that could be lowered down grooves in the sidewalls. This stone is not only dense and immensely heavy, it has an under-reported quality: in the desert, lit by bright sunlight against pale sand, Aswan granite appears not red, but an intense glowing violet. The Egyptians must have thought this rock possessed some kind of metamorphic power. In total, the King's Chamber, with its protecting portcullis kill-slabs which would have crushed all beneath them if they were released, uses around 3,000 tonnes of red granite. And what wonders that protean rock would have guarded. We can only begin to imagine what originally lay around the granite sarcophagus, itself still in situ. Just think of the treasures of Tutankhamun's tomb – a relatively insignificant, minor king: over a hundred walking sticks, childhood games, scores of packed duck lunches, earrings, rings, necklaces, leopard-face gold ornaments; gaudy, fake, bejewelled slippers, made just for show; beds, gloves, amber scarabs; blue lotus flowers, laid in a wreath; dried herbs, tiny ivory combs, giant golden ankhs – over 5,000 items.

Today there is a strange austerity to Khufu's burial place – curious, when the world it intended to perpetuate was highly sensuous. No treasure, just that empty sarcophagus, so heavy and huge, the chamber must have been built around it – facing the setting of the sun to expedite the king's journey to the afterlife. There is a chance that the air channels into the central burial chamber itself were originally directly aligned to stars in the night sky[47] (no longer, sadly, as the axis of the earth itself has shifted – a result of the weight of human activity). A place of ascension from the potent earth, at a time of significant geo-seismic activity, when planet Earth would have seemed to rock with a kind of primordial power.[48]

The sarcophagus, weighing 3.75 tonnes, must have been brought into the Pyramid before completion of the building works. Cut with a copper saw – whose indentations are still visible, with imperfections smoothed over – it seems a little sub-standard as the resting place of an almighty king and for a Wonder of such near-perfection. As well as the pocks on the sarcophagus, there is one crack in the burial chamber itself, which is also unusual in that it sits directly above the Pyramid's entrance, so it's easy to locate – not a typical robber-proof arrangement. Could the King's Chamber itself in fact be a decoy? Is Khufu, the Great King, buried elsewhere within one of the other unexplored caverns of the Great Pyramid?

In truth, this is unlikely. Despite three granite portcullises and granite plugs originally blocking the entrance to the burial chamber, and an external limestone seal, the Pyramid has been scoured clean and sucked dry. The looting and desecration in Egyptian tombs is ghastly. Iron filings are often found where coffins have been sawn and hacked apart.[49] All that is left in that central burial chamber of the Great Pyramid, indeed in all of its chambers so far discovered, are echoes and ideas.

In some senses the audacity of those tomb-raiding chancers is the essence of the spirit that drove the creation of all seven of the listed Wonders. However mystical, spiritual, they were also ultimately motivated by a drive to win. To possess wonderful man-made things, to profit from them, to take great risks in order to approach and enjoy a better life.

Above the gabled chamber of the burial room itself is a vaulted space that once contained red ochre jottings of the Great Pyramid's original builders, which, along with hieroglyphs and Khufu's cartouches, have been written over and blackened out by the soot inscriptions of inquisitive vandals – ranging from the Englishman Lord Nelson, to the Scottish diplomat and amateur archaeologist Patrick Campbell, who entered on 27 May 1837, through to medical sisters serving in World War I. General Howard Vyse, exploring too in 1837, was particularly delinquent, gunpowdering the space directly above the room of the sarcophagus. Vyse discovered four additional chambers which he named for influential friends: Wellington's Chamber; Nelson's Chamber; Lady Arbuthnot's Chamber and Campbell's Chamber. (He then dedicated his findings, *Operations carried on at the Pyramids of Gizeh*, to HRH Princess Augusta Sophia – a flattering gift, a transfer of timeless royal power by association.)

Above these relieving chambers, faced with rough stone, there is that space, a mystery – at the time of writing, the Egyptian–Japanese team is still virtually exploring above the burial point. There seems to be an empty chamber, 98 feet long, within the Pyramid itself. Is it structural? Or is it there to hide more treasure, perhaps even the body of a king?

The red ochre hieroglyphs in the relieving chambers have been eagerly alighted upon as proof of Khufu's ownership. But the material used also has significance. Red ochre, the colour of the sun, of blood and fertile soil, was not being employed by chance. In some of the very earliest underground burial structures known to man – such as the Hypogeum on the island of Malta – red ochre covers the half-rotten corpses of the entire community who were laid to rest there, possibly in the anticipation that their flesh would be reborn. Red ochre, reminiscent of wounds and the blood of menstruation and childbirth, was used in this 6,000-year-old mass grave, and elsewhere in Neolithic structures, almost certainly to represent the cycle of life and death. We now understand that chemically we are all stardust, that we are all part of the matrix of the universe, that at death the constituents of our bodies will become another form of life. The Stone Age and the Bronze Age got there first. By sponsoring wonder-generating projects such as the building of the Great Pyramid on the Giza Plateau, as a means of re-joining the 'indestructibles', Egypt's kings and pharaohs were living the concept of molecular chemistry. For the Old and New Kingdom Egyptians, death began the journey to another life in the universe. Pharaoh-kings, buried in the time-travelling resurrection machines of first mastaba tombs, then pyramids, then rock-cut burials, were being prepared for their journey through the skies back to the stars.

In 2020, inside an old cigar box in a university collection in Aberdeen, a small fragment of wood was discovered. The wood was cedar and had originally been found inside the Great Pyramid in the Queen's Chamber in 1872 by Waynman Dixon, an engineer working for the Astronomer Royal of Scotland, Charles Piazzi Smyth. The wood was in pieces, but had once been a small board, perhaps a cubit-rod or ruler, inserted in the narrow air shaft that leads out from the chamber itself. Other objects had also been in that shaft – a dolerite ball and a copper hook – perhaps to allow a spirit exit or entrance through the shaft? Or was it a worker's joke – a Bronze Age 'I was here'? What came to be called Dixon's ball and the hook are now held by the British Museum, along with a section of Tura casing stone* from the Pyramid that Dixon also helped himself to.[50] But now the wood has yielded a great surprise. When the organic fragments were sent off for analysis and dating, it was clear that the tree it came from had grown between 3341 and 3094 BCE, so over 500 years earlier than expected, 500 years before the historical date of the Pyramid's construction.

Should we move the Pyramid's age back 500 years in time? Or was the cedar tree – almost certainly from the Levant (modern-day Lebanon, Syria and Jordan) – so august because its own inner core was half a millennium old? Was this small plank cut to use in construction? Or was the wood a regional antique brought into the Pyramid to connect the Great King to his ancestors? Was it part of a funerary gift? Either way, that carefully chosen ancient piece was used to connect Khufu across time itself which, according to the Egyptian worldview, moved both forwards and back. Because this was an age without the ticking tyranny of clock-time. Time and space were capacious possibilities through which the Ancient Egyptians believed they needed to plot a course. Time was multidimensional, not linear, and constantly renewing. Although the Egyptians devised many of the timetables we live by – a 365-day year, for example – time belonged to the gods, and the Great Pyramid was Egypt's gargantuan attempt to keep time itself turning.[51]

So the Pyramid and its construction is the grandest of religious gestures – but activities detectable on the Giza Plateau show it was so much more too; a buzzing political and economic centre where many had the chance to marvel at this great Wonder of North Africa.[52] Somewhere that was transformational, that catalysed Egyptian civilisation. Because the Great Pyramid overlooked a vibrant river-city, and arguably it was not just an endeavour made by the Ancient Egyptians, but – as a director of excavations on the Giza Plateau has put it so well – the making of them as a nation and a people.

The great pyramids at Giza would not have existed without the power of the river. Indeed, the Nile made Egyptian civilisation possible. Although Herodotus is credited with nominating Egypt 'the gift of the Nile', this label was probably a phrase coined by his predecessor Hecataeus

---

* The documentation that came with the casing stone said that it had been removed from the rubble generated by road works in the area.

*Albumen print of the Pyramid of Khafre during inundation, showing the
Pyramid reflected in the Nile, taken by Antonio Beato in 1860–82, presented to
King George V.*

of Miletus, and a fact so ingrained in the psyche and physical experience
of Egypt that it was manifest in deeds before written words.[53] The very
name for a journey in Ancient Egyptian was the glyph for a riverboat. And
although it can be hard to credit now, it is vital to understand that water
would have been all around the Great Pyramid, that this Wonder was a
riverside attraction. The Nile flowed much closer to the Giza Plateau than it
does today, only 1000 feet or so from the pyramid complex for ten months
of the year, and for two, almost lapping the Pyramid's foundations.

Photographs, even from the early twentieth century, show the Nile
flooding close up to the Pyramid's base. The rise of this great river would
have been 23 feet every year, and for six to eight weeks during the inundation, the Pyramid would have been reflected from top to bottom in
those dark waters. Then, as now, the water and its alluvial floods brought
fertility; there would have been immediate abundance, darnel and canary
grasses, Egyptian clover in carpets, tamarisk and fig trees.[54] The waterway,
one of the longest rivers in the world, would have been thick with craft:
one-man skiffs skimming reed banks, cargo boats winding through the
sandbanks and reed beds, beefier barges rocking the waters with their
wash. Islands of crocodiles too, who could (and frequently did) mount
the banks at night to snatch mummified remains from less well-protected

burial places. We should imagine along the glittering line that is the Nile the waters glowing an intense, inky blue from the blue lotus flower – famed for its aphrodisiac and psychotropic qualities.

As well as the formal shop-fronts at the port there would have been ad hoc riverbank markets (as there still are on some stretches of the Nile today) where enterprising individuals would lay out wares on linen cloths. The river was also a larder – Nile perch and catfish were a regular meal. Even the hip bone of a young hippo has been discovered in detritus layers at the Giza site, suggesting it was hunted down and then consumed. The Nile water was canalled right up to the monuments on the plateau itself, from a tributary now vanished – allowing access for builders during the Pyramid's construction, and for pilgrims once it was finished. In front of what is now the Great Sphinx, a harbour wall is still just visible; excavations to expose the ancient port that was once here have already begun and will take at least two decades to complete.

The Great Pyramid looked out not over the desert, but over a riverine port.

We should remember that Khufu's name comes from the great god Khnum who was the source of the Nile, and therefore the source of life in Egypt. The king was believed to travel to the afterlife not on foot, but in a boat, through the ocean of the sky.*

Little surprise perhaps, then, that next to the Great Pyramid, glorious boats were buried. In 1954, a young Egyptian archaeologist discovered, under rubble at the base of the south face of the Pyramid, forty-one sealed limestone blocks. Within, preserved in the airtight conditions, was a giant river barque. Deconstructed but undamaged, the hull consisted of 1,274 separate pieces of wood – mainly of cedar – held together without a single nail. The most frequently used Ancient Egyptian word for shipbuilding is 'binding', because most boats were made of bound reeds, and modern versions still ply the river today. Weighing in at 20 tonnes, 138 feet long, the boat's wood shows evidence of at least one journey in the waters of the Nile, surely to carry the king. Boat pits have also been

---

* It is somewhat perverse that we think of Egypt as a desert culture, because not only was the Nile always present, but this land was once far more verdant. Recent research analysing fossil evidence and mineral deposits shows that the whole Arabian peninsula – and what is now Egypt – was significantly greener; it was only five thousand years ago, with the earth's tipping, that the marked desertification that we see today began.

identified, adjacent, on the eastern side of the Pyramid and above the royal causeway. Remarkably, after thirty years of exploratory work, in 2011 the remains of another boat were excavated.[55]

Those beautiful vessels were there to help the Great King in his journey through the afterlife, with the first one discovered having been rowed by oars; the other, waiting to be fully analysed, would have been sailed.[56] In the later tombs of the Valley of the Kings, solar barques transporting the king across the sky and on to the afterlife glide in painted form across many walls. The recent removal of the first boat from the Giza Plateau to the new Grand Egyptian Museum, as the wooden remains dwarfed workers and experts all around, gave a sense of the royal barge's original magisterial scale.

It's vital for us to remember that the pyramid's riverside location was itself a religious entity. The Nile was considered divine. The personification of the Nile's inundation was the deity Hapy, the non-binary god with bluish-green skin, aquatic plants in their hair (lotus leaves or papyri) and pendulous breasts, worshipped in particular at the cult centres of Elephantine Island and Gebel el Silsila, a ten-hour drive today from Cairo – the narrowing gorge of the Nile.* On Elephantine Island I have explored inside the underground channels within the rocks at the Nile's edge in this picturesque place, where hills of sand rise above the fast-running river. A deafening, echoing, crashing collision of Nile flood waters here meant this was where the god-head-power that caused the Nile to flood was believed to dwell. Khnum, you will recall, was the god whose spirit was thought to have generated those primordial earth and water pyramids; a creator deity who formed humanity from the Nile's fertile earth. Khnum's sacred turf, 500 miles south of Memphis, was also a political and trading hotspot, which could facilitate trade with Nubians to the south, delivering exotic goods that proved the pharaoh or king's glory – ebony, gold and panther skins.[57]

---

* Again in the Aswan area, another deity of inundation was worshipped, that god so special to Khufu – Khnum, the curly-horned, ram-headed deity, said to reside on Abu ('ivory' or 'elephant' in Egyptian), Elephantine Island. Gebel el Silsila is a riverside site rimmed with rock-cut tombs and sandstone quarries, used in particular from the time of Pharaoh Seti I onwards. The much later wall decorations on the Khnum temple at Esna give us a sense of how potent and life-giving Hapy was thought to be – the fertile soil left after the floods was associated with the creator gods (there are similarities here with the Greek myth of Prometheus).

Religion in Egypt was both an ecstatic and an economic expression.

So although the hulk of the Great Pyramid gives an impression of solidity, and of the magnetic pull of mass to one point, although it feels like a destination, this pyramid was in fact all about movement and travel, about connections along the great Nile River, which ran south to north, joining the seas of Arabia and the Mediterranean, and ultimately the Indian and Atlantic Oceans. Akhet-Khufu's horizon was a maelstrom of activity, a massive and intensive collective effort, a landscape designed for the dead that was full of life.

The Great King in his great Wonder tomb was not alone. The whole Giza Plateau was a necropolis, a city of the dead. The walls and piles of ancient rubble surrounding the three great pyramids, ruins that visitors scramble over, and are whistled down from by long-suffering guards, are in fact the remnants of the burials of thousands of women and men. These mini-pyramid mastabas for Khufu's queens, and the nobles in the court of both king and queen, have been laid out in a grid pattern. Potentates were buried here in their own mastaba tombs, amongst them Khufu's early overseer of works, Hemiunu. Overlooked by time and by tourists, originally these transits to eternity would have been decorated in low-relief with depictions of kingship, and aspirational scenes imagining all the things Khufu might revel in in the afterlife. Stretching out from the great pyramids, in this field of tombs for royals and courtiers, one can only imagine the jostling between rivals to be buried closest to the king and to his cosmic power.

So, a state affair, and a family affair too.

One tomb in particular helps us to appreciate the Great Pyramid Wonder in sharper focus. In 1925, inexplicable patches of white plaster were discovered on the eastern side of the Pyramid. The patches led excavators to a tomb shaft, to an empty room, and then below that into a re-sealed burial chamber. The chamber had been robbed, but still contained a concealed canopic chest (the repository for internal organs post mummification), a jewellery box complete with twenty decorated silver bracelets, gilded wooden furniture, a sedan chair, a bed, an elaborate canopy that would have protected the bed itself, small seats and a beautiful throne – recently reconstructed, made of cedar wood decorated with blue faience tiles, gold foil, gesso, ebony panels inlaid with gold hieroglyphs, and copper with a cordage seat. First explored in 1837 by those two English tomb-raiders, Howard Vyse and his engineer-aide John Shae Perring, this was the burial place of Hetepheres I, King Khufu's mother, no less. The mastaba burial of Hetepheres I hints at both the treasures which would originally have been buried with her son, and at what forms of beauty and richesse mattered to his family in life.

The Great Pyramid was joined, over a space of decades, by others: by the tomb-temple of Khufu's son Khafre and then of his grandson Menkaure. Khafre also built, as a guard for the whole site, the remarkable Sphinx – a crouching lion with a royal head, the face possibly modelled on Khafre's own. This astonishing custodian (partly hollow and filled with dead-end shafts and tunnels – investigations are ongoing and slowly the Sphinx will give up his secrets) was also built up from the bedrock. Facing directly west to east, with traces of red, blue and yellow pigment indicating the guardian was once gaudily bright, called in modern Egyptian Arabic 'Father of Dread' or 'The Terrifying One', the Sphinx is a fittingly monstrous sentinel for an astonishing ancient Wonder.

Immediately after Khufu's death and burial, the Great Pyramid would have been the site of a royal funerary cult, where sacrifices and offerings were made, administered by the cult's high priests. Did these men respect the king, and the Wonder which their generation had created? The interiors of other tombs show that burial officials themselves often ransacked the goods inside, sealed the tomb behind them and then exited down pre-planned, pre-built escape shafts. And of course, along with his treasures, the body of Khufu himself is missing – that cavernous burial chamber, that day blind sarcophagus, is empty. However sublime the king was believed to be, it seems his burial was not beyond desecration; Khufu's carefully mummified body and the treasures intended for the afterlife are yet to be found.

But the legend of Khufu endured. Mortuary priests continued to serve his cult for 400 years until at least the Eighth Dynasty, in around 2120 BCE. Alabaster jars were inscribed with Khufu's name at sacred sites close to Luxor. Pretty quickly, though, after these grand experiments (the pyramids of father, son and grandson, and the giant Sphinx who adorned the valley), even though the faithful still visited to pay their respects, burial practice returned to more modest, slightly less expensive tombs. Mortuary temples, where the living could convene, grew gradually grander and more sophisticated. Eventually the desert mountain El Qurn ('the horn') above the Valley of the Kings, sacred to the protecting cobra-goddess Meretseger (she who loves silence), became a natural pyramid, overseeing the new tombs beneath, which would become the temporary homes of the dead. The valley's tomb builders at Deir el-Medina surmounted their own burials with mini-pyramids, a budget-version of Khufu's Wonder, and the pyramid-building tradition was taken up instead by Nubian rulers in what is modern-day Sudan.

Four hundred years later, in the New Kingdom, the Giza pyramids once again became the popular target of religious pilgrimage, with Khufu the subject of a revived religious cult. But this time the giant guard-dog of the Giza Plateau, the Sphinx, rather than King Khufu, was worshipped as an incarnation of Horus in the Horizon, Horemakhet.[58] The first extant depiction of the Great Pyramid, rather tall and thin, comes courtesy of a plateau stele created by a scribe called Montuher who lived on the cusp of the Old and New Kingdoms. And again, between the giant, flexed and curling paws of the Sphinx is another flamboyant inscription – this time recording a fervent dream of the Pharaoh Thutmose IV that he must clear sands from Giza's wonders, as indeed he did. As I studied this record of respect, one wet February, an unexpected storm stained the Sphinx's stones a battle-ship brown and a double rainbow joined Khufu's, Khafre's and Menkaure's pyramids one to the other. I was processing the news that my father had died just hours before, and I was washed, as Pharaoh Thutmose seems to have been 3,500 years before, with a sense of awe. I felt utterly and poignantly wonder-struck by the remarkable things that mortals, in their short lives, attempt to achieve.

From the mid-seventh to the mid-fourth centuries BCE, Saite Egyptians from the Nile Delta restored Giza's mammoth constructions, and it seems that visitors came to Giza with a semi-mystical idea of Khufu in mind, buying vast numbers of scarab beetles engraved with his name. Mortuary cults for the pharaoh-king continued in an impressive number of locations across Egypt. The historian Herodotus visited in the fifth century BCE and wrote at length about the Great Pyramid in Book Two of his *Histories*: 'The pyramids also were greater than words can say, and each one of them is equal to many works of the Hellenes, great as they may be . . .'[59] The wondrous nature of the Pyramid was doing its job, forcing the world to remember its inhabitant and its ingenious builders.

Khufu (given his Greek name Cheops by Herodotus)[60] does not fare well at the historian's hands. Herodotus commemorates the king as a kind of pantomime villain – in particular recounting that Khufu sold his daughter to a brothel so she could be paid in stone blocks to build the Pyramid (and adding that the daughter also loaned out her body to collect massive stones to construct her own memorial).[61] We also hear that Khufu forced his workmen to slave during the construction of the Pyramid and its causeway. Herodotus was told by a local that writings on the outside of the Great Pyramid (probably the work of those Saite restorers from the century before) translated as the number of beetroot, onions and garlic the workers ate – the equivalent of £5 million worth.[62] The well-travelled historian reported this fact in all seriousness, yet I'm sure the Egyptian guide at the time would have howled with laughter at his curious visitor's gullibility. All these accounts reveal a *Grimms' Fairy Tales* gruesome gloss that the pyramids and their founder had acquired.

On a happier side note, we hear from another, later Greek historian and geographer, Strabo (who was born in what is now the eastern Black Sea region of Turkey), in an early version of the Cinderella story (and a faint pre-echo of the narrative of the Taj Mahal in India), that the smaller pyramid of the plateau was built when Rhodopis, a beautiful Greek courtesan, while bathing in the coastal Egyptian town of Naukratis, had her sandal stolen by an eagle. The perfumed shoe was dropped in the lap of the Pharaoh Menkaure. Enraptured, the king ordered a search for the shoe's owner, and when Rhodopis was found, he constructed his pyramid for her as a token of his love.[63]

Romans were more dismissive of the Great Pyramid Wonder, seeing it as a rival to their own engineering marvels. Pliny the Elder, the travelling general, author and naturalist, adjudged the pyramids as 'the idle and foolish ostentation of royal wealth', although in his *Natural History* he also perpetuated the narrative that there was a channel running under the Great Pyramid which communicated with the River Nile.[64] Perhaps this was something those Roman investigators were trying to discover when they penetrated into the lower chamber, leaving trophy graffiti.

There are even independent scholars today who still question whether Khufu's monumental tomb could have been broken into to lay the body of the Macedonian leader, Alexander the Great, to rest. It is one of the Seven Wonders which still sparks earnest fantasies.

In the fourth century CE, the pyramids were further hijacked by a fascinating character, a Christian woman called Egeria. The details of Egeria's life are scant, but her legacy is great. She embarked on a bold pilgrimage – probably from northern Portugal – right through the Holy Land, writing an account for her 'sisters'. We are not sure whether this was a community of nuns, or just like-minded female friends. Either way, Egeria's journey was quite the adventure. One can only begin to guess at the complication of organising such a trip 1,700 years ago, travelling as she did to modern Jordan, Israel, Palestine, Syria and across to Egypt. But, almost as if to justify her mission, Egeria was compelled to see a Judaeo-Christian God all around her. Thus, in her estimation, the great pyramids at Giza became, somewhat surprisingly, the granaries of the biblical Joseph. Those were the stores the wily Jewish hero had put to one side that would save Egypt from the great plague and subsequent famine.[65] It was a misidentification that stuck right through the mediaeval period and beyond. In St Mark's refulgent basilica in Venice, high in the glittering ceiling, a fine gold mosaic tells the story. Joseph oversees workers stashing bushels of wheat into the elongated, windowed pyramids – at a stroke connecting the Venetian maritime power to the East, and to notions of good management, with the Venetians styling themselves as a chosen people.[66] This was a time when women in Venice typically walked through the streets veiled, so strongly associated the Venetian empire was with the Muslim-majority southern ports of Alexandria and Damascus.[67] It is little surprise that Egypt's wonders were on the Venetians' minds. As antiquity continued to judder into the mediaeval age, seeking gold, grain, and a granary of wisdom, the Pyramid was reopened by that Caliph al-Ma'mun sometime between 813 and 833 CE, most likely in 832 CE.[68] There are stories of the theft of emeralds the size of eggs; the plunder of a solid-gold cockerel; and even that al-Ma'mun found remnants of Khufu's mummy still lying in his sarcophagus, albeit much deteriorated. Others were inspired by the Great Pyramid to offer more sober reflections. The late-twelfth-, early-thirteenth-century Egyptian scientist and researcher Al-Idrisi described in his pioneering work *Anwar* why it was important to study the pyramids, to assess their measurements and chemical composition and to document their inscriptions. Al-Idrisi provided a handy traveller's guide to the best routes to the site – clearly already a prestige destination. The Scribe of Saladin, Al-Imad Al-Işfahani, visited at the invitation of a local dignitary, again in the early 1200s CE, and spent happy hours there debating the pyramids' purpose and their sponsors. Al-Idrisi mentions, too, the female-guardian spirit of the plateau (fascinatingly, Saite visitors 600 years before spoke of a shrine to the goddess Isis next to the Pyramid), a popular belief amongst Arabic writers.[69]

Another regional historian from the fifteenth century, Al-Maqrizi, quoting the twelfth-century CE text, *The History of Egypt and its Wonders*, by Ibrahim Ibn Wasif Shah, suggested that an ante-diluvian pharaoh created the Pyramid as a giant waterpark, connected to the Nile by canals and reservoirs. Al-Maqrizi also wrote that Khufu, plagued by nightmares of the sky falling, the earth turning upside down, a monster deluge and his people being kidnapped by the stars, had constructed the three great pyramids to keep his treasures and his books safe.[70] A number of Arab writers at the time believed the pyramids were built by Idris – the name they gave to the Greek god Hermes, originally the ancient Egyptian Thoth.[71] The Pyramid was becoming a lightning rod for untethered imagination.

That massive geo-seismic event in 1303 CE loosened the majority of the Great Pyramid's remaining limestone casing stones. Nine decades later, in 1395, the pilgrim Lord of Anglure from north-eastern France recorded that blocks of stone and these fallen veneers were being taken for use in the construction of mediaeval Cairo. Some can indeed still be seen on Muhammad Ali Pasha's Alabaster Mosque, in Cairo' old town, built between 1830 and 1857 by an architect from Istanbul and in the Ottoman style (inspired by the splendid Sultanahmet Cammi, the Blue Mosque, which still dominates the Istanbul skyline today). But much of the silver-bright casing stone, brought so carefully from Tura, was in truth ground down to use as lime, building material for other generations, other civilisations to force new structures on the inhabited earth.[72]

The stones of the Pyramid were being repurposed, and its purpose was changing. Fact-finding missions by colonial explorers such as George Sandys (whose detailed, dramatic *A Relation of a Journey begun An: Dom: 1610* was presented to the future Charles I, still the Prince of Wales, with observations floridly printed on soft paper, and bespoke-drawn rubrication – faded red lines of ink so the work appeared like a hand-written

Taking a picnic to the summit of the Great Pyramid, 17 February, 1938.

Illustration from Generis Splendore *by Hans Jacob Breüning showing pin-figures also climbing to the top of the Great Pyramid* (1612).

manuscript) contained fine engravings, showing excited caravans of Westerners approaching Khufu's tomb. Sandys' account is a page-turner. His mind was clearly blown when he encountered crocodiles for the first time, and we owe him some debt of gratitude for overturning the tenacious misconception that these pyramids were granaries built to house Joseph's grain supplies. This son of the Archbishop of York, having explored the Great Pyramid inside and out, published his proof that Giza's pyramids were indeed the burial place of an Egyptian king, and animatedly described the Sphinx as a Colossus. This beautiful book was clearly much-thumbed in the royal library, seeing that it was re-bound with ostentatious, embossed, bark-brown leather in the early nineteenth century. A German adventurer named Hans Jacob Breüning, publishing an account just two years after Sandys in 1612, sandwiches his eager description of the pyramids between illustrations of two mummified human remains, and a page featuring a handsome dragon. There is haptic pleasure in researching these works. Breüning's German volume has been covered with a robust pig-skin binding, locked with clasps – as if the privileged knowledge within it needed protecting.

The first European systematic survey of the Pyramid was completed by John Greaves, the Gresham Professor of Geometry, and also the Savilian Professor of Astronomy at Oxford, in 1639.[73] In 1646 Greaves published his *Pyramidographia* – an attempt at a sober understanding of the construction of the great monument, drawing on Arab and Persian sources as well as Greek. Sir Isaac Newton, the definitive Enlightenment natural philosopher, who by his own admission stood on the shoulders of giants, used Greaves' work to measure the dimensions of the King's Chamber.[74]

The reports of European travellers such as these show there was a theatre of international tourism in play by at least the seventeenth century. Visitors were actively encouraged to climb to the peak of the Pyramid (illegal now, although still a pursuit for socialites and soldiers alike up until the 1970s). In Sandys' volume, men are shown eagerly clambering into the entrance blown open by Caliph al-Ma'mun, and in Breüning's book, two triumphant free-climbers are waving from its summit. Visitors were also challenged to try to clear the Pyramid's base with an arrow from on high, while Janissary guides from the ruling Ottoman empire impressed the impressionable by firing pistols into entrances to 'dispel robbers'. Many of these visitors from the modern world reached the Great Pyramid and the Giza Plateau by Nile river-boat – just as ancient construction teams, travellers and pilgrims had done.

Nathaniel Davison, a British diplomat, was the first we know of in modern times to crawl his way up inside the Pyramid from the Grand Gallery, through a tunnel in its south wall, into the stone attic above the King's Chamber, in 1765. Sporting a pigtail, one of the very last of his age to do so, Davison described having to force his way through mounds of bat dung as he approached.[75] I too have found myself having to do this in tombs in Egypt, and I feel for Davison. The stench is overwhelming, the caress of hundreds of disturbed bats panic-inducing. But in truth, Davison had no right to be there. He not only left his name brazenly graffitied across the Pyramid's walls, but, ahistorically and incongruously, this extraordinary example of Ancient Egyptian engineering is still called Davison's Chamber today.

Forty years later, Napoleon's savants followed – 167 of them. The Pyramid was studied minutely and scientifically – the findings published in the monumental *Description de l'Egypte* – across two decades up until 1822. The work was so extensive, that the constituent books were printed in a huge form, in what were called 'elephant' folios. Whole mahogany cabinets were built to store the books – of such a scale that turning a single page is quite an effort. The *Description* was scholarly work, with a non-scholarly legacy, and a trigger for European Egyptomania – sparking baseless theories such as John Taylor's in his *The Great Pyramid*, that a unit of measurement, the 'pyramid inch', existed.[76]

And in 1858, the first photographic coffee-table book about Egypt was produced. Crowd-sourced in advance by elite subscribers, including dukes, a marquis, and a pageful of esquires, the peerless photographs for this magnificent collection were supplied by Francis Frith, who put turbaned human figures and donkeys into the empty, rocky desert landscapes for scale. Again, a huge volume (officially a 'mammoth print'), the 1858 edition has helpful little maps and a biblical tinge, entitled as it was: *Egypt, Sinai and Jerusalem*.

Meanwhile, visiting Western clerics used the Pyramid as a whipping boy for Christian zeal. Popular works such as *The Land of the Pharaohs: Egypt and Sinai* by one Rev. Samuel Manning, LL.D., published by the Religious Tract Society (with a suitably religious address: 56, Paternoster Row, 65, St. Paul's Churchyard), wrapped stories of Moses and Herod the

Great into Victorian travelogue and monotheistic censure. The enslave-
ment of the Jewish population was a narrative set in the shadow of the
Giza pyramids. The Great Pyramid chapter in this particular publication
finishes with a biblical homily about the passage of time that would have
seemed anathema to Khufu, even if his Egyptian belief in immortality
went on to inform Christian ideas of resurrection and the afterlife. 'The
grass withereth, the flower fadeth: but the word of our God shall stand
for ever.'[77]

Western interest painted layers of ahistorical meaning onto the Pyramid's sloping profile. But then it was those two British explorers, Colonel
Howard Vyse and engineer John Shae Perring, who (after, unforgivably,
dynamiting an opening into the core blocks on the southern side in an
attempt to find another entry-point) stumbled upon Khufu's red-daubed
cartouches while exploring inside the relieving chambers in the nineteenth century. Khufu's involvement in the creation of the oldest of the
Seven Wonders – never doubted by the ancients – was rubber-stamped
by the modern world.

The Great Pyramid was a Wonder around which its creator, Khufu,
would have been thought to circle in the form of a falcon, while his
people circumambulated as a means to connect to the universe, and
from which their king ascended to the stars, to help ensure the cosmos
never descended into chaos. 'The earth is made into steps for the great
Pharaoh to move towards heaven, so he may ascend towards heaven.'[78]
What wonder – for the great king not just to rise from the dead, but to
move through those nights up to the skies above a plateau whose name
means 'Khufu belongs to the horizon'.[79] In our lifetimes, newly identified
solar boats (watching the wood currently being preserved and analysed in
laboratories at the back of the new Grand Egyptian Museum as thrilling
as any forensic crime-show), satellite pyramids, empty chambers and internal shafts have all been discovered. What other secrets, one wonders,
do the Pyramid and the Giza Plateau hold?

Although the recent discovery of a pyramid-shaped tomb-covering,
10 feet high, in the shepherd-saturated mountains of northern Lebanon,
has encouraged some to question whether this was a 2,000-year-earlier
inspiration adopted by the Egyptians, the truth is simpler. Pyramids
were men playing with the power of the earth, and the power of the

human mind to bend the earth's raw materials to their will. These Ancient Egyptians, with little interest in the past and the future, did not consider themselves to be standing on the shoulders of giants. Khufu *et al.* knew that in order to maintain the giant wonder of the universe, their involvement with it must have gargantuan scale and ambition.

Khufu's father's title was 'He who makes things perfect, Horus, Lord of Ma'at'. Ma'at was an underlying principle of Egypt – a goddess and the world's first abstract concept: a notion of order and justice and a righteousness which renewed creation. The Pyramid was intended as a compliment to the understanding of the Ancient Egyptians that Ma'at – balance and harmony – as well as mathematical systems governed the universe. No little irony that this Wonder did so by generating one of the most intrusive buildings on earth for close on 4,000 years, the tallest man-made structure until the spire of Lincoln Cathedral was raised in 1311, a structure that rose from the sweat of the brow of an entire generation.

The Great Pyramid Wonder was a state-sponsored sycophant to individual ambition, and also celebrated our hyper-connectivity with other planets and the rest of the cosmos. Our next Wonder comes from the playbook of man's control of Ma'at, and planet Earth's finite resources.

Many still consider a trip to the pyramids a once-in-a-lifetime experience. The Hanging Gardens of Babylon, which made water the gift not of Mother Nature, but of man, is a fantastical creation whose exact location may still not be identified in our lifetimes; but which remains the most famous Wonder of all the seven collected in the ancient world's Wonder-lists.

CHAPTER 2

❖

THE HANGING GARDENS OF BABYLON

c. 691–550 BCE

I raised the height of the surroundings of the palace, to be a Wonder for all peoples. I gave it the name: 'Unrivalled Palace'. A high garden imitating the Amanus mountains I laid out next to it, with all kinds of aromatic plants . . .

KING SENNACHERIB DESCRIBING HIS NEW GARDEN AT NINEVEH,
ON THE CLAY PRISM OF SENNACHERIB , c. 691 BCE

'The Walls of Babylon' engraving produced by Philips Galle after designs by
Maarten van Heemskerck in 1572; gardens are featured on the roof of the palace.

After he has travelled twelve double hours, it is light.
Before him stand shrubs of precious stones,
he sees them as he draws nigh.
The carnelian bears its fruit;
vines hang from it, good to look at.
The lapis lazuli also bears fruit; pleasant to behold.
For thorns and thistles there were haematite and rare stones,
agate, and pearls from the sea.
And Gilgamesh walked in the garden.

EPIC OF GILGAMESH IX.170–95,

DESCRIBING THE GODDESS INANNA'S GARDEN, C. 2100 BCE

When Alexander the Great was a teenager, around 340 BCE, in the wild-wooded hills of the Macedonian palace at Pella in what is now northern Greece, Persian ambassadors came to his father's court with high tales of the Orient.[1] We are told that Alexander made it clear he had no time for incidental fripperies; that his interest lay in the roads and military installations that would allow him to stretch south and to subjugate.[2] But others in this palace-citadel, protected still by woods thick with the calls of owls and eagles, must surely have hung onto the visitors' accounts of wonders such as the Great Walls of Babylon and its Hanging Gardens, which lay 1,000 miles north-east of the Giza Plateau in Egypt, 1,600 miles east of the Greek mainland. Now, as then, the stepped and well-watered royal gardens of an Ancient Babylonian king burn bright in the popular imagination. They are indeed, arguably, the most 'famous' of the Seven Wonders; for many, they are top of the list. They are also, ironically, the only Wonder which may, just possibly, not have existed.

The exact site of these fabled Hanging Gardens in the Middle East has never been securely identified. The 'Father of History', Herodotus, who probably visited Babylon in the fifth century BCE, does not mention them. Herodotus' slack-jawed wonder is reserved for the city of Babylon's great walls.[3] In some Seven Wonder lists – including that early version by Antipater of Sidon (the Greek poet of the second century BCE who started life on the Lebanese coast and moved to Rome) – it is again Babylon's *walls* that make the cut: the gardens simply are not an option.[4] Archaeological remains between the Tigris and the Euphrates in what was Mesopotamia, and is now Iraq, which *might* be gardens in a palace setting in ancient Babylon, are ambiguous. There is no hard evidence that they were ever planted.[5]

The Great Walls of Babylon, famed since 1700 BCE, definitely existed – they have been identified in a series of archaeological digs running along the line of the Euphrates.[6] Stretching at least 30 miles, these fortifications were made of mudbrick encased with stone. Some areas would have been crusted and burnished with brilliantly glazed and coloured tiles. One section, over one mile long, may well have been demolished by Alexander the Great to erect the gargantuan funeral pyre of his beloved, much-mourned companion Hephaestion (Alexander did get to Babylon as planned).[7] Babylon's inner-city wall was said to be wide enough to turn a horse and chariot on[8] – and so would have been easily wide enough to support the weight of earth for ornamental planting: perhaps these enclosures doubled as giant window-boxes, from which flowers, herbs and shrubs could tumble down? Sections of Babylon's kaleidoscope-bright inner walls can still be seen – even touched – in museums in Iraq, Istanbul and Berlin. They are astonishing. They are truly wonderful. They are an extraordinary exercise in colour and design and engineering from 2,600 years ago.

So are we perhaps talking about an elevated arboretum above a vivid fortified enclosure? A winding line of wind-washed green that seemed to hang on top of the world below? Impressive certainly, definitely a site that would be talked about, but arguably not one of <u>the</u> greatest and most wondrous creations of all time. Could our second Wonder be a confused memory, a phenomenon that has somehow escaped the extant archaeological record, or was simply made up?

To try to dig to the truth, we must start at the beginning of this Wonder's recorded history. Who tells us that there *were* Hanging Gardens of Babylon at all? That these existed in Babylon, or were indeed *hanging*?

We start with the wonder-biographers. In the early fourth century BCE, Ctesias of Knidos – an author, general, courtier and physician (who tended to the wounds of the Persian King Artaxerxes II, no less) – apparently described the Hanging Gardens in some detail in his work *The Persika*. Coming as he did from the tumbling port city of Knidos in Asia Minor (famed home to the fully naked sculpture of the love-goddess, the Knidian Aphrodite), which was built on raked cliffs that slope down to the sea, Ctesias' interest in elevated engineering is understandable. And his time spent in the Persian court (Persia had taken over the territory of Babylon by Ctesias' lifetime) means he could well have heard of a verdant sensation which the Persians inherited.

But we have a problem, because *The Persika* of Ctesias survives only as ghostly fragments, as references mentioned in the works of others.[9] Ctesias' work *Babyloniaca*, describing the territory the gardens would have inhabited, has been completely lost. So Ctesias is a diminished source.

Granular description was added to Ctesias' account by a flamboyant historian of Alexander the Great's campaigns called Cleitarchus, who may himself have gone to Babylon, and who certainly met eyewitnesses from the fourth century BCE, namely, the followers of Alexander and their descendants. We hear from Cleitarchus of complex mechanisms for raising water, and the bitumen from the Dead Sea used as waterproofing along with reeds and lead-lining, to prevent the well-watered plants, clearly in some elevated planting scheme, from dripping on passers-by. He also describes gorgeous 'royal lodges' dotted through the grounds at Babylon.[10]

These vivid accounts were then expanded on once again in the first century BCE by the historian from Sicily, Diodorus Siculus, in his monumental *Universal History* – almost certainly deriving his ideas from those accounts of Ctesias and Cleitarchus, which, respectively, had been written 300 and 200 years earlier.[11]

And the tantalising references do not stop there: the Greek geographer Strabo quoted at length another of Alexander the Great's companions, Onesicritus, who relates, in elaborate prose, that Babylon's garden was square and was raised at different levels – it is this staggered arrangement that must have earned the epithet 'hanging'. We hear it had arched vaults made of baked brick and bitumen, on top of which giant planters were watered thanks to mechanical screws designed to raise water from the Euphrates.[12] Onesicritus wrote this account from his calm little hometown-island of Astypalaia in the eastern Aegean. Only 8 miles across, Astypalaia must have seemed a far cry from his campaigning adventures with Alexander – where, by his own account, we hear he witnessed artificial rivers and lakes, towering walls, and exotic fruit-filled gardens.[13] It was Onesicritus who arranged that conference for Alexander in India with the naked wise men, the *gumnosophists*.[14] Although dismissed as an exaggerating, unreliable source (Onesicritus claimed to be Alexander's

admiral but was in truth only his helmsman), at the very least, the details
which this soldier-pilot supplies testify to a burning interest in the East.
Another author, Berossus (in a work dedicated to the son of another of
Alexander's right-hand men, Seleucus, and quoted in the first century
CE by the Jewish historian Josephus),[15] a Babylonian priest who doubtless had access to Babylonian archives, provides additional particulars.
Berossus writes in around 290 BCE that these were gardens *within* the
palace itself.[16] Given archaeological evidence from the region, where
palace walls protected against both marauding humans and animals, this
feels like a pretty likely scenario. Berossus speaks of lofty stone terraces
like mountains, a hanging 'paradise'. Based, eventually, on the island of
Kos, home of the father of medicine, Hippocrates, Berossus may have
been particularly interested in the medicinal plants that were said to have
grown in this horticultural wonderland.*

Berossus also tells us the Hanging Gardens were commissioned in
604–562 BCE by the Babylonian King Nebuchadnezzar II for his wife
Amytis as a token of his love, and to help prevent her pining for the mountains of her homeland – Media, in what is modern-day Iran.[17] Ctesias also
tells us the gardens were built for a homesick wife (interesting, given that
in his own life, he cared for King Artaxerxes' wife Stateira and tended to
his own mother Parysatis. Perhaps an example of an empathetic historian
delighted to find a past that matched his own narrative?). Ctesias, we
are informed, also excitedly described the exploits of the semi-legendary
warrior-queen Semiramis, with whom the gardens came to be associated.
This glamazon heroine took time off from her horticultural pursuits to go
into battle dressed as a man, to make love to a different soldier each night,
and then to kill them.[18]

So, many fine, high-octane, enchanting, memorable words, recording
what people believed to be true, but there is rather less hard evidence in
the ground.

The gardens themselves are therefore a tantalising lacuna, but their very
elusiveness is their strength: the gap they leave, we have filled with our
dreams. For 2,500 years the Hanging Gardens of Babylon – apparently

---

* Author of the *Babylonica* and the *Assyrica*, a kind of guide for Greeks to the East. Berossus' treatise on Babylon survives, but the work dealing with the Babylonians' northern
neighbours, the Assyrians, is entirely lost. It is in this missing treatise that a written record
of an alternative location Hanging Gardens could possibly have been set down.

with no extant visible trace – could be whatever over fifty generations of wonder-chasers have wanted them to be, and so they have grown, by degree and delight, by the day.

But the Hanging Gardens of Babylon are a Wonder worth investing time in, and worth investigating, because they speak of an innovative age, the Iron Age, where new, efficient iron tools were changing our relationship with the planet. The Hanging Gardens were, we are told, laden with imported decorative shrubbery, all kept alive with an innovative water system that irrigated plants not for survival but for show. Babylon's River Euphrates was embanked with an artificial bitumen lining to control flooding. Mesopotamia was already a region rich with pistachio forests, heaving herds of sheep and goats, and access to luxury goods – carnelians from the Indus Valley, lapis lazuli from Afghanistan – but iron allowed its rulers to become phenomenally wealthy. Woodlands were cleared, terraces cut into hillsides, rivers diverted. More food was produced more efficiently, so populations had fuller bellies and therefore more time to think, to dream, to create. But pollution levels also started to rise. Fascinating studies in the region show that even today, the milk of goats herded by Bedouins in remote desert districts displays significant levels of heavy metals – ancient residues in the soil. Iron technology was turning agriculture and horticulture into an action of extreme intervention.[19]

The Hanging Gardens are also, in truth, a mystery which may be solved. Not only was Mesopotamia credited as a dynamo of civilisation and innovation, where mankind achieved extraordinary things against the odds, but as a culture that adored gardens and their making. The most ruthless, pitiless rulers of a territory spanned by modern-day Iraq and Syria would come back from campaigns with prisoners of war, looted treasures, and also with roots, cuttings and seedlings. Magnificent gardens from this time and place are not just a possibility but a probability. 'Gardens enhance the pride of cities', chanted one Babylonian hymn.[20] The acquisition of plants from all quarters was effected with vim and vigour. This was a time and a place that took the ownership and artful display of flora dead seriously.[21]

It was truly a pioneering age, that had the time, expertise, technology and wherewithal to move not just Nile-ferry-loads of stone blocks, but wagonloads of delicate flowers and trees (and often the earth to go with them), for examination and transportation. Khufu's inheritors of pharaonic power, such as the female Pharaoh Hatshepsut, might have tried to import exotic plants like frankincense trees from the Arabian Peninsula, but Babylonia's rulers would move whole forests. The Hanging Gardens come from a new epoch when humans do not just try to be an effective part of nature; we try to make nature an effective part of our everyday lives and experiences. Just think of it – this is the exact epoch when the Book of Genesis was written down, which declares in Chapter 1 that God tells man he has dominion over the living world: 'God blessed them. And God said to them, "Be fruitful and multiply and fill the earth and subdue it and have dominion over the fish of the sea and over the birds of the heavens and over every living thing that moves on the earth."'[22]

And now, on modest tablets that sit in the storerooms of the British Museum, we can read brilliant new evidence on the ground for exactly the kinds of plants cultivated 2,600 years ago by the Babylonian elite.

Whereas in the Neolithic and Early Bronze Ages, Arabia and the Middle East had been surprisingly green, well watered and lush (our evidence includes newly discovered riverbeds and petroglyphs from 5,000 years ago showing cattle-herds roaming where now only camels and goats survive), by the seventh century BCE the desertification of much of the region was well established.[23] Verdant, cultivated landscapes at the time of the Hanging Gardens symbolised exceptional fortune and knowhow. Mature gardens demonstrated a dynasty's staying power. It takes at least a human generation, twenty-five years or so, for most trees to reach their adult height, so ownership of established, exotic trees is a representation of endurance. Expeditions to seize trees are first recorded in *The Epic of Gilgamesh* – the poetry about these timber missions pounds keenly.[24] One early-ninth-century Assyrian king proudly lists the specific trees he grew – forty-two varieties – many of which were seized from foreign lands.[25] Other rulers of Mesopotamia imported cedars from Lebanon, oaks and fruit trees, spices from what is now Turkey, gram beans from India to produce gram flour. Exotic grasses were employed for their sculptural qualities. We hear too of pomegranates, pear, fig, hazelnut and olive trees, as well as the vine – wine had been produced in Asia from at least 8,000 BCE, as clay analysis from terracotta pots in Georgia has recently shown. On decorative steles from his palace, Ashurbanipal, the king of the Mesopotamian kingdom of Nineveh, is shown reclining under a vine-terrace.[26]

So we know, then, the region could acquire exotic specimens and nourish serious planting schemes, but the plot thickens. Unequivocal archaeological evidence for hanging gardens at Babylon might be conspicuous by its absence, but the existence of ancient hanging gardens a hundred miles to the north, in the city of Nineveh, is indisputable. Because new evidence, and the persuasive detective work of scholars, suggests that our second Wonder could quite possibly not only be a daydream made flesh – as the majority of later historical accounts would have it – by Nebuchadnezzar the Great in Babylon in the sixth century BCE, but also in gardens further to the north in the wider province of Babylonia in Nineveh, the Bible's 'city of sin',[27] in the seventh century BCE by Sennacherib, the self-styled 'Favourite of the Gods'.[28]

The story of the Hanging Gardens of Babylon is then a tale of two cities; a tale of two emotional reactions to history; and a tale of two kings – the Babylonian Nebuchadnezzar the Great whose power base was Babylon, and the Assyrian Sennacherib who ruled from the mighty northern city of Nineveh, just shy of the modern city of Mosul.

This is an investigative trail that leads us through a remarkable time and place – the seventh-century BCE Near and Middle East, from the shores of Lebanon and Syria to the Arabian Gulf. To understand and imagine Babylonia's elusive garden Wonder, first we have to think back twenty-seven centuries and out to a vast geographical landscape, strategically connected, whose inhabitants were on the rise.

Just south of modern-day Baghdad, Babylon (a historic site most recently inhabited in the tenth century CE, as the small village of Babel) enjoyed an excellent strategic location. Not only framed by the Rivers Tigris and Euphrates, Babylon was also fed by the Royal Road from Susa to Sardis, and by the Khorasan Road, one of many silk routes which would ultimately connect to the home of another of the Seven Wonders, the Temple of Artemis at Ephesus.

Flourishing from around 700 years after the Great Pyramid was built,*

---

* From c. 850 BCE Babylon had been controlled by a relative newcomer-dynasty, the Chaldaeans. Originally Semitic speakers from the Western Levant, by the time the Chaldaeans were in charge in Babylon, their language was a form of Aramaic. Aramaic became the lingua franca of Babylonian territories under the Persians. Prophet Abraham, many contest, was born in Ur of the Chaldaeans in southern Iraq, although Urkesh (north-eastern Syria), Uratu (eastern Anatolia), Kutha (central Iraq) and Şanliurfa (Edessa) in southern Turkey are also possibilities.

then passing hands between Babylonians and Assyrians for eight centuries, in 609 BCE, just eighty years after Babylonia had been occupied again by the Assyrians, a new history-maker came to Babylon – King Nebuchadnezzar II. Nebuchadnezzar – whose name in Babylonian is Nabu-kudduri-uṣur – blasted the Babylonian Empire back onto the international scene, with a lightning-strike of campaigns in Egypt, Palestine and Syria, triumphing at the Battle of Carchemish in modern-day Turkey in 605 BCE and then bringing the King of Judah and other Jewish prisoners to Babylon in 597 BCE, and the entire Jewish population in 586 BCE, and so earning the condemnation of both the Old and New Testaments.[29]

Assyria, meanwhile, was a kingdom whose centre of operations comprised what is now central and northern Iraq, a territory of mountains and rainfalls and tributaries, whose power base lay east of the fast-flowing Tigris. Nineveh was an older settlement than Babylon, with heft, right from the time the pyramids on the Giza Plateau were being raised. With continuous influence dating back to at least the seventh millennium BCE, Assyria controlled Babylon from 732 to 626 BCE – and at its height territories in what is now Turkey, Palestine, Israel (called by the Assyrians Bit-Omri), Egypt, Iran, Jordan, Lebanon, Iraq and Syria. Today Nineveh abuts war-ripped Mosul, where the River Tigris flows now more sluggishly. Students sip tea at riverside cafés, with the devastated historical city, virtually obliterated after three years under the ISIL caliphate, just visible on the river's east bank.

Both ancient territories had natural and logistical advantages. Unlike the unity of Bronze Age Egypt under Khufu, here there was the chance for extreme rivalry and conflict. Both kingdoms had leaders who were ferociously ambitious.

As crown-prince, Nabu-kudduri-uṣur (we will call him Nebuchadnezzar from here on) had reconquered Babylon. He went on to rule for forty-five years and to rebuild his city in honour of the gods, adding an additional palace, and new gardens. Nebuchadnezzar trumpeted his slash and burn triumphs across the region; in the high hills of Lebanon, famous for its cedars, he ordered his image to be carved on rocks. On the weathered stone he fights with lions and is about to tear down a giant tree to build his temple doors. Remote now, in a herb-thick pass above Wadi El-Sharbin, at the edge of Lebanon and Syria, in this carving in

Babylonian cuneiform, Nebuchadnezzar boasted long and loud of his dominion over the natural world:

> Strong cedars, thick and tall, of splendid beauty, supreme their fitting appearance, huge yield of the Lebanon, I bundled them like reeds and I perfumed the river with them . . . and I put them in Babylon like Euphrates poplars.[30]

King Sennacherib the Assyrian too had listed the natural resources – often thought to hold special, magic powers – which he had taken from the earth. He says; 'I tore open mountain and valley with iron picks,' and:

> I built other palatial pavilions of gold, silver, bronze, carnelian, breccia, alabaster, elephant tusk, ebony, boxwood, rosewood, cedar, cypress, pine, elammaku-wood and Indian wood for my royal abodes.[31]

> . . . fossiliferous limestone . . . a charm stone efficacious for winning acceptance [from the gods] . . . for making bad weather pass without damage . . . breccia which looks like dragonflies' wings, efficacious for assuaging throbbing in the brow, and which brings joy of heart and happiness of mind as a charm stone . . . *girimhilibû* beautiful and pleasing to behold, and with the ability to prevent plagues infecting a person.[32]

> I diverted the course of the flood-prone river from the city-centre, and directed its outflow into the land which surrounds the city at the back. For half an acre along the watercourse I bonded four great limestone slabs with bitumen and laid reeds from reed thickets and canes over them.[33] [A replica reed-marsh inspired by southern Babylonia.]

For those with extreme power, this age was about weaponising your control of nature, to maximise your domination over your domain, cement your right to rule, and worst and outdo your rivals.

The city of Babylon, which itself covered an area of 850 hectares (the same size as entire historical estates in England such as Blenheim Palace near Oxford or Highclere, the 'real' Downton Abbey), gained a reputation for hosting the biggest and the best – of all things. Everything here in

Babylon under Nebuchadnezzar became about being the ultimate expression of itself: the central temple, Esagil (meaning 'House Whose Top
Is High'), which had walls decorated not with washes of bitumen and
gypsum, but actual panels of lapis lazuli and alabaster; the awe-inspiring
ziggurat (the original Tower of Babel), 300 feet square at the base and as
high, a tower in seven ascending sections, the top storey dressed in dark-
blue glazed bricks to match the sky, named Etemenanki ('House of the
Foundation Platform of Heaven and Earth'). Nebuchadnezzar's Southern
Palace alone spanned 1,066 feet by 722. Around the double-depth walls
a moat was built, its entrances stopped with 'bars of shining iron'. And
we hear from a later source that in Babylon's extreme gardens, luxuri-
ously decorating a substantial area outside the Ishtar Gate (a ceremonial
entranceway dedicated to the goddess Ishtar in Nebuchadnezzar's palace
extension), the terraces of the garden were 50 cubits (that's around 82 feet)
high.[34] Nebuchadnezzar, it seems, did not do anything by halves.

Mass production of mudbricks allowed for construction on a gargantuan scale. Some were glazed and tinted to form stunning decorations.
Fragments of bricks, both glazed and unglazed, have been painstakingly
pieced together – one pacing, roaring lion from the 30-foot-high, 184-foot-
long central throne room at Babylon was only recreated in 2013.[35] From
one of our sources for a Seven Wonders catalogue, the Pseudo-Philon of
Byzantium, we hear that there were cross beams in Babylon's hanging
planting schemes made of palm tree trunks.[36] Clever to use palm wood as
an architectural feature because it does not rot, but contains water instead
like a sponge, helping to nourish both plants and soil. Sources describe
water being twisted up in hidden channels in the garden and then cascading down as waterfalls into pools to irrigate and delight.[37] We know
that King Nebuchadnezzar received splendid tributes of copper from the
people of Magan, who lived in what is now Oman, where date palms
flourished.[38] Amongst the man-made valley oases of the Magan, fed by a
sophisticated *Aflaj* water distribution system pioneered in the Bronze Age,
palm-trunks are still sometimes used as waterproof planters. Visiting these
quasi-miraculous *Aflaj* systems – teeming with butterflies, songbirds and
mint-green frogs in raw-rock mountains just above a punishing desert –
one has to wonder whether Nebuchadnezzar was inspired by word of what
the Magan people had achieved in terms of water engineering. These fine
water-works certainly bring an Eden-like quality to the landscapes.

The hall of the Babylonian king too was alive with soaring, stylised palm trees and flowers rendered in gorgeous glazed-brick murals. Here Crown Prince Belshazzar, son of King Nabonidus, possibly the grandson of Nebuchadnezzar II, was supposed to have seen a vision from God – the writing on the wall, at his famous feast. Here too, two centuries later, Alexander the Great died, on 11 June 323 BCE (one researcher puts this death at precisely between 4 and 5 p.m. in the afternoon).[39] Alexander's cause of death is disputed, but malaria is an extremely strong possibility, very likely given the marshy hinterlands of the great Euphrates River, and the presence of all those babbling water-features in the ornamental park of Babylon's palace. Indeed, a clay tablet from Babylon, which I've held in the palm of my hand, is stored along with many thousands more in the wood-cabineted hush of the British Museum and offers a description of Alexander's death that forms part of our evidence for Babylon's royal gardens. At the end of his world conquest, and having taken Babylon, feverish, the great vanquisher was moved by boat across the River Euphrates to a royal garden, where he was laid to rest in a vaulted, or canopied, bed. Here Alexander was still able to bathe and sacrifice, until he was moved back across to a palace on the other side of the river, where the most famous man in the world – ancient and modern – possibly with the Hanging Gardens of Babylon in view, died.[40]

But there is a problem. Not only are the Hanging Gardens in Babylon *not* mentioned by the Greek adventurer-historians Xenophon and Herodotus, who almost certainly both visited the city, but an elegantly worked piece of stone, 20 inches wide by 22 inches tall, the so-called East India House Inscription (and its two duplicates, probably laid as a pavement), ordered up by Nebuchadnezzar II, systematically, eloquently recites the great works of the Great King – but a garden? Let alone a hanging garden? This does not get a single mention. The East India House Inscription (so called because it was displayed in the London headquarters of the East India Company) was created under the purview of the Great King himself.* It could be that the Hanging Gardens were for the private enjoyment of the royal family – a kind of exclusive, secret garden – so did

---

* The East India House Inscription was found in Babylon sometime before 1803. It was given to the East India House Museum by Sir Harford Jones Bridges – before Babylonian cuneiform had been deciphered – and was then donated to the British Museum in 1938.

not form part of the catalogue of publicised works. But for once, absence of evidence could also be evidence of absence. Wonders are rarely kept under a bushel. We have to widen our search.[41]

So if we travel a hundred-odd miles north, and a hundred years back in time, to Ancient Nineveh, on the outskirts of modern-day Mosul, we get to meet both evidence of formal gardens, arranged in a hanging design, and their ambitious architect, King Sennacherib.

The Assyrian King Sennacherib ruled for twenty-five years, from 705 to 681 BCE. Assyrians admired Babylonian culture, but they also wanted to dominate it. In Assyrian texts the two rival powers are frequently gendered, Assyria as a husband, Babylonia as a desired wife. And Sennacherib, renowned for his military attacks on others 'like a wolf on the fold' (as Lord Byron described it in his poem 'The Destruction of Sennacherib'), descended on Babylon in 689 BCE. Since his eldest son had been executed by one of Babylon's allies, he destroyed much of the city in a red mist of pain, rage and zeal.[42]

Not shy of vaunting his ravening drive far and wide, Sennacherib's inscriptions are still to be found in the west of his empire, carved into rock faces in the North Beqaa valley in modern-day Lebanon, where locals trade animal skins and felted tunics (and warlords' heroin) above the Orontes River, flowing into Lake Homs. King Sennacherib is shown taking giant timber trunks – cedars of Lebanon – for his building campaigns. Additional inscriptions have only recently been identified – eroded by natural forces and the bullets of target practice – overlooking settlements where refugees from the Syrian Civil War outnumber the locals, and where, at the time of writing, the attenuating conflict and proxy war is still churning behind the ridge of Beqaa's hills.[43]

King Sennacherib moved the Assyrian capital from Ashur, 60 miles further north, to the ancient city of Nineveh – a grand project demanding titanic impact to justify its scale. Nineveh city (the city of sin) did excess well. Sennacherib, who travelled personally to inspect mountain springs as potential sources of irrigation, ordered that reed-marsh to be created mimicking southern Babylonia and (as we are told in his Standard Inscription) 'tore open mountain and valley with iron picks to dig a canal'. Sennacherib's vision was game-changing.[44] He built walls, temples, a new palace complex which was more like a city itself, with ceilings made of cypress and cedar, multiple windows and silver and bronze decorations, across an area of 1,476 by 722 feet, ten times bigger than Luxor's great temple by the Nile. A second palace served as an arsenal and somewhere standing soldiers could be stationed – atypically, the women in Sennacherib's harem also commanded their own military units. Women's names during Sennacherib's rule appear in inscriptions and tablets more than in the courts of other kings. Just listen to how Sennacherib lionises the creation of his palace (and, interestingly, his love for his wife):

> And for the queen Tashmetu-sharrat, my beloved wife, whose features Belet-ili [the queen of the gods] has made more perfect and beautiful than all other women, I had a palace of love, joy and pleasure built. I set female sphinxes of white limestone in its doorways. By the order of Ashur, father of the gods, and heavenly queen Ishtar [the slightly later form of the Sumerian love and sex goddess Inanna], may we both live long in health and happiness in this palace and enjoy wellbeing to the full![45]

Could the historical reality here lead to these stories about gardens commissioned as a love-gift for a beloved female consort, or perhaps be the model for Babylon's own, later, ornamental gardens?

On the prism cylinder of Sennacherib from c. 694 BCE (a truncheon of clay, tightly packed with writing – one copy now in the Iraq Museum, another in the British Museum – originally found hidden in the west wall of the city of Nineveh), both the king's palace and his gardens are immortalised in quite some detail.[46] Moreover, the creation of Nineveh's palace and grounds is described in positively ecstatic terms. From the Great King himself (although careful respect and reverence is given to the gods) there is a Pygmalion-esque sense of control and sorcery, a god-like pride in the power to conjure something that appears to live from out of stone. The palace, we are told, was raised to such a height to be 'a wonder for all people'; and next to it, 'A park imitating the Amanus mountains [so elevated and on a slope, surely?] . . . with all kinds of aromatic plants, orchard fruit trees, trees that sustain the mountains and Chaldea, as well as trees that bear wool [probably cotton from India], planted within it.'[47]

One drawing of Sennacherib's South-West Palace, from a stele now lost (the Original Drawing IV 77), seems to show not just a garden but a pleasure garden, even a water attraction. Figures cross giant ponds with horses, on boats and on history's lilos – inflated animal skins. One man seems to be swinging from a rope into the water – for military training purposes, or as a spectacle, or simply for pleasure?

Inflated cow/buffalo-skin lilos known as 'mussuks', still in use in 1865 (River Kullu, Himachal), and indeed still used today in Afghanistan. Pradesh Albumen Print, Samuel Bourne.

And by his own account Sennacherib's garden was mystic, wonderful, a fairy-tale. The entrance seems to have been through an open portico, facing the planted areas, which were arranged in layers, including a roof garden. Giant *lamassu* – bull-figures with human faces – made of both stone and fine metals, some weighing in at 30 tonnes, would have protected the king and his family here.

We are also told Sennacherib's garden was artfully irrigated, cotton and olives were grown here, and both imported and exotic animals were displayed. Artificial, highly engineered terraces were constructed with water travelling on elevated and underground aqueducts, delivered to the upper levels by a screw system developed, it has been argued, by Sennacherib himself. The engineering (a pre-echo of Archimedes' screw) was cunningly concealed within artificial, bronze trunks, like a counterfeit version of trees' natural vascular systems.[48] The aesthetically pleasing machines seem to have worked by winding water up with a turning inner spiral. Running alongside stairs that ran up and down the slopes of the garden, they terminated in decorative pavilions. There was an upper attraction where trees were planted above a walkway, their roots visible to those who promenaded below. In Nineveh, a tributary of the Tigris, the Khosr, brings water aplenty, and this supply was amplified by canals, inspired by those that Assyrian troops had seen on campaign in Urartu (Ancient Armenia).

> . . . and at the prompting of my intelligence and the desire of my heart I invented a technique for copper and made it skilfully. I created clay moulds as if by divine intelligence for cylinder-trunks and screws, tree of riches; twelve fierce lion colossi together with twelve mighty bull colossi which were perfect castings; twenty-two cow colossi invested with joyous allure, and plentifully endowed with sexual attraction.[49]

Sennacherib was clearly thrilled with the water-manipulation he introduced: 'I provided the land festooned with spiders-webs with water . . . I diverted the flood-prone river . . .'[50] The aqueduct to Sennacherib's palace brought water from the Jerwan conduit – through 2 million dressed stones over a distance of 31 miles, starting at Khinnis, in what is now the remote Kurdistan region of Iraq.[51] The Jerwan concourse, with its pointed arches, is still visible, and the Shallalat dam – also in operation at the time – was functioning right up until the twentieth century. At Khinnis an image of Sennacherib is carved into the rock alongside representations of the gods – hubristic blasphemy that draws vehement damnation in the Book of Ezekiel. The proud carvings pock the rock-face here. Sennacherib was a man of vision and action.

Perched on the northern citadel, the rebuilding of Nineveh's royal palace and its gardens took twelve years to complete. Nineveh was Sennacherib's new capital – but crucially, was called Old Babylon in some

Assyrian sources.[52] The entire region was often described as Babylonia. So when ancient sources describe Babylon, could it be, as argued cogently by the scholar Stephanie Dalley, that they are in fact memorialising Nineveh?

It was certainly a splendidly impressive complex. Employing an understanding of Pythagoras' theorem of the hypotenuse in both Assyrian and Babylonian building projects, a century before the mathematician from the Greek island of Samos was born, walls were decorated with reliefs and glazed storyboards. (We know of this mathematical understanding because schoolboys' clay teaching tablets from the time show geometric diagrams exploring a version of the theorem, along with scrawlings-out. Children were being raised to use complex mathematical applications. On one of my favourite tablets from Babylon a frustrated schoolchild has drawn an unkind caricature of his master – the maths must have been a bit tricky that day.) Originally brightly coloured, carved stelae have also survived from the palace of Sennacherib's grandson, Ashurbanipal – from these we can get further sense of the horticultural landscape in Nineveh. Gardens in Nineveh were clearly a place for feasting, listening to music, playing board games, engaging in archery practice, and also worshipping, mounting processions to the great goddess Inanna-Ishtar (that fluid deity responsible for both life and death, both pleasure and pain). A relief contemporary to Ashurbanipal shows pillars with what are approaching Ionic capitals, and a freestanding altar – or it could be a brazier, or a stand for lights. The king is framed in a portico. On another, columns are mounted on lion-bases, there are finely worked outdoor tables and chairs, footstools for the royals – even what seems to be a tame pet lion. So one can imagine how the gardens of this particular dynasty might become legendary.

But again there is an issue. What is so strange is that one of the richest resources in the region of Mesopotamia was clay, and onto this clay were written some of the earliest records available. And in the landscape of what is modern-day Iraq, baked clay is almost indestructible. So – unless it has yet to be excavated or deciphered, or was actively destroyed – why not a garden tablet? Sennacherib's grandson, Ashurbanipal, was obsessed with the possibilities of what clay tablets could do – how they could buttress his power and influence and inform the future. Ashurbanipal is shown with a reed-stylus for writing in his belt. He pulled down an entire

'The Garden of Sargon Khorsabad', stone panel carved in bas-relief, from Sargon II's palace, c. 710 BCE – gardens were a status symbol for royalty.

palace, only to replace it with another – with the biggest library in the world right at its heart.[53] Twenty-six thousand tablets from this palace, discovered in a layer a foot thick, are still being studied in the labyrinthine, wood-lined, worn-carpeted back-rooms of the British Museum. Could it be that this rebellious ruler actively ate into his grandfather's gardens? Proof of a more urbane, a less bucolic, a more cerebral mind?[54]

So the Hanging Gardens still prove tantalisingly elusive, even in Nineveh. Time to return to Babylon.

Babylon was lower-lying than Nineveh, with ready access to the waters of the Euphrates. A garden here would have been wonderful, but tablets describing royal gardens in Babylon give the impression of something a little functional, rather than theatrical, more akin to a formal kitchen garden watered by irrigation channels. Lists of plants grown at the time and used to prepare feasts include mangel-wurzel, sea-blite, radish, shallots, gourds, fennel, anise, fenugreek, mint, pennyroyal, rue, turnip, thyme, dill, cucumber, cardamom, coriander, marjoram, mint, purslane, pomegranate, pear, fig, roses, jasmine and lilies.[55] On one tablet we hear sadly of species of plant either lost to us or impossible to identify: 'bird-dung plant', 'hound's-tongue plant' and the horrible 'slave-girl buttock' plant.[56] Ebony, rosewood, walnut, terebinth, oaks, tamarisks are also on record as having been grown here, and the Euphrates, or desert, poplar – a tree whose bark has had some success in de-worming programmes. So from the evidence we have, the planting in royal schemes here was done with cogent purpose.

In Babylon's palace, architecture and horticulture met. Stone-carved depictions of carpets show that real, woven rugs were often decorated with lotus flowers. In the gardens themselves there were colonnaded pavilions, arches of blue-glazed tiles, and outdoor seating, shaded by pines and vines, with palms present to provide their distinctive rustle – natural air-conditioners. Then, as now, date palms and date-palm oil were not just decorative, but drivers of the economy; in some senses the date palm was the fuel of North African, Middle Eastern and Arabian civilisation. Dates self-preserve, so can be a food supply in both good times and bad; they have been described as the petrol of antiquity. In remote regions of north-west Saudi Arabia and southern Jordan, you can still find dates carefully stashed 33 feet high in rock crevasses, a shared larder for the Bedouin who pass through these high desert plateaus. Dates did not grow naturally further north. Tamarisks were here too, the salt-cedar that appears in the *Epic of Gilgamesh* [57] and which provided wood for the bows so beloved at this time and in this place, and – thanks to their polyphenolic compounds – balms for the wounds bows and arrows inflicted. Nature was, for all kinds of reasons, a welcome guest in royal courts.

Gardens in the ancient world were a statement of status. But a place too for restoring mental balance. Trees were planted thickly in Babylon's gardens, we are told, '[so that] by their great size or other charm, [they] could give pleasure to [the] beholder'. [58] Anyone who has spent long stretches under Near and Middle Eastern sun can easily imagine the cool and balm that dappled water under rustling foliage provides. The spiritual wonder of an oasis in the desert – which is still awe-inspiring today, where drinkable, cold water burps up beautifully, mesmerically, miraculously from under miles of sand, to encourage the proliferation of dragonflies, finches, butterflies and the palms and plants that create their own orchestra of sound – must have been an extraordinary phenomenon to witness in a man-made pleasure-garden. Shade, fragrance and flowing water were all highly prized commodities in the Near and Middle Eastern Iron Ages.

Gardens were somewhere to lose yourself psychologically, a poem planted: 'I am yours like this field which I have planted with flowers';

'You don't have to die to go to paradise, provided you have a garden'.[59] The poetry of the day luxuriated in the garden metaphor – as a place where spirit and soul could flourish.

Indeed, the entire metropolis of Babylon was known as the Sacred City, and when Greek authors described the gardens of Mesopotamia as being like a theatre, surely they were not just referring technically to the shape, rake and architecture – but to the garden's fundamental ritual purpose. Greek theatres were often associated with places of healing. Think for instance of the famed theatre at Epidauros, which was attached to the sylvan sanctuary of Asclepius in the Peloponnese. Or Athens' theatre on the slopes of the Acropolis, built to honour the cult of the god of nature and the vine, Dionysos. Dramas performed in these spaces were part of a holistic process, a collective katharsis, a balm for mind and body. There were theatres too, serving the same purpose, in late Babylon (using old, neo-Babylonian bricks). Gardens, for the ancients, had a psychological as well as a physical purpose; they were wonderful in many ways.

Fantastical too, because gardens also gave comfort at night.[60] Night culture was vital here in Mesopotamia. Not only did the night skies blaze with stars in a way we no longer know, they were a book to be read. Babylonian astrology-astronomy (the line between these two disciplines could be a little blurred, and the Babylonians pioneered both) has come directly down to the modern world – much of its understanding unchanged. The sun, the moon and Venus were the most important of the planetary spheres, and it was in the security of protected gardens that stars could be safely stared at, observed without the dangers of nature red in tooth and claw around about. Not only did the planets 'predict' wars and natural disasters, the night sky was thought to bring both disease – shedding afflictions like dew – and healing. Recent brilliant investigative work has plotted the process of 'astral irradiation' – where ointments and amulets, sometimes even people, would be left under particular stars in Assyria and Babylonia to catalyse their special magic powers.[61] Alexander the Great, let us not forget, was brought out to a garden in Babylon when he was terminally ill. This celestial healing was thought to be fired by the presence of the goddess Inanna-Ishtar, in the form of her star, today's Venus. On cylinder seals from the time, figures are shown reclining outside, with Venus' eight-pointed star hovering above them. Inanna-Ishtar was a goddess who never really slept – simply retiring to her chambers at night (in Mesopotamian culture it was thought taboo to disturb someone who seemed to be sleeping), where she could also keep a divine half-eye on her favourite night-time activities, the lovemaking of women and men. I picture the goddess dozing like a dolphin, with one eye open, one eye closed.

Spirits of all kinds were believed to inhabit these bucolic places. So the experience of this Wonder would have been a charged, numinous one. Trees themselves were thought of as gods – in particular the god Nin-gishzida, who guarded the gate of heaven, the threshold between life and the afterlife. Wonderfully, this was a tree therefore who could 'talk'. On Nineveh's garden stele the sovereign is shown with the magical tree of life. Sprites were believed to fill these cultivated places with perfumes and sweet song. Earlier descriptions from nearby Nimrud describe a 'garden of delight' where 'the paths are full of scent; the waterfalls [sparkle] like the stars of heaven on the garden of pleasure'.[62] Flesh and blood entertainers were here too. On the walls of Ashurbanipal's palace at Nineveh there are rapturous representations of musicians – lyre and harp players – walking through gardens with tamed lions. Real lions were imported or bred to be hunted in these royal enclosures – big cats were sacred to Inanna-Ishtar – and images on wall carvings show them being released from cages to be killed by the king. The dead beasts are then laid out and re-blooded with a libation of wine, a brutal offering to Babylonia's premier goddess.

In Babylon alone there were 180 shrines to Inanna-Ishtar, but Nineveh was said to be particularly 'beloved to Ishtar' – also known locally here as Mulissu, a presence since at least 1700 BCE. Inanna-Ishtar's temple and ziggurat at Nineveh overlooked the palace gardens; her spirit was believed to have guided Sennacherib to seek out particularly rich seams of stone to build and decorate the palace – from the very mountain range, the Amanus mountains at the Gulf of Issus in modern-day Turkey, which his gardens were aiming to replicate. In fact the city of Nineveh itself was probably named after Inanna-Ishtar – Nina being a Sumerian name of the goddess. Ishtar, in all her guises, was certainly the fairy godmother of all this Assyrian new build.

Babylon too was built around Inanna-Ishtar's temple, and as night approached, and her star Venus was seen to rise in the twilight sky, she would have been adored. Just listen to this poem of the time, 'The Lady of the Evening':

> At the end of the day, the radiant star, the Great Light that fills the sky,
> The Lady of the Evening appears in the heavens.
> The people in all the lands lift their eyes to her.
> The men purify themselves; women cleanse themselves.[63]

Thinking of all of this – of the sacred sensuality of the nature that powerful Near Eastern dynasties chose to nourish and contain within their domain – we can imagine why an aura of wonder would have evolved around a city-garden. A plain old garden, let alone a hanging garden, would have exhorted a feeling of connection to the power of the natural world, and of the power derived from that connection. Virgin landscapes in the Iron Age were being evermore moulded and mutilated by axes, saws, scythes, ploughs; it is pertinent that those who could, those with extreme wealth and influence, attempted to recreate a natural paradise within their palace or city walls.

Apart from the inner circle of the royal family, who would have witnessed and admired these art-saturated, sensuous, spirit-filled landscapes?

Both the Babylonian and Assyrian empires stretched from modern-day Iran to Cyprus, from Turkey to the Nile Valley and northern Saudi Arabia/Jordan, and their empires were polyglot. Royal gardens were sacred – but they also served a diplomatic purpose – so we need to populate the Hanging Gardens, whether in Nineveh or Babylon, with the women and men who would have enjoyed (as well as constructed and serviced) this elusive Wonder first-hand.

High-status locals and foreign diplomats would have been able to experience the gardens at festivals and at great trade delegations, often masquerading as diplomatic gift-exchange parties. On tablets and stelae we hear and see what these visitors ate: pomegranates, cakes, grapes, wine – helpful to wash down the dried locusts also on offer.[64] Captive kings (some billeted under house-arrest within the palace itself) are shown bringing wine and food to their new overlord. All-comers had to cover their faces in the presence of the Great King, whether that be Sennacherib, Nebuchadnezzar or Ashurbanipal. The prevalence of eunuchs might be a little surprising to modern readers. Eunuchs had been a part of Assyrian culture since at least 2000 BCE. Originally castrated captives (castration and full dismemberment were a punishment for sodomy as well as a torture meted out on enemies), by the 1300s BCE eunuchs often held high-status positions. They are shown with governors and kings, making libations, attending cult practice, and acting as counsellors. The state of the eunuch had become something not to punish, but to praise and, in some cases, to desire.[65]

Of course, the beautiful gardens in Babylon and Nineveh were built on the sorrow and sweat of slaves. Sennacherib boasts that he 'uprooted people from Chaldea, Aram, Mannay, Que, Cilicia, Philistia and Tyre . . . and made them carry the head-pad [a cruel contraption for carrying great weights balanced on individuals' heads], and they made bricks'.[66] Bone evidence from both the Bronze and Iron Ages shows children as young as five with compacted neck-joints – a result of continuous hard labour. Written clinically into one clay tablet, along with a list of other 'possessions', we hear of the vicissitudes of one slave, which surely must be similar to the experience of so many. This was an individual who escaped, tried to buy his freedom, but was then re-sold, and sold again.[67]

Sennacherib had of course also famously attacked and taken Jerusalem – Jewish captives are shown on Assyrian sculptures; abject, disorientated, afraid. We have to imagine that those who were not executed were fated to become labourers on the king's almighty projects. This was a time when mercy was conspicuous by its absence. Many in the generation of those Jewish families' grandchildren would be taken again, only this time Judaeans from the south by Nebuchadnezzar the Great – he who destroyed the temple of Jerusalem, who forced Daniel into the lions' den and who perpetrated the Jews' Babylonian Captivity.[68] These were those Israelites who 'by the waters of Babylon . . . sat down and wept'.[69]

One shocking frieze featuring the royal garden at Nineveh shows Ashurbanipal (Sennacherib's grandson) and his wife relaxing in their garden while birds play and sing in the canopy of the trees. Musicians entertain, Ashurbanipal and his queen are attended to by courtiers, an arbour of vines protects the royal couple from the sun. It all seems rather blissfully idyllic. Then a ghastly surprise – in a pine tree, there hangs the head of the King of Assyria's arch-enemy Teuman, the King of Elam from what is now south-western Iran. A branch has been forced through Teuman's open mouth. Defeated in the Battle of Ulai in 653 BCE – attacked because of his 'insolent messages, his boasting, his plots' – his hand decorates a tree on the far right of the scene.[70] Elsewhere on the stone reliefs, on public display in the British Museum, the vanquished have their tongues cut out and have been flayed alive. Over two thousand six hundred years later, it is still shocking and deeply upsetting to witness. The palace world was one of extremity, the garden paradise a place too of nightmares. Sennacherib himself was assassinated – it was said while praying at a temple at one of the gates of his great city in a palace coup, by one of his own sons. The goddess Inanna-Ishtar, we should never forget, was a deity of violence and death, as well as of love and life. We should never be lured into a sense that these gardens were ravishing, romantic places.

Horror is an experience of the gardens that, tragically, endures. While researching this book I have come close both to new discoveries here, in what is now Iraq, and to new destructions. In 2014, ISIL fighters, who had taken over the city of Mosul, implemented a spree of desecration. Surrounding one of the splendid *lamassu* – the giant figures set to protect the city, with the face of a man, the wings of an eagle and the body of a bull – the ragbag of fighters clubbed away the *lamassu*'s head. A pathetic video shows one man futilely gouging at the mythical beast's front leg. The mini-mob then destroyed Nineveh's ancient Nergal gate (Nergal was the god of death and pestilence) which the *lamassu* had been guarding. But there was more.

On one neighbouring hillock stood the mediaeval mosque of Nabi Yunus – otherwise known as the prophet Jonah recognised in Judaism, Christianity and Islam, he who escaped in the belly of a whale and was sent to tell Nineveh it was a City of Sin. In fact, the shrine the mosque covered was almost certainly not that of a biblical character at all, but rather of a seventh-century CE representative of the Christian Church of the East, Henanshisho I. But for ISIL these were degenerate religious men, the prophet Jonah the wrong kind of prophet – so the extremists rigged the mosque with explosives and then detonated it, telling locals to stand at a distance of a third of a mile to watch, filming the explosion and expelling all the Christian families who lived locally. As it turned out, by blowing up the mosque, these vandals also blew their cover.

When Mosul was liberated in 2017, archaeologists desperately picking through the wreckage discovered that under the destroyed mediaeval mosque there were a series of tunnels. Although researchers had been wanting to explore the archaeology here since the nineteenth century, the ground had been considered too hallowed by locals. ISIL had no such compunction. Its members had drilled down through the floor of the mosque itself, creating fifty new tunnels to store weapons and, critically, to loot artefacts – carvings, statues and treasures – from what lay beneath. Because here was buried an Assyrian palace.

In an episode of daredevil proportions, a local archaeologist and an Iraqi filmmaker entered the tunnels to take over 1,000 photographs as a record. Both the men were arrested on exit but managed to smuggle out their memory cards. Limestone slabs inscribed with the names of Ashurbanipal and Esarhaddon (Sennacherib's son, the Neo-Assyrian king who conquered Egypt, rendering Nineveh's empire the largest the world had known, the man who went on to rebuild the Babylon his father had destroyed) were discovered, as well as bricks bearing Sennacherib's name. Appearing like ghosts in the light of their phones as they explored, there are also three women, waist-high, staring face-on – not, as normally, in profile. Too deep-set to hack out, they survived the ISIL attack and appear to be carrying some kind of a box. Are they women at council? Goddesses? Priestesses? Seers?

Sickening as it is, the very destruction of these unique artefacts proves the power of history's artistic wonders. Then and now they generate identity and confidence. Their creation and preservation are a way to connect to your ancestors and to other cultures. Exceptional works craft a kind of immortality for the maker and for the things made. Wonderful things hold more value than their mere beauty. Profits from the sale of stolen 'blasphemous' artefacts by ISIL have, at the time of writing, already reached $35 billion. And because such objects are also freighted with meaning and memory, they are targets for destruction. Their very annihilation helps to explain the potent value of physical wonders, and of wondering.

The despicable endeavours of ISIL constituted a kind of crude, accidental archaeology. The presence of those women in these tunnels is fascinating. Because remember that in many of the accounts describing the creation of Babylonia's gardens, women are cited as the motivation for their creation. Psychologically women had long been associated with the narratives of gardens, as witnessed by the story of Amytis and the myth of Semiramis – it now seems that physically they were too.[71] We hear they were there in statue form, serving an apotropaic function:

> In the upper rooms within the private apartments I opened up latticed windows. I placed feminine protective statues in their doors, fashioned from alabaster and ivory, carrying flowers and holding hands. They radiate poise and charm, they are so beautiful that I have made of them a wonder.[72]

And discoveries at the end of the last century also revealed that in the North-West Palace of Nimrud, elite women had been buried with their finest possessions under trees in the palace courtyard itself.[73]

Sifting through the (scant) evidence for female agency at this time, it is clear that female heirs were frequently given gardens and orchards as part of their dowry – including the income derived from them. Witness the Babylonian dowry tablet, now held in the British Museum: 'a 3-panu [hectare] orchard, extending to the fallow area . . . from the irrigation dyke . . .'[74] In general, it must be said that this was an acutely unequal world, with women punished more severely for the same crimes as men, judged to be compassionate creatures but also emotional saboteurs, and denied many inheritance rights. A little unexpectedly though, some women, especially elite women, were literate. We are lucky enough to possess a fantastically snippy retort from one princess, Serua-eterat, to her sister-in-law, Assur-Sharrat – the self-same queen who is depicted reclining luxuriantly in the garden at Nineveh with her king – bemoaning the fact that Assur-Sharrat is not bothering to learn to write:[75] 'Why do you not write on your clay tablet? Why do you not rehearse on your exercise tablet? . . . people will ask whether you really are a royal!'

Classical tradition, recall, posited that the individual responsible for these gardens was feisty Semiramis, the great queen who has taken on an afterlife of her own. Semiramis is almost certainly based on a flesh-and-blood character, the real Queen Sammu-ramat of Assyria, the dynamic consort of Samsi-Adad V. Sammu-ramat, who flourished around 830–800 BCE, ruled after her father's death, helped to expand Syria's borders, rode into battle with her son and oversaw building projects.[76] An agate eyestone – quite possibly personal to Sammu-ramat, perhaps worn against her breast (as peasant women in Greece still wore seal stones from Knossos up until the 1940s to ward off disease and help to ensure breast-milk) – is inscribed with the words:

> To Ishtar, her lady.
> Sammu-ramat
> Consort-Queen of Shamshi-Adad
> King of Assyria
> gave (this) for her well-being.[77]

Sammu-ramat's dates do tally with the existence of gardens in Mesopotamia – but with the evidence we have so far, not with gardens that were 'hanging'. Even so, Semiramis continued to be associated with gardens through time; in the pastoral *Primavera* painted by the Renaissance master artist Botticelli, for instance, the figure of Venus-Aphrodite (theologically the distant descendant of Inanna-Ishtar) is very Semiramis-like.

The other figure associated with the gardens was Queen Amytis. According to Berossus (via Josephus, you will recall), this second wife of Nebuchadnezzar was missing Kurdistan's vertical beauty, her mountains and foothills. A daughter of the King of the Medes – who controlled huge swathes of Asia – Amytis would have been used to luxury at every turn. She was also extremely well connected. Her brother was the last Median king, the brother-in-law of both Nebuchadnezzar II and King Croesus of Lydia – whom we will soon meet as a patron of the Temple of Artemis at Ephesus. Maddeningly, the Medes did not write their own history down, but later sources tell us that lofty constructions of stone, topped with soil, gave enigmatic Amytis what she craved. Sadly, we have no written evidence that gives Amytis herself a voice. There is even a chance that this lovesick, homesick theme was inserted into Berossus' account by the later author Josephus, who was inspired by the advent of a new artform – the novel.[78] Because when Josephus was writing his histories, there was a pioneering entertainment model starting to circulate – developed by a fascinating individual called Chariton from the town of Aphrodisias in Anatolia, what is now Turkey. Chariton developed light-read romances, inspired by the love-interests of the patron goddess of his home town, Aphrodite. So we hear for instance of a young, female, intercontinental traveller who, 'on arriving at the River Euphrates . . . beyond which lies the vast continent . . . then was filled with longing for her home and family'.[79] The emphasis on Amytis could possibly have arisen as later writers collided the Seven Wonders' traditional and historical narrative with the tender preoccupations of this brand-new, romantic (in every sense of the word) art form.

The Hanging Gardens of Babylon, which surely must once have existed in some form, given their incidental evidence, and reputation, and the obsession of the Iron Age in tampering with nature (in contrast to the preoccupation of Egypt in becoming a part of the cosmos), evolved during antiquity into a vehicle for fabrication as well as for fact.

We must remember that even if hanging gardens are incontrovertibly missing from contemporary factual accounts, Babylon's walls are conspicuous by their presence. Could it be that Babylon's and Nineveh's gardens were such a natural and organic extension of great walls – protecting the cities and palaces themselves – that the two became synonymous? It is, after all, Babylon's walls rather than her gardens which appear time and again in ancient Wonder-lists.

Themselves described as a Wonder both by Nebuchadnezzar in Babylon and by the father of the mightiest of Assyrian kings, Ashurbanipal, in c. 669 BCE – 'a wonder for all people' – the walls of ancient cities had a perceptible character and a kind of mystical power. In the oldest extant work of human literature, the epic poem that sits somewhere between fact and fantasy, the *Epic of Gilgamesh*, we hear that the Seven Sages (the number seven saturated with significance here) themselves must have laid the foundations that protected the hero-king's wall around Uruk, 'a copper band . . . that none else can match'.[80] The walls of Babylon had names and identities: the inner was called Imgur-Enlil (the god Enlil approved), the outer Nemetti-Enlil (Enlil's bulwark). Into the walls themselves, rival kings laid cylinders. Propagandist time-capsules, these catalogue the rulers' exaltation and reconstruction of both the inner and outer compounds. Conquering Assyrian kings, when they briefly held Babylon itself, restored the very walls they had once attacked. And when Nebuchadnezzar then took back control of Babylon, he too built up again what the Assyrians had destroyed. 'I raised its top like a mountain, I built it perfectly, and filled it with splendour, for the wonder of all the people.'[81]

The walls of Babylon and Nineveh were raised to create and enshrine a symbolic political, as well as a physical, barrier.

In fact we can still wonder at some sections of the walls of Babylon with our own eyes. Remnants of Babylon's extraordinary Ishtar Gate and processional way still impress museum visitors from across the world in sections that are on display in Iraq, London, Berlin, Brooklyn, Istanbul and Paris.[82] The precision and aesthetic acuity of the pairing of blue and gold glazed tiles in a rainbow-ring around Babylon must have been, indeed still is, truly astonishing. Because by the sixth century BCE the walls of Babylon shimmered with mind-blowing natural and supernatural imagery: mustard-yellow dragons; wild white bulls; snarling lions and wreaths of flowers, all in procession in a sky-high space of lapis-blue. The lions, sixty or so, were white-furred with golden manes, or golden with russet-red. Babylon's wall dragons were fierce composite creatures – sporting a snake's head, a lion's body and ripping eagles' talons on their hind legs; they stalked towards the double gate of the goddess Inanna-Ishtar, connected by a 157-foot-long passage. 'I placed wild bulls and ferocious dragons in the gateways and thus adorned them with luxurious splendour so that mankind might gaze on them in wonder'.[83]

These chimeras prowled not just on the walls but also as statues along the 820 feet of the processional way (itself 79 feet wide) to the Ishtar Gate (called, intimidatingly, Ishtar-sakipat-tebiša, 'Ishtar Repels Her Attackers'). The dragons' presence was proudly proclaimed: 'I cast seven [note the symbolic number seven again] bronze savage *mushushshu*, who spatter the enemy and foe with deadly venom'.* Surviving bronze dragon heads, now in the Louvre Museum, Paris (itself, of course, boasting its own glass pyramid, a version of Giza's pyramidical wonders), clearly had eyes and skin decorated with a jewel inlay, and tongues of iron. As the creatures of Inanna-Ishtar, the goddess in charge of the army and in charge of desire of all kinds, these magnificent beasts represented war and passion, a hybrid-feral-feline incarnation of sublime ambition.

The scale of Babylon's walls was also staggering – no matter the source you choose to read. Herodotus reports 480 stades or furlongs (a whopping 55 miles) in length, and 200 royal cubits high, or about 335 feet,

---

* This is a dedication by the usurper King Neriglissar, a factotum of Nebuchadnezzar who married one of his daughters.

Ctesias suggests 360 stades, or 41 miles, and 50 fathoms (around 300 feet) high; Cleitarchus says 365 stades (that's 42 miles) long, 50 cubits (about 75 feet) from top to bottom.[84] Archaeology shows there was in fact a network of walls around Babylon's city proper, including double walls with a passageway between them, and reaching out too into the farmland between the Tigris and the Euphrates. Aristotle's comment, 'Babylon, they say, had been taken for three days before some part of the inhabitants became aware of the fact', makes sense. Babylon's vast, bright, kaleidoscopic defences were attacked and also sabotaged by successive administrations – again, proof of their totemic value.

We have found Babylon's great walls, which may possibly have been planted like a kind of roof-garden, but are we closer to identifying our garden-Wonder? Is there sufficient evidence not just in the reports of later wonder-seekers, but in the history that is carved in the rocks and stone of the Near East, impressed onto Assyrian and Babylonian tablets, in the earth of war-torn Iraq? Like Egypt's pyramid-Wonder being, in truth, a complex landscape of construction rather than a singular monument, perhaps the Hanging Gardens of Babylon is in fact a family of gardens. A conflation of memories of impressive, elevated planting on the mega-palace of Babylon, introduced by Nebuchadnezzar, 100 years after Sennacherib's pioneering works at Nineveh, which were utterly remarkable, and which were extended by his grandson Ashurbanipal. Babylon's garden was relatively modest at only about 390 feet long; but the walls that surrounded it – raised by Nebuchadnezzar to outdo his historic rival – a legend rebuilt, were unparalleled, not just an arch of colour as could be found at Nineveh, but a whole ring of blue and gold.

All ancient literary sources agree the gardens were built at Babylon. But Quintus Curtius Rufus (author of a history of Alexander the Great and of a Wonder-list) ascribes them to an Assyrian king who conquered Babylon. The Tigris rather than the Euphrates is sometimes named (with Diodorus Siculus positioning Nineveh on the Euphrates, not the Tigris), and descriptions of the palace of Babylon seem to match what we know of the palaces of Sennacherib and Ashurbanipal as well. The name Babylon can be translated as 'Gate of Gods', so, some argue, Babylonia refers in select sources to the entire territory encompassing both Nineveh and Babylon. The Old Testament Book of Judith (considered apocryphal in the Hebrew and Protestant tradition) describes Nebuchadnezzar as a king of the Assyrians ruling Nineveh.[85] Arabic sources employing data from 'Old Babylon' seem to be using latitude that corresponds better to Nineveh or Nimrud. It is all a bit of a muddle.

So, should this Wonder better be called the Hanging Gardens of Babylonia – a term used to refer to both Assyria and Babylon? Is it a memory sparked by centuries' worth of garden creation, including a cascading garden with dramatically staggered planting and a garden wonder-land to the north which found itself on the wrong side of history? A new generation of archaeologists in Iraq could well, one day, find the answer. Until then we have to lay out the patchwork of evidence in front of us, and endeavour to fill it with informed conjecture rather than fake certainty.

Today if you walk along the banks of the Tigris or the Euphrates, there is a wariness to your few companions in the landscape – the shepherds, goatherds and subsistence farmers you pass, men half-expecting you or someone else to take what is rightfully theirs: their grazing lands, their footpaths, their marshes, their homes. The Hanging Gardens encapsulate the tension of human civilisation – being driven to imagine, to plan and create, but needing to heed where our dreams lead us. Needing to be aware of the fallout – for good and for bad – of the fact that a notion made flesh impacts many. The rulers of Babylonia used their autocratic might to create manufactured paradises for their personal use. Whatever they were, however wondrous, the Hanging Gardens of Babylon would not have been idylls. They would have been exquisite, exacting expressions of potency, expressions of belief, manifestations of ingenuity and the start of a dangerously domineering relationship with the natural world.[86]

The creation of gardens in Babylonia, at the peak of the Iron Age, was when iron tools were allowing men to manipulate nature in a way unimagined before. One of my favourite artefacts from the period is a tiny ivory cube, just the right size to fit in a small bag, on whose faces are carefully calculated in neat cuneiform the number of daylight hours for each season: the cosmos catalogued. Yet the ancients knew that nature would always fight back, always win – so when they looked at woods and saw roads, at swamps and saw cities, at deserts and made gardens, they understood that in many ways this was an act of impossible will. Better than us perhaps, the populations of three millennia ago knew that what they were creating was a phantasmagorical and temporary gift. Time and again in Bronze Age mines or at hunting grounds we find gifts left to the earth as compensation for what had been taken. It was not without significance that the first words put into the mouth of the Mother Earth goddess Gaia, who enters the written record in the Greek world at exactly the time Nineveh's gardens and Babylon's walls were being rebuilt, deal with this problem. Gaia says, to survive the interventions of mankind, she wants to 'rid herself of the burden of humanity'.[87]

And indeed, in the palaces and homes of both Assyrians and Babylonians, a bearded character would appear in myths or on wall-art – the *lahmu*. The *lahmu* is frequently seen wrestling with wild or domestic animals, or both at the same time, holding these struggling creatures in a kind of headlock. An idea was being communicated that the dynamic equilibrium of the world and its resources was delicate and could only be maintained by the active effort of humans and gods alike.[88] For the inhabitants of the lands between and around the Tigris and the Euphrates, the cosmos was believed to have emerged from water. Both Babylon and Nineveh enjoyed atypically plentiful supplies of sweet water; Babylon from a system which canalised waters from the Tigris and Euphrates across a flat plain, while Nineveh benefited both from rainfall and from the tributaries into the Tigris that ran from Persian mountains. The gardens were a test of human ingenuity for people who understood that all the resources of the world were finite. It seems appropriate that Inanna-Ishtar – a fidgety, flighty, feisty young woman who was believed to wander through the heavens as a ball of light, the morning and the evening star – was so adored here. This young goddess of desire, a symbol both of fertility and of beauty, and of that nagging human drive to want more, to do more, to be more, embodied the ambition to manipulate the wildness and beauty of the earth, the very ambition which built gardens so wildly extravagant, they could never be forgotten.

The Hanging Gardens of Babylon are perhaps something else too, an incarnation of longing. An attempt to crystallise and capture the wonder of elsewhere.

In 612 BCE, a combined force of Babylonians, Medes and their allies attacked Nineveh. While Nineveh was to a large extent destroyed, from the classical and Hellenistic period on, through the time of the Sassanids and the early Islamic empires, Babylon kept going. It seems plausible that the idea of the great gardens was transported to the great Babylonian palace in the east which still stood. So Nineveh was wonderful, and was then destroyed – but its wonders could not be forgotten.

In 539 BCE, Babylon too was taken, by Persian forces. The Persians, whose own empire stretched from the Indus Valley to the Aegean, were ferocious adversaries. Babylon, effectively ruled by King Nabonidus's son Belshazzar, fell, and its captive population of Jewish exiles were allowed to escape their captivity, a population transfer imagined in paintings and literature across 2,500 years. In 400 BCE, the Greek historian-general Xenophon passed by and described the place as desolate; but the gardens had a long afterlife. As a dreamy, paradisiacal, water-tinkling haven they were beatified. In truth, though, the Wonder-walls and gardens of Babylon mark the beauty that starts the beginning of the end, the end of a temperate, sustainable relationship between humankind and the rest of the natural world.

Babylon was taken by Alexander the Great on his road to global dominion. It is via a description of Alexander's first entry to the city, written 400 years after the event, that we hear in detail not just of the garden but of the remarkable engineering it boasted to support mature trees, their roots and even the earth they were planted in. The staggering impression from these descriptions of the gardens does force us to consider whether Alexander could have died with the Hanging Gardens of Babylon to the fore of his mind, perhaps also written on his heart. Because, for Alexander, Babylon was a city of destruction above delight.

In around 335 BCE, as a young man beginning his campaign of conquest, Alexander had dismantled the seven-storey ziggurat in the city, vandalising work started by Persia's King Xerxes in the fifth century – probably adding to the allure of the tale of a legendary Tower of Babel.[89] A decade later, when Alexander found he had failed to become 'king of the world', he returned to Babylon. It was in Babylon that he buried that beloved companion Hephaestion[90] (who had died in either Ecbatana, western Iran, or the city of Tabriz, in East Azerbaijan province, Iran). It was in Babylon where Alexander gave up on his angry, ravening life.[91] He died here, aged thirty-two, of infected wounds, fatigue, a broken heart and almost certainly malaria – a malign gift of the marshy landscape and the sophisticated water-engineering in this great city. Before Alexander lay dying in Babylon, we're told he was planning to build a pyramid greater than the Great Pyramid Wonder itself.

When Alexander passed, the power he had amassed splintered and scattered, taking with it word of wondrous gardens – gardens which spawned both darkness and light.

Within forty-eight hours of Alexander's death, his empire was diced up and disputed by the leader's once-loyal generals. Just a few years later, the walls of Babylon themselves would be broken down by a warrior Demetrius, the son of another of Alexander's loyal companions, Antigonus.

It would be the same Demetrius whose siege of the city of Rhodes would catalyse the creation of our sixth Wonder, the giant bronze statue of the sun god Helios, the Colossus. Demetrius' attack on one of the citadels of Babylon was so ferocious, sections of the fine glazed wall-tiles vitrified – they turned to solid glass. The likelihood of any formal planting surviving such an attack is simply impossible, which might perhaps be why the gardens became a myth as fast as they became history. The very point of a garden is that it is full of life, that there will always be a spring after the winter. We do not want to imagine or memorialise a garden as blasted.

So the entrancing, visionary idea of the gardens as a long-lost Wonder lived on, inspiring gardens in Alexandria (some of which around the Mahmoudiyah Canal have endured until today), in Herod's Winter Palaces in Judaea and in paintings in the arching splendour of Nero's Golden House in Rome. In Latin accounts these lofty pleasure-garden-arboreta are described as a *miraculum*.[92] In Jordan today, in Herod's desert-wind-blasted, tottering fortress of Machareus overlooking the Dead Sea, where John the Baptist was imprisoned and then beheaded, archaeologists have identified a garden-section within the fortifications, fed by cisterns; and in Israel evidence is coming to light of Herod's dramatic hanging planting schemes using container-pots, artificial hills, and cascading rows of shrubbery. While writing this book, a hanging-garden-homage nightclub in Durham in the North of England and a multi-purpose '1,000 Trees' building on Suzhou Creek in Shanghai have opened, and student accommodation in Birmingham, inspired by Babylon's Wonder, has been proposed. In Athens, one of the more salubrious night-clubs and strip joints, decorated with images of Babylon's Ishtar Gate and palm trees, is called Babylon. The Hanging Gardens' allure has never faded.

Although mudbricks were picked away at, and carried off by locals to use in building, some of Babylon's treasures – the surface of the processional way, remnants of Alexander's pyre for Hephaestion and the seven-storey ziggurat – endured for the following 2,300 years, only to be destroyed during the Iraq conflict of 2003.[93] At the time of writing, the palace-complex of Nebuchadnezzar at Babylon, a sinister sham poorly reconstructed by Saddam Hussein in 1987 – with the dictator's name inscribed in the baked mudbricks just as were those of Babylonian kings – lies empty, a shell. Possibly, just possibly, the truth of the garden and its location still lies underneath.

This Wonder is as much a story of collapse as it is of creation.

Typically the ancient world was a place with a fetishistic reverence for the past.[94] So, when the Assyrian and Babylonian kings rebuilt their palaces, they dug down into foundations, often excavating and re-mounting earlier foundation stones. One such king, Nabonidus, the last king of the Neo-Babylonian Empire in the sixth century BCE, wrote: 'I deposited with my own inscription an inscription of Hammurabi, an ancient king, written on an alabaster tablet which I found inside a ruined temple; I placed them forever.'[95] This is the present parlaying with the past, and the past enjoying its power over the future. These wishes were often buried under and within walls; history, physically and psychologically, acting as a foundation for life to come – an inclination we still have which helps to explain our perpetual interest in phenomena such as the Wonders of the World. Neuroscientifically, we cannot have a thought about the future unless we access the foundation of a memory.

The Hanging Gardens of Babylon are a Wonder with a unique charge. From the Garden of Eden to the Buddha's Sacred Garden at Lumbini in Nepal where the seeker of enlightenment was said to be born, garden paradises have long been a trope employed by the West to 'understand' the East. Paradise is an old Persian word meaning a walled garden – derived from *pairi* (around) and *daeza* (wall). But despite this spiritual dimension, ancient Eastern gardens were also frequently credited by Western sources as filled with carnal delights of all kinds: fruits, frankincense, the forbidden fruit of sex. Add to that the fact that in the Judaeo-Christian tradition, Babylon was a name to be feared – think of the Whore of Babylon, the Tower of Babel – and it is easy to understand why the gardens have been at the fore of our collective imaginations.[96] The Hanging Gardens of Babylon, for at least twenty-five centuries, have triggered an oxymoron of understanding – a locus both very good, and very bad. They are as much an idea as a place.

But in their own day, the Hanging Gardens were surely constructed to understand and to own a man-made version of the wilderness of the wonderful mountains in the north of both the two great cities, Babylon and Nineveh – mountains that extend into what is now Turkey, Kurdistan and Lebanon. For those in Mesopotamia, mountains were places of great promise and of great peril, where both death and magical transformation were possible. A mountain without humans brought wonder but little comfort; a mountain landscape with the comforts of *kalam* (culture/the cultured world) was truly wonderful.[97] The Hanging Gardens were both.

Babylonia's recondite Hanging Gardens were a secluded Wonder for the hyper-elite, an object lesson in the manipulation of nature. Our next Wonder was built, officially at least, to adore the natural world and a female spirit of mountain-sides, to encourage and to allow access for many – pilgrims, merchants and asylum seekers – from far and wide across the Mediterranean Sea and three continents. It was also a Wonder that reminded humanity to respect and fear the raw power of nature, and the power of women as well as of men. It was, too, the first time we encounter a Wonder that emerged from an increasingly commerce-driven world. An astounding antiquity that turned a pretty profit.

CHAPTER 3

THE TEMPLE OF ARTEMIS AT EPHESUS

c. 550, REBUILT c. 340 BCE

I have set eyes on the very wall of lofty Babylon, supporting a chariot road, and the [statue of] Zeus by the Alpheios [in Olympia], and the Hanging Gardens, and the Colossus of Helios, and the huge labour of the steep pyramids, and the vast tomb of Mausolos; but when I saw the temple of Artemis, reaching up to the clouds, these other marvels dimmed, they lost their brilliance, and I declared 'Look, apart from Olympus itself, the sun has never shone on anything that can compare to this!'

ANTIPATER OF SIDON, C. 140 BCE[1]

'The Temple of Diana at Ephesus' engraving produced by Philips Galle after designs by Maarten van Heemskerck in 1572.

One dark night, a figure could be seen slipping from one column to another in Artemis's imposing Temple at Ephesus on the western edge of Anatolia. The individual's actions were odd; they did not look like a thief, but perhaps instead a crazed adorant, someone dipping to deposit shells or goat-bells, offerings for the great goddess of wild nature who called this Temple her home. Was that an ordinary he, or a she, climbing the inner wooden stairs to the roof? Surely not! Only authorised Temple personnel, high priestesses and priests were allowed this close to the innermost sanctuary. But then, suddenly, there was a suspicious spurt of light, and spits of flame from the points where the shadowy figure had been. Fire! Fire! Panic! Sound the alarm! Because this nocturnal visitor to the Temple of Artemis was no acolyte; this was an arsonist.

The results must have been sickening to witness and hard to process: a total devastation. But despite the fact that, on 21 July 356 BCE, the ancient Temple at Ephesus was destroyed in a terrible day and a night of heat and flame, none of this could be spoken of. Captured, racked and then executed, the criminal who chose to play with fire should, by rights, be nameless. The Temple authorities at Ephesus were so appalled by this blasphemous, murderous act, so petrified it would inspire copycat atrocities, they not only exterminated the arsonist, but made it a crime punishable by death even to speak his name.[2]

And yet here we are, talking about him. The fire-raiser was called Herostratus, possibly a desperate slave mounting the most astonishing of protests; but what seems certain is that the purpose of this wild rampage of destruction was, explicitly, to gain notoriety. The news of the attack was eventually leaked by a non-Ephesian, a libertarian historian and rhetorician called Theopompus from the nearby island of Chios, eight miles across the Aegean.[3] As soon as the identity of Artemis's desecrator came out, Herostratus' story belonged to everyone. 'Herostratic fame' has come to mean fame acquired at any cost. Herostratus' terrorist crime against our next Wonder became a popular morality tale – because he achieved the infamy he craved: he was famous for being infamous.

The flames that consumed the Temple of Artemis at Ephesus in the fourth century were lit the very night that Alexander III of Macedonia – later to be Alexander the Great – was born.[4] Tongues wagged: Artemis – the goddess of nature and childbirth – it was whispered, was so busy in northern Greece, super-birthing a world-class megalomaniac, she neglected her earthly temple home. Seers muttered that this prophesied the degradation of Asia by outside forces.[5] The arson became not just legendary, but an archetype; a meme for notoriety through negative and nefarious activity. Valerius Maximus, a Roman collector of historical anecdotes, who travelled to the Ephesian coast in the first century CE, tells us that Herostratus was tortured and then confessed to his deed – declaring that he indeed had burnt the Temple down in a quest for immortal fame. A strangely apposite strategy, given that the root of our 'fame' is the ancient Greek *pheme*, *fama* in Latin – a negatively charged word that originally meant rumour, gossip, slander.

Herostratus certainly got his wish; his reputation was immortalised and 'embalmed in . . . history, like a fly in amber', as Maximus, put it.[6] 'Herostratic fame' became quite the thing.* The incendiary of Artemis's Wonder was commemorated by Chaucer in his *House of Fame*;[7] by Cervantes in *Don Quixote*;[8] in Colley Cibber's *Richard III* of 1699,† where we hear: 'The aspiring youth that fired the Ephesian dome, / Outlives in fame the pious fool that rais'd it.'[9] Herostratus was the subject of Jean Paul Sartre's existentialist short story about misanthropy, *Erostratus*.[10] The arsonist was even commemorated by Adolf Hitler in a hideous anti-Semitic address to the Reichstag: '. . . it is clear to me that there is a certain Jewish international capitalism and journalism that has no feeling at all in common with the people whose interests they pretend to represent, but who, like Herostrates of old, regard incendiarism as the greatest success of their lives . . .'[11]

But Artemis's archaic destroyed Temple at Ephesus had already burned such an impression in the ancient world's imagination, like a sunlight photo on zinc, it would be an inspiration for the re flowering of culture in the region. The new Temple of Artemis at Ephesus, rebuilt in the Hellenistic period after its infamous demise, is the Wonder for which the phrase 'phoenix from the ashes' might have been invented.[12]

The Temple of Artemis at Ephesus should be considered wonderful for other reasons too. Despite the pyro-maniac Herostratus' best efforts, the Temple is the first of our Wonders which was accessible not just to

---

* As recently as 2001, the Armenian director Ruben Kochar produced a film about a modern-day rebel named *Herostratus*.
† A work published by Rivington and Sons in 1777.

kings, but to commoners, and the only one of all the Seven Wonders of the World where women, mythical and historical, can be found right at the heart of the Wonder's narrative. Many processed here to adore the goddess Artemis, or fled here to seek her protection, in addition to the stream of travellers who journeyed from one Wonder to another simply to marvel. The Temple of Artemis also nourished a kind of power that differed a little to that exemplified by the Giza pyramids and the towering monuments of Babylon, power that drew its strength from offering comprehensive sanctuary as well as lionising control and attack.

Artemis's Temple is also a Wonder with many lives, with a complex backstory. And to understand it, you have to learn to read the remains of the sanctuary – now a little distance from the main Hellenistic and Roman site at Ephesus – with a forensic eye.

The Temple site, just off the main road to the small town of Selçuk in Turkey, and beyond the tomb of an unknown fifteenth-century Ottoman prince, is ragged and marshy. Bullfrogs chant incessantly at the wrong time of day, and midges can whine. A peacock calls. Earnest visitors from as far afield as China and Brazil take selfies and try to conjure the mood of marvel despite the lack of many visible remains. Men bring dog-eared postcards in the hope of a sale and local dogs copulate listlessly at the Wonder's edge.

At first – truth be told – there seems to be little to see. Foundation stones are flooded, or emerge from weed-choked ponds, perimeter walls are covered with grasses, colonnades lie buried. A single erect column offers a happy nesting place to a family of storks. Elsewhere, antique fragments appear nearby as architectural salvage in the Great Isa-Bey Mosque, just visible across the fields, and in aqueducts and in the sixth-century CE Basilica of St John high on the hill above at Ayasuluk. Soberingly, the majority of the remains of Ephesus' Wonder have made their way to museums in Britain, Italy, America, Germany and Austria.[13] So there are scant remnants in situ, given the extreme praise reserved for the Temple by ancient authors, from Antipater whose quote opened this chapter, to the Roman-period travel-writer Pausanias who tells us that this was once the largest building in the ancient world. A temple which was destroyed and rebuilt, destroyed and rebuilt again, and which was the subject of admiration and speculation for close to a millennium.

It was a Wonder to which, in its day, most arrived by boat. Travelling up the Turkish Lycian coast from south to north, as traders did when they sailed from Babylon's Levantine territories, heading west past what was once the kingdom of ancient Karia (soon to be home to another of the Seven Wonders, the Mausoleum of Halikarnassos), the volcanic rippling of the coastline softens as Ephesus approaches. Now the land is flat, wetlands reach down to the shore. From the sky – from the gods'-eye view – Ephesus' specialness is apparent. The eastern Aegean islands of Chios, Kos and Lesbos lead like stepping-stones to a fertile river-mouth at the edge of Anatolia, to meadows protected by mountains. Ephesus sits in an apple-bite curve of the coast, beyond that a sparkling sea, with the sparkling possibilities of trade and exchange. So, access to the sacred Wonder was typically by Ephesus' sacred port. The great Temple of Artemis at Ephesus is the first of our Wonders which is as much about seawater as rivers. A place which incarnates a salty fertility, the possibilities of escape, and intercontinental potential.*

Ephesus – on that sliver of coastline that separates (or joins, depending on your outlook) the Eastern and Western worlds – had long been both a pivot and a pawn in the powerplay between the two. Originally situated on the high hill of Ayasuluk, it was occupied in turn by those Bronze Age superpowers, the Anatolian Hittites and the Greek Mycenaeans; by Phoenicians and by allies of the Egyptians; then by Cimmerians, Lydians, Persians and Greeks. This was a site on the frontline of history. Dominating the mouth of the Kaystros River – the 'Little Meander', as it is known today (a smaller version of the larger Meander River which physically meanders through the landscape here) – with a sea-port and natural harbour, Ephesus was coveted by players in the region across a 3,000-year span. It marked the crucial western end of the two main land highways from the Euphrates: the *koine hodos*, the common highway, and the Royal Road to Susa, at the foot of the Tagros Mountains, in what was once Persia, modern-day Iran. The line of the ancient Royal Road – which can be traced running 2,000 miles east, its branches linking Ephesus to Nineveh and Babylon – is still visible from the air above the site.[14] So Ephesus was a magnet for pilgrimages and profane journeys from the East and the West.

___

* At the time of my last visit to the site, a project was underway to connect the Temple to the seaboard by canal once more, as it had been in antiquity.

You approach Ephesus today, in late spring, through fields hazed by magenta-pink peach blossom, along ancient roads, many dead-straight, because 2,600 years ago – when an early version of the Temple was built – this was already a popular pilgrimage site. Within half a century, Ephesus had become one of the busiest and largest cities in the ancient world, the centre of Rome's Asian road network, with a port that could accommodate at least 800 ships. One of the reasons Ephesus' great Temple became legendary was its accessibility – this was a Wonder that was relatively easy and relatively safe to reach.

Originally, before human activity interrupted the site's natural beauty, there was a fresh-water spring next to the sea, protected by a backbone of tree-rich mountains. Recent excavations have shown that a sandy beach once abutted this miraculous water source, and that some kind of simple, sacred space was established before Ephesus was a settlement. In remote locations along the Turkish coast today – like the quiet, almost inaccessible village around Kargi Bay – this combination of salt and fresh water still feels more than a little magical. Bullrushes tower next to the fresh-water spring, attracting their own ecology of mammals and birds, while flying fish and dolphins swim through the brine nearby, with fertile hills above. Even today in the low-lying Ephesian landscape, with flocks of storks and cranes skimming other-worldly mudflats and mounds, there is a strange, spiritual feel to the Temple's hinterland. It is easy to see why early populations would want to worship the fertility and paradisiacal brilliance of earth and sea in the form of a nature goddess here.

Other temples of Artemis were built around the wonder of a fresh-water supply too. Travelling 600 miles south to Jerash, in what was ancient Arabia and is now northern Jordan, current excavations, ongoing at my last visit, of Artemis's huge temple-complex, which in its heyday stretched a third of a mile from one end to the other, have revealed two subterranean pools, directly beneath its holiest portion. The goddess honoured at Ephesus was responsible for the stuff of life – her sanctuary was naturally abundant. This was a Wonder founded on a wildly beautiful natural phenomenon, and was rightly respectful of the value of that natural world.

Ephesus is a site with a deep and diverse history. Where now there is a crusader castle, a Byzantine church and classical fragments – all sunning

spots for the local cat community – there is evidence of habitation on the
hills above the Hellenistic and Roman settlement reaching right back to
the seventh millennium BCE. Simple building on the Temple site itself
starts in the second millennium BCE. At the time of the Hittites (the
Asian super-power who once controlled much of what is now Turkey,
northern Iran and Iraq between c. 1680 and 1120 BCE), Ephesus was
called Apasa, the chief city of the region of Arzawa for close on half a
millennium. Arzawa was a distinct entity – just as Ephesus would come
to be the administrative centre of the distinct province of what Rome
called Asia from the second century BCE onwards. So we should imagine
somewhere with a natural attraction, but also the opportunity to be a
strategic hub for the power-players of the day.

In the fourteenth century BCE Mycenaean Greeks took Ephesus as a
bridgehead into Asia. The Temple of Artemis starts its life at this time,
where there is evidence of the worship of the fresh-water spring, Hittite-
style. Clues include a bronze figurine of a Hittite priest and a cult statue
that is clearly influenced by Minoan Crete.[15] Visitors and prehistoric
influencers would have travelled here across the seas from what is now
called Europe. Early Ephesus sat on a ribbon of internationalism and
sophistication. Developments in the vicinity had great form: the remnants of one palace-settlement further inland at Beycesultan appear, for
example, to show evidence of under-floor heating back in the second
millennium BCE – a thousand years before such engineering is officially
recognised in archaeology.

But there was always a passionate, primal timbre to the rituals and
beliefs at Ephesus. Sacrificial puppies, buried alive in c. 900 BCE, were
found in a pit here, indicating the worship too of the sorceress witch-
goddess Hekate. Hekate, whose very name links her to Artemis (the
adjective *hekatos* means 'far-darter'), is a deity often associated with the
hunting goddess. She is sometimes described in Greek myth as Artemis's
half-sister or as her alter ego (and on occasions she is fused with Iphigenia
– the virgin girl paired with Artemis in the Greek myths).[16] Hekate is also
the hex whom the mythical character Medea summons for aid. Hekate
helps Medea to punish Medea's faithless lover Jason, to poison his new
princess-bride and murder her children. Like Artemis, Hekate's cult was
served by eunuch priests.

This earliest sanctuary at Ephesus, which would be continually adapted, and eventually serve as the foundation of the famous classical Wonder, was clearly a mystical, bucolic, hallowed space with a far-reaching reputation and international DNA. Excavations here have revealed ivories from northern Syria, decorated with the image of a griffin and a tree of life. There are representations of the Egyptian god Bes, a kind of sublime, priapic male midwife. Archaeologists also discovered Egyptian scarabs. Bears' teeth (the bear was a creature special to Artemis) from Greece, drilled to be worn as necklaces, were uncovered. A beautiful gemstone, delicately carved with the image of a stag and an ibex, was a reminder of the animals hunted here throughout the Stone, Bronze and Iron Ages. A slim, beautiful ivory distaff from the late seventh century BCE shows a young girl holding a wine jug and libation bowl, with a bird of prey high on her head. Called 'The Hawk Priestess', this is a demonstration of Artemis's love for the falcons who hunted so superbly. There are also lovely pots, again decorated with the head of a hawk, or foxes being hunted. Fat amber beads too emerged from the earth; also the stumps of wooden posts, bronze-buckled belts and delicate ivory hands. Smooth bracelets and chunky necklaces with beads like gobstoppers were discovered here, designed to hang on an image of the goddess, who may well have taken the form of a flat, human-shaped wooden plank. The earliest image of the female deity here must have twinkled with dangling ornaments like a millionaire's Christmas tree.[17]

And then there is the gold. Crescent-shaped brooches proud with roaring lions. Gorgeous golden goddess figurines, their headdresses cascading down their backs, decorated with undulating meander designs (sometimes known as a 'Greek key' design), some wearing pearl necklaces and drop earrings – all have enchantingly enigmatic smiles. A gold bull's head, with a lion sitting between its horns, double-headed axes, luscious golden rosettes, animal-shaped appliqués. All left in the Temple of Artemis as offerings to a goddess who clearly mattered – to the inhabitants of Ephesus and the many who would come to attend her cult.

While the Hanging Gardens of Babylon (or Nineveh) were being enjoyed, others were champing for influence in the Near East. At the end of the Bronze Age, when cities and communities fell one after the other in a domino-line of devastation following the disruption of climate-change events (evidence of which has recently been excavated from the Sea of Galilee), and after attacks by the 'Sea Peoples' – probably Phoenician pirates

– in the Iron Age Greeks returned to take control of Ephesus, establishing a place to worship Artemis, at the latest in the ninth century BCE.

This was a busy epoch. The Artemis Temple – the Artemision – witnessed many local regime changes, many fluctuating local influences. King Midas of Phrygia – who burns brighter in legend than he does in history by turning all he touched to gold – finally had his nearby lands subsumed by the Lydians, who became allies of the Assyrian King of Nineveh, Ashurbanipal. The Lydians, first accomplices of the Persians (whose territories would come to stretch from Iran in the East to western Anatolia), then friends with the Greeks, halted just shy of Ephesus at coastal territories also dominated by Lycians and Ionians. When one group of semi-nomads from the Caucasus, the Cimmerians, attacked Artemis's sanctuary and the early structures at the Temple at Ephesus, the Lydians petitioned the strong-man of the day, King Ashurbanipal, for help. Cimmerian prisoners-of-war, captured as they ravaged the countryside round about the sanctuary, were then sent as captives to Ashurbanipal's court. These Cimmerian prisoners witnessed and attacked one Wonder, the Temple of Artemis at Ephesus, only to become slaves toiling in the shadow of another, the grand monuments and gardens of Babylonia. And just as Babylon was relishing its spoils as the newly dominant force in the Near and Middle East, to the west, another culture was on the rise, Ephesus' neighbours the Karians, a brilliant civilisation, surprisingly neglected by history, but who would be responsible for their own ebullient tomb-Wonder 60 miles down the coast at Halikarnassos.

Detail of Lekythos vase showing a Battle of Greeks against Amazons, note the women's trousers, c. 420–410 BCE. Amazons were central characters at Ephesus.

Ephesus was a site at the sea-rim of an energetic geopolitical cauldron. So if we think back twenty-seven centuries, to the eighth century BCE, and the early Iron Age, we should try to imagine the excitement of the audacious construction works here.

The first, archaic stone-built Temple of Artemis at Ephesus, dating to the late 700s BCE, was a wonder for a wide world because – at a time when the pecking order in the Eastern Mediterranean and the Near and Middle East was still in flux – it constituted the tidal flow of cultural and political sway between East and West. It was also worthy of wonder because it was a temple to humanity's testy relationship with the natural world: by worshipping the goddess of nature, women and men at Ephesus were trying to work out what their contract with the rest of nature should be. Unlike the elite, exclusive palaces of Babylonia, people of all degrees could come here, from farmers to heads of state. With a packed-earth floor, built at about the same time that Sennacherib was planting his well-watered gardens, this structure was ground-breaking: the first ever colonnaded Greek temple. An archetype for everything we think we know about classical architecture. And it was huge.

Ephesus' double colonnades – copied in the later iterations of the building – themselves paid homage to earlier architectural forms from North Africa: the great temple-complexes of Egypt, at Luxor, Karnak, Abu Simbel *et al*. These monstrous glades-turned-to-stone represented giant papyrus reed beds. In Anatolia, the Temple of Artemis was an architectural version of the forests of pine and dwarf-oak through which the hunters of the goddess of the hunt, Artemis, were thought to run.[18]

Walking through the canopies of stone-columns, still standing on the banks of the Nile at Egyptian Thebes, humans emerge like sprites, tiny at their bulging bases. The acoustics are other-worldly, sounds ricocheting from one pillar to another. In an open courtyard, this is a megalithic grove – impressive because it is both relatable and remarkable. Ephesus was similar but with key differences – it marshalled those stone trunks into something cleaner, more angular. The distinctively shaped peripteros at Ephesus – a portico and colonnade running around the central temple – has been copied right up until today and all around the world, and appears to be one of the very first of its kind.

Flanked by patient market-gardeners, in the marshy ground on the sanctuary site today there are still tantalising hints of the earliest

Comparison of the crowded Hypostyle Hall in the Temple of Karnak in Egypt and columns arranged in double colonnades in the Temple of Artemis. Only one still stands in Ephesus.

monumental temples here: the ghost of that eighth-century BCE building, made primarily of smooth yellow limestone; a surrounding wall from the extended seventh-century Temple, there to stop flooding – a measure that did not work. In the seventh century the entire Temple was destroyed by flash floods when over 5 feet of sand, silt and gravel washed from mountain run-off into the nearby Selinus river,[19] churning over the Temple's clay floor and crashing columns to the ground. Flash floods are petrifying in this part of the world. The waters rise by feet in moments, they rip through buildings, swarm trees, plucking and snatching those in their path, and deposit muck and material from many miles away before they vanish as quickly as they appear.

To combat the squelching meadows of water that helped to give the sanctuary its mystique, Artemis's Temple was raised, and raised again, originally by 6 and a half feet and then, in the sixth century BCE, by 8 feet. Perhaps even a further 13 feet by the end of the fourth century. But Artemis's glorious home was never moved, however treacherous, however unstable its flood-plain foundation. Eventually, in the fourth century CE the Temple fell for the last time, and no one would ever build here again – the ancients clearly felt there to be something magnetically holy about the particular spot the Temple inhabited for 1,800 years. The Temple's footprint was as much a Wonder as the Temple itself.

If we focus primarily on the engineering genius of Ephesus' great Temple, we can sometimes forget who, and what, it was all constructed for, and therefore how it actually felt to witness the Ephesian Wonder first hand. Because this Temple was the earthly abode of a truly almighty goddess. While ancient deities were immortal, their interaction with the world was inescapably corporeal. For many, the Sanctuary of Artemis at Ephesus was a Wonder because of the real, radioactive, sublime power it was thought to hold: because of the centrality of Artemis to all human life.

So who – or what – were the faithful adoring at Ephesus? Well, the answer varies across time, and depending on whom you ask. The Ephesian Artemis is a brilliant example of an idea that matters – our place in nature – and how that relationship was intended, understood and realised in both the East and the West. Asiatic Artemis was complex and compelling, a goddess of mountains and rivers and estuaries and untamed land. And whereas the perhaps more familiar Greco-Roman version of the deity – the Artemis-Diana we meet in the oldest halls of the Louvre Museum, for example, or in the Tivoli Gardens near Rome – is frequently represented as a hunter with a bow and arrow, Ephesus' Artemis was not an elegant woman poised, artfully, with a flowing chiton. The goddess at Ephesus was a mistress of the beasts – their protector, not primarily their nemesis. Asiatic Artemis was a patron of the wild world – a channel for Mother Earth's potency. An Eastern creation who came to play host to a Western version of herself.

The Artemis of Western origin, many Greeks said, had been born on the sacred Cycladic island of Delos, 100 miles west of Ephesus. Her mother Leto, a Titan (whose name, interestingly, may have its roots in the Lycian word for 'woman'; Lycian was a language spoken along the coast from Ephesus), had ranged across the Mediterranean for nine days, racked by birth pangs. Leto finally found in stony Delos an island that would take her in – an island blessed ever since with fertility. Clinging to a palm tree, she birthed Artemis and her twin brother Apollo. A single palm tree still stands on Delos in memory of the myth. Leto's tree was first documented in Homer's epic poem, the *Odyssey*, where the adventuring war-hero Odysseus recalls the distinctive botanical landmark on the windy island.[20] Delos today is still wind-whipped and wondrously atmospheric, a giant heritage and excavation site. Only a few archaeologists and guardians are allowed to stay overnight here, whereas all tourists and visitors must leave by 4 p.m. Thus, Delos sustains an other-timely, other-worldly feel.

While Artemis's brother Apollo, the god of the sun, roared through the heavens in his horse-drawn chariot, Artemis's elements were woods and water and the night. Her great Temple at Ephesus (the *Latorculi Alexandrini*'s first entry in the Seven Wonder list, you will recall) was an incarnation of the security that comes from standing not against nature, but within it.

Artemis in the mythology of the Greeks was an unusual goddess, a female figure who stood apart from the rutting sexuality that was the norm of ancient life and myth. The story went that on the eve of her wedding, Artemis begged her father Zeus to allow her not to marry. In most cultures at this time, women were controlled, either by having to have sex, or by not being allowed to. Artemis's agency, and her choice, makes her attractively odd. She was a virgin whose sphere was consummation, a guardian to virgin-girls and to boy-bridegrooms alike, and a huntress who also protected her prey. As a deity she was framed as both a normal member of normal (cosmic) society – and as other. Chaste and yet fertile, Artemis was a potent mystery. A creature so fecund, she needed no other man or beast to reproduce. She was parthenogenetic, a virgin-creator, although she chose never to burden herself with childbirth or children.

And one of Artemis's favourite haunts was credited to be Ephesus. In fact, many other Greeks said Artemis was not born on Delos at all, but at Ortygia, a grove rich in olive trees close to the Ephesian sanctuary.* For at least five centuries, from the time the Temple in the Wonder-lists was being built, the birth of Artemis was celebrated in the steep, well-wooded land that rings Ephesus, and under skies pleated with layers of clouds – pale grey, oyster, lemon-pink, like chert – as a secretive, mysterious celebration – orgiastic in the true sense of the word.

And then, in the sixth century BCE, Artemis's special sanctuary was given an injection of cash. The Temple's patron was the King of Lydia, Croesus, a potentate so rich, the ancient world buzzed with stories about this billionaire ruler and the projects he sponsored. We still cite Croesus' name as an example of excessive wealth. Croesus' name in its original Lydian was probably Krowisas, 'Karos the Noble', and he was, you will recall, that brother-in-law of Nebuchadnezzar II and of Queen Amytis in Babylon. The historian Herodotus recorded that a serious building project was begun at Ephesus in the sixth century BCE, and recent archaeology indicates that a brand-new version of Artemis's Temple was indeed initiated around 580–570 BCE after the damage of those terrible flash floods. From the digs, a monumental statue base, an altar, and a ramp have all been recovered.[21] The new monster Temple of Ephesus was 425 feet long and 225 feet wide.[22] That is almost double the dimensions that the Parthenon in Athens would come to have when it was built 150 years later. The Parthenon continues to dominate modern Athens today; just think of the impact a temple twice its size would have had twenty-five centuries ago. The Artemision – the name the Temple was given in classical sources – boasted 127 columns, a 60-foot height, possibly with an opening in the roof above one statue of its goddess.[23] Ebullient marble capitals, over 6-and-a-half-feet long, with giant rosettes – transported to

---

* Confusingly, the island of Delos is also sometimes known as Ortygia.

the British Museum in the nineteenth century – still dwarf those few who pass, as they sit lonely in the gloom of the museum's storerooms.

Despite the fact that the foundations were on marshland, and in an area prone to regular seismic activity, the Temple that was raised was astounding in ambition and scale. We get a rather sympathetic glimpse (even if this is a flight of fantasy) into the great stress of the construction of Artemis's new Temple from a later Roman source, the scientist-adventurer Pliny the Elder. Pliny relates that the Cretan architect Chersiphron, working on the site with his son Metagenes, was so strung out by the apparent impossibility of placing the Temple's lintel (a giant stone beam) over the building's entrance doors, he considered suicide. The architrave alone has now been estimated to weigh 24 tonnes, so this would indeed have been a daunting task. Fortunately, that night the guardian goddess Artemis heard Chersiphron's prayers and magicked the lintel into place herself.[24] While the pyramids were an enormous engineering challenge and the gardens of Babylonia a conceptual innovation, the gargantuan Temple of Artemis was an astonishing feat of construction and creative design. Many of the limestone blocks used for construction would have weighed over 5 tonnes. Sketches of the Temple's excavation in 1840 show the crowds of local farmers pressed into service to re-raise the blocks, so they could be wilfully removed to museums in the West.

According to the historian Livy, in 557 BCE the sixth king of Rome (Romulus being the first), the Etruscan Servius Tullius, in concert with Latin tribes, built a tribute-temple to Artemis based on the example in Ephesus.[25] This is a story now backed up by archaeological identification in Rome. Sections of the temple's walls can be found in elegant neoclassical villas in the Via Tempio di Diana in the multimillionaires' quarter of the Aventine Hill. In high-end restaurants visited by the discerning wealthy of the city, staff and chefs nip to and fro, some unaware of the significant stones built into the foundations. Up above them starlings swarm in vast murmurations just as they would have done above the copy-cat Temple of Diana. This appears to be a Wonder that was talked about, that was inspirational almost as soon as it was raised.

Croesus' intervention and bank reserves (Croesus is the man, after all, who helped to bring the world the cash economy) made the continued reconstruction of Ephesus' archaic Temple a success. Not, though, before he had threatened the city of Ephesus with erasure.

As the last in the line of the Lydians, ruling from c. 560 to 546 BCE, King Croesus had the opportunity to benefit luxuriantly from the work of his royal ancestors. From his magnificent capital at Sardis, 80 or so miles inland from Ephesus and situated as a terminus on the arterial Royal Road, which led to Persia's capital Susa, he was a political player with very deep pockets. Electrum (a naturally occurring alloy of gold and silver) washed into his territories via the River Pactolus – which flowed from snow-capped Mount Tmolos, right through Sardis's central market-place. This gift of the river was used to make the world's earliest coined money. Croesus sponsored the distillation technology that separated this electrum into its constituents of gold and silver. It could also be that the very first gold coins ever minted carried images of the Ephesian Artemis. This would make the goddess commander of Ephesus' Wonder the original privy seal – an image and stamp used to represent the authority of a reigning monarch.[26]

Croesus' Lydian capital at Sardis, still being excavated, was itself a wonder to behold. With direct road-links east to the territory of the Assyrians and south to Babylon (it is still possible to drive along much of this road in modern-day Jordan and Iraq), Sardis was hyper-connected. On the city's great north–south highway, it boasted its own riverside temple to Artemis.* Columns from this Artemision, the fourth largest Ionic temple ever built, still stand in the strange, volcanic landscape. As does the temple's free-standing altar, like a giant stone bunker.

Sardis's acropolis is – literally – a gold mine, and the large-scale cottage-industry refining that took place, where gold and silver were separated out, has been identified here. Stories from antiquity describe Croesus' wealth being in the form of gold dust as well as solid gold. We hear of the gold bars Croesus grandly dedicated to the great Sanctuary of Delphi on the Greek mainland – the holy place considered the navel of the earth by the Greeks. And excavations at Sardis have also proved the gold-dust speculation to be true.[27] Gold to be refined and silver to be recovered ensured the River Pactolus was the gift that kept on giving. It would be the direct source of the funds that enabled the Temple of Artemis

---

* Sardis's Artemis, like the Artemis at Ephesus, had attributes very like the goddess Kybele, an Eastern nature-deity who was sometimes referred to as the Lydian Kubaba.

to be completely rebuilt in the sixth century. Croesus' earth-given cash would ensure Ephesus's Wonder would end up being ground-breaking and world-famous.

The River Pactolus also yielded enough wealth to train and subsidise an unbeatable army. In 560 BCE, as Croesus blazed west to beat down a challenge to his throne from his nephew and half-brother, the first city he attacked was Ephesus, the most strategic settlement in the region. Herodotus tells a story that the people of the town, in desperation, ran a woollen rope from the columns of the Temple to their city, high on Ayasuluk Hill, covering a 7-stade (or just under a mile) distance (note the magic number seven in play), so that Artemis's divine protection, the sanctuary she promised, could leach out along that line to keep their homes and their families safe.[28]

But quickly the inescapable reality of the situation dawned on the Ephesians and they realised that not even the goddess' protection could keep them out of harm's way. They knew that they were beaten; Croesus was now in charge. The Ephesians' loss, though, would prove to be the Temple's gain. Nominally ruler of the city, Croesus decided to throw his weight around. He sponsored expensive carved column drums for Artemis's new Temple – a number of broken examples of which are still held by the British Museum. These would have been animated with bright paints and tints. In the British Museum's labyrinthine storerooms, there are also fragments of the inscriptions that Croesus left in the stones of Artemis's Temple, trumpeting his generosity. In Greek and Lydian, again and again, Croesus declares: KING CROESUS DEDICATED THIS.[29] One interesting rogue historical reference from a Jewish polymath called Nicolaus of Damascus (a close friend of Herod the Great), writing around the time of Jesus' birth, tells us that Croesus had held a lifelong ambition to be involved in the construction of Ephesus' great Temple. Whether true or not, it reflects an emotional reality of the age – a desire to be associated with the biggest, the best, the most unique, the most wonderful.[30]

Indeed, in the archaic period no other sanctuary boasts the wealth of gold found at Ephesus' Artemision. There is jewellery, predominantly women's, probably donated by female visitors: earrings in the shape of boats, mini-goddess pendants, floral-headed pins, brooches like birds of prey.[31] Also discovered were electrum coins, an embossed golden falcon, drilled amber, fragments of ivory perfume jars.[32] There are fertility symbols – currently held by the Istanbul Archaeological Museum, protected behind its shady gardens, where kittens and cats play happily in the courtyard. In the Ephesus Museum the gold on display from the site is breath-taking, with delicate bracelets, ornamental pins and finely decorated bands. And commanding the whole room, there are those tiny, captivating, enigmatically smiling gold female figurines. Perfectly formed, just three inches high, their arms neatly beside their sides, waists cinched, one with a dimple in her chin, these offerings to Artemis have enormous charm. All the gold at Ephesus is of exceptional purity, much straight from Sardis. Interior columns of the Temple itself were gilded with silver and gold. A silver plaque, detailing the taxes raised to pay for the works on Artemis's new super-Temple, was said to have been displayed on site.

Croesus also donated golden oxen (we do not know whether they were solid gold or gilded) – the living versions of which, their horns too gilded, draped in garlands of flowers and herbs, would have been led to the sanctuary to be sacrificed. The Temple's sacrificial altar – in front of the entrance – was surrounded by its own colonnade with stalls for the waiting tribute-animals. It was all part of a complex that had become grander and more audacious than any other temple ever seen in the Eastern Mediterranean. By the time Pliny the Elder was writing in the first century CE, we hear that 'many kings' (not just Croesus) had presented new columns to Ephesus – a measure of the jaw-dropping impact this monument must have had, to be perceived as the gift of not one, but many regal potentates, and a reminder that success has many fathers.[33]

So at Ephesus fabled wealth met immense significance.

Croesus' version of Artemis's Temple was a brilliant collision of Western and Eastern influences constructed by master-builders whose traditions drew from all points of the compass, and whose skills were in demand across the Eastern Mediterranean. Using a lucent blue-white local marble, the lead architects, as mentioned, are recorded as being Chersiphron and his son Metagenes from Knossos,* along with one Theodorus from the nearby island of Samos. When it came to working on mega-sanctuaries, Samian Theodorus certainly had form. Because Theodorus was also

---

* Knossos had used wooden columns (tapering to the bottom) to replicate wood canopies – might Chersiphron have been aware of these when he designed the stone trunks at Ephesus?

involved in building the imposing complex to the goddess Hera on Samos. This vast site, like Ephesus, is marshy, with reeds still growing in Hera's sanctuary (called the Heraion). Here frogs are your companions at night, and marsh-marigolds by day. Indeed, Samos' sanctuary consciously tried to out-do the earlier complex at Ephesus – encouraging Herodotus to nominate the Heraion as the largest temple in the world, much to Ephesus' chagrin.[34]

A Gorgon's head, we are told, was raised on the front face of Artemision's eastern pediment. Gorgons were originally a decorative feature from the Near East – a nightmarish incarnation of our fear of the ferocity of the natural world (and of society's fear of women).[35] Another Gorgon from exactly the same date survives and still glowers down from within Corfu's Archaeological Museum. Its fearsome stare and head curling with snakes shocks even today. The Artemision Temple showed this Eastern-leaning influence throughout: the elegant Ionic order (Ionia loosely spanned the Cyclades in the Aegean Sea and the Eastern seaboard of the Mediterranean), which adapted floral patterns and decorations from Eastern art; the fact that human figures were used within the Temple architecture itself (think of all those beautiful women described in the decorations of public buildings in Babylonia, and the regal figures in Egypt); and that dreadful, serpent-haired monster. We mis-identify this Wonder if we

Marble column drum from the Temple of Ephesus decorated by Scopas, 340–320 BCE. Currently on display in the British Museum. Figures almost life-sized.

A Greek gorgon, c. 590–570 BCE from Corfu, similar to that found on the Archaic stone Temple of Artemis. Like Artemis, this Gorgon also protected animals.

describe it as 'Greek'. The Temple of Artemis was an oriental, monumental home for the Asiatic goddess, the deity appearing in the form of a cult statue, built in local marble but drawing inspiration from a wide Eastern Mediterranean radius.

Yet even though Croesus' name was inscribed again and again in Greek and Lydian on Ephesus' great Temple columns, the rich king never lived to see his work finished. Because Croesus and his verdant, rich, gold-packed territories were blasted by a Persian invasion.

So that he be whispered of far and wide as a dread example, the story goes that the Persian Emperor Cyrus II decided that the Lydian king's fate was to be burnt alive on a pyre. As the flames started to lick, Croesus cried out the name of the Athenian philosopher Solon, who had taught him that you cannot appreciate happiness until you are dead. Presumably on hearing these touching pearls of wisdom, howled in a dying man's anguish, Cyrus suddenly had a change of heart. But it was now too late and the Persians could not put out the flames. Then, miraculously, Croesus appealed to Artemis's twin brother Apollo and, in a stunning *deus ex machina*, was saved from death by a god-conjured deluge of rain.[36] A later version of the tale declared that on hearing Croesus wildly chanting the Ephesian *Grammata* – a magical language of spells understood only by Artemis and her familiars – Artemis herself, the goddess Croesus had so honoured with the most splendid temple on earth, intervened to save the once-so-rich king.

In truth, the historical fact of the matter was as dramatic. Croesus almost certainly threw himself on that pyre, rather than become an under-lord to a Persian king. Self-immolation was considered an honourable end for disgraced leaders at the time.

Croesus' failure against the Persians left western Anatolia, and ultimately mainland Greece, open to Persian attack. But not before the bully Cyrus had had his come-uppance. On campaign in the East, the Persian emperor met a formidable enemy, a real-life Amazon, Queen Tomyris. Although accounts differ, Herodotus tells us that the warrior-queen slashed Cyrus' neck clean through, crucified his decapitated corpse, and then drowned his severed head in a skinful of wine, hissing, 'I warned you I would quench your thirst for blood, and so I shall.'[37]

With its dynamic, high-roller patron out of the picture, the energy in the Ephesian project dimmed. Because of local infighting and the Persian Wars, Artemis's stone temple would linger as a building site and not be fully completed until 430 BCE – 120 years after it was begun. By this time others were already beginning to copy Ephesus' greatness – most notably (although still only about half the size of the Ephesian original), the now world-famous Parthenon in Athens and the temple that housed our fourth Wonder, the giant Statue of Zeus at Olympia. One tantalising reference tells us that an 'extremely archaic' panel depicting the Ephesian Artemis was painted in c. 400 BCE by a woman, Timarete, the daughter of an Athenian painter. Waspish comments by the Roman author Pliny the Elder, who remarked that Timarete 'scorned the duties of a woman and practised her father's art', ensured she was remembered infamously. A fifteenth-century CE version of Timarete's Artemis painting shows the goddess poised, with one hand fluttering over her chest, like the sculpture of Aphrodite at nearby Knidos – a life-size, naked artwork by the maestro Praxiteles which became the most famous representation of the goddess of sexual love in antiquity.

So the bulk of the foundations for the fourth century BCE Wonder at Ephesus, which appeared in many Seven Wonders lists, were delivered in the sixth century and then sporadically in the fifth century BCE, in a rush of geopolitical turmoil.

*

All this matters, because to start to understand the Wonders as the ancients did, we need to focus not just on their manifestation, but on their inspiration. To get to the heart of the Temple of Artemis at Ephesus, we must investigate the perceived power of the goddess for whom this giant Wonder was created.

Artemis herself would originally have been understood to inhabit a cryptic lump of wood – now called a xoanon. An enigmatic figure to be pulled out from behind a containing curtain in the Temple at political adjudications, for example – rather as we might bring a bible into a courtroom. This cult statue was a reminder to all present of the life-changing seriousness of the decisions being made. Treated like a living being, this wooden form (originally flat, like a plank) would be washed in sea or spring water, draped with flowers and clothes, decorated with gold, moisturised with oil, fig milk or even grape juice – a ritual process called *kosmesis* (which gives us our word cosmetics).

Legend had it that back in the Age of Heroes, this wooden statue was brought all the way from Tauri in the Crimea by the anti-hero Orestes and his sister Iphigenia (whose sacrifice had been demanded by Artemis, who had then saved her victim, whisking Iphigenia off across the Black Sea from Aulis to Tauri).[38] But just as the mediaeval world saw a vigorous trade in relics, with lakes'-worth of the tears of Mary of Nazareth, a forest of fingers of John the Baptist and the remains of the one true cross encircling the earth twice over, so in antiquity there were 'original and unique' wooden statues of Artemis in sanctuaries across the Near East and the Greek world. Another popular story was that the wooden goddess had been miraculously washed up at the mouth of the River Kaystros – and that the Artemision Temple was built on that very spot, and never moved, despite the number of times it was re-constructed.[39]

When Artemis was being imagined as a wooden plank, zoomorphic gifts were left for her in her bucolic Ephesian sanctuary. Crude pottery figurines of animals from the Bronze Age, possibly dedicated by Mycenaean Greeks, were found in the foundations of Artemis's Temple, as well as that hoard of amber decorations.[40] These are truly beautiful things: birds and human faces carved out of this magical stone immortalising plant and animal life from prehistory. Three millennia later, the amber totems still have a charged presence up close. The amber here at Ephesus was possibly traded by Phoenicians from Lebanon, where over 400 outcrops of the semi-precious stone have been identified, or from Sicily. Believed to be the tears of the granddaughters of the sun god Helios, amber's Greek name, *electron*, derives from a term meaning 'beaming sun' – and gives us our word electricity. Amber can bear a static electric charge – proof, in the ancients' minds, that the glowing, fossilised sap had supernatural properties. It would have been a worthy gift for the goddess of nature and the rapture of the natural world.[41] The incarnation of Artemis, probably in the seventh century BCE, around the time the gardens in Babylonia were being cultivated, then evolved from a plank decorated with gold, fine cloth, and jewels, into a more anthropomorphic form with lions on her shoulders or flanked by deer. In all her iterations at Ephesus, Artemis's connection to nature – nature in goddess-form – was being remembered and imagined.

Artemis's cult was celebrated and maintained predominantly by the female of the species, usually young maidens – *parthenoi* (etymology explaining why Artemis was 'parthenogenetic' – a maiden or virgin-creator) – and unmarried women. But there were special high priests too, the *megabyzoi* – eunuchs, men who castrated themselves for the goddess. The idea was that Artemis's ferocious female fecundity could not stomach the threatening, polluting challenge of male presence. Early ivory figurines of these eunuch priests have been discovered at Ephesus. Their name *megabyzoi* means 'drones' or 'the serving ones'. Artemis's priestess equivalents were the *melissae* – 'the honey women'. We can imagine the entire Temple being conceived as a giant beehive. Later cult statues of the goddess show Artemis's dress covered with fat bees, flanked by their hives. She was also depicted with manifold breast-like appendages which could well be pollen sacs. The Temple of Artemis was an outsize home for a busy population, a safe-house for golden treasure, and a celebration of the sophisticated, carefully balanced systems of the green planet.

Honey, bees and their hives, like gold, were transported along the coast here.*[42] Honey collection dates back at least to 5500 BCE in the Eastern Mediterranean, and beekeeping to the second millennium. Stone-cut hives were common in prehistoric and ancient Greece, represented on

---

* A tradition that still continues today in some Greek communities. I spent one very happy summer on the nearby island of Ikaria with Ikaria's water-borne 'Odysseus of honey' – searching from one islet and from one bay to another for the finest flowers for the beekeeper's colonies.

Mycenaean gold signet ring depicting lion-headed figures carrying libations towards a seated goddess, fifteenth century BCE. Lions were often associated with potent goddesses such as Artemis, Gorgons and indeed Inanna-Ishtar.

signet rings from Mycenae. Like Artemis, bees were thought to be able to procreate without sex. The goddess Artemis was a queen bee in her Temple Wonder. Ephesus started to mint coins with bees on them – a clever move that suggested to travellers and traders that this was a place sweet with the lure of a hive and its fruits, somewhere blessed with fertility and magic by a vital goddess, and somewhere safe to store your cash and other golden treasures.

All this fabulously fecund iconography demonstrates the Ephesian Artemis's connection to an older goddess who originally held sway in Anatolia – the Great Mother of the East, Kybele, whose rock-cut shrines are still just visible across Karia (often in remote, mountainous locations – beware the barb-collared sheep-hounds who menace if you dare to venture on Kybele's territory). Kybele was an ancestor of and influence on the huntress goddess and a cousin to the Lydian-Karian nature goddess Kubaba – whose symbol was also a bee.

Kybele, like Artemis, came from the mountains (her name possibly a version of the Karian for mountain, *kubaba*). Another goddess of nature and wild animals, Kybele can still be found in sites across Turkey. Some of Kybele's statues are complete with metal-hammered *mammae* – bulls' testicles (similar to the pendulous sacs on representations of Artemis at Ephesus). One such statue, accessible only by scrambling up thorny goat-paths, now lies collapsed east of the Marsyas River at the wonderful remote settlement of Gergakome, sacred to the Karian mother. This colossal Kybele statue was felled in the fifth century CE by Christian forces.

Until recently she was believed to be another Artemis (Artemis's twin brother Apollo was also honoured here) but the discovery of stone lions' paws (Kybele was usually flanked by big cats) makes the identification clear. Kybele was there too in the minds and the myths of the ancients – believed to be the protecting deity who kept the young god Dionysos safe along with the nymphs of the Nysa Mountain.[43]

Like Artemis, Kybele appeared at rock-cut windows; like Kybele, and unlike other deities, Artemis was often called 'great'. Kybele would eventually simply be known by the Romans as Magna Mater – the Big Mama – a divine force who was thought to control the access between life and death. Both goddesses (like Kubaba) were served by eunuch high-priests. The Artemis worshipped at Sardis, Croesus' royal capital, recall, was a goddess who appeared very like the mountain deity Kubaba. The Asiatic Artemis at Ephesus, in the same way, took on the guise of Kybele, the Mistress of the Animals and the Mother of the Gods. So, when we think of the Temple of Artemis and the goddess that the sanctuary honoured, we must suppress all notions of a classical, wispy-toga-ed Diana-figure and think instead of a summation of nature's primal power.*

Artemis at Ephesus was considered to be a goddess who decided whether humans lived or died. And at Ephesus this petrifying power, on occasion, took an enlightened and positive form.

One of the least dispiriting, more encouraging aspects of ancient civilisation was that where conflict was a clear and present danger, so too there was the provision of sanctuary; and not just a calm place to contemplate

---

* Some have even suggested that the evolution of Artemis begins with Egyptian deities: the cat-loving goddess Bastet worshipped at Bubastis, north of Heliopolis, and Neithin, a goddess of the bow, a ruler of animals, a lover of dancing, protecting the weak, and a merciful killer, bringing a quick, clean death (see Ionescu, 2022). The scale of Artemis's Temple at Ephesus also recalls the Goddess Queen of Crete, the Potnia Thea, commander of all living animals. And if you travel through the Albanian Alps today, in remote villages relatively untouched by the modern, outside forces which have controlled this strip of the Balkans – from the Ottomans to the Communists – a form of Artemis is still honoured. The last of the traditional lahute players, with their stringed instrument similar to those used by ancient Greek bards, drink raki and sing songs of the goddess-sprite Zana (whose name derives from Diana, the Roman equivalent of Artemis) who lives in the high hills, protects young girls, and runs with the wild deer still hunted there. Like the Gorgon, Zana's stare could turn men to stone.

the divine, but a location that offered real, physical, political asylum.*
All religious complexes at this time were classified as sanctuaries, a place
where special rules applied, but the Temple of Artemis – a monumental
Wonder of the world – was an intercontinental asylum par excellence.

For centuries Ephesus was regarded as one of the most effective and
distinguished sanctuaries in the ancient world. Recent excavations and
re-analysis of finds here show that asylum-seekers were actually given
their own special zone within the sanctuary. Many flocked to Artemis's
Ephesian home, often waiting eagerly, desperately, to ensure that their
petition for security had been accepted. The coastal location meant that
many could arrive by boat. By the Roman period, accommodation blocks
for refugees stretched over the whole north-eastern zone, where their
keepers, cult officials and priests, also slept. It was said asylum-seekers
could be found in Artemis's sanctuary 'like nesting birds'.

That story of the citizens of Ephesus being protected from Croesus'
attack – when a rope was stretched those 7 stades from the Temple to
the city – may be apocryphal, but it was prompted by an historical truth:
the fact that the Temple of Ephesus, which came to be walled with military patrols around the perimeter, had a reputation far and wide as a
monument which offered asylum to those who qualified for Artemis's
protection. In theory, any bona fide plaintiff had to be taken in. Sanctuary could be extended as a diplomatic gift – a facility which perhaps was
sometimes abused. The philosopher Apollonius of Tyana, from Cappadocia in Anatolia, with wonderful nimbyism, complained, around the time
of the birth of Jesus, of the number of robbers Artemis's precinct housed.

Sanctuaries in the ancient world were all holy places, safe homes for
gods, spirits, divine heroes and supernatural forces, but the precise kind
of sanctuary they offered wildly differed. Many – such as the Temple of
Artemis at Ephesus – were also massive depositories of wealth, operating
exactly like a bank. Fortunes in the form of gold, bronze, ivory and other
luxury items were stored within temples. Wealthy individuals would
leave personal riches in these divine-banks for safekeeping – with the

* Ephesus had seen its own fair share of conflict. Having attacked the Persians with fire
and flame at Sardis, the Greeks were routed here in 498 BCE. Athenian forces suffered
another defeat at the hands of the Spartans in 406 BCE in a naval battle just off the coast.
Once Alexander the Great had come and gone, his inheritors, the Ptolemies, would fight
the Rhodians here in 258 BCE, for control of Rhodes island.

notion that none would risk the ire of the monuments' deities to steal them (though of course thefts did happen). Some temples – like Artemis's at Ephesus – were safehouses of wisdom and knowledge, operating as archives, protecting the laws and memories of a community. As sacred spots, all were governed by rituals, and by customs and codes to prevent pollution. And all, in theory at any rate, could offer *asylia* – the right to protection to women and men fleeing persecution – the ancient Greek word that gives us asylum.

The notion was that in a sanctuary no war or violence could pollute the deity's home – and that all, male or female, slave or free, citizen or foreigner, if granted access by the goddess' gatekeepers, had a right to shelter, to security of mind and body within the sanctuary's precincts. The churn of a region where kings, dynasties, factions and political ideologies were all fighting for the upper hand meant that many were displaced. The battle for democracy in the Athenian Empire, for example, resulted in the displacement of at least 50,000 refugees.[44] These historical narratives are frequently played out in Greek drama – think of Aeschylus' tragedy, performed in 463 BCE, *The Suppliant Women*, where the Danaids, Egyptian women, flee to Greece and seek asylum-status to escape forced marriage to their cousins.

Aeschylus' drama reflected a real situation. In Ephesus, asylum-seekers would have had to petition a representative of authority to be allowed to stay – in the case of the Temple of Artemis, either priests, or, more likely, priestesses. Refugees seeking asylum would wrap strands of wool around their staffs – the images of the Ephesian Artemis that have survived show tassels dangling from her arms, a signal perhaps that she was the sanctuary giver.[45]

As with so many real-life experiences in the ancient world, the history of refuge and safe haven at Ephesus was understood, remembered, and reinforced by the telling of a wonderful tale.

It was said that the god of wine and ecstasy and excess, Dionysos, had made war on the ancient tribe of warrior-women, the Amazons – worshippers of Artemis. The Amazons were themselves such ferocious fighters, they were suspected of being daughters of the Greek god of war, Ares. (Quite why Dionysos attacked Amazonian women is not clear – perhaps because the Amazons favoured fermented mare's milk, *kumis*, for their community high rather than the grape wine of the god of the vine?)

The story went that Dionysos came upon the Amazons at Ephesus; they fled, in fear of their lives, across a narrow channel of water to the island of Samos. But the god pursued them there and effected a bloody slaughter. Dinosaur bones discovered on this spot were shown off by ancient tour guides to prove that a 'giant race' had fallen here.[46] Then, raconteurs recounted, a cluster of surviving Amazons made it back across the water, and attempted to return to hide near Ephesus, in a sacred grove – at the very site on which the great Temple of Artemis at Ephesus would later be built. This Amazonian association brought an exotic mystique to Ephesus' premier sanctuary.

There were other sanctuary myths and histories attached to this Wonder too. It was said that here the Amazons, on another occasion, sheltered from another of their perennial foes, the semi-divine bad-boy-hero Herakles. In one account this was where the Ephesian gold-loving tyrant Pythagoras – himself credited with rebuilding the Artemision in the late seventh or early sixth century BCE – trapped a woman, hiding within the temple-complex, against her will. After this point we get onto firmer ground historically speaking, because Artemis's sanctuary at Ephesus was indeed used as a high-level hiding place, where the remarkable female admiral Artemisia I (one of the very few XX-chromosome naval captains attested to ever in history, and grandmother of the Artemisia II who would help to build the Mausoleum of Halikarnassos, our fifth Wonder) fled to hide after the Battle of Salamis. Artemisia sought protection here for herself and her wards – the illegitimate children of the Persian Emperor Xerxes. The Egyptian Ptolemaic Princess Arsinoe IV, sister of the more famous Cleopatra the Great, hid here at Ephesus as well – before she was brutally murdered – only briefly enjoying the goddess's protection.

Originally proponents of divine power, complexes like the Ephesus Artemision came to be centres of real, political significance, places offering both success and succour, in a dog-eat-dog world.* And for some reason, this particular monument's protecting powers became both a real attraction, and the stuff of legend.[47]

---

* In reality these sacred sanctuaries at the edge of cities – the sanctuary of Ephesus was three quarters of a mile from the main town – were an extension of territory and sacred sovereignty. From at least the eighth century BCE this was an arrangement the Greek world was used to: the sprawling Heraion at Samos; the picturesque Amyklai near Sparta; the intimidating Artemision at Ephesus.

Oh Amazons of Ephesus
Bestow on me eternal virginity,
and countless names like my brother Apollo,
a bow and arrow like his, too, the power to bring light,
a saffron hunting tunic with a red hem,
that reaches to my knees.
River nymphs to care for my buskin boots,
and to feed my hounds.
Give me all the mountains in the world.

CALLIMACHUS ODE, 'HYMN TO ARTEMIS AT EPHESUS'[48]

Amazons were inescapably present at Ephesus – in the myth stories of the sanctuary and in the elaborate art that decorated the Temple itself. The Amazon race, those ferocious warrior-queens, princesses, cavalry-women and foot-soldiers, it was said, regularly scent-marked the sanctuary at Ephesus, their safe-space, with wild night-time corybantic dancing around the city. The image of these potent, bare-breasted women was popular, fetishised on vase-paintings and in Greek drama.[49] The language used to conjure up the sight of the Amazons of Ephesus' Temple is decidedly titillating. In one fragment of a lost play, real Ephesian girls, imitating Amazons, were said to shake out their hair with their hands for Artemis's pleasure, suggestively drop down on their hips, then twerk up from their haunches and waggle their backsides like wagtails or lapwings.[50]

The Hellenistic poet Callimachus also describes the Amazons of Ephesus, armour-clad, rattling their quivers and stamping their feet under a great oak tree. Often shown with a palm tree (that tree so beloved of Artemis, since she had been born under one on the wind whipped island of Delos), these are clearly war-dances. The girls are frequently depicted wearing trousers (the living Amazons, the real Saka-Scythians, from Thrace and Central Asia, did invent trousers and did wear them). On one vase, with spears and shields emblazoned with snakes, these adorants dance in front of a life-size statue of the goddess. On another the young women have short tunics and Scythian hats, while pipes play 'off screen'. We can imagine the fire-pits roasting and the heady drugs that Amazons were renowned for enjoying perfuming the Ephesian sanctuary. Ecstatic dancing traditions went on for hours – a ritual said to have been inaugurated by the seven daughters of the Amazonian Queen Hippo, princesses

Glaukia, Protis, Parthenia, Lampado, Maia, Stonychia and Kokkymo.*

Ephesus was a site where the Amazons, and Amazonian qualities, were commemorated, adulated and also feared. In fact it was claimed by some that the Amazons had founded Ephesus itself.[51] The untamed goddess had appropriately salty female acolytes.

> Zeus has made you [Artemis] a lion among women, and given
> you leave to kill any at your pleasure.
>
> HOMER, *ILIAD* 21.483–4, TRANS. LATTIMORE (1951)

The Temple of Artemis was a place of sanctuary – but we should not imagine that this meant its presiding deity was in any way comforting or safe.

Artemis was a goddess not to be messed with. With Zeus as a father and a Titaness as a mother in the Greek tradition, Artemis had strong genes. She was, moreover, the product of a rape, and was often a reminder of the pain as well as the pleasures of sex.

Think of the terrible story of Helen of Troy, raped aged ten (some sources say she was just seven) by the middle-aged Athenian hero-king Theseus in the Sanctuary of Artemis-Orthia on the outskirts of Sparta. That was a sanctuary where the goddess demanded the ritualised whipping of young Spartan boys to toughen them up. Or indeed, the fate of the young virgins at Artemis's sanctuary in Brauron near Athens who, aged ten to fourteen, lived in a quasi-boarding-school environment. They wore masks and yellow dresses resembling bearskins and learnt a bear dance called the *Arkteia* (the bear was one of the animals sacred to Artemis; that's why necklaces of pierced bears' teeth were found at

---

* Archaeological digs are increasingly identifying the real women on whom these stories are based. Bone evidence shows warrior-women from the period with fingers warped by excessive bow and arrow use, hips turned square thanks to the time spent in the saddle. Gold-covered buried fighters that had originally been identified as men are now proving through further study and bone analysis to be women. These graves can be found in Azerbaijan, Kazakhstan, Afghanistan, Iran, Georgia, Armenia, the wider Caucasus and eastern Turkey. A number have died from battle wounds – axe attacks to the skull, arrow heads in the ribs and back. The burials date from c. 1500 BCE to the first century BCE. I have had the privilege of seeing some of these, even to hold the swords buried with their female owners. It is little surprise that these real warrior women became legendary. And their connection to Ephesus, to Artemis's Temple and to other settlements in the region, is fascinating.

Ephesus). This period of ritualised, Amazonian 'wildness' prepared elite Athenian girls for a new chapter in their lives and demonstrated devotion to Artemis in return for her protection. But was Artemis really acting in the best interests of girls and women here? Or was her protection actually a form of patriarchal control? If a girl dared to desecrate these sacred rites, Artemis would unleash her wrath – if she had sex outside marriage, Artemis would send a plague and famine on her hometown. For the Greeks, the safe transition of young girls into marriageable material was essential for society to function correctly. If a girl died before she bore children, she was said to have 'been killed by the arrows of Artemis' for some unknown violation. By indoctrinating girls to lead a chaste life and punishing those who strayed from the 'natural path' to motherhood, the Greek Artemis kept (male-dominated) society working as it should.

This is precisely why the Eastern, Artemis-worshipping Amazons were so terrifying – proving women can own their sexuality and still have status and standing in society.

Artemis was also a goddess who punished the hubris of men, and who demanded gifts of the first fruits of the earth and of the humans on it. It was for this reason that the Greek hero Agamemnon's daughter, Iphigenia, was to be sacrificed, slaughtered like an animal on the altar of Artemis because Agamemnon shot one of the goddess's deer in the deity's sanctuary. The King of Mycenae had forgotten to give up the first fruit of the season, having boasted he could hunt a deer just as well as the goddess, and so Artemis took the first fruit of his body, his eldest daughter.[52]

This gruesome story of child sacrifice may be a pointer to a harsher historical truth from the age when Artemis's sanctuary was first established. In 2020, I was escorted to a dig in the backstreets of the port town of Chania – ancient Kydonia – in Crete. A Bronze Age mansion here had been rocked by earthquakes, around 1250 BCE. Stepping over the prehistoric crevices in the floor, I was taken to the spot where archaeologists have recently discovered vast numbers of bones of slaughtered animals, and the skull of a young, high-born woman, decapitated and left as an offering to appease the gods. I was looking at evidence of virgin sacrifice. Suddenly ancient stories felt horribly real: the teenager Iphigenia slaughtered by her own father on the instruction of Artemis to ensure fair winds for Troy; and Achilles' Trojan lover, Princess Polyxena, sacrificed on the hero's grave in retribution for his death.[53]

The Greeks were very honest with themselves. The gods were not excessive, rather they were representative of the excesses of mankind. Their sanctuaries were places you could come to face up to the presence of a deity and to human horrors.

There is a ferocious intensity to Artemis in the Greek tradition. Her mood turns on a twist of wind, very like the raw nature she represents. She was said to have punished the handsome huntsman Orion, hanging him in the sky as a constellation (the star, recall, that drew Egyptian pharaohs as they ascended to eternal life from the pyramids), and to have transformed Actaeon into a stag to be devoured by his own hounds.[54] She morphs hunters into the hunted. Ancient hunts frequently happened after sunset, especially under a full moon when the star becomes a searchlight in the sky. Artemis is a charged lunar goddess bright with the thrill, and the horror, of the chase. Following a hunt by night in the hills of Greece and Anatolia is still an intense, extreme experience. Hounds at bay pound the earth with a thundering beat. Their eyes glint threateningly in the moonlight. The air is pierced by yelps of triumph and the frenzy of a kill.

At the time her archaic Temple was being raised, we hear Artemis described in a Homeric Hymn (27) as loving the lyre and dancing, piercing cries and shadowy groves, the bow and hunting and cities of just men.[55] But in Homer Artemis is also 'she who showers arrows' – on humans as well as on animals.[56] Ancient authors warned of the dangers of disrespecting her rites and altars. And the goddess' displeasure was fatal. During the Roman Empire's first pandemic, the Antonine plague, which killed at least 6 million, the city of Ephesus was advised that the only chance of salvation was to make a golden statue of the goddess and to sing her praises. And when a crowd from the city of Sardis harassed a delegation from Ephesus who were bringing new cloaks for the goddess, forty-five of the hecklers were sentenced to death.[57] Artemis had zero tolerance for disrespect.

The Temple of Artemis is a Wonder with diverse genetic make-up and influences from both East and West within its deity, its design and its dogma. It is a work of mankind, trying to understand the power of the natural world and the power of women. Which is one reason why the Amazons became a prominent decorative theme in both the final iterations of the Temple – the one added to by Croesus in the sixth century BCE, and the other rebuilt after Herostratus' catastrophic fire 200 years later.

Framing the central door of the Temple were two stone Amazons, with two more represented up in the eaves. Five bronze statues of Amazonian women – with short chitons, a breast bare, carrying their bows and arrows, battle-axes and distinctive crescent shields (*pelte*) – also decorated Ephesus's Wonder. Some have battle wounds. Roman authors (and ancient tour guides) recounted that in the fifth century BCE there was a competition to raise these bronze lovelies, to celebrate the end of the Persian Wars, and peace between all those in the Delian League (a league of Greek city-states whose political, financial and spiritual HQ was on the sacred island of Delos, Artemis's birthplace) and Persia in 459 BCE. The top talents of the day bid for the commission – the resulting fake women warriors were shown with expressions ranging from vulnerable to merciless, and in different poses. The winning sculpture was by Polykleitos, the runner-up by Pheidias – the sculptor who would also come to carve our next Wonder, the Statue of Zeus at Olympia.[58] A Roman stone copy of one Amazon – where the bare-breasted female fighter has used a broken belt to hitch up her chiton – is now held by the Metropolitan Museum in New York. Another shows an Amazon felled by her wounds; yet another, lost to time, immortalised an Amazonian girl riding a rearing horse, her spear aloft. The Emperor Nero so loved this particular piece, he confiscated it from the Roman who had stolen it from Artemis's Temple and paraded 'Lovely Legs' (as she came to be called) in Rome.

The original bronze sculptures were ranged on the Temple of Artemis's pediment, positioned carefully at either side of the Temple's three top-storey, peek-a-boo, open windows (a frame of which was eventually built into St John's grand basilica nearby, which still surveys the site from the hill of Ayasuluk), where subsequently a wooden statue of the goddess was regularly revealed – displayed in the opening by Temple attendants to impress the crowds waiting below. So these freighted warrior-women would have glared down on visitors as they approached Artemis's home, flanking the goddess. A fragment of the altar from the Artemision still shows a bare-breasted wounded warrior, staring out challenging, woeful, from the grained white marble. Of course, in many ways there has long been an orientalising contest to 'create' the most impactful Amazons, a rush to embody the idea of a threatening female and the threat of 'the East' – since Amazons were thought to originate in Thrace and the Caucasus – all wrapped up into a monstrous regiment of women.

The design of one of Ephesus' Amazons can be appreciated via this Imperial Roman-period replica of an Hellenistic original, a marble statue of a wounded Amazon woman, first–second century CE, from the Villa Borghese.

But at Ephesus, Amazons seem to have been respected as well as feared, and could be found as a notable presence beyond the Temple too, in the city itself, where images of the sculptures were also portrayed on the tall walls of the theatre and on high-end marble panels in prominent public buildings. Amazonian shields were even depicted as decorative features in wealthy homes, painted on their walls and grouted into mosaics. Many of these features have survived and can still be seen when one walks through the ancient site of Ephesus city. And just listen to the ancient travel writer Pausanias, knitting Amazons into the allure of Ephesus and the renown of the Temple Wonder:

> But all cities worship Artemis of Ephesus, and individuals hold her in honour above all the gods. The reason, in my view, is the renown of the Amazons, who traditionally dedicated the image, also the extreme antiquity of this sanctuary. Three other points as well have contributed to her renown, the size of the temple, surpassing all buildings among men, the eminence of the city of the Ephesians and the renown of the goddess who dwells there.[59]

The original statue of Artemis herself, her body made of vine-wood or ebony, was probably destroyed in that fire attributed to Herostratus in 356 BCE, so, maddeningly, we don't know exactly what form it took in the archaic Temple – but Hellenistic and Roman versions from the mid-fourth century BCE onwards (which seem likely to be versions of the earlier model) make up for any disappointment.

Standing boldly in the Ephesus Museum, two of Artemis's cult-statues – both found in the Prytaneion or central Council Chamber of the city – leave no room for doubt that we are in the presence of a goddess.* One 'beautiful' Artemis stands nearly 6 feet tall, while the other 'great' Artemis towers 9-and-a-half-feet high. Artemis's clothes and body are completely encrusted with bees, lions, griffins (griffins – half lion, half eagle – were a mythical creature often associated with the Amazons), cows, horses, sphinxes. The goddess from is thick with those heaving, hanging pouches; strange, sensuous swellings that might be ostrich eggs, bags of gold, bulls' testicles, breasts, pollen sacs, palm-dates, giant acorns, leather purses, drops of nectar or sacs of honey – a produce which is still a

---

* We hear from Pausanias of a further statue in Ephesus of Artemis Protothronia – Artemis of the First Seat – with an image of Nyx, the primordial goddess of the night, sculpted above her. The artist Scopas – who was almost certainly responsible for the carving on at least some of the Temple's columns and pediments – also completed a family trio of Artemis, Apollo and Leto. A second century CE version of the goddess from an imperial garden (now in Naples' Archaeological Museum) polymastic with twenty-one 'breasts' is also clearly inspired by the Ephesian goddess.

'Great Artemis' from Ephesus. The Artemision, the Temple of Artemis, forms the summit of the goddess's high polos hat.

speciality of this pine-rich region. Whatever those curious, bulbous decorations are, they are unforgettable. One interpretation of this remarkable adornment is that the scrota – if indeed this is what they are – gave the goddess the fertility she needed to birth bees, just as the souls of the initiates in her cult would be reborn through their connection with her. So Artemis was not just parthenogenetic, she could bring forth many kinds of life, beyond human. Great Artemis's polos, her cylindrical crown, is topped with an image of the temples of Ephesus. Most prominently, on the top tier, is the Artemision itself. Ephesus' Temple Wonder is the summation of all the power of the great Asiatic goddess.

Lit by candlelight, the strange, captivating carvings on Artemis's body would have been thrown into eerie relief and flickered with life. Artemis's decoration, which becomes increasingly neat and symmetrical as time goes on – rectangular cells, containing sphinxes, and bees, and griffins, and grapes on the vine – suggests an understanding of the intelligent design and intelligent balance of the natural world. Or perhaps it represents an idealised version of nature, controlled and perfect, as mankind would ideally want it to be.

Once the Romans took over Ephesus in 129 BCE, Artemis was promoted within and beyond her sacred city with even more universal appeal, not as a local, or even an Anatolian goddess, but as an empire-wide deity. The Roman addition of zodiac signs to her body reminded her worshippers that her domain was the night sky as well as the day. These cosmic attributes were also designed to make her more transportable, transposable and multi-relevant – like a Korean pop star who then starts to wear the bling of LA and the tweeds of the UK as proof of pan-national relevance. And so the Artemis adored in Ephesus became an international celebrity.

Artemis was in all ways a goddess of plenty. And she was understood to be a successful businesswoman in her own right. Her temple-estate at Ephesus (as with churches from the mediaeval period onwards, ancient temples owned land and commercial assets) was the wealthiest in Asia; the goddess owned salt-pans, herds of animals, vineyards, quarries and pastures. (There were many real-life businesswomen in Ephesus too. It is tempting to imagine them inspired by this divine, and divinely successful, role-model.) With money no object, the most expensive artists of the day were hired to furnish the goddess's Wonder-complex.

The new fourth-century BCE Temple, post Herostratus' arson attack, whose chief architect was the local star Paeonius, was marginally smaller than Croesus' original but was elevated by 9 feet or so – partly to have maximum theatrical impact, and partly to help deal with the constant issue of the surrounding wetlands and the threat of earthquakes. The spongy, marshy landscape provided some cushioning against geo-seismic activity, but the drainage here alone must have been a gargantuan, costly task. Everything had to be carefully thought through – the foundations had been packed out with layers of wooden charcoal, goats' fleeces, sheepskins and wool. The design of the columns too, drums sitting one on top of the other with no mortar, encouraged shifts rather than collapse during earth tremors. (Although some damage was inescapable; sections of the Temple Wonder would be destroyed in 23 CE, as a result of a massive earthquake.)

Because so little of the fourth century BCE original remains, for a live impression of the scale of this monumental architecture at Ephesus it is worth visiting the Istanbul Archaeological Museum, where prime fragments of the neighbouring temples of Priene, Miletus and Didyma are kept. Here, curling lips the size of mantlepieces smile down, corkscrew locks the length of ballroom curtains hang from monumental heads. Sculpted at the same time, with Paeonius as their overseer, their confidence, their playful gravity, as well as their beauty, is spectacular. The lautitious lower shafts of the columns in Didyma are decorated in a similar way to those of Ephesus – it has been estimated that each column would have taken 20,000 man-hours to carve. As the colossal works of art at Ephesus were hoisted into position, which were just like these others only on an even grander scale, we should appreciate the forceful impression they would have made.

According to the Roman-period author Strabo, Praxiteles (who created the iconic sculptures of Aphrodite at Knidos and Herakles, and Hermes carrying the baby Dionysos, which would be put on display in Olympia) also fashioned sculptures for Artemis's Temple.[60] Fascinatingly, the bases of a sculpture by Praxiteles of Artemis and her twin brother Apollo and mother Leto have just recently been unearthed in the Arcadia region of the southern Greek mainland. We can perhaps imagine the maestro warming to his theme at Ephesus, and to the life-story of his divine patron, trying to represent her control of wet, writhing, wonderful nature in stone.

And we should also try to imagine the other assaults on the senses that would have accompanied time spent at the Temple of Artemis's staggering sanctity.

Our Pavlovian response to the mention of ancient sites is often to imagine antiquities trapped by the weight of time, by sheer mass, by loss and abandonment – while in their heyday they were in fact all about crushing crowds, saturating experiences, churn and shift. Ephesus in particular, as a busy international port, was a chameleon place. Sailors and merchants docking from many oceans, bringing incense from the Arabian South with stories of mountains like castles and caravanserais a thousand camels strong; Scythians with furs from Thrace; Phoenicians with finely spun glass and coarse wine that gave poets a headache worth writing about; pepper, silk and ebony coming from India along the Silk Roads.

For many reasons the Temple of Artemis was a temple of experience.

And one thing is clear. Artemis was worshipped at Ephesus in a heady and cryptic way – with women at the centre of ritual. An appreciation – or imagination – of Amazonian customs was paramount. There was also a massive procession at the time of Artemis's birthday around 6–25 May – the month of Thargelion in the Ancient Greek calendar – when a parade of gold and silver statues, glinting in the lamplight, including an image of the goddess, were carried through the city.

When we experience something, we do so with a number of our senses. To ignore the soundscape of the past is to etiolate the historical experience. Music would have been heard around the sanctuary of Artemis at weddings, funerals, sacrificial rites, dances, during athletic training, military and religious marches. There were paeans for Apollo, dithyrambs for Dionysos, and no doubt solo contests for *kithara*, the lute-like instrument whose name gives us our word guitar, and the pipe-like aulos; competitive choral contests too. That hissing rattle of the sistrum, the percussion of choice for priestesses, would have been punctuated by chants and ritual. Sometimes you would have heard pan pipes, a tortoise-shell lyre, the clash of men and boys performing Pyrrhic dances in armour. There was musical experimentation, men travelling to Ephesus for inspiration. As the composer, choir-leader and concert-promoter Damon (working for the Athenian leader Pericles) said at this time, there is an ethos of music, which affects character, emotion and action.

And Ephesus certainly loved its music. Bronze horns were famed here. One instrument-maker designed the perfect lute and hung it in the goddess' Temple as a gift. The chief priest of the Artemision, the eunuch portrayed beautifully on an ivory offering bowl in the site, complete with pearl necklace and a giant shell-shaped headdress, controlled a huge choir. I have walked through private Ephesian homes, still being excavated, where whole rooms are devoted to the Nine Muses and to music and poetry. On the walls, brush-fine frescoes still show the Muse Urania with her blue, wafting chiton, the demi-goddess of the heavens and of astronomy. Particularly charming is the recent discovery, from this residential quarter, of a signet ring with a carved gem showing a mouse playing pipes. (Interesting that one of the treasures excavated from a private room here was an Egyptian 'antique', a golden figurine of a priest of Egypt's sun god Ammon; a revelation of Ephesus' connectivity and the interest of the cultures of antiquity in one another.) It was no coincidence that an inscription dating to c. 200 CE has been found close to Ephesus at Aydin (ancient Tralles), belonging to one Seikilos (described by some as Seikilos of Ephesus but probably an itinerant musician from Sicily), the oldest surviving complete Greek musical inscription, including musical notation.

> While you live, shine out
> don't succumb to grief
> life exists only briefly
> and Time demands his due.

The goddess here was honoured with dances steeped in mystery and meaning. An ancient wind instrument, the syrinx, was often used; examples from 40,000 years ago – the Hohle Fels flute – have recently been discovered. The syrinx, being thin and tubular, gives us our word 'syringe', and bound together, syrinxes become what we call panpipes. The syrinx has gruesome origins. It was said that a virgin called Syrinx, a nymph, who loved to hunt in the woodlands, was an acolyte of Artemis. But one day the god Pan conceived a tumescent desire for her. He was determined to rape the girl, and Syrinx was only saved when Artemis turned her into a hollow reed – which then sighed by the banks of rivers as Pan passed, panting with breaths of frustration – the disturbing origin of pan pipes.[61]

It was from a similar woody location dedicated to the goddess that the messenger god Hermes kidnapped Polymele, the finest of many beautiful, young girls who had gathered to participate in a dance for Golden-Bowed Artemis.[62] Rapes like these were blasphemy to Artemis. Imagine taking on the goddess in charge of all of this: threatening virginity was a serious business in antiquity. From the Code of Ur Nammu in the twenty-first century BCE we hear: 'if a man de-flowers the virgin wife of a young man they shall kill that man'. In the eighth century BCE Gortyn Code, the fine for raping a virgin (4 obols) was eight times that for a non-virgin female.*[63]

---

* Male virginity caused more suspicion. Hippolytus, the son of the uber-male hero Theseus and the Amazon queen Hippolyte, was so disgusted by sex and so devoted to Artemis that he presented a problem in the Greek mind. His tragedy was to be targeted by the goddess of sexual love, Aphrodite, in revenge. Escaping his stepmother's accusation of rape, Hippolytus was caught in the tack of the horses of his chariot and dragged to his death.

Depressingly, real Ephesian girls were given perfume bottles decorated with images of Amazons being pursued by men – their erect or horizontal spears a sinister, priapic innuendo – in the sanctuary of Artemis at Ephesus and beyond. Were these stories shared to ease young girls into the initiation of marriage? Somehow to offer them comfort by connecting them to ancient rape narratives? Female children were given toys of Amazon women to play with – we find these sometimes buried in their graves in Asia Minor.[64] Is it wishful thinking to hope these represented, even subliminally, some kind of feisty role-model? Or were they storybook preparations for the certainty of forced marriages and the likelihood for young girls of sexual abuse?

The young virgins' dances to honour the goddess were accompanied by the sound of pipes made of fawn bones. These bone pipes make a magical, haunting, memorable sound. And participation was not just for selected performers, but for pilgrims who travelled to wonder at the Artemision Temple and to pay their respects to the goddess from across the Eastern Mediterranean. Broken bones in the sanctuary show both sacrifice and feasting took place here; miniature copies of the Temple were hawked around the site; oracles were shared along with portions of sacrificial meat – blessed like holy water from Lourdes. Excavations have revealed the jewels and gifts that were donated, or lost – some with provenance in the Indian subcontinent.

The Temple was a sanctuary for hard cash as well as for humans. The travel-writer Pausanias tells us the Artemision was 'the first for size and wealth' of all the Ionian sanctuaries, and over 1,500 golden artefacts have been discovered to date in excavations, more than anywhere else in the region: earrings with the birds of prey sacred to the goddess, brooches with lion and falcon heads set within a flower, gold heads of barley containing real barley seeds, slim golden snakes, enchantingly beautiful gold bees and those hauntingly beautiful, enigmatic miniature goddess-figurines.[65]

Curiosities would have been held here too. Sacred belts, dedicated by virgins, were given to the virgin goddess at her Temple. Then there is the enigmatic 'Diopet of Ephesus'. Currently, bizarrely, the Diopet is in the North of England, in the storerooms of the Liverpool Museum. It is a 4,000-year-old, 16-centimetre-high greenstone axe, decorated with tin inlays, apparently found at the Temple, and brought to England in the nineteenth century. This prehistoric axe was probably revered as a

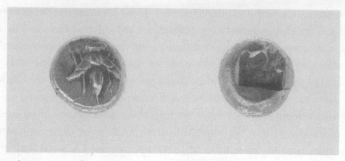

An electrum coin from Ephesus, c. 550 BCE, featuring a bee on the obverse and a square punch on the reverse.

thunderbolt – how a number of prehistoric stone axes were understood and identified by the ancients 1,500 years or so after they were made. This tallies with a reference in the Acts of the Apostles, where we are told that 'the city of the Ephesians is temple keeper of the great Artemis, and of the sacred stone that fell from the sky'.[66]

Back in Ephesus in what is now Turkey, the local museum, flanked by family restaurants in Ottoman-period wooden homes and proudly being refurbished, contains a display of electrum coins, buried in the foundations of the Temple. Some of these coins, featuring the Artemision itself, are a very helpful source for the design of the archaic, classical and Hellenistic temples, and indeed of the cult statue within. Some show children in front of the statue of Artemis throwing dice – or rather *astragaloi*, knucklebones – literally dicing with fate.[67] Others bear images of bees, lions and deer – all creatures beloved by the goddess. And in sources for other sanctuaries of Artemis we hear that fawns and deer were allowed to roam free, and could not be killed, so we might also have to consider the wider sanctuary a little like a deer park.[68]

When we imagine the feel of the Artemision, we should too think of priestesses being prominently present. We have personal testimonies, from these disciples of Artemis, hearing in the Roman period that one Vipsania Olympias and her adopted sister Vipsania Polla 'completed the mysteries and sacrifices in a dignified way'. And (fortunately, given the popularity of the cult all year round, and the attendance of so many at festival time), another priestess of Artemis, Quintilia Varia, dedicated a latrine.

Another author, Athenaeus, from the Egyptian coastal town of

Naucratis, quoting the local resident Democritus of Ephesus, delivers a vivid description of the riot of colour that he had heard marked out Ephesus' celebrations:

> The Ionians' robes are dyed violet, purple, and saffron, and have lozenge-shapes woven into them; animal-designs were woven into the tops of them . . . They also had quince-coloured, purple, and white sarapeis, and some that were sea-purple. Also kalasireis made in Corinth; some of these are purple, while others are dyed violet, or are dark blue . . . [some] flame-red or sea-green. In addition, there are Persian kalasireis, which are the most beautiful of all. You could also see . . . aktaiai; this is the most expensive type of Persian garment. It is woven compactly, to make it strong and light, and is covered with gold beads; the beads are all attached to the inside by means of a purple thread . . . After the Ephesians surrendered to luxury, he says, they wore all these items.[69]

There were two great festivals in the goddess' honour, the Ephesia and the Artemisia.[70] During the month of Artemesios, equivalent probably to our March or April, the month-long Ephesia festival for Artemis must have been ecstatically exuberant. Starting at the Temple, activity bled into the settlement of Ephesus too. Along the sacred way, mossy and calm today, hugging the lee of the hill above, dancing and music was a central ingredient, revels at just the right time of year – to welcome the arrival of the spring.[71] We can imagine the young men and young women who participated, using ropes and lamplights and laurel and myrtle to guide themselves through the intricate dances the goddess demanded. The rites that started in the sanctuary and then spilled out into the town and surrounding countryside would have been charged: an exciting celebration of the power of the moon and night, of nature, and – initially at least – the potential for female potency.

For the duration of the Ephesia – a pan-Ionian affair – a truce was observed for the entire month. Thucydides described this as a kind of national festival of the Ionians of Greece and Asia,[72] a giant party – where visitors from all over Ionia were welcome, travelling in by land and sea. Women would gather with their children to spectate and seem to have been prominent in the festivities. Once the Romans were in charge, the revelry included night-time dances, where virgin women, slaves and free (not the married), met to dance by the light of the moon – echoes of Amazonian myth are clear. When Apollo – in the form of the sun – dips and dives to greet his rising sister at this time of the year, the full moon in this part of the world sits like a giant pearl above hills and the sea. Walking through the sun-abandoned sites, owls, nightjars and jackals cut through the still air. The pale burnish on the stones is uniquely special. The moonlit majesty was appreciated by ancient authors, as it is by the modern.

During the Artemisia, which were games that took place every four years, a statue of the goddess was paraded through the streets, escorted by young maidens (a sight immortalised by the most famous painter of antiquity, Apelles). This perfumed, clothed icon travelled from the theatre to the sacrificial altar and on within the Temple sanctuary. All were here to buttress a very serious idea; that the goddess' realm included civic duties: the curing of disease, the extension of credit, the protection of ephebes (young men), and citizen decrees. Today the festival route is predominantly closed to the public but passing through the soft-white fields of almond-blossom and cicada-heavy pine-trees, one can imagine what an evocative experience this would have been. As time went on, the route of the procession was mapped to include monuments that spoke of the city's history, and that connected to the story and purview of the goddess. And although Artemis required her Temple attendants to be de-sexed (as we know, the men were eunuchs, while the women were just expected to remain virgins), during the Artemisia men and women could choose their fiancées or fiancés. A vivid novel written in the Roman period by Xenophon of Ephesus describes a love-affair sparked during one of the Ephesian festivals:

> And so when the procession was over, the whole crowd repaired to the shrine for the sacrifice, the order of the procession was dissolved, and men and women, ephebes and girls, gathered in the same spot. There they saw each other. Anthia was captivated by Habrocomes, and Habrocomes was bested by Eros. He kept gazing at the girl and though he tried, he could not take his eyes off her: the god pressed his attack and held him fast. Anthia too was in a bad way, as with eyes wide open she took in Habrocomes' handsomeness as it flowed into her, already putting maidenly decorum out of her mind: for what she said was for Habrocomes to hear, and she uncovered what parts of her body she

could for Habrocomes to see. He gave himself over to the sight and fell captive to the deity.[73]

The Artemisia festival fielded sports such as the pankration, the pentathlon, and long- and short-distance running. The Artemisia took place elsewhere in the Greek world (the island of Delos, for instance, hosted a month-long festival in the goddess' honour), but was observed in Ephesus with particular intensity and panache. Semi-professional athletes would travel into the port from cities across the Eastern Mediterranean and the Near East, and in particularly great numbers from Alexandria, to compete. There was an accompanying arts festival too – we hear of poetry, comedy and rhetoric contests, of flute and lyre recitals. Ephesus became very much the festival city. The high priest, astrologer, and Emperor Nero's prefect of Egypt, Tiberius Claudius Balbillus (who was born in Alexandria and who lived out his life in Ephesus), was honoured here with the Balbillean Games from 79 CE. Commemorated by his granddaughter in an epigram scratched onto the Colossi of Memnon near Luxor in Egypt as 'wise Balbillus', the races and contests in his honour celebrated his astrological interpretation of the night sky. With her command of the night, this would have been a pursuit appreciated by the goddess. From about 104 CE rites around the Ephesian Wonder involved even more music, more divination (the inspection of entrails), more donors and sponsors, more initiates to Artemis's mystery cult.

In a fictional account from the second century CE, when both Ephesus and the festivals were at their absolute height, the Alexandrian novelist Achilles Tatius says the wine flowed freely and drunkards were everywhere. The festivities were mounted with such passion, in such a full-blooded way, the devotion to Artemis proved, temporarily, to be a brake on Ephesus' advancement. Having used their claim that Artemis was born in Ephesus as a legal stick to beat their Roman overlords with (arguing taxes should only be due to the goddess, not to the emperor), the imperial regime in Rome doubted Ephesus' ability to establish a successful cult to the divine emperor and chose to invest, initially, in other towns in the region. The devotion of the city to their goddess just seemed too sincere.

One of the great benefits of these international crossroads was the opportunity to engage in what is called the critical mass of the cognitive group – to be exposed to new ideas, to think deeply. Pertinent, then, that one of Ephesus' most famous sons was the philosopher Heracleitus. This pioneering seeker of wisdom, we are told, played knucklebones in the Artemision's sanctuary and then dedicated his greatest work, *On Nature*, to the Temple archives. Bronze versions of these knucklebones were manufactured in the classical period; in fact a number were found during excavations at the Temple site (but were swiftly taken away to the Louvre in Paris where they are still on display). Heracleitus's philosophical gold was held safe in the Artemision Temple, through the Roman period.*

Renowned for declaring, 'You never step in the same river twice', the fragments of the philosopher's work that survive in fact demonstrate thinking that is a little more nuanced:

Ever-newer waters flow on those who step into the same rivers.

We both step and do not step in the same rivers. We are and are not.

Ephesus would maintain its reputation as a city of learning. The Library of Celsus (which, despite its name, was built in the Roman era as a tomb for Tiberius Julius Celsus Polemaeanus, a man from Sardis who became pro-consul of all Asia) held at least 12,000 scrolls, with a sophisticated climate-control system, where stone niches in the walls prevented papyrus scrolls from getting damp. After its completion in c. 120 CE the library was open to the public.

Trade and religious tourism made this a truly cosmopolitan city. Study of the bone evidence is revealing that the population here at Ephesus was multi-ethnic: Asian, African and European, with visitors from Marseille to the Caucasus.[74] At its peak during the Pax Romana, there were between 200,000 and 250,000 residents. We hear of non-Ephesian women dedicating a cloak to Artemis's sanctuary. Many foreigners flooded in to visit the great Artemision, which, at least by the Hellenistic period, had secured its place on the majority of the extant Seven Wonders lists.

---

* Himself described as wondrous, Heracleitus conceived of human nature as being composed of fire, which could destroy excesses such as drinking. We can imagine Heracleitus as a counter-balance to the high-octane port-city hedonism he saw around him. He escaped into the inner Temple, not from men, but from mankind.

A number of inscriptions record that many foreign visitors were granted citizenship here. The Temple had become one of the Mediterranean's biggest attractions and one of Asia's biggest international banks.

So word of the Ephesian Wonder would have spun out on trade, pilgrimage and military routes. The Greek general, philosopher and historian, Xenophon, for example, who used the Temple of Artemis at Ephesus as a safe-vault for the treasure he acquired on campaign in the East (many sought the service of Artemis's Temple as a kind of pawn-broker), retired (as an exile) to the Peloponnese in Greece in the 4th century BCE, having instructed Artemis's chief-eunuch Megabyxus to use his wealth to construct something that would be 'pleasing to the god' – should anything untoward happen to him. But Xenophon was so enraptured by his memories of Artemis's Temple, once he had safely retrieved his loot, that he commissioned a scaled-down replica of the Artemision on the busy road (a highway broad enough to allow two-way traffic in some places) from Olympia to Sparta, complete with orchards, meadows for pasture and hunting grounds, a tithe from this estate near Skillous being offered up in sacrifice to the goddess each year. Both Ephesus and Skillous, coincidentally, had a River Selinus flowing through them – Xenophon must have thought this was some kind of a divine sign that Artemis belonged in both places. Xenophon and his sons would organise a hunt in the goddess's honour – roe and fallow deer, and boar (which are still assiduously tracked and hunted by all-male hunting parties in the Peloponnese). In this transplant sanctuary of Artemis there was even an effigy of the goddess made out of cypress wood.

The Ephesian Temple Wonder immortalised by those scribes in Alexandria was the version restored and rebuilt by the father of Alexander the Great, Philip II of Macedon, in the fourth century BCE. At the Battle of Chaeronea in 338 BCE Philip had taken control of Greek lands. Philip's 'patronage' at Ephesus was honoured by a grand statue of the northern king within the sanctuary itself. With the work overseen by Paeonius and another local, superstar architect called Demetrius, the Temple was raised on a plinth of ten marble steps. Then Alexander, aged just twenty-two, rocked up in 334 BCE to finish what his father had begun.

Alexander and Artemis had history. Remember, it was said that Alexander was born on 20 or 21 July, when the sun rises hot here at 5 a.m. and sets hotter at 9 p.m., the very night that the archaic Temple of Artemis at Ephesus had been burnt down.[75]

And now, the appetitive warrior from Macedonia was in Anatolia. Alexander had enjoyed great victory at the Granicus River to the north. He'd sneakily smitten the Gordian Knot, on the ancient road between Lydia and Babylonia, and was heading south to Ephesus to act as Ephesus' 'liberator' from the Persian overlords who had controlled the site since the triumph of Sparta (an ally of Persia) in the Peloponnesian Wars. En route Alexander accepted the surrender of Croesus' old capital city of Sardis and celebrated his triumph by building a temple to Olympian Zeus on Sardis' citadel. Hearing he was on his way, the garrison of Greek mercenaries at Ephesus asked for two war boats – triremes – and then, with the Persian troops, disappeared. Oligarchs had held the city in what has been described as a brief reign of terror, plundering the Artemision and tumbling that statue of Alexander's father, Philip II. Democrats there had been expelled for supporting Alexander. Barrelling up to Ephesus, Alexander recalled these men for their loyalty. And then, in an act that garnered him huge praise, he stopped the vengeful lynching of the oligarchs who had despoiled Artemis's Temple and who had at first opposed him. The conquering hero also told the city they no longer had to pay tribute to Persia, but instead could redirect this tax to the great goddess, Artemis. Accompanied by Persian magi, also in the city at the time, Alexander paid for sacrifices for the goddess and mounted a procession with his army in full battle dress, as if ready to fight for Artemis's honour.

As soon as he was in charge, Alexander decreed all land within a stade of the Temple building to be inviolable. And, just two decades after the arson attack that had destroyed the old Temple, in 334 BCE, Alexander proffered an opinion that Artemis's grand edifice should be re-styled, with his own name emblazoned as benefactor.[76] A sensitive situation for the Ephesians to find themselves in; but Alexander the Great's offer to help with the rebuild was gently rebuffed – the ravening conqueror tactfully being told by Artemis's chief priest that it was inappropriate for a 'God' to pay for another 'God's' home. Instead, locals, as ever passionately protective of their beloved deity, pawned personal possessions to help with the building works. The reconstruction began in earnest in 323 BCE, the year of Alexander the Great's death. Ephesus' new, Hellenistic Temple was now raised up on a thirteen-step podium, the columns lowered a little to

58 feet to help with the aesthetic balance of the building. One hundred and eighty feet tall and 360 feet long, this was a magnificent, breathtaking sight. One flourish was a new form of delicate Ionic capitals – a design innovation that came to be copied throughout the region.

Karia's most skilled stonemasons were summoned in to work at Ephesus – and clearly in huge numbers. Just as the construction of the Great Pyramid sparked a new, dynamic era for the Egyptian state, this was a re-renaissance for Ionia. The nearby site of Didyma, where a temple to Artemis's twin brother Apollo was also raised by many of the same creatives, bears an architect's sketches in the marble, identified in 1979 – a hint at the complexity of planning involved in projects such as these. Thirty-six columns were carved at Ephesus, it was said, by that renowned artist Scopas. A child of Paros, the Greek island rich in the very finest marble, and also responsible for work at the Mausoleum of Halikarnassos (our fifth Wonder), Scopas was praised for combining technical brilliance with emotional understanding. His work was so exquisite, he instantly became a celebrity.

One drum – from a column that was originally 60 feet tall – survives today in the British Museum. Acquired at the end of the nineteenth century, it was such a weight, fifteen men working together could drag it just fifty paces a day, down to the British frigate, HMS *Terrible*, waiting on the Anatolian seaboard. The column drum arrived in 1873 and immediately became a *cause célèbre*, commanding full-page spreads in the *Illustrated London News*. Still on display, on close inspection, the sophistication of the work is indeed remarkable. Almost life-size, the god of the underworld, Hades, his captive Persephone and a draped woman – Alcestis or Eurydice, between Thanatos (death) and Hermes Psychopompos – are all portrayed. (Hermes Psychopompos – what a beautiful name! – was the ferrier of souls between this world and the next.) Presses of international tourists jostle past, many unaware of the life-and-death drama playing out in front of them. An appropriate narrative of the underworld, given Asian Artemis's purview over death as well as life.

With the splendid harbour of Ephesus nearby, which at this time would have welcomed in boats from ports across the Mediterranean, it is no surprise that the materials used for the Temple construction were so rich: planks of cedar for the roof, cypresses for the doors, vine-wood from

Cyprus for the stairs, which were said to reach to the roof itself. The core of the cult statue of Artemis – made of ebony, or blackened grape-wood, or black stone – was decorated with gold, silver and ivory. The walls and architraves were made of a local marble. Another painter employed to embellish the Temple, Euphranor the Isthmian, decorated the interior with images of Odysseus feigning madness, yoking oxen to his plough, as if to trample his baby son; and also created a sculpture of Artemis with her brother and mother, which ended up in Rome.

And Alexander, even if rebuffed as a patron, was, flagrantly, still present within the sanctuary. The stellar painter Apelles (who trained at Ephesus, we are told) painted a giant portrait of Alexander within the Temple itself, styled as his divine father Zeus, in a pose derived from our next Wonder, the Statue of Zeus at Olympia. Ephesus's Alexander was seated on a throne and reaching out of the frame with his fingers, wielding a thunderbolt. Across the next 500 years, Alexander would enjoy adoration in his own cult in Ephesus. The city honoured the Macedonian leader with temples and priesthoods and sacred games. In some ways Alexander had become the totem for the energetic compulsion that built those Wonders in the first place.

And although the sanctuary started life as a celebrant of the divine feminine, the hard truth is, from the time of Alexander the Great on-wards, Ephesus became a site that was typically the pawn of strong men, and a witness to the strong-man narrative of the ancient world. Ephesus suffered one regime change after another. Briefly held by the Seleucids, it was temporarily renamed Arsinoeia after the wife of Lysimachus – Alexander's bodyguard and one of his childhood companions. Lysimachus attempted to steal Artemis's influence by resettling the city uphill away from the Artemision – the location of the city today. The city and its sanctuary then went on to belong to Ptolemy II (the sponsor of the Lighthouse Wonder at Alexandria) and was also host to Hannibal of Carthage along with the fleet he hoped would save him when he was fleeing from Rome's wrath at the end of his life. Later Ephesus was handed over to the Pergamene kingdom, whose king, Attalus III, bequeathed the city to the new power in ascension, Rome. Ephesus' strategically vital position is written in its choppy political narrative, as the city's patron, Artemis, became entangled in those political ebbs and flows. Rome, in particular, would have great impact on the size and feel of the Artemision Temple.

Since the fourth century BCE, the Romans had merged Artemis with their local goddess Diana.* As they expanded their territorial reach, Romans took this hybrid goddess with them, in sanctuaries dedicated to Artemis from Tunisia, to Spain, to Jordan where, initially, the goddess was represented with many breasts, just as she was in Ephesus. At the city of Jerash in modern-day Jordan, the rich elite – with Artemis as the civic patron – were buried in tombs decorated with the distinctive *peltes* shield of the Amazons. These still survive, adorning the evocative site which stretches over its fertile, well-watered valley. In the National Archaeological Museum of Naples, after negotiating the graffiti-strikes and Italian hen-parties on Naples' streets, one can see an impressive polymastic Roman Artemis from the second century CE, rescued by the sixteenth-century Cardinal Farnese and restored in the nineteenth century. It is one of the museum's most popular objects. The adoption and embrace of Artemis was a message to Roman citizens across the empire that they needed to procreate, and a sign to the subjugated that Roman reproductive power led to Roman expansion and domination. As an inscription at Ephesus from the first century CE puts it:

> . . . the goddess Artemis, patron of our city, is honoured not only in her native city, which she has made more famous than all other cities through her own divinity, but also by Greeks and barbarians, so that everywhere sanctuaries and precincts are consecrated for her, temples are dedicated and altars are set up for her because of her manifest epiphanies . . .[78]

Ephesus was wrapped into the Roman province of Asia from 133 BCE, and from 129 BCE was its capital. Physically, psychologically, this was where Asia and Europe could be controlled, and Ephesus became a blisteringly busy port.† The Artemision Temple itself, in effect an incorporated company, boomed. Artemis owned property in the Kaystros Valley,

---

* Notably at Lake Nemi near Rome, where a sanctuary was dedicated to Diana Nemorensis (Diana of the Woods) around 300 BCE.
† A beautiful mosaic featuring the sea-king Triton from the Roman period, originally unearthed in the 1870s – with Tritons also decorating the homes of the well-to-do in that swanky housing sector – were reminders of how much wealth came to Ephesus from the sea.

salt-flats and marble-quarries. The Artemision leased out fish-farms, deer-parks, horse-studs. It produced crops and cattle and franchised out the sale of frankincense, brought in from southern Arabia for regular, pricey sacred rites.[79] Slaves were dedicated specifically to serve the goddess. A third of the population would have been enslaved at this time and another inscription from Ephesus shows that slaves here had 'TAX PAID' tattooed onto their foreheads. Whether as a tourist attraction or an agro business, the sanctuary of Artemis was becoming phenomenally wealthy, and breaking lives along the way.

So the Romans got greedy, sending tax collectors to cream off these revenues. The Ephesians reacted by welcoming in one of Rome's most formidable enemies – the 'Black Sea Poisoner' Mithradates VI Eupator, ruler of the Kingdom of Pontus, who was burning his way through the region, inciting revolt. On arriving in Ephesus, Mithridates' henchmen slaughtered the Romans who cowered under Artemis's protection. Savagely ironic, since one of the Ephesians' griefs against their Roman masters had been that they had attacked a slave in the Temple (a place of refuge) a couple of years before. It was said that in just one night 80,000 Roman civilians – women, children and men – were cut down by Mithridates' troops, and by locals who prayed this would be the end of the Roman yoke. Mithridates then declared everything within a bow-shot of Artemis's Temple to be sacred, protected land. The sanctuary-status of Ephesus' wonder was clearly being used for political gain and popular favour. It was said that during his brief occupation of Ephesus, Mithridates stayed in an inn used by Alexander the Great while he was in the town – one megalomaniac emulating another.

As you might imagine, the Romans hit back. In 84 BCE Ephesus was deprived of its freedom, and fined a huge sum – 20,000 talents. High-minded principle dissolved into *realpolitik*; as a port city, the Ephesians could use the Pax Romana that the Romans promised. Ephesus formally became an asset of Rome. The 'greats' of the Roman world started to pass through: Cicero, Pliny the Elder, Pliny the Younger, the Emperor Hadrian. Ephesus had become an outpost of the ideas, and sensitivities, that made Rome tick.

In 41 BCE Cleopatra of Egypt's half-sister Arsinoe IV was sheltering in Ephesus, banished there after a power-struggle with Cleopatra for pole position in Egypt, but also safe and secure. Weeks before, Mark Antony had revelled in a sensuous meeting with his Egyptian lover Cleopatra at Tarsus in southern Anatolia – with the Roman general dressed as Dionysos, to her Aphrodite.[80] The Queen of Egypt had won her man, dazzling him with her gold and her brilliance. Her younger sister Arsinoe represented a threat to her hold on power, a rival Ptolemeid for forces to gather around. Arsinoe had already been humiliated, paraded in Caesar's triumph in Rome in 46 BCE as a captive, but now Cleopatra persuaded her new love to get rid of this troublesome sibling. Arsinoe was murdered in Ephesus in cold blood – on the very steps of the Temple of Artemis where she sought sanctuary from the goddess. Debate still rages as to whether or not it is Arsinoe's bones (the remains of a young woman in an elite grave were re-examined in 2007) that are buried on Ephesus' Curetes Street in an octagonal tomb. The base alone is now in situ, and fragments of the tomb are held in storage on site, while two of its fabulous Corinthian columns are in the Ephesus Museum in Vienna. In 33–32 BCE, Cleopatra and Antony wintered in Ephesus, clearly comfortable with the fact that the sororicide, on Queen Cleopatra's orders, had taken place in one of the premier Seven Wonders of the world just eight years before.

Mark Antony had originally arrived in Ephesus without Cleopatra, drunk, dressed as the god of wine, Dionysos-Bacchus, and attended by satyrs and maenads – the male and female counterparts of the god's retinue.[81] He claimed to be Bacchus reborn. One suspects the significance of re-invading the Amazon-themed sanctuary, as the god himself was said to have done back in the mist of myths, was not lost on the Roman general. Sheltering in Artemis's Temple at the time were those who had supported two of the murderers of Julius Caesar, Brutus and Cassius. With the exception of two men in the group, Mark Antony chose to forgive them. It is worth noting that an alternative, later Roman source, Dio Cassius, asserts that also sheltering in Artemis's Temple were two brothers of Cleopatra, whom Mark Antony pulled out and put to death.

Mark Antony wintered in the city, along with 300 Roman senators and 800 ships, conceiving his doomed rebellion against Rome. It was from Ephesus that Antony and Cleopatra would set sail for the Battle of Actium, across the Mediterranean in the high-cliffed Greek mainland opposite the island of Zakynthos. Mark Antony followed the example of Alexander the Great and King Mithridates the Poisoner, and declared that the whole area between Artemis's Temple right up to the city's edges was a sanctuary zone.*[82]

It was to Ephesus that Octavian (the future Emperor Augustus) headed after he had defeated Antony and Cleopatra in the Battle of Actium – over a period of six months, stationed in the city and plotting his new world order. He was, one suspects, somewhat salty with the city council and the authorities at the Artemision, whom he had already written to six or so years before, demanding the return of a golden statue of Eros bequeathed as a gift to the goddess by his uncle and adoptive father, Julius Caesar. While his rivals, Pompey and Antony, had used the resources of the Temple to bankroll their campaigns, Augustus chose to de-escalate the Artemision's political muscle. He returned some of the Temple's properties in the city, and offered the goddess what the goddess was due: an anti-corruption job, attempting to discourage other pretenders from using Ephesian resources as blood money. He also, however, encouraged an imperial cult to be established in Ephesus, where he was to be worshipped by the people of the city as a demi-god.

By the first century CE, Ephesus was the fourth largest city in the Roman Empire, beaten only by Rome, Alexandria and Antioch. Roman visitors started to flood there. It was as a traveller to Ephesus in 29 BCE that Strabo witnessed the rites to the goddess, providing us with vital clues to their celebratory nature.[83] But as Roman influence escalated, the celebrations at Ephesus took a brutal turn. Gladiatorial fights and hunting games were introduced. Ephesus is in fact the first Romanised city to provide extant evidence for the sickeningly corrupt, and corrupting, fights of man against beast – organised as early as 71 BCE by one entrepreneur, Lucullus. The popularity of these 'entertainments' is immortalised on stelae and sculptural reliefs from the region. With cash to splash

---

* Although rather brilliantly, as Strabo tut tuts, this meant creating a zone where normal rules didn't apply, and so became a kind of duty-free, black-market paradise, an arrangement that was therefore nullified by Augustus. Augustus' measure was clearly only partially effective, since his lieutenant Marcus Agrippa (responsible for victory at the Battle of Actium and the construction of the original Pantheon) wrote to the Ephesians that some from the Jewish community sheltering there who had mis-managed Temple funds should be treated as Temple robbers and so be forcefully removed. Whether for convenience, or genuinely religious purposes, we should never forget the sense there was of these man-made constructions – particularly one as splendid as Artemis's Temple – being surrounded by a protective and inviolable sacred force-field.

around, the wealthy dignitaries of the city organised these blood sports, a sickeningly inverted version of Artemis's woodland hunts, to impress and bind the Ephesians in a pact of dubious commission.

Excavating the sacred route from the Artemision Temple into the city itself, flanking an ancient road, in 2007 sixty-eight individuals were discovered. The surviving headstones confirm these were gladiators, and, sadly, their bones bear witness to the trauma they suffered. One has a flat, deep, healed blade strike on the front of his skull; others show fatal blows from a blunt instrument on the base of the head; there are terrible lesions on femurs, shoulders and ribs; and, horrifically, one skull has deep, pierced holes in the bone, which match precisely the span of a trident, discovered near the port – exactly the kind used by the net-and-trident gladiators known as *retiarii*. The number of dental cavities in these Ephesian individuals indicates a diet of barley and beans (gladiators were often fed carbs to give them a layer of fat which would bleed theatrically but could pad against a killer-blow), and a lack of the production of saliva – the result of 'dry-mouth' fear.[84] Now in Artemis's city men were hunting other men for sport.

Marble relief fragment showing combat between a gladiator and a lion. Greek inscriptions include the words 'first (fight); second (fight); third (fight) and fourth (fight). He was taken away for burial.'

*

Soon the public spaces in Artemis's city – the theatre and the agora, as well as the city's synagogue – would be accommodating a new kind of pilgrim: members of a fledgling cult who, initially, desperately, might find themselves forced to meet gladiators and beasts in the arena. The very first of these pilgrims was a Jewish convert – Paul the Apostle, or St Paul, as he would become. Paul made his way to Ephesus to diminish Artemis's power rather than to nourish it. Standing and calling to all who would listen, we are told that Paul denied the goddess and those who served her – decrying her cultic, special-magic language, her trinkets and her totems. There was plenty for him to despise. The *megabyzos*, the eunuch Temple warden, was still in charge at the time of Paul's visit, along with his companion, the high-ranking priestess who performed public sacrifices, maintained Artemis's cult and distributed money to the choral composers and singers, the *hymnodoi*, on Artemis's birthday.

Originally from Tarsus in what is now southern Turkey, where Mark Antony had made his dramatic entrance to meet Cleopatra dressed as Dionysos, Paul came twice to Ephesus, in 52 and 55 CE, drawn by the size of its population and the reputation of its supernatural power. Paul also wrote that he 'fought with wild beasts' at Ephesus, although this was almost certainly metaphor rather than fact. When considering Ephesus at the time, we need to reorientate ourselves a little, to understand that all seven of the ancient Wonders come from a time when buildings, monuments, and statues themselves were believed to possess a spirit and a god-given potency. When the sculptures of the Temple of Artemis at the city of Ephesus would come to be blinded by Christian incomers, or their foreheads scoured with crosses, or their eyes put out, it was not the weakness of these inanimate objects but their strength that was being identified and diminished. Paul travelled to Ephesus partly because he needed to meet its pagan demons head-on.

Paul's testimony, history by accident, tells us of the wealth and goddess-worshipping piety of the city, partly thanks to the fury of the Ephesian silversmiths who complained that any challenge to Artemis's authority would mean a massive hit for their businesses. For centuries these families had made an enviable turnover selling tourist nick-nacks (mini Artemis Temples, just as tourists buy mini Big Bens or Eiffel Towers today) to the visitors who came by land and sea to the goddess' great city.* The journalist-politician Tacitus – as governor of the province of Asia from 112 to 113 CE – had direct experience of the town as a pagan city.[†][85] And despite the assertion in the apocryphal Acts of John that John the Evangelist came here and found the incense from Artemis's festival so thick, it veiled the sun, and that the Christian God broke the altar into pieces, an edict of 162 CE shows in fact that the Romans extended Artemis's festival at this time, on the face of it as recompense for the affront of a Roman doing business on her holy days. Nonetheless, it does seem likely that John did return to Ephesus towards the end of his life, in around 95 CE. He died here and was buried on the hill overlooking Artemis's sanctuary. Yet archaeology shows that Artemis's lovely altar, decorated with Amazons, was not broken at this time. Instead there were additions and renovations: a banqueting hall within the Artemision and a covered portico to the sanctuary to protect from rain,[‡] at a time when the eruption of the Taupo volcano in New Zealand seems to have caused severe climate change, including excessive rainfall in the region. So for a while, Artemis, in her Temple Wonder, stood strong.

Ephesus, however, was in a region that was the seedbed for the new Christ cult, the cult of a boy-god who promised that – without the need for any god's or goddess' intervention – each and every individual could have power over their own life and death through the miracle of resurrection.

In 262 CE there was a catastrophe: a massive earthquake, which toppled walls, split mosaics and tumbled the decorations in those rich Ephesian homes to the ground. Incense-burners were hurled about, catching fire on the Temple altars, where they burned with offerings to the goddess. The flames spread, reaching to the huge roof beams, and soon the Temple of Artemis was destroyed in a second conflagration – a horrible repeat

---

* In 1 Corinthians I.11, written in Ephesus, we hear of an Ephesian woman with employees (Ephesus, recall, was home to a number of successful businesswomen), whose staff, on business in Corinth, brought back news of the spread of Christianity on the Greek mainland to Artemis's hometown.
† A note of Tacitus's governorship is recorded in an inscription at nearby Mylasa.
‡ Running from the Magnesian Gate and dedicated by Titus Flavius Damianus and his wife Vedia Phaedrina.

of the scenes of Herostratus' arson attack 600 years before. The Temple which had been built to protect and honour the power of nature and the earth had felt nature's blade-hand. Five years later, Goths from Crimea and Scythians came to finish off the job, plundering what was left of the Temple's treasures – Asia's reserve bank. The famous Library of Celsus was looted. From this date on, although Artemis was still honoured in her ruined Temple Wonder – possibly up until 401 CE – there is no more evidence of her mysteries, her frenzied rituals and dances, being mounted.

After the earthquake only the *cella*, the inner sanctuary of the Artemision, was fully restored, while the rest of the building was patched together with reclaimed material, probably on the orders of the Emperor Diocletian. Then, from the newly Christian city of Constantinople, the New or Second Rome, the Byzantine Emperor Constantius II ordered an empire-wide removal of all pagan statues. One Christian, Demeas, took it on himself to pull down the statue of Artemis which had overlooked the bustling, elegant boulevards of Ephesus' town centre, surveying her own sacred processional route. He erected a wooden Cross of Christ in her place. The act of theological vandalism was commemorated with an inscription: 'Demeas, tearing down the deceitful image of the daimon Artemis, set up this sign of truth. He honoured God who drives away idols, and the Cross, the victorious, immortal symbol of Christ.'

In 401 CE came the hammer-blow. Ephesus was under attack. Statues of Augustus and Livia had crosses scored into their foreheads. Artemis's name was scoured out of inscriptions on the portico of the Prytaneion (the council chamber) and the harbour baths. The Basilica of St John was raised on the hill above, using choice building fragments from the old Temple. And Proclus, one of the last of antiquity's pagan philosophers, declared in his *Twentieth Oration*: 'In Ephesus he [the archbishop of Constantinople John Chrysostom] despoiled the art of Midas' – a reference, surely, to all that glittering gold craftsmanship that once adorned Artemis's sanctuary. In the sixth century the Byzantine Emperor Justinian appropriated the giant Gorgon's head that had decorated the centre of the eastern pediment for his public-art display in the Byzantine capital, Constantinople. The cruciform Christian church Justinian founded with his wife Empress Theodora still partially stands on Ayasuluk Hill, overshadowing the wide, fecund, marshy plain where Artemis once reigned.

*

But the goddess still clung on, albeit in a rather different form.

If you walk a little further out of the settlement, south-east of the Temple site, to the wider reaches of Roman Ephesus, you find evidence of another potent, sublime, virgin woman associated with the city: the Virgin Mary. Because the first ever church dedicated to Mary of Nazareth was raised in Artemis's city. The episcopal church of the Virgin was built on top of the portico on the south side of the Olympieion, a temple erected by Hadrian to Zeus Olympios. It was here in 431, 433 and 449 CE that the vitally influential Councils of Ephesus took place. At Ephesus, Mary was declared *Theotokos*, the Mother of God, a statement of status that would change world history. Picking through the tumbled brick and marble ruins of the church today, where grasses blow softly, and friendly packs of dogs sun themselves at dawn, it is hard to imagine this was the site of a seismic theological decision. Artemis might have lost her mysteries, but another virgin, another divine birth, another protecting veil would come to be celebrated here in the form of the new Marian cult.

Legend has it that the Virgin herself was taken to Ephesus by St John, where she lived until she died at the age of fifty-one. So in addition, on the western slopes of Mount Aladağ, 4 miles south of Ephesus, travellers and the faithful from all three Abrahamic faiths make a steadfast journey to tie prayers of petition to bushes and fences at the modest building where Mary was said to have breathed her last mortal breath. This is the very glade at Ortygia where Artemis was believed, by some, to have been born.

Christian pilgrims also came from far and wide to see the hills that witnessed the awakening of the Seven Sleepers – seven brothers and their dog who were, legend had it, walled up inside a cave above Ephesus during the Roman Emperor Decius' persecutions of 250 CE, but who then, miraculously, woke up as if from slumber, a hundred years later, disturbed by unsuspecting masons. Believed to be buried in a cemetery at Ephesus, the Seven Sleepers became the subject of fervent adoration. Currently under excavation, their cemetery was finely decorated throughout the Byzantine period. Recently images of Mary Magdalene have come to light and, also, some of St Paul from the fifth century CE in the so-called Grotto of St Paul. The Sleeping Seven is clearly a fairytale, but it does point to historical persecution of Christians in Ephesus at this time; and is also a reminder that the magic of the number seven endured through the Christian age. Still today in the twenty-first century, locals animatedly fathom from genies or djinns, via coffee grounds or other forms of divination, the whereabouts of Mary's lost tomb, the aura it has left through Ephesus, sharing their conviction that Mary's body itself will be rediscovered within all of our lifetimes.[86]

But when it came to the structure of Artemis's Temple itself, an earthquake and the Sassanians delivered the *coup de grâce* in 614 CE, ravaging the pride of the once-famed cosmopolis.[87] The *Parastesis Syntomoi Chronikai*, a kind of tourist guide to ancient, potent artworks seized by Byzantine authorities for re-use in Constantinople, tells of statuary and materials from Artemis's Ephesian home. It relates that one great door, 'darkened with the deception of idols', was re-purposed in Constantinople's Senate House. Today, in Istanbul, where this would have stood, market-traders sell religious nick-nacks, instant Covid tests and fans made in China. The Temple-door story is almost certainly a fancy (the Senate in Constantinople has bronze doors and we are told that Artemis's main doors were made of carved wood), as is the assertion that columns from Artemis's Temple were re-used in Emperor Justinian and Empress Theodora's great church, the Hagia Sophia (a building which would itself end up on later, mediaeval Seven Wonders lists). The sage-green serpentine columns, claimed to have originated in the Ephesian Wonder, might not be from Artemis's temple (apart from anything else, they are the wrong size, shape, height and stone), but nonetheless Theodora was the beneficiary of a theology, established at Ephesus, which maintained female power in the form of 'Mary Mother of God'. As one contemplates Theodora's initials at Hagia Sophia, carved boldly into the capitals of the columns said to belong to the mighty goddess – the initials of a poor young girl who ended up as a super-empress in charge of a million square miles of Byzantine territory – the potency of the *idea* of the Artemision Temple and its divine patron is inescapable.

Stones and statues might have been looted, or cannibalised, or ground down into mortar, but nothing could eradicate the impact this Wonder had made. Because as the centuries ploughed on, many came from far and wide to marvel at Ephesus. In the early mediaeval period, around 700 CE, one of the first tourists to the site from the far West was a young religious pilgrim-adventurer, the Anglo-Saxon daredevil Willibald. In an account of his travels via Rome and the Holy Land, dictated to his female relative just before he died, the nun Huneberc (whose endeavour was disapproved of, and so whose name was recorded in a cryptogram – only deciphered in the mid-twentieth century – making Huneberc the first female English author to have composed a full-length work of literature), we hear the intrepid young man made Ephesus one of his destinations. Committed to a monastery in Bishop's Waltham, southern England, from the age of five, Willibald's adult life was the very incarnation of adventure. Sailing out from Hamblehaven near Southampton, still a small-boat maritime centre today, Willibald's father, a Wessex chieftain and under-king, died in Italy on pilgrimage to Rome – so his sons had to carry on without him. Willibald – the first Englishman to make this kind of *peregrinatio religiosa* – marvelled at the lost city (he makes no specific mention of what must have been the tumbled ruins of Artemis's Temple, but so visible is it from Ephesus' hill, it would have been impossible to avoid). We only know of this journey thanks to Huneberc's diligent account, the *Hodoeporicon* or *Relation of a Voyage*:

> [They] sped on towards Asia, to the city of Ephesus, which stands about a mile from the sea. Then they went on foot to the spot where the Seven Sleepers lie at rest. From there they walked to the tomb of St John, the Evangelist, which is situated in a beautiful spot near Ephesus . . .[88]

The Wonders, and their fine locales, have an enormous pull across time and space. And although its harbour had completely silted up by 1244 CE, Ephesus was also one of the Wonders which lived on vibrantly in the mind, in literature and in art. The Roman poet Horace had listed it amongst other locations that would be a theme of singers for generations to come – and indeed, it is where Shakespeare sets his *Comedy of Errors*, a version of a play by the early Roman playwright Plautus. Plautus' original, called *Miles Gloriosus*, presents themes of pride before falls and the possibility of 'even a slave' being heroic and glorious. The soap-opera, domestic-drama action takes place in Ephesus' residential district, the district where so many had been made rich by living alongside a world-class attraction.

In 1624, England's Earl of Arundel sent out his amanuensis, Revd William Petty, on a mission of 'marble raking' to seize antiquities from

Asia Minor, including some from Ephesus. Clearly with no little sub-terfuge (the ambassadors Sir Thomas Roe and Sir Peter Wyche at the time advised on how to remove particular marble pieces 'by stealth'), by 1627 Petty had acquired '37 statues, 128 busts, 250 inscriptions, together with a large number of altars, sarcophagi, fragments of sculpture, and an invaluable collection of gems.' Antiquities ripped from their home. The totemic eighteenth-century English historian and politician Edward Gibbon imagined Artemis's Temple animatedly, even though it had yet to be excavated, and Ephesus' Wonder was described in the penny magazine of the Society for the Diffusion of Useful Knowledge in 1845.

But it took the son of a Shropshire lad, raised in East London's Hack-ney, to physically drag the Temple of Ephesus from the alluvial river mud. In the 1860s, John Turtle Wood, in Ottoman Turkey to build a railway, was lured to channel a path to the past rather than the future. And so from 1863 to 1875 Wood gave up on engineering, and a paid job with the Smyrna and Aydin Railway Company, and started to dig.

After six years of tribulation, even a brush with a kidnapping attempt by local 'brigands', John Turtle Wood identified the top of the Temple's columns 20 feet beneath the soggy surface of the hummock. Even the celebrity archaeologist of his day, Heinrich Schliemann (yet to discover Troy), was impressed – and came to visit the Temple site on 16 December 1869.

Appropriately enough, given Wood's profession as a creator of in-frastructure, the amateur enthusiast discovered the processional sacred roadway to the Temple first and followed it to his goal. Uncovering frag-ments of columns, he eventually dragged that entire column drum, fifty, occasionally sixty paces a day, through the marshy ground, to be shipped back to the British Museum. Woods cuts a rather lonely figure – his journals describe the incapacitating infections and fevers he and his wife endured, falls that laid him up with fractures, and a constant battle for funding. He communicated his progress in over 500 letters, now in the British Museum's archive. It is clear that many of the finds were intended to remain in a new local museum, with the most valuable being sent to the Ottoman Sublime Porte in Istanbul. In fact, lack of the resource of supervision by Ottoman officials meant the majority of the Temple's re-mains left the country – either ending up in London's British Museum or, between 1885 and 1909, on camel and then train from Izmir, in the newly created Ephesus Museum in Vienna. The shocking volume of transport of antiquities from Ephesus paved the way for Turkey's Law on Historical Artefacts.[89] On his return to England Woods wrote a popular account of his digs, changing dates and details for dramatic effect – academics today have to winkle-pick through these detailed site-reports, plans, sketches and photographs from his excavations to jigsaw-puzzle the truth back together. *Discoveries in Ephesos*, published in 1877, was quite the hit.

I lived for a year in Marine Parade, in Brighton, on the UK's south coast, where John Turtle Wood died. I like to imagine him there – that bright grey light from the sea, a very English version of the Eastern Mediterranean brilliant blue that led him to unearth Artemis's Wonder – thinking of that site in Anatolia, where the water and springs by themselves gave a sense of sanctuary and security. Where the possibilities of human involvement in the tree-loved hills were so great.

The Temple at Ephesus was a human creation that endeavoured not to turn its back on the power of nature: mankind knows that nature fights back, and will always have the upper hand. But even so, the wonder-makers, like their counterparts in Mesopotamia, looked at mires and saw settlements, at woodlands and saw sacred roads. They determined to create new worlds and to create their way out of a crisis. They did that very human, out-vying thing and looked at what others did, and they decided to do it bigger and better. Of all the majestic monuments that decorated the Hellenistic world in the fourth century BCE, Artemis's magnificent Temple was stand-out extraordinary. The wonder of Ephesus was where the majesty and magnificence of the mountains, the haunt of the goddess, were turned to stone and brought within mankind's reach.

Women and men believed that Artemis had been born in Ephesus, that her cult image had miraculously appeared there, and they knew that by honouring her with a massive temple, they had made their city rich. Little wonder that we hear, from the Acts of the New Testament, in response to a suggestion that Jesus should replace the wild, protecting virgin huntress: 'When they heard this they were enraged and were crying out, "Great is Artemis of the Ephesians!"'[90]

An inscription from Ephesus encapsulates the urgent need that both Ephesians and visitors to the Temple must have felt to adore her:

Artemis of the beautiful quiver, from my family. For she is the leader of every city as midwife in childbirth, increaser of crops, and giver of fruits. Bring a gold and ivory statue of her from Ephesus and place it joyfully in a temple; she will ward off pains and undo the destructive enchantments of plague, consuming with blazing torches in torchlit nights the symbolic figures of wax made by the arts of the magicians. When you have carried out my instructions for the goddess, honour her with hymns and sacrifices as delighting in the bow, invincible, un-approachable, with unerring aim, the famous sharp-sighted maiden; in dances and feasts let maidens and boys all over the salty lands of the Maeonian River Hermos celebrate her, crowning her with broad myrtle crowns and calling on the pure Artemis of the Ephesian land, that she shall be your uncorrupted helper for ever. But if you do not execute this instruction, you will pay the penalty of fire.[91]

It is a fitting mark of respect to this great goddess that a NASA mission beyond earth's atmosphere to the moon – to Diana-Artemis's star – has finally been named not Apollo, but Artemis I.

In Ephesus, the Artemisian Wonder, which understood the power of wilderness and the need to keep mother nature on side, on her terms, would often be viewed by moonlight or torchlight in nocturnal festivals led by young girls. Artemis, who begged Zeus to allow her to be light-bringing, wisdom-bringing, was invoked by women who would make supplication, 'by Artemis', more than any other Greek deity. Our next Wonder, the Statue of Zeus at Olympia, was all about the glaring brilliance of a mid-summer sunlit sky, and not about virgin girls, but the bellicose ambition of mature men, teenagers and prepubescent boys – to achieve and to win.*

---

* Artemis has a strange coda on the nearby Greek island of Patmos. Patmos itself was said to be raised up from the seabed on the request of the goddess – originally called after her, the child of Leto, Letoia. The submerged island had been revealed to Artemis while she sat, rather companionably from the sound of things, on Mount Latmos on the mainland in Karia (with Selene, the goddess of the moon), surveying those waterways which had brought her so many worshippers. A temple to Artemis is said to lurk under the very church on Patmos where St John was visited by Jesus and inspired to write the Book of Revelation. But John was not polite to his pagan host. An account in the pseudo-gospels tells how John, appalled by the clouds of Artemis's incense at Ephesus, blocking out the sun, demanded the destruction of her statues and sanctuaries – returning himself, once the cultural vandalism had been effected, to live with the Virgin Mary in her little house above the site until 120 CE. Even after burial, it was said that you could still see John's breaths, puffing above his tomb, while he waited for the Second Coming.

CHAPTER 4

❖

THE STATUE OF ZEUS AT OLYMPIA

C. 432 BCE

The wish to witness the ancient masterpiece of Phidias was so intense, that to die without having seen it was considered a huge misfortune!

EPICTETUS, *DISCOURSES* 1.6.23, A STOIC PHILOSOPHER
(BORN INTO SLAVERY) DESCRIBING THE POPULARITY OF
THE STATUE OF ZEUS AT OLYMPIA DURING HIS
LIFETIME IN THE FIRST CENTURY CE

'The Statue of Zeus at Olympia' engraving produced by Philips Galle after designs by Maarten van Heemskerck in 1572.

Just over 300 miles west of Ephesus, in south-western Greece, as the classical stone Temple of Artemis was finally reaching its completion, an intimidating golden god was being raised: the giant statue of almighty Zeus in colossal form, 41 feet high, glowering from within his temple in his sanctuary at Olympia. Zeus was Artemis's father (the king of the gods raping the Titaness Leto, who then gave birth to those twins, Artemis and Apollo),[1] but also, counter-intuitively, her evolutionary child. Because when the Statue of Olympian Zeus was being fashioned, Artemis, in her prehistoric guise as Mistress of Animals, had been around for at least two millennia. On the other hand, a dominant male god at the head of the Greek pantheon – a supreme, smiting father figure like Zeus – had existed only 800 years.[2] The first appearance, in the Aegean, of a thundering male deity, in the thirteenth century BCE – Zeus mark 1, if you like – coincides with a time when Bronze Age communities were ramping up their military activity, privileging the role of warrior armies, and of generals, and of their divine equivalent – a lead-from-the-front male god who rained down thunderbolts on his enemies.

By at least 522 BCE, almighty Zeus was looming as the patriarch of the Olympian pantheon, a twelve-strong divine family who inhabited Mount Olympus in northern Greece. King of success and power, Zeus was a god who ruled men with violence and with intimidation. In Zeus's world, failure was not an option. Understanding this Olympian Wonder, Zeus incarnate, is to understand ancient mettle and might.

To get to Zeus's sanctuary-home at Olympia is necessarily a pilgrimage. A traveller from Ephesus would have had to negotiate the Anatolian coast, cross the Aegean and brave the Rhodope, Olympus and Pindus mountain ranges. From the west and south, the journey would have been via vast stretches of the Mediterranean at its most dangerous. From the north, along bandit roads. A steady trickle of travellers beat a path to Olympia year in, year out, but once every four years there was a flood of men. All pilgrims summoned in by horn-blowing heralds who had tramped thousands of miles and ridden across Greek territories from modern-day Georgia in the Caucasus to Sicily in Magna Graecia, clarion-calling those from the Greek world who wanted to be hailed as heroes, or to come as spectators to buttress the Greeks' sense of ethnic (Hellenic) specialness. A truce was declared from the time of the heralds' announcement through the duration of the Games, the first of which was dated to

776 BCE. In an age that was by default pugilistic and bellicose, this meant an interruption of typical life. There were compelling reasons for ancient Greeks to comply: a serious fine of 2 minae (200 drachmas) per soldier in combat. When Sparta attacked the city of Lepreum during the Olympics in 420 BCE, for example, the city-state was fined 2,000 minae – loosely equivalent to £500,000 in today's money.[3] We should not imagine, though, that the Olympic truce was primarily designed to generate peace in the world; it was designed to ensure the safe passage of athletes and pilgrims to Olympia, so that these men could fetishise competition in the presence of the king of the gods.

The able-bodied travelled to Olympia by boat, foot, mule or donkey. Many came with a caravan of the enslaved and other 'possessions'. Because participation in the Olympics was a public display of belonging and primacy, only Greeks were invited and many people were excluded. All those classified as barbarians – those who 'bar-bar-bar-ed' in non-Greek languages – were not eligible to join the Olympic festival. The destination of each and every chosen pilgrim to Olympia was, from the mid-fifth century BCE, also to its great god, Olympian Zeus, in giant statue form. They also came to see the Wonder Statue because Olympia was Zeus's sanctuary, and the king of the gods (Zeus Panhellenios, Zeus of all the Greeks, as he was known elsewhere) was presiding over an event trumpeted to some extent then, and to a greater extent now, as a cause for celebration across the 'civilised' world. It was believed that anyone who fought in the month before the Games was 'accursed in the eyes of Zeus'.[4]

For those who did come, this was an essential and chauvinistically Greek show of solidarity and one-ness against an external enemy, an opportunity to flaunt city-state and tribal strength and superiority, and a way of healing the trauma of living through an age of consistent warfare and strife. So, although peace was the machinery that allowed the Games to proceed uninterrupted, it was not the goal. The Olympic Games were a quest for omnipotence: who better to bestow this than the king of the gods himself, in monumental form.

The only Ancient Wonder of the world on mainland Greece – the Statue of Zeus the All-father at Olympia, still one of the largest indoor sculptures ever made – was the incarnation of an idea. An idea of individual agency and perfect power.

For those travelling from Athens, the pilgrimage to Olympia would have been a five- or six-day journey, past the eerily beautiful land that is arcadian and still, appropriately, called Arkadia, and along hill passes and by bright rivers. Some journeys would have been made by torchlight and special tour boats would have been laid on by entrepreneurs to import visitors and contestants alike from the islands and coastal communities, fishing skiffs and trading boats pressed into service. Olympia was serviced by its own ports – some remains still visible today on the isthmus that connects the Cape of Katakolo with the Peloponnesian mainland. In the little harbour of Pheia, much of the ancient town is still under the waves here – thrillingly, walls, jetties, streets are clearly visible 16 feet or so below the water's surface. Upmarket tourist developments, including the Pheia hotel, peer down on waters that would once have thronged with ancient craft. But the coastline and seabed itself are protected because there are so many extant antiquities, and pottery fragments are regularly excavated. This tranquil spot was once buzzing. Approaching from the sea must have been awe-inspiring, exhilarating. The ample beach of sandy Pylos reaches out, with the towering Taygetos mountain range looming behind.

Today's tourist-truce-route to Olympia is a bit of a confection – beautiful, but fake. The real path to the Olympic experience was, and is, more rugged. Some of the old pathways are just track, some rock-cut, with rutroads. Today the ancient route from the sea, retraced in part by modern tourists piling off cruise ships, is flanked by signs of modern internationalism – a China City supermarket, a Nissan Olympic car dealership, Silk petrol stations. Heading further inland from the coast on B roads, the wild mountain and river landscape soon starts to engender a real sense of occasion. The ancient pilgrims would be distinguished by the baggage trains they brought with them, and by their hats – typically worn for travelling (but used infrequently at other times). One rather brilliant anecdote tells us a boxer travelling from Alexandria in Egypt claimed that bad weather delayed him in the Cyclades – although it turned out he had made a detour to the Ionian islands to do some business and was peremptorily disqualified for his dishonesty.[5]

Think of pilgrimages to Mecca or Lourdes – part of the devotion of the journey was the adventure of arriving, the novelty of experiences along the way. The appreciation of this Wonder came with difficulty, dedication and a theatrical reveal baked in.

The journey to Zeus's sanctuary at Olympia was the largest peacetime migration, not just of Greeks, but of humans, in ancient history. All aiming for one thing – a sacred space. Because in every way participating in the Olympic Games was a religious experience.

Ten months of preparation built up to this sublime, shared devotion. To describe the Olympic Games as an ultimate sporting event gets us only ten per cent of the way there. The emotional investment was enormously high, because these games were believed to have begun as an immortal affair, and to be conducted under the watchful eye of the Olympic sovereign. They were thought to bring Greek men (and some women) closer to their gods and to supernatural power.

The story went that the Games had started when the super-hero Herakles initiated the contests at Olympia in honour of his father Zeus. He had cleaned out the Augean stables of King Augeas at nearby Elis, measured out the stades in Olympia's stadium (which explains why the Olympic stadium is longer than others, thanks to Herakles' enormous, heroic feet), and taught men how to wrestle. It was Herakles who was said to have first fenced off Olympia's sanctuary. A monstrous ivory shoulder-blade – almost certainly a dinosaur bone, such bones do appear in fossilised layers here – 'belonging' to Herakles' great-grandson Pelops was displayed at Olympia in a specially built shrine, the Pelopion.* Other bones of the hero were stored in a bronze chest in an outbuilding of the Temple of Artemis Kordaka, just outside the eastern edge of the Olympia precinct.[6]

Alternatively, some said, the Olympic Games were kick-started because a local king, Oenomaus, loved his daughter Hippodameia so much, he raced with her prospective suitors all the way from Olympia to Corinth, eventually dying in the attempt when the semi-divine Pelops, lover of Poseidon, and an ardent new suitor of Hippodameia, tricked the king's charioteer into replacing the linchpins of Oenomaus' bronze axles with beeswax, which melted and generated the mother of all chariot crashes. The triumphant trickster Pelops – who gave his name to the region, the

---

* The bones of dead heroes and monsters must have appeared to be scattered all about. Two 10-foot-long tusks belonging to the Pleistocene *Elephas/Palaeoloxodon Antiquus* were unearthed in 1994 by roadbuilders. Disintegrating tusks and skull fragments, dating back to c. 200,000 BCE, are currently on display in the Elis Museum.

Peloponnese – then founded the Games, perhaps as a funeral rite for the assassinated king. Pelops was buried – so the Greeks told one another – in the sanctuary at Olympia under an imposing mound of earth. One version of the legend (surely to keep foreign, Eastern visitors on side) had Pelops arriving from the East to change the course of history (or at least myth).

Or, others declared, Zeus himself had established the contests as a celebration of his triumph over his Titan father, Kronos. Little surprise that Zeus had daddy issues. The godling's siblings, when they were new-borns, had been slowly eaten, one by one, by their abusive father Kronos. Hidden away in the snow-capped, stalactite-jagged Idean Cave on Crete by his mother Rhea, Zeus had only escaped because she replaced this, her favourite baby, with a stone. The location of the father–son battle at Olympia was the hill that overlooks the site – still called the Hill of Kronos today – affording a great vantage point over the sanctuary below and adorned with trees and a comms tower. Victorious Zeus, the myths went, invited the gods of Mount Olympus to participate in his celebratory games, though most events were won, rather predictably, by swift Apollo. And so, before men even saw the Wonder that resided here, they were pumped up with an invested expectation, a knowledge that they were about to enter the ultimate god's earthly kingdom, a place thick with myth. And they knew that the god himself was present – in wondrous form.

Yet despite the fact that the Olympic Games were in honour of Olympian Zeus – whose Statue in the sanctuary, completed in c. 430 BCE, was swiftly considered a Wonder of the world, and which cost more to build than the temple it was housed in – the first stop for these ardent travellers was in fact not Olympia, but the traditional old-school city of Elis, 23 miles to the north. It was at Elis that hard-core training for the Games took place over forty days and nights, all presided over by the original Olympic committee, nine Elean elders, the Hellanodikai, or 'Judges of the Greeks'. What went on in Elis gives us a sense of how carefully laden with ceremony and import this ritual of might and main, of ascendance, was. Disarmingly, Elis is now arable and meadow land, disturbed only by lone hunters coming down from the mountains where Herakles himself was said to have killed the Erymanthian boar, but this was once the region's metropolis. The Hellanodikai here were chosen by lot from within the oligarchy, their names scratched onto *ostraka* – broken pottery sherds – and theirs was a serious task. Planning, overseeing athletes' training in Elis – themselves training for ten months to do so – officiating at religious ceremonies in the sanctuary. The Hellanodikai kept the Games legal, clean and sacred. They dressed in purple robes to mark out their kingly status; once the Games started they would preside as judges, and award prizes, sitting opposite the only woman officially allowed to witness the contests, the High Priestess of Demeter, who watched, enthroned, above an altar – the very marble blocks of which, rebuilt in the second century CE, are still in situ at the Olympic stadium, a prototype venue which would be copied across the Greek world.

For a place that is so peaceful today, with a remote pastoral stillness, Elis was a wildly busy city. The site at Elis is now being re-excavated and the new digs at the heart of the ancient settlement are revealing just how central the Hellanodikai were to the psyche of the city-state, and how central Elis was to Olympia. The judges' living quarters were right next to the marketplace, the agora. These taste-maker, standard-setting men assembled in a grand stoa that edged the agora's western side, and its footprint is still visible today, dusted with pine-needles. The purpose of the Olympic hopefuls' time in Elis, overseen by the Hellanodikai, was to fine-tune their already finely honed bodies, and to find out their ranking in the contests to come.

Many aristocrats in the Ancient Greek world regularly spent eight hours a day in the gym. Doctors actively prescribed exercise as a cure for mental and physical health challenges. Greek men were thought to be *kalos k'agathos* – beautiful of body and therefore noble, beautiful of mind. Beauty and physical strength were indeed a gift of the gods. The Greek body in some ways 'belonged' to the gods; ritualised physical effort was an act of worship. When athletes such as the unarmed-combat-sport hero, the *pankratiast*, Timanthes, lost form back at home (in Cleonae, a town on the road to Corinth), unable to string his bow, he killed himself, immolating his body on a pyre.[7] The training at Elis was overseen by *gymnasts*, who drew up the individual programmes; a *paidotribes*, who supervised; and an *aleiptes* or masseur. A three-pronged coaching team. The days the athletes spent at Elis were hyper-intensive.

There is new evidence from Elis, from the latest digs at the time of writing in 2022, of pop-up altars to Zeus in the Hellanodikai's stoa, with shrines and sanctuaries around the agora: because whatever the political, economic and diplomatic spin-off of the Games, at their heart these were superstitious proceedings which aimed to tap into the cosmic power of a god-inhabited universe, and of the ultimate of all Greek gods, Zeus, whose name derives from the proto-Indo-European *Diei*, meaning 'sky' or 'shining' – giving the Western world the words *deus* or god, and deities – godly things.[8]

And unlike the many thousands of local versions of the Olympian gods and goddesses worshipped by the Greeks, not to mention a myriad of nymphs and dryads and assorted spirits, the Zeus at Olympia, Zeus Olympios, was thought to belong to each and every Greek citizen.

After about a month of intensive training in gymnasia (recently identified in further detail after ground-scanning investigation and waiting to be fully excavated), it was time for the sublime Olympic jamboree to leave Elis for Olympia itself. A rut-road (the ruts 53–57 inches apart, 3–4 deep and 8–9 wide) winds its way inland through the Peloponnese from the sacred territory of Elis to the Olympic sanctuary. The holy highway runs through a bosky landscape which in its day would have been thick with holm oaks, myrtle and oleander, all of which still grow there.[9]

These woodlands are a home to eagles, who softly surprise as they glide close from low branches. The birds would have been there in antiquity too, augurs of victory, thought to be Zeus's messengers and sometimes the god himself in avian form. It was even by then an ancient tradition: King Khufu, you will recall, appeared regularly, in the Egyptian mind, as Horus in the form of a falcon. The Greek god's spirit must have seemed to be luring the Olympic caravan to his home. Over two days the participants (athletes and project-management officials from Elis) stopped to purify themselves at the Piera spring – still flowing in the village of Aghios Ilias under an old oak tree. Here at the spring, clogged with plastic bottles today, they made sacrifices, and then continued on across flat floodplains towards the sea, crossing the River Alepheios, Zeus's favourite river, along the old road to what is now the city of Kalamata – cheered on, one has to imagine, by local crowds and well-wishers. Finally they arrived into Olympia via their finely paved processional route, the Sacred Way. From c. 456 BCE, the Temple of Zeus, the greatest building on site, would have loomed on the skyline.

If Elis was the Olympic village, Olympia was a pilgrim's destination, a monastic complex cum mosh-pit. The central sacred space here was originally called simply *Altis* – the Grove, an area still soft with wild olive and oak and poplar and plane trees. Fertile from the waters where the River Alpheios meets its tributary, the Kladeos, the Altis has a unique and animistic feel. The ground here is moist and mossy. Mosquitoes sneak onto your skin at the wrong time of day. Zeus, the god of the sky, and of the waters that came from the sky to feed the earth, would have approved of the dewy fertility here. The famous Athenian speech-writer, Lysias (who would have been a young man as the Statue of Zeus was being built), in his *Olympic Oration* described the sanctuary as 'one of the most beautiful places in Greece'.[10] From numerous classical sources we hear there was an ancient olive tree, from which the victorious athletes' wreaths were cut – quite possibly, itself an object of worship in a time before history.[11] These centuries-old plants (which can live for over 2,500 years; it is remarkable to think of the history they have survived) still command the roof canopy – reaching high above the younger trees around them, and visible at quite a distance. Herakles was credited with introducing olives to the sanctuary,[12] and fascinatingly, recent study has shown that it was indeed around 900–800 BCE that walnuts and olives appeared in the Peloponnese – a time contemporary with the generation of a number of heroic myths.[13]

As pilgrims began to head down into the valley, they would have heard the birdsong from Olympia's woods. And then they would have felt the flies on their faces, and then they would have smelt the odour of shit. This was the excreta of mass crowds. Anywhere between 50,000 and 100,000 together in a space that feels busy when just 5,000 visitors come today. Greeks and their households drawn together from tiny islands and major cities from all points of the compass. Mainly men – eating, drinking, making love, working out, dragging in reluctant animal after animal, from doves, to rams, to goats, to bulls, all to be sacrificed. I have attended festivals in India where goats and buffalo are still sacrificed in huge numbers by pilgrims; the earth and stones run sticky with blood and the air is filled with bleating.[14] It was said that even one of the founding fathers of the Games himself, the hero Herakles, was bothered by the flies here, and called on his divine father Zeus to help to banish them – hence Zeus's epithet at Olympia, *Apomuios*, 'Averter of Flies'.[15] A wish wished rather than granted – the flies remained perennially notorious. Even if visitors managed to brush these irritants off their limbs and faces, they would have rested, horrifically, undetected, on teeth and nails.

Buried for centuries under landslides and the flood sands from the Rivers Alpheios and Kladeos, with more sections being discovered every excavating season, this was not a settlement, but a super-sanctuary with multiple extensions. And it was undeniably Zeus's stamping ground. Olympia takes its very name from Zeus's palatial mountain home to the north and east, Mount Olympus – at 9570 feet, the highest peak in Greece. Olympian Zeus's cult was lovingly tended all year round here at Olympia. His great altar was smeared with ash from the sanctuary of Hestia, his sister, on the 19th day of Elephebolion (the end of March); and every month, precious incense from the south (which would have started life teased out of frankincense trees in the rocky deserts of modern-day Yemen and Oman, and been traded up through Arabia, across the Red Sea, and on into Egypt and the Levant) was burnt on altars around the temple – sixty-nine of them at one point – to please the god-king. The Games here were meant to incarnate justice, and Zeus, represented as strict, stern, but fair in his great wonder-Statue, was being projected as a divine father, in harmony with the cosmic order, a dispenser of the Greek notion of justice, *DIKE*. *DIKE* was evolving at this time – a word that originally derived from the Babylonian for 'finger' (think of our index finger or the decimal system), and is used in the word *iu-dex*, a judge who could point out the right way. But by the fifth century BCE, *DIKE* was being understood as a portion of justice meted out individually, the exciting notion that individual men had the capacity to be just. The king of the gods was central to the ethics and the identity, as well as the founding narrative, of this Wonder-site.

And from the fifth century BCE onwards it would have been impossible to miss the godfather of Olympia. Now, a single, recently re-erected column is all that is prominently left of Zeus's great temple. But originally this would have been a fierce beauty. Today tourists pick their way through the ruins, past tumbled column drums like cut swiss rolls and weeds growing in the marble flagstones. The inner limestone of the temple is exposed, harvested from a local quarry on the River Alpheios's banks near Louvro village (the overgrown, pine-tree-shaded quarry only recently discovered, a winding 10-mile path away from Olympia itself), the soft-rock romantically thick with fossilised sea-shells, themselves dating back over 35 million years – like the fossilised sea that is found in the bedrock of the Great Pyramid.[16]

This was a stone visibly thrumming with nature.* But in its heyday the conglomerate shell-rich core of the architecture would have been masked with polished and painted gypsum-plaster – a stucco made from marble-powder – to resemble expensive, imported marble, and would have appeared simply splendid, one of the finest ever examples of the stolid might that is Doric architecture. Designed, the sources tell us, by the architect Libon of Elis, paid for by the city with the spoils of war, the Temple of Zeus took over fifteen years to raise and was finally completed in 456 BCE.[17]

This was a new home for the god, moving a few yards away from Zeus's original, strange shrine at Olympia – not a wooden or stone temple, but a congealed mound of ash deposited by the burning of centuries' worth of animal sacrifices to the deity, just under the shadow of Mount Kronion. Many of the visitors to Olympia would have made their own mini sacrifices on this steaming mound. Recent research has identified animal remains – sheep, goats, oxen and pigs. Deep in wells here, the heads of bulls have been found, their skulls smashed by a spear-strike. Animals must have been brought in from local markets or from Olympia's own estates. Each one had to be inspected to check it was the right age, gender, colour – and was unblemished. So many were dragged in, having been first purified in the waters of the River Alpheios. (The over-kill was so great here, a rumour circulated in antiquity that the muck from the victims' dung travelled in a submarine channel all the way to Sicily.) But the greatest gift of all here at Olympia, followed by an almighty feast for the Olympic faithful, was the Hecatomb, the sacrifice of 100 bulls – supplied by the Eleans – slaughtered for the mighty god Zeus, next to his Wonder-filled temple-home.[18]

Dark, muddy, gelatinous with bone and fat, and held together as a kind of ash cement when mixed with water from the Alpheios River, the original Zeus mound was a reminder of the prehistoric roots of Greek religion. This monument to blood and death (and to rebirth, since the choicest entrails, bones and fat-cuts were offered to Zeus while the rest

---

* Appropriate, given that Zeus was the god of fertility and life as well as of thunderbolts and lightning.

was eaten to sustain life) was matched, like a negative print of a photo, by a nearby sacrifice pit, where a black ram was slaughtered, its blood and entrails offered to the hero Pelops – buried, you will remember, in another tumulus mound within the sanctuary. And the organic, carnal shrine gives us the earliest evidence of Zeus's belligerent worship at Olympia. Over 6,000 offerings – figurines of the warrior-god Zeus, mortal warriors, chariots and charioteers, as well as images of bulls and horses – have all been retrieved from the remains of this pile of bone and ash. Analysis of the remains shows there was continuous combustion from the late eleventh to the early sixth century BCE, when the altar was shifted a little, but the sacrificial mound was never decommissioned. The accretions of old sacrifice – bone, fat and skin – here were so solid, a stairway could be carved into them. From around 700 BCE, the offerings ardently donated were personal possessions, including bronze tripods which would have supported massive cauldrons. The scale of these cauldrons and their costly three-legged stands – attached or welded on – proved you could afford to cook serious amounts of meat for those loyal to you. Weapons and tools of war were left here too, even life-size bronze sculptures.

The new temple – and then its *pièce de resistance*, our fourth Wonder, the Statue within – would have felt like a fresh start in a sanctuary which, up until the sixth century, must have seemed a little like a hotch-potch holy hotel for Greece's most powerful deities. Because, like its key role-model the great Temple of Artemis at Ephesus, the Temple of Zeus at Olympia was in every way a statement building. Painted in fairground-bright colours throughout, the roof was fringed with 100 lion-heads, spouting rainwater in the wet season, all made of the finest marble from the island of Paros, just as Parian marble was used in Ephesus. A straggle of these lion-heads can still be seen abandoned in the tall grasses of the site today. The roof tiles themselves – also of marble – were cut so very thinly they acted like glass, so an alabaster light, soft and creamy, would have poured into the interior. Drawing inspiration again directly from the Temple of Artemis at Ephesus, the temple was raised up on a platform 10 feet high and its outer colonnade boasted six columns front and back, and thirteen down each side, matching the height (34 feet) of those of Athens' great Parthenon exactly. This was the biggest religious building in the Peloponnese. It was only a fraction smaller than the Parthenon; because the Athenians' premier monument, completed in 432 BCE, extended its footprint deliberately in order to worst Olympia's best efforts.[19]

I have been lucky enough to investigate beyond the ropes here. Gaining access to the interior of Zeus's home at Olympia allows one to appreciate the dramatic gradient of the temple's entrance steps; they encourage a stately, imposing advance into the inner sanctum. The design of the building's entrance was partly to ensure emotional and visual impact, but there was a practical purpose too, because the land on the site of Olympia slopes fairly steeply down to the banks of the River Alpheios (ancient architects had the same engineering headaches as their modern equivalents), meaning the Altis was on a tricky angle.

On the east pediment of this doggedly muscular Doric construction was a vigorous scene of that homicidal chariot race between Pelops and Oenomaus, overseen by Zeus and anxious-looking seers. On the west pediment, with rational Apollo surveying, was the battle between Lapiths and Centaurs in Thessaly, the Centaurs abusing Lapith women and attempting to rape them. Greek heroes in the furious fray are being bitten and kicked. Attacks on Amazons were also celebrated above the temple doors. The labours – or rather contests, from the Greek word *athloi*, which gives us our word athletes today – of Herakles hectically decorated either end inside the porches. The appetitive hero Theseus was immortalised too.[20] While the Temple of Zeus might have followed the design of the Temple of Artemis in Ephesus, in its treatment of women it certainly did not mimic its spirit.[21]

The interior of the Temple of Olympian Zeus also anticipated the giant billboards celebrating today's athletes and heroes in sports stadiums. The temple had its own painted panels lauding athletic, heroic, splendid physical specimens.

Then twenty years later, into this pumped-up setting, came the giant Statue of the god himself. Because of course, in a place where men were attempting to become god-like, the ultimate god took the form of the ultimate man.

Measuring the size of a three-storey home (41 feet, on his pedestal rising over 44 feet tall), and yet seated, crouching, with his head skimming the ceiling, like Alice in Wonderland after taking her Drink Me spiked potion, the godhead must have seemed extraordinarily intimidating. It was said that if he stood up, this Olympian Zeus would 'unroof' his temple-home.

Every age is a Golden Age for those who have the gold. Using around a ton of the metal, and a similar weight of ivory, Zeus's Statue in Olympia, in the spirit of competition, was made of the most precious and expensive materials available at a time when Greek city-states were expanding their territorial reach – with colonies in southern Italy, Anatolia and North Africa. With a glistening skin of hippopotamus ivory, this glowering Zeus was decorated with precious stones, polished bone and ebony.[22] Glass lilies were set, and animals were carved into Zeus's robe. Mythological scenes were depicted on his gilded throne; his massive head was crowned with golden olive shoots. Every detail must have been ardently worked over. In Zeus's left hand was a multi-metal sceptre, the perch of a glaring eagle; and in his right, a statue of Nike – the winged goddess of victory – itself over 6-and-a-half-feet tall. Nike was a mini-me of Zeus, also chryselephantine (overlaid with gold and ivory), also crowned with a wreath made of olive shoots. Coins from Olympia were struck with Nike's image too – not, as is often erroneously imagined, representing victory in athletic contests, but victory in war.

Zeus's hair curled onto his shoulders (the heft of two heavy locks hinting this hair was also made of gold), and his ivory skin was dressed in perfumed oil to counter the damp of the Altis plain – oil which then dripped off and formed a pool in a rectangular, dark-limestone basin rimmed with Pentelic marble, so that the domineering deity, in this oil-slick reflection, became twice the god he already was.

With a marble base from the quarries at Eleusis near Athens (21 feet wide, 32 feet deep – the ghost of which is still just visible on the temple floor – and standing over 3 feet tall), the decoration scheme of the throne, as with the temple itself, was not comforting: six images of conquering Nike sinewed up the throne legs; the arms of the seat were formed by the body of a sobering Sphinx (the Sphinx at Greek Thebes ate young boys); on the struts was represented the dash for Herakles to seize the girdle of the Amazon queen (slaughtering Amazonian women as he went); and on the sides, a chilling display of the twin deities Artemis and Apollo, hunting down Niobe, the sister of Pelops, and her children for daring to claim that she was more fertile than their mother Leto. Zeus's feet were perched on a stool formed by rampant lions, and again an Amazonomachy, a battle against Amazonian women, decorated the footstool's front. The message was clear: Olympia and its Holy of Holies were, in every sense, somewhere that weakness was abhorred, for in Zeus's domain, there were only winners and losers.

A special staircase was constructed within the Temple of Zeus to allow access to Zeus's head. A chance to immerse yourself in the monstrous possibilities of mankind, of the possibilities of (male) minds and (male) bodies. Imagine that mature, vital, virile power, the luscious beard signifying that Zeus was a fully grown patriarch, more potent than those erotic, downy-chinned, sweet-lipped young gods such as Apollo or Hermes.

Zeus was designed by the Athenian sculptor Pheidias, the creative *enfant terrible* of his day who had already made not only those ferocious Amazons at Ephesus but also two giant Athenas for Athens: the Athena Promachos, with a gleaming spear and helmet, which could be seen reflecting the sun as sailors approached the city's port at Piraeus; and, freestanding, concealed within the Parthenon, the Athena Parthenos. Olympia's monumental Zeus, the future Wonder of the World, was Pheidias' last great work and would indeed be the artist's crowning glory. Everything about the colossal Statue aimed to prove Olympia's superiority: this Zeus was taller than the Athena on the Acropolis, the Nike bigger than Athens' Nike. Pheidias could well have seen a sitting Zeus decorating the rich Treasury of the Siphnians at the sacred site of Delphi, and rendered that idea here at Olympia in 3D. Athens dedicated their Athena in 438 BCE; so, the Eleans adapted their Temple of Zeus to accommodate a sculpture that would be even more gob-smacking. The construction of the Statue would have taken around five years, probably between 438 and 430 BCE – awls, adzes, rock-drills, specialist saws, all breaking Olympia's peace with their sound. It continued through the seasons: early spring, when the air is saturated with humidity and the sound of birdsong; across late summer, when the stadium's edges were spotted with daisies, red anemones and wild irises; into autumns when purple Michaelmas daisies covered the slopes; and through winters where the doused, brumal surroundings sparkle the valley with frost.

Inside this Father of all Zeuses was a timber frame holding a wooden skeleton, onto which the hippopotamus ivory – which, up close, seems to live, with its own veins and twisting, repeating internal cells – was carved and shaped and smoothed, so that no joints were visible. Recent research by one scholar, Kenneth Lapatin, has shown that the sheets of ivory were almost certainly soaked in vinegar to make them malleable.

The level of skill required to achieve this is still breath-taking, and it was appreciated by the ancients too, who described the petrifying potency of the godhead – modelled, it was said, on the canonical poetry of Homer in Book One of his *Iliad*. Zeus in this popular passage is described as being so replete with strength, a mere frown from his broad brow can rock Mount Olympus itself.[23] The Zeus Statue was an awe-inspiring collision of art and engineering, emphasising the Greeks' growing ambition to be not parochial, but international, to be world-beating and relevant to the known world.[24]

Materials were brought in for both the Statue and the temple on rafts along the Alpheios River, still navigable today. Additional supplies would have come in from the port of Pheia – that marble from Paros, hippopotami tusks from Egypt, mood-lifting incense from Arabia. Destroyed by a violent tsunami around 551 CE with waves 60–65 feet high, Pheia doubtless possesses other clues that will eventually emerge from the seabed. The whole project was a massive engineering challenge. Pausanias reported four columns supporting the throne – perhaps as a buttress to its massive weight. And of course, there was the highly skilled, but somewhat more quotidian, question of maintenance and health and safety. In a marshy area, where subsidence and staining from the moist air were a problem, the 'burnishers' of the Statue – said to be descendants of Pheidias himself – were given the full-time job of maintaining the god, right down to the Roman period.

And the sponsor of this Wonder? Truth be told, for both the Statue and the temple, funding must have been mosaiced together. It would have been politically convenient and impressive to say it all derived from the spoils of a single war, but the latest archaeological investigations suggest the bill would simply have been too high. Regional spend, philanthropy, income from Olympia's own estates probably provided the bulk of funding.[25] Thrillingly, Pheidias' own workshop was identified in 1958 on the site of Olympia – just a stone's throw from the position of the great Statue, which sat at the western end of the temple.[26] The identification was helped by the discovery of tiny chips of the very materials the sculptor used – hippo and elephant ivory, rhinoceros horn – all brought to Greece from Africa, probably via Egypt. Here too was water-buffalo bone, pigs' teeth, amber, chalk, gypsum, quartz, shards of paint and pigment, ancient glass and a recently identified erotic graffito currently being investigated.*²⁷ Even the artisans' bronze tools were in situ – chisels, terracotta moulds for the gilding and gold decorations (dumped together as refuse) – and, satisfyingly, the base of a black painted jug or pot, inscribed 'PHEIDIO EIMI' - 'property of Pheidias'.²⁸ Clearly not shy about coming forward, it was also said that he had himself commemorated in an inscription below Zeus's feet that read, 'The Athenian Pheidias, the son of Charmides, made me.'²⁹

The original workshop-building has exactly the same orientation and heavy-set design as the temple, presumably so the master craftsman could try out lighting states and interior effects. It was converted into a Byzantine church sometime between 435 and 451 CE, and graced with anachronistic crosses. I have been fortunate enough to walk through the workshop space during its restoration. Now daisies and grasses grow where once there was a hive of activity. Tortoises and kittens lie peacefully in warm corners. Pheidias was in his fifties when he started his work at Olympia, and we know he returned to Athens in around 432 BCE (where it was said he was murdered by his political opponents), so it makes sense that we are looking at a four- or five-year project. As the sound of creation clanged out of the workshop, and preparations were made within the temple itself, the sense of expectation on the site must have been palpable.³⁰

The maestro worked, it seems, supported by friends and allies. Panaenus, described by some sources as a brother, by others as an artistic cousin (Panaenus had already depicted the Battle of Marathon in the masterpiece that was the Painted Stoa in Athens, through which Stoic philosophers walked, giving us our word stoicism), decorated movable screens to conceal and protect the Statue, each commemorating the 'all-time greats' of Greek mythology in the temple's interior. A more mysterious figure, the beloved Pantarkes, was a boy from Elis who won at wrestling in the eighty-sixth Olympiad (436 BCE) and who also appears to have been involved. Pantarkes' name, it was said, was inscribed on Zeus's finger – 'Pantarkes is beautiful' – and Pheidias' (apparent) crush was featured placing a ribbon of victory in his own hair in one of the struts of Zeus's throne.

---

* From the mid-fifth century BCE onwards, there is evidence of the production of other bronze and chryselephantine artworks in neighbouring buildings. We can imagine the Statue of Zeus sparking a copycat trend, the very wealthiest wanting to sponsor statues on the site that recalled and resembled the giant Olympian Wonder.

Tip-toeing my way carefully around the remains of the great temple today, past the top-quality mosaic depicting the semi-divine mermenkings, the Tritons (another copycat detail of the Temple at Ephesus), who decorated the entrance floor of the pronaos from the Hellenistic period onwards, immediately the pull and power of the sea within the building is present. Moving carefully on through spaces that once held those giant painted frames, the scale and sheer solidity of the building still overawe. To have an anthropomorphic figure dominate all this must have been quite remarkable. Zeus would have faced the rising sun in the morning, as it shafted its way through the open doorway. Then, just before twilight, Apollo's chariot, pulling that ball of flame, the solar orb, would have set directly behind Olympia's giant monster-man.

As with so much of the activity at Olympia, the creation of this anthropomorphic Wonder was all about striving and competing, about rencontre and conflict. In Greek society at this time, poets, playwrights and politicians were all in contention – artists and sculptors too. Those who won out were celebrated. Just think of how the Parthenon in Athens physically measured itself up against Olympia's temple. The home for the Wonder itself, the great Temple of Zeus, was partly paid for from the spoils of war against Pisa; another 26-foot-tall bronze statue of Zeus in the sanctuary was funded by booty from a conflict with Arkadia. The painted screens shielding the Wonder and preventing access under the throne commemorated the recent, key battles of Salamis and Marathon. The rooms of the Olympia Archaeological Museum are thick with the weapons that were once offered here: shields, helmets, greaves, spears, arrow-heads, daggers, breastplates – only a minute proportion are on display while the store-rooms heave with shelf after stacked shelf of metal.* This is indeed the world's largest collection of bronze objects – all dedicated by ancient pilgrims as thanks for success in conflict or in the hope of future victory. Speakers travelled to Olympia to deliver polemics of exclusive panhellenism, the notion of *homonoia*, apartheid-unity; the Sicilian orator,

---

* Warrior figurines are dedicated here from 900 BCE, the spoils of war from the late eighth century. The earliest dedications to Zeus are on a bronze greave (Olympia B67 in the museum's catalogue reference) from the seventh century, and possibly an Italian buckle (Olympia BE 656) from the eighth – so far the earliest evidence we have for the worship of Zeus on the site.

Gorgias, declaimed a rousing polemic encouraging Greeks to focus their looting and raiding not against each other, but against 'barbarians' – in particular against Persia. It was at Olympia that Herodotus, the Father of History, originally from Asia Minor, chose to performatively read out his account of the Persian Wars:

> Here are presented the results of the enquiry carried out by Herodotus of Halikarnassos. The purpose is to prevent the traces of human events from being erased by time, and to preserve the fame of the important and remarkable achievements produced by both Greeks and non-Greeks; among the matters covered is, in particular, the cause of the hostilities between Greeks and non-Greeks.[31]

It was a rendition that was said to bring tears to the eyes of a young boy in the crowd, the father of scientific history, Thucydides.[32]

The Iron Age – when Olympia started to flourish – had been a time not just of increased dominion over nature but of total war. Bone evidence from between 900 and 500 BCE and across Greece shows shins smashed, collarbones broken, eye-sockets pierced with arrows. The sixth and fifth centuries had seen costly revolts along the Anatolian seaboard, and the fifth saw sustained warfare with Persia. Individuals were at Olympia to represent the firepower of their city-state, an overt tussle with their Greek neighbours, allies and enemies. Success came through *agwn* – struggle. The word as it first appears in Homer's *Iliad* meant simply a space in which to come together to compete, and rightly gives us our word agony.[33] The competitions in the Olympic Games – javelin and discus throwing, boxing, wrestling, running, horse and chariot races, a race in full armour – were all acutely punishing, and tacit training for full-scale warfare.

Wealthy men and city-councils paid huge sums to import statues (often war booty from other lands) and stumped up for improvements to the structure of the sanctuary at Olympia. Zeus's guidance and approbation for acts of institutional violence were also sought at the sanctuary itself where military divinations and prophecies were proclaimed by resident seers. The oracle was delivered at the top of the old altar of Zeus, as these seers interpreted cracks in the skins of sacrificed animals[34] and the curl of flames from the thigh-bones burnt at the very top of his conglomerate, congealed concrete of gore. Recent archaeology at Olympia substantiates, precisely, the description of this kind of oracular sacrifice in the *Iliad*,[35] known as empyromancy, where thigh-bones were de-fleshed, wrapped in fat, drenched in wine and then burned. The killing business done, the sacrifice was then followed by a massive feast, the meat from 100, sometimes up to 200 bulls being dispersed to the crowd. The advice delivered by seers practising empyromancy in the sanctuary of Zeus was then taken on into the battlefield. So we should also imagine Olympia as a seasonal war cabinet. If Zeus's oracle was vindicated, a tithe (a tenth) of all spoils were brought back to be dedicated to Olympian Zeus – another reason the site was so heaving with statuary and dedicated weaponry and armour.

As well as being founded on *agwn*, Olympia was all about *arete* – what we would translate as virile virtue – a very male kind of manliness; and about *kleos* too – the need to be heard of, to be spoken about. Here at the Olympia sanctuary, Zeus was being portrayed as Lord of all Contests, and the purpose of his Statue was to celebrate struggle, to witness success, and to burn an impression into the minds of all who visited – to be spoken of far and wide.

The riches and spoils of war within Zeus's temple would have gleamed out like a pirate's hoard. The shield of a soldier who had run from Marathon was displayed here; twinned statues of Hesiod and Homer; and the helmet of the triumphant Athenian General Miltiades rescued and now on show. Pausanias reports there were twenty-five blazing bronze shields dedicated by winners in the Hoplitodromia, an excruciating, punishing footrace where men ran naked except for their helmets, greaves and carrying their shields. Far-flung Greek communities – Gela and Syracuse in Sicily, Italian Sybaris, Byzantion, Chalcedon in Asia, Kyrene in Libya, Megara on the mainland *et al.* – had treasuries running almost parallel to Zeus's temple itself, leading up to the stadium, where wealth (some of it sham) was laid out to be wondered at, rather like an international expo where guests were allowed to touch, and marvel, but never to buy. The treasuries were shop-windows for rival powers. Post holes in the stadium confirm that precious loot from rival communities, shields in particular, were hung as trophies to awe crowds and spectators alike.[36] A gold bowl found at Olympia is inscribed in Corinthian letters, a dedication of the Kypselids from the late seventh century. This beautiful bowl is a rare find – Olympia was a site with a giant 'X marks the spot, treasure be here' sign on it, so was consistently looted across the centuries. If this had not been the case, the finds from Zeus's Olympian sanctuary would have been some of the very richest on earth.

The original stadium ended right at Zeus's altar – the athletes at Olympia were running to, and for, Zeus's effable and ineffable power. They were running to be lauded and to be awarded by the god in statue form. The festival here was a religious rite which, come the fifth century BCE, spanned a full week. And since the Greek year ran from one summer solstice to another (the month of Hekatombaion was loosely equivalent to our July), in some sense what happened at Olympia was the beginning and end of everything. The origin of the Games almost certainly stemmed from funerary rites which celebrated the cycle of life. These were very like those immortalised in Homer's *Iliad* – where boxers, wrestlers and equestrians were awarded prizes, horrifically for us, of enslaved people, as well as of livestock and luxury goods such as the bronze three-legged cauldrons which turn up across the Greek world in the eighth century and were found in huge concentration in Olympia.[37] Possession of these man-made goods and human slaves showed that, as a man, you had arrived.

Imagine you inhabit a world where you know that Zeus, the king of the gods, has given birth to all gods and all men. Imagine that mature, bearded, divine-male power now presiding over one of the most popular sanctuaries in the Greek world, and then imagine that you are an athlete, already the *übermensch* of your own village or city-state, and suddenly you have access to that divine power before competing in front of all who matter, everyone who you think counts. Boys were included too – because the races here were divided into age groups: twelve to seventeen or eighteen, and the over-eighteen categories. In front of another Zeus statue in the sanctuary, this time wielding his thunderbolt and standing before the Council House – Zeus Horkios (Zeus of the Oaths) – you swore that you were pure, that you had trained for ten months, and would bring no miasma to the sanctuary, ethical or physical. This was a once-in-a-lifetime opportunity. A sacrifice to Zeus sealed the deal. An occasion you would never forget; something you would always talk about.

The great god's name, and the impression the Statue left, would have been on the lips of many from antiquity – either eyewitnesses, or the audiences of travellers' tales, in Europe, Asia and the edges of Africa.

On day three of the Olympic contest, after the full moon, the Statue attracted even more concentrated focus, because a full twenty-four hours was reserved for the rites of Zeus himself.

A procession of athletes, *paidotribai* (the athletes' coaches), priests, and the Hellanodikai would convene at Olympia's committee room.[38] First came the competitors, then ambassadors, bearing gifts from their city-states, then those 100 oxen ready for the slaughter. The beasts would be garlanded with flowers and ribbons, their horns probably gilded, then their throats would be slit one by one, their thighs offered straight away to the all-seeing god. Other cuts were consumed in the committee room; one memorable historical detail is the tale of a member of the Pythag-orean vegetarian cult, on pilgrimage to Olympia, who offered a bull made of dough and decorated with herbs.[39]

The athletes arrived purified, stripping naked to prove to the god they had honed their bodies in his honour. Gymnastics takes its name from the Greek word *gumnos* (naked), and a large section of the gymnasium at Olympia has recently been uncovered. Here, typically couples would hang out to watch one another; there are numerous accounts of men exercising all morning and making love all afternoon. A swimming pool accessed by steps at either end was eventually provided to allow the athletes to cool off and wash. Much beautiful flesh would have been on show in the gymnasium. There were laws to prevent loitering and pandering. The sweat, oil and dust of the competitors was – literally – bottled and sold as a quack potion called *GLOIOS*. There were rub-downs with sea-sponges soaked in olive oil. The rites for Zeus seem to have been all about being uber-macho – in the true, Greek sense of the word – all about fighting, about male achievement (over-achievement?) and male love (over-love?) of all kinds. A kind of eroticised ambition with a capital E. Because the Greek godlet Eros, consort-son of the goddess of sexual love, Aphrodite, was thought to inspire desire, yearning, ravening of all kinds – including worsting and beating others, proving your prowess, proving you could win.

Ready for competition, the Olympic athletes cursed and hexed their fellow competitors (curse tablets have been found wishing rivals to be headless, heartless, hopeless), but if the athletes cheated they were them-selves displayed in a kind of hall of shame – their names emblazoned on a row of other statues of Zeus, known as the Zanes, close to the treas-uries – which declared to the inhabitants of heaven and earth that these contestants were now husks, disgraced individuals who deserved neither pity nor support. Humiliation was fiscal as well as reputational – if athletes were busted for bribing others, or having been bribed, not only were they fined, but a portion of that penalty income was used to erect those lines of bronze Zeuses. Then, as now, preparation for the Olympics was a highly expensive business, so this would have bankrupted participants. What went on here under the watchful gaze of that giant, gleaming, gimlet-eyed Zeus really mattered.

It is no coincidence that Olympia was also believed to be somewhere the mirror-world – the underworld – could be accessed: close to the hippodrome was said to be the very spot where Hades' pounding chariot, hitched to four black horses, disappeared through a chasm in the earth to his Greek hell.

And also then, as now, the Games took place at the hottest time of the year, the dogdays of summer: July or mid-August, whenever the second full moon rose after the summer solstice. This was harvest time – surely a reminder of the Games' connection to prehistoric fertility rites which tried to comprehend nature's life cycle. We can track the rise and fall in participation at the Games by the number of temporary wells sunk to meet the thirst of the crowds here. The wells start in noticeable numbers from 700 BCE, with a huge increase around the time the Statue of Zeus was being raised.[40] The greatest cause of death during the Games themselves was not heat exhaustion for the competitors, but heatstroke amongst the crowds. The ground-breaking philosopher and scientist, Thales of Miletus (from modern-day coastal Turkey, 40-odd miles down the coast from Ephesus), the first of the Seven Sages of Greece (note, again, the appearance of the number seven in ancient culture), was said to be a high-profile heatstroke victim when he visited the Games as a septuagenarian.

As well as the five days of sporting events, the chryselephantine Statue of the king of the Olympian gods would also have witnessed competitive partying. Half of the activities at Olympia were not sports, but other games: hymn-singing contests, philosophy riffs, all spiced up by evening parties and 'middle of the day marriages' which hundreds of prostitutes, male and female, would have been ready to serve. Feasting was de rigueur; very like a festival today, you could wander around to choose from food or drink stalls, or there were show-off gestures. In 416 BCE the

Athenian golden boy, aristocratic companion of the philosopher Socrates, Alcibiades, won first, second and fourth positions in the four-horse chariot race, and laid on roast oxen for all present. In terms of archaeology there have been more iron spits for roasting meat found in Olympia than anywhere else in the Mediterranean.[41] Again, the atmosphere of a post-sacrifice feast is brilliantly conjured up in the *Iliad*, and we should imagine the reality at Olympia mirroring Homer's poetry:

> . . . the feast laid out, they ate well
> and no man's hunger lacked a share of the banquet.
> When they had put aside desire for food and drink,
> the young men brimmed the mixing bowls with wine
> and tipping first drops for the god in every cup
> they poured full rounds for all. And all day long
> they appeased the god with song, raising a ringing hymn . . .[42]

There was a soundtrack too. As well as a distinctive trumpet called the salpinx (with a long, slim bronze horn, and often a fired-bone tip, an instrument which could also be heard at Ephesus) used as the starting signal, trumpeters met in a specially constructed building, where the sound of the horns echoed out seven times (that symbolic number again); at Olympia there were even official trumpet contests.[43]

Zeus's Peloponnesian home was also where you came to see the ancient world's celebrities. Heads of state, authors, artists and veterans all flocked here. This was where the globe-trotting general-historian Xenophon met Ephesus' chief eunuch priest, the *megabyzos* from the Temple of Artemis, and tried to arrange to retrieve some of the loot Xenophon had left in Artemis's sanctuary. Where Pythagoras displayed his golden thigh. Herodotus, the Father of History, shared his take on world history from the back porch of Zeus's temple.[44] In fact, many philosophers and sophists were here selling their wares. There was Gorgias, the philosopher and rhetorician from Sicily who came to speak to a crowd of 20,000; Themistocles, a 'man of the people' politician and a driving force behind the democratic ideal; and Plato too, the philosopher who described the kind of erotic passion and ambition that derived from joining together for festivals – plangently on display at Olympia. We should also imagine the ideas of Alcibiades' messmate and Plato's mentor, Socrates, being discussed in the sanctuary: exciting, radical ideas about human agency and potential. The chance, for the first time in history, to imagine the possibility of utilising your own mind to change the world. The chance for every common man to be a philosopher, a lover of wisdom. Olympia was a collective experience which, for the first time, lionised the possibility of the individual. There would have been hawkers and poets and orators reading out their latest works, singers singing, souvenirs and sex of all kinds on sale.

While I was writing this book, a clay fragment – the oldest extant written record of the verses of Homer's *Odyssey* from Greece, dating to the third century CE – was discovered in Olympia, inscribed onto a sherd of a tile, close to Zeus's temple. Was this a dedication to Zeus? A teaching-aid, lost in the press of the festival? A bit of tourist tat – a memento of a memorable visit, just as the visitors to Ephesus would take home models of Artemis's great Temple? From Book 14, the thirteen lines are a little mundane, describing the creation of a pigsty at Odysseus's home:

> This yard was built high, visible for miles,
> blocks of stones topped with thorn twigs of wild pear.[45]

So perhaps this was an athlete or trainer, or one of the thousands of visitors, simply trying out the art of writing in their spare time. In the fourth century BCE a high-class, high-end hostelry was sponsored opposite Zeus's temple to try to deal with the huge influx of crowds here – one can still walk through its ruins. Accommodation at Olympia remained a real issue, and most visitors slept on matting, in tents, or on the bare earth in what must have come to resemble a shanty town.

Tens of thousands came, many entirely to be seen. There was PR branding and sponsorship. When Alcibiades entered his seven chariots, tents for his team were donated by the city of Ephesus, food for twenty-eight horses by the island of Chios and supplies for entertainment and parties by their near-neighbour, Lesbos. When he won, the bon viveur supplied that roast-oxen feast for all the attendees – up to 50,000 of them. After Alcibiades had wiped the floor with his rivals, the award-winning Athenian playwright Euripides, no less, wrote Alcibiades' victory ode: 'Victory shines like a star, but yours eclipses all victories.'[46]

And men came here simply because they knew they would get an audience. In 153 CE a troubled individual, originally from the Hellespont region of Anatolia, Peregrinus Proteus, attacked the popular philanthropist Herodes Atticus (who had recently built a beautiful nymphaeum – a shrine for nymphs – for Olympia, and was also responsible for a grand theatre set into the Acropolis at Athens). The remains of the nymphaeum still stand, and one can imagine what a delight its flowing water would have proved in the low-lying sanctuary in that midsummer heat. A furious mob threatened to stone Peregrinus to death, and he was saved only by taking refuge inside Zeus's temple. Such a flagrantly provocative act makes one wonder whether Peregrinus (accused of parricide at a young age) had mental health issues. A decade later, he returned to Olympia, swearing he would kill himself 'like Herakles' by burning himself on a funeral pyre. He was true to his word, dying a few miles from the sanctuary itself. Peregrinus' sorry tale was recorded by Lucian of Samosata (who also visited Ephesus and described the statues there of Amazons leaning on their spears). Olympia was such a magnet for interest, news and tittle-tattle. It was where you came to make your mark, and as an author, historian or journalist, to collect the news of the moment.[47]

And what about the athletes who swarmed in to worship this Wonder Zeus with all their waking hours, with their sinews and their sweat?

The ultimate prize at Olympia was to be the winner of the stadion, the running race. Across Greek city-states, from the fourth century BCE onwards, it became custom to name the year itself after this victor – and since all Greek dates stemmed from the 'first' Olympics, a kind of ground zero of time in 776 BCE, this became, by definition, the winner's year. Olympia was the most prestigious of all the Panhellenic contests (Delphi, Isthmia and Nemea being the others). All athletes started at the eastern end of the stadium, facing and racing westwards – in other words, towards the god. Zeus stared out from his temple in the direction of the stadium, daring weakness. The smell and smoke of sacrifice would have poured into his sublime home. He would have witnessed the footfall of pilgrims crushing in, and after each race, the tang of triumph or of disappointment.

Passing the exquisite sculpture of Nike, winged Victory, by Paeonius, which still survives in the Olympia Museum, and whose wing-flexed power is still breath-taking, the sporting victors of the Olympic Games would have progressed to be crowned within the pronaos of the Temple of Zeus, as the god watched with his rock-crystal eyes, with sprig-crowns from the olive tree next to the sanctuary, said to have been planted by Herakles himself. Each victorious athlete was allowed to erect a bronze self-portrait statue in the sanctuary. One decree, insisting that these should be no more than life-size, suggests winners seized the opportunity to turn themselves into giants;[48] their success here meant they could become a little more like Zeus himself.

So far, we have only heard about the men who built, and worshipped, and competed in front of the ancient Greek mainland's Wonder.

Yet although famously billed as an all-male contest, women did in fact participate in the sporting contests at Zeus's renowned sanctuary[49]; and, as new archaeology is increasingly showing, goddesses as well as gods were worshipped here.

Indeed, the sanctuary at Olympia was originally sacred to female deities – in particular to deities of the earth: Rhea, Zeus's mother, who birthed the god in a cave in white-capped Mount Ida, that still lowers over central Crete; and Gaia, the god's grandmother, Mother Earth. The setting here is nourishingly, naturally fecund. A statue of the mother goddess, a matreon, was erected on a towering column at the end of the fifth century BCE. An altar to Artemis had already been raised in the sixth: in the fourth, a Doric temple, a metroon, to the mother goddess, too. Behind Zeus, on his throne, were six tall statues, each 6-and-a-half feet, of the three Charites and the three Horai, all Zeus's daughters and spirits of the seasons and fertility and the cycles of life. Aphrodite – the consort-mother of Eros – was honoured with an impressive temple at the starting point of the Games. Aphrodite's birth was inscribed under the feet of the Statue of Zeus. Demeter was present too, the goddess of harvest whose sanctuary on the Hill of Kronos was discovered only in 2006; and Eileithyia, the goddess of childbirth whose sanctuary only came to light in 2016. The sanctuary of Eileithyia and her son, called Sosipolis, was also open only to women. While maidens and matrons, their heads wrapped in a white veil, could attend the cult, burning incense and chanting, an elderly priestess alone was allowed access to the inner sanctum here, given the job of bringing in barley cakes and bathwater for Sosipolis the boy god.[50]

The other goddess prominently present, who would come to be framed in the Olympian pantheon as Zeus's wife – Hera – held sway here too in no uncertain terms. In fact, the holy of holies, the altar to Zeus – that odd, huge pile of ash and bone on a marble slab – was originally closer to the temple of Hera and her husband. Though initially made of wooden columns, the first stone temple built at Olympia may have possibly belonged to a female divinity of the harvest and was at the very least shared between Zeus and Hera. A tantalising, and striking, monumental head dating to the early sixth century and excavated here could be a sphinx, or a Medusa, or Hera herself.* The exquisite donations at the Heraion included a marble sculpture of Hermes (unearthed in 1877) holding baby Dionysos by the mega-star sculptor Praxiteles, whose work also adorned the Temple of Ephesus; a bronze of Zeus by Cleon from the northern Peloponnese; and a gold and ivory figure by Leochares, the sculptor-architect from Athens who would also help to build the Mausoleum of Halikarnassos, our fifth Wonder. Hera's cult endured, and seems to have been particularly strong in the fifth century BCE – at precisely the time the giant Zeus Statue was being built and enjoyed.[51] Was the Olympic sanctuary a place that started out to honour and nourish the competition we have with the rest of nature to survive, where female deities were prominent, and which evolved to become a place that honoured conflict between individual groups and individuals?

And just as goddesses have been written out of the story of the sanctuary, so women have been written out of the story of the Olympic Games. Because not just men, but women travelled here too, in the same configuration, from Elis along the Sacred Way, to marvel at the Olympian Zeus and to run in honour of Zeus's wife, Hera. Their foot races, which took place in their own festival, the Heraia (on a different year from the all-male Olympic Games more familiar to history, but possibly more frequently), were organised by a separate, all-female, sixteen-strong committee, also based at Elis.[52]

These sixteen, post-menopausal women, 'the oldest, most noble, and most esteemed of all', also wove a robe (possibly a veil) for Hera every four years.[53] Pausanias tells us that these women arranged theatrical ritual dances, and even acted as mediators between disputatious local towns.[54] The female athletes all had to be unmarried, and according to Pausanias, who visited the sanctuary, they ran with their hair flowing free, wearing

---

* Until more clues come out of the earth, we simply cannot confirm the identification.

a chiton, fastened just at the left shoulder, to the knee.[55] The winners were given wreaths of olive – stored on an ivory and gold table in Hera's temple, exactly as the wreaths for the men were – and a portion of a cow sacrificed to Hera. A ritual celebratory feast must have taken place. Niches on the columns of Hera's temple, still visible, may have been incised to display portraits of the winners.

We must never forget that an all-powerful, smiting Zeus was a late-comer to the Greek pantheon.

No men were allowed to participate in the all-women games – although the jury is out on whether or not they were allowed to spectate.[56] Bear in mind that if, on the other hand, married women turned up to the all-male games and were found anywhere within the sanctuary area north of the River Alpheios, they could be thrown from the nearby Mount Typhaion. And a cautionary tale was told about the Olympic site. The River Alpheios, manifested on the east pediment of Zeus's temple as a reclining figure, had begun life as a hunter, who developed a burning passion for a young nymph, Arethousa. Alpheios stalked Arethousa deep into the thick woods of the Peloponnese, but the goddess Artemis was so horrified by the idea that Arethousa's virginity might be spoiled, she turned the nymph into a stream which then wound its way under the sea towards the island of Ortygia near Syracuse, Sicily. In desperation the hunter turned himself into a river, the River Alpheios, and pursued Arethousa there. In another version of the story Alpheios hounded Artemis herself, who, mid-orgiastic celebration at a nocturnal gathering with her acolytes, smeared her face with mud to escape his advances. The message relayed by these unsettling myths was twofold: it made the point that Olympia was a place where virgins had to be protected, and that Artemis's power reached far from its Ephesian core.

Investigating the truth of Zeus's sanctuary, a re-analysis of the structures around the Wonder should also give us pause. Because across the site, a number of what were originally identified as ceremonial ramps, but now seem to be disability ramps, have been identified.

The games at Olympia would not just have been a celebration of an idealised body beautiful, but a recognition of the body traumatised. Just as the craftsmen who worked on these Wonders would have been sur-rounded by the gnawing debilitations of war – cities gutted by destruc-tion, collapse a more common experience than creation, men de-limbed,

burned; even Philip II, once fully sighted, died glass-eyed, with only one
eye intact[57] – so Greece was a land of the war-wounded. Sixty per cent of
180 individuals examined recently from Amphipolis in northern Greece
show osteoarthritic lesions.[58] Amputees, paraplegics, stroke victims, farmers crippled by repetitive work, the many thousands for whom a simple
eye-infection meant blindness were there too.

The wide slope that leads up into the very temple of Olympian Zeus
itself could, in fact, be a disability ramp.[59] Up until recently it has been
presumed that this was an entrance way for carriages – but the ramp
could too have been for those who were lame or in the wheelchairs that
we see represented on Greek pots. In the fourth century BCE in the Sanctuary of Asclepius (admittedly, a god of medicine), as many as eleven such
ramps have just been identified. Disabled Athenian veterans were given
pensions. Prosthetics had been in use since the time of Ancient Egypt.
And recent analysis by career surgeons of scenes on vases and Greek
reliefs, showing the treatment of war-wounds, makes it clear that the
understanding of the body and how to mend it was very highly tuned at
the time Zeus's temple was being raised.[60] Indeed, many who participated
in the violent Games at Olympia would themselves have suffered terribly,
especially from the contact sports there. As well as head injuries, breaks,
fractures, internal bleeding and seizures, we know some died. The grave
of a boxer from Alexandria, for instance, from the second century CE, has
recently been identified.[61] All this suggests that the differently abled were
not necessarily excluded from the sanctuary.

Disability was so present in the ancient world, it appears to have been
viewed not as a miasmic curse, but as an impairment that could be taken
on board.[62] Living in ancient society was all about being useful. Even if
those chosen to race naked were the least externally traumatised by war,
the spectators – possibly as many as 50,000 of them, don't forget – would
have been physically diverse.[63] The Statue of Zeus was completed at a
time when the issues of health were paramount in the minds of many. A
plague (a form of *Salmonella enterica*) had ripped through Athens from
430 to 428 BCE. Day by day more and more were dying, always crying
for water, their tongues bloodied, their skin breaking out in ulcers, their
lungs constricted. It typically took seven to ten days to die. Those who
survived were often left blinded or incontinent.[64] Contained in the city
by military command, one third of the population, around 60,000, was

eradicated. As the plague stalked the streets for two years, Thucydides tells us there was a slip in morals as people dealt with terrible afflictions, deformities to genitals, fingers, toes and eyes.[65] Pericles, the great general – a kind of Zeus of the streets – saw his two sons fall victim to the pandemic. He was fined,* and subsequently died himself, either of the pathogen or as a broken man.[66]

Olympia's god-Wonder was built at a time when few were complacent about the physical, natural and political challenges of life. The perfect, potent head and body of Zeus represented all the achievements of humanity but, in traumatic times, none of its challenges.

In short, what was happening here at Olympia related to older fertility and hunting cults, and to the role that women and others could play in early Greek communities, but the Zeus who was immortalised by Pheidias, and who was adored by so many during the Olympic Games in particular, was all about the works of man and the hyper-abled. From the complicated mechanical mechanism that released horses from their traps in the hippodrome, to the hysplex starting mechanism for foot races, the cult of Olympian Zeus was less to do with union with nature and the cosmos, with the world and the humans within it, and more about privileging and developing ways to trounce and to triumph over the world and its challenges, or over those in the world whom you chose to view as your competitors. It was all about ascendance.

The Sanctuary of Zeus is where the Greeks were performatively Greek, to those of all kinds whom they chose to view as outsiders. It stemmed from an age when, for the first time, after that invention of coined money by Croesus in Lydia, individual men had cash in their pockets and were economic actors. Now, to succeed, you could be not only a pharaoh, or a Babylonian king, not just a high priest or priestess, or an all-conquering general, but an individual with nous and heft. The Statue of Zeus was the incarnation not simply of a god, but of men who could become god-like in their actions.

*

---

* Pericles was fined by the Athenians, as Thucydides tells us, on charges of financial abuse – in reality, the Athenian people were angry about his mismanaged leadership during the plague and punished him for it. It is worth noting that Pericles remained in his position as a general. Then (as in recent times) disgraced leaders could have surprising staying power.

The reputation of the Zeus at Olympia didn't simply draw travellers in, it reeled out around the Eastern Mediterranean: in Cyrene in North Africa and at Siwa, Greeks had given the great god there the name Ammon, equating him both with their sun god Ammon and with the Olympian Zeus, and erecting a copy of the original Wonder-Statue in the Libyan desert. The base for this sculpture still exists in the sands of this magical, palm-protected oasis. An exaggerated figurine of an African man has very recently been discovered in a religious context in Elis – brought by an international trader, or perhaps by a visitor of African origin.[67] In Alexander the Great's commanding birthplace, at Pella in Macedon, in northern Greece, games replicating those at Olympia were mounted in honour of Zeus at Dion – only this time in the shadow of Mount Olympus itself. And when Alexander chose to have himself represented seated in the painting in Artemis's Temple at Ephesus, was he drawing a not so subtle parallel between himself and the Olympian king of the gods?

The Greek Seleucid King of Syria, Antiochus IV, who sacked the Temple of Solomon in Jerusalem (already sacked 350 years before by Nebuchadnezzar II of Babylon), ordered that Solomon's sanctuary should be renamed the Temple of Olympian Zeus and erected a statue of Zeus there, specifically to defile the place so sacred for the Jewish population.[68] In 167 BCE Antiochus snugged the back of the Olympian statue with a massive cloth dyed with Phoenician purple and woven with Assyrian patterns: quite possibly the 'temple veil' famously stolen from the Jewish people's centre of power.[69]

In the late summer of the same year, over six centuries after Olympia's Wonder was made, we are told by Livy that Lucius Aemilius Paulus, commander in chief of the Roman army, went on a tour of the great sights of Greece, culminating in Olympia, and visited Zeus's Statue, where he felt himself to be in the presence of the god, in person. This was a Wonder so monstrous, so impossible, it was believed to breathe. But in 146 BCE, when the Romans had taken over the Greek world after they sacked Corinth, twenty-one gilded bronze shields, trophies of victory gathered by the Roman general Lucius Mummius, were draped on the external walls of the temple – a triumphalist warning.

Pheidias' Statue – the most written about artwork in antiquity – came to be the ultimate representation of Zeus himself. The Olympian Zeus was replicated by the Roman Emperor Augustus, who also stole the idea of characters from Zeus's throne when he built a temple to Apollo on the Palatine back in Rome. In the State Hermitage Museum in St Petersburg, an entire hall, the 'Jupiter Room', was constructed in the nineteenth century to house a 11-foot-high Roman replica of Olympia's Zeus. Sculpted sometime between 69–96 CE, this marble giant, complete with gilded bronze, was excavated from Emperor Domitian's villa 12 miles from Rome near Lake Albano, Italy. Coins cast by Hadrian showed the emperor seated in the guise of the god. For Roman citizens, Zeus – the god they came to call Jupiter – was exactly the kind of masterful, virile, vanquishing deity Romans felt comfortable to promote and to adore.

Alexander the Great's coinage celebrating the Statue of Olympian Zeus and the ruler's connection to the god's power. The lion's mane headdress makes reference to Alexander's 'ancestor' the hero Herakles.

The Statue of Zeus at Olympia was a Wonder not just because of its conception and construction, but also thanks to its kudos. When Pheidias completed his work he asked for a sign from the god that the deity was pleased. Zeus responded, we are told by Pausanias, by striking the ground with a thunderbolt.[70] The evidence of this thunder-strike was eagerly shown to gullible visitors on Zeus's temple floor. Competitors travelled from one set of Games to another and victors were formally awarded jubilant home-comings – walls of cities were smashed open to allow their four-horse chariots of glory to enter. These Olympic heroes were immortalised in poetry and sculptures, given free meals for life and permanent tax-relief. The whole point of the Games in the king of the gods' sanctuary at Olympia was that its glory should be spread, heard and spoken of. In a word-of-mouth culture, the might of Olympia's lambent, towering Zeus, wreathed in clouds of incense, would have been ardently described. How could such a triumph of art and design not be a topic of conversation? It was a Wonder which became an icon in an instant.

Five hundred years after the completion of the extreme Zeus, when the Roman Emperor Caligula ordered the head of 'Jupiter' to be removed in 41 CE, so he could replace it with his own (eventually planning to transport the original to Rome), the god was said to have cackled with laughter, crumbling the scaffolding from under the feet of the lackeys instructed to decapitate him. Within days the emperor had been assassinated, dreaming of Zeus's wrath the night before his murder.[71] His successor Nero played it a little safer – painting an image of Zeus's head as Jupiter the Thunderer on the domed throne room of his palace (Domus Aurea). Nero, a great Hellenophile, bequeathed additional facilities at the Olympic sanctuary, a kind of athletes' club complete with swimming pool. Lovely Roman mosaics from the period, where tesserae dolphins splash about joyfully – are currently being excavated and restored. The Emperor Nero seems to have added to the gaiety of Olympia, but his hubris also risked the god's punishment when he turned up to Olympia to compete in 67 CE and, surprise, surprise, despite being thrown from his chariot, won all the races he entered.[72]

Olympia's Zeus was a Wonder too because it signified not just power, but, seated as it was, the power of potential. The potential of divine wrath, and the potential of the Olympic competitors to find the hero within themselves. Those who entered Zeus's temple would have stood or knelt, bowed, crawled or scraped, with the heart-stopping thought that one day, this divine wonder of the world might just stand up.

The extraordinary Statue of Zeus was demonstrably one of the greatest draws of the ancient world because Pausanias, that travel-writer extraordinaire, devotes seventy pages to conjuring up his visit to the sanctuary at Olympia – close on twice the space he allows for Delphi, considered the navel of the ancient world. The seated Zeus of Olympia was replicated on personal items – on carnelian intaglios held close inside clothes to keep their owner safe; on terracotta oil-lamps; even on other outsize statues – such as the giant, seated sculpture of the god of healing, Asclepius, at another wooded Peloponnesian sanctuary, Epidauros. World leaders, from Alexander the Great to Emperor Hadrian, chose to emblazon Olympia's

Zeus on coins which would be used for trade around the world. Pheidias' Zeus was popular, the Marvel superhero of his day.

But Zeus of Olympia, as it transpired, was not omnipotent. A passing reference in the work *Timon the Misanthrope* by Lucian of Samosata (that acute writer originally from Asia Minor, who definitely visited Olympia as well as Ephesus) suggests the sanctuary was plundered: 'they have laid hands on your very person at Olympia, my lord High-Thunderer, but you had insufficient energy to wake the dogs or to call in the neighbours; surely they would have come to your aid and caught the ne'er do wells before they had finished packing up their loot'.[73] And in 267 CE, an invasion from north Germany by the Heruli tribes – a people with roots in the Caucasus and Scandinavia – forced the inhabitants of Olympia to cannibalise the precinct so they could turn the great temple into a fortress, pulling down other buildings to establish a protecting wall around Zeus's sanctuary.[74]

The temple itself was also damaged by a serious earthquake at Olympia in 280 CE. The Olympic Games were banned by the Christian East Roman Emperor Theodosius I in 393 CE, and the site was ordered to be vandalised in 424 CE by his successor, Theodosius II. What religious extremism could not destroy, flame did, as a terrible fire ripped through the settlement during Theodosius' reign, probably in around 426 CE.

In 2007, in a ferocious wildfire in Olympia, sixty people tragically lost their lives and only a concerted effort from air and land contained the flames. This modern experience helps us to understand how devastating these fires would have been. A decade after the conflagration in 426, Pheidias' temple was turned into a church by the burgeoning Christian community at Olympia, with Zeus's temple itself being reconsecrated to the Christian God. The celebrations in honour of Zeus had taken place, unbroken, since 776 BCE – 1,169 festival years in total. There would have been a great deal to destroy and loot. By the time of the 269th Olympiad, the Altis alone boasted at least 3,000 bronze, wooden and stone statues and sculptures, left by victorious athletes and their grateful communities. Recent research confirms that earthquakes, followed by tsunamis, finally crashed down the monumental columns of Zeus's temple in that massive geo-seismic event that also flooded Olympia's port of Pheia.[75] Eventually covered in landslides from Mount Kronos and sand from the River Kladeos, the Olympic site was abandoned by the ninth century CE, and was only re-discovered in 1766, and the Temple of Zeus in 1830.

But the Statue of Zeus itself had fled the sanctuary long before the modern age, ending up in Constantinople at the end of late antiquity. Transported in the most careful and complex way – on boats with reinforced beams – the original, rather than a copy, was a great trophy for the Byzantine emperors, who ordered the acquisition of high-end antiques to decorate the centre of the city they styled a 'New Rome'. Along with the world-famous Aphrodite by Praxiteles from Knidos, and the statue of Hera from her massive sanctuary on Samos, ripping the body of the king of the gods from his sacred home, which pulsed with the cultic devotions of the pagan world, was a defining statement.

So we should try to imagine lugged-about Zeus in Constantinople, the city now commonly called Istanbul. Pheidias' Wonder seems to have been situated inside the display-estate of the eunuch-vizier Lausos, right in Constantinople's historic heart, where today pigeons are fed, lottery tokens and slush-puppies are sold close to the ancient hippodrome. Our source tells us the Olympian Zeus was displayed around 420 CE next to a cistern which provided drinking water and a veritable smorgasbord of statuary, including an Athena carved out of green stone, giraffes, tigresses and even unicorns[76]. Trying to envisage Zeus's location in central Istanbul, I was caught up in our own twenty-first-century plague, as Covid shut down the historic centre of the city. Streets once thrumming were eerily empty. But the city's abandonment allowed me to poke around a little, and there, behind a bus shelter, defined by a small, raised bed, could well be the Byzantine walls which last protected this gargantuan Wonder.

By the fifth century CE, Zeus of Olympia had probably shed most of his gilding – a gift for opportunists – as it was described by eyewitnesses not as glinting with gold, but as casting out the lustrous gleam of ivory. And that empty wooden interior left Pheidias' creation vulnerable. In around 476 CE, Olympia's Wonder was destroyed by flame: a terrible city fire that spread out from Constantinople's copper market close by in the ancient bazaar. The destruction was immense, wiping out the art-collecting eunuch's palace and contents. Even if Zeus had, by some miracle, survived that conflagration, riots and incendiary terrorism in 532 CE would have sealed his fate. The statue that had been honoured with an ashen mound for over 1,000 years had become just that, burned to ash.[77]

But Zeus was not forgotten. It seems that the artists of Constantinople were inspired by the god's thundering face, and so in the newly Christian city, Zeus became Christ. Motivated by the Ancient Greeks' notion of their ultimate, divine king, Christ *Pantokrator* or 'Ruler of All' appeared in similar guises to Olympian Zeus in mosaics and frescoes, seated on a throne, or simply glowering. As John of Damascus writes in the early eighth century, 'he divided the hair into a parting so that his face would not be hidden. For this was the way the Greeks painted Zeus'.*[78] And this indeed would be how Jesus Christ, the God-King, would be imagined for centuries to come. In fact, he still stares down today, a one-minute walk across the hippodrome from where the Zeus statue was possibly last seen, in the fine, golden mosaics of the Hagia Sophia – the church built by Emperor Justinian and Empress Theodora which, rumour had it, also preserved columns from another Wonder, the Temple of Artemis at Ephesus.

Fifteen hundred years later, and over 5,000 miles away in the United States of America, the memorial of Abraham Lincoln was produced in Washington. Here the president was portrayed sitting, poised, potent, as Olympia's Zeus had been, bearded and frowning, just waiting to rise up and change the world with his manly actions.

The word 'idea' is first delivered to us via a poet from Thebes called Pindar – who, beautifully, describes a competitor in the Olympic Games of 474 BCE as being *ideai kalos* – a beautiful boy, beautiful in form.

> And I praise the lovely son of Archestratos
> Whom I saw at that time
> Beside the Olympic altar
> Winning victory with the valour of his hands
> Beautiful in form [*ideai kalos*].
>
> OLYMPIC ODE 10, LINES 100–104

So a real, beautiful, physical thing at Olympia, a thing that was seen, a beautiful boy, unleashed an unfeasibly potent phenomenon – ἰδέα, 'idea'.

---

* Although it was said that the first man to paint Jesus in this way in the fifth century CE found his arm withered as a result of tangling with the pagan world, fortunately his disfigurement was healed, miraculously, by the Archbishop of Constantinople, Gennadius.

Thanks to Plato, the word 'idea' then became an abstract description of a perfect thing: a perfect king; a perfect mathematical equation; a perfect relationship. That ideal of the real could, Plato argued, then be realised and made manifest through the power of human thought to change reality. Thus a young worshipper of the Olympian Zeus unwittingly generated the word 'idea' as an abstract notion. Zeus's Olympic Games were an incarnation of human agency. This Wonder was part of an intellectual revolution, the notion (ironically) that women and men were no longer mere pawns of the gods, or of nature, or of mortal potentates, but rather the power of their minds, of their deeds and words, could change the world. They could be the authors of their own destinies.

The Wonder of the Olympian Zeus perpetuated its own tenacious idea: the power of contest, that virility and divinity could be one. The artwork also embodied the potency of human wit and will, and the belief that if we put our minds to it, we can achieve anything. While our first Wonder, the Great Pyramid, was built for a single man and involved the subjection of hundreds of thousands, the Zeus at Olympia encouraged the empowerment of the individual at a mass event. It was the embodiment of ambition.

In the sanctuary at Olympia, in 338 BCE, a beautiful chryselephantine statue of the Macedonian hero Alexander the Great – plagiarising many of the materials used for the Zeus Statue – was constructed alongside images of Alexander's father Philip II, Alexander's mother Olympias, and Alexander's paternal grandparents. The work was done by the artist Leochares (whom we will soon meet again at the Wonder in Halikarnassos). The gold and ivory used were an indication of the mortal family's divinity, their placements a nod of homage to Pheidias' great Statue. Dedicated to Zeus by Philip II in thanks for victory at the Battle of Chaeronea, in which the Macedonian dynasty defeated other Greeks and took charge of the Greek world, the building, sections of which are still standing, was then completed by Philip's vaulting son and heir. Alexander chose to decorate the Philippeion's roof with a giant marble poppy – a nod perhaps to his own delight in poppy juice and its effects. This construction in Zeus's Olympic sanctuary was Alexander's family laying claim to their divinity and potency and to the fact that their ancestor, Alexander I, a Macedonian, asserted his Greek descent through his ancestor Herakles (no less), and so had been allowed to participate in a sprinting race at the Olympic Games – as a Greek, not as a northern barbarian (*Makedones* means 'highlanders'). For Alexander the Great's family it had been a suppurating wellspring of shame that Alexander I's name had been eradicated from the victors' list. Alexander's father Philip II would not allow this at Olympia, so he constructed his Philippeion – a temple to his own power (its tholos or small-mountain shape was another sign of divinity), filled with a glimmering *tableau vivant*. Recently restored, today the Philippeion is one of the few buildings in the Olympic sanctuary that stands proud. It is no coincidence that, when Alexander was born on 20 July 356 BCE, the night the Temple of Artemis was burnt down by Herostratus, we are told that the announcement was sent to the king along with other, equally good news, that his team of horses had won at Olympia.*

A visit to Olympia was both the most visceral of experiences and a visit to an idea, to a touchstone of myth and meaning. I travelled to Olympia, on the very day the ancient site was being locked down as a result of the first outbreak of Covid-19 in March 2020, and once again, the day before a national quarantine, in the autumn of that year. In a strange echo of the past, this remote region of Greece was being hit hardest because of the number of travellers who still beat a path to one of the Seven Wonders of the World. The Korean, Japanese, Chinese, Canadian and Croatian visitors (many having arrived by cruise ship to the Bay of Katokalo, the site of Olympia's old port) whom I passed at the locked gates were devastated. We chatted about how they had made this trip of a lifetime because they wanted to honour the possibilities of human effort, achievement and excellence. For the first time since 1944, the Olympic Games (of 2020) was cancelled. But then, in 2021, despite the fact the pandemic still raged, the Games were remounted. Alexander and Philip, and indeed the presence of that 100-foot-high Wonder-Statue of the king of the gods, were the continuation of that axial idea – that human agency and ambition can surmount most challenges.

Having decorated Olympia, and liberated Ephesus, Alexander the Great would go on to besiege one of the most idiosyncratic Wonders

---

* And no coincidence that when Alexander effected a grand political gesture in 324 BCE, recalling political exiles, his audience of 20,000 gathered at Olympia.

in the world, and the city that raised it. A Wonder built to honour not the power of the living, but the power of the dead. A five-day sail from the Greek mainland, if the southbound Etesian winds were kind, past islands like pyramids, like mountains, like crouching lions – the giant, gaudy, sky-scraping tomb that was the father of all mausoleums is our fifth Wonder: the Mausoleum of Halikarnassos.

CHAPTER 5

THE MAUSOLEUM OF HALIKARNASSOS

351 BCE

. . . it was and is a wonder.

EUSTATHIUS, *COMMENTARY ON HOMER'S 'ILIAD'*,

TWELFTH CENTURY CE, TRANS. NEWTON (1862), 73

'The Mausoleum at Halikarnassos' engraving produced by Philips Galle after designs by Maarten van Heemskerck in 1572.

In Washington, President Abraham Lincoln, assassinated in 1865, stares out under his colossal, classical canopy from that gargantuan seat, as you will recall, just like the king of the gods, Zeus, in Olympia. The dedication of the Lincoln Memorial in 1922 embodied a world the West wanted to believe in; a world where heroic Bronze Age Greeks from the time of the Trojan War survived the Dark Ages to resurface in a blazing star-shower of political ideas and physical beauty during the 'Greek Golden Age'. This Greek miracle was then eagerly plagiarised and amplified by the Romans, whose republic was – culturally and politically – an inspiration for America's own. Think of America's Senate and its written constitution. The Greeks gave the world Zeus; and they gave the world the Mausoleum, on which Lincoln's own tomb in Springfield, Illinois, and Ulysses S. Grant's in New York are modelled. This is how the story of cultural inheritance goes.

Only the Greeks didn't. The Mausoleum of Halikarnassos,* our fifth Wonder, was built in what is now southern Turkey for a Karian king. The Karians were a remarkable people who changed the course of ancient history, yet they swim in the slipstream of other, noisier cultures of the fifth and fourth centuries BCE. Investigating Halikarnassos' Wonder is an object lesson in recovering civilisations who have been etiolated from the historical narrative. It is also an object lesson in aesthetics, a summation of what humans do when they choose to use the natural landscape as a stage set for cultural experiment, and for creative endeavour.

The Mausoleum is, too, a monument that is about family rivalry, and about the covetous competition between societies, that can result in remarkable art.

How people choose to be buried tells us a great deal about them.

The Karian King Hekatomnos, born in around 420 BCE, had founded a dynasty from the Karians' new power-base on the rich plain of Mylasa – modern-day Milas, just inland from the Aegean coast of Anatolia. Today Milas is a charming town where Ottoman-era houses crowd in on ancient remains. Rimmed by protective mountains, Milas feels a secure and strategic place to start a bid for regional domination.

---

* The name may be Luwian-Pelasgian in origin and mean 'the blessed spring-city beside the sea'.

It was where Hekatomnos ruled, and where his son and heir, Mausolos, buried his father. Overseen by the majestic mountain sanctuary to Zeus at Labraunda, Hekatomnos' tomb, only fully identified by archaeologists in 2019, during the writing of this book, reveals the ruler's remarkable wealth and hints at his and his son's worldview. One bright spring day, being given the chance to investigate this tomb during excavation was a once-in-a-lifetime experience. A call from the authorities came through and within the hour I found myself clambering down a wooden ladder, through earth-shafts 60 feet deep, while rescue and restoration work was being completed around me. The level of preservation of this splendid, stygian burial at Uzunyuva is remarkable, and its discovery is a staggering story. The king's delicate wreath-crown of solid gold olive leaves and spiralling tendrils was temporarily looted (spending an illegal five-year holiday above a Turkish restaurant in Edinburgh, Scotland), but originally it accompanied other gold gifts for the dead king in his tomb, approached by a long chamber-corridor. The wall-paintings and carved sarcophagus are still in situ and are sumptuous. On the sarcophagus there is a dramatic scene of a lion-hunt, a funerary banquet, women and men in mourning. A family group – almost certainly including Hekatomnos' son, Mausolos, as a child and again as a young, moustachioed man – is shown in delicate, confident relief on the sides of the sarcophagus. The brilliance of the work is breath-taking – birds are feather-fine, the tousled hair of the hunter seems to twist with the rush of attack, the lion's claws rip through earth made of stone. Sixty miles from Ephesus, it had been the Karians who supplied many of the master-masons to build Artemis's Temple Wonder, and their extraordinary skill is on display here.

The wall paintings too – in soft shades and fluid brushstrokes – flow elegantly, immortalising the Karian dynasty and wrapping its narrative up with rich mythological and hunting scenes. With airlocks and protective clothing, the restorers are racing against time to prevent this paint – undisturbed for 2,300 years – from flaking to the floor. Because this was a tomb that was robbed by an organised gang, there are still enormous pits in the floor where they continued to dig. Another home that seems to have been prepared for the dead king at Berber Ini, a magnificent rock-cut temple-tomb, dominates the old road that linked the sacred mountain site of Labraunda with Halikarnassos (modern-day Bodrum) on the coast. Gilded rosettes stud the star-shaped roof, reminiscent of

Egyptian tombs. Decorated with both Ionian and Doric orders, this enigmatic burial place shows the influence of West and East, of Greece and
of the giant rock-cut tombs of Persian emperors. Karia was a culture that
drew inspiration from all directions. And it would be this collision of
influences that catalysed the unique Mausoleum of Halikarnassos.

The tomb at Mylasa was glorious enough, but Hekatomnos' eldest son,
Mausolos, was determined to outdo his father. At almost exactly the same
time that Herostratus was burning down the great Temple of Artemis
at Ephesus, all who sailed into the harbour of ancient Halikarnassos,
40 miles to the south on the western coast of Turkey, would have been
greeted by the image of a remarkable, technicolour death monument,
being raised to the sky.

The Mausoleum of Halikarnassos, the burial place of Mausolos, King
of Karia, was a bold, creative endeavour. It was also a Wonder with
historical significance – a statement of extraordinary hubris and hope,
planned and delivered by a pioneering man alongside a highly intelligent woman. With no little irony, though, down time, this giant tomb
came to be thought wonderful because it was trumpeted as embodying a
faithful woman's selfless devotion to her husband-brother, a sign that the
brilliance of some men is to devastate women by dying.

Mausolos's giant tomb also sparked a cultural phenomenon – the mausoleum. Mausoleums would be replicated from Moscow's Red Square
and the tomb of Lenin, to Ataturk's mausoleum in Anitkabir, Ankara,
Turkey; from that Lincoln tomb in Springfield, Illinois, to the Shrine
of Remembrance, Melbourne; from St George's Church in Bloomsbury,
London, to the National Parliament of Tokyo. So who was the instigator
of all of this – the man who has had such impact on world culture?

Mausolos came to power in 377 BCE. His field of operations was both
land and sea. In 360 BCE he powered up the Lycian coast in what is
now south-west Turkey, beaching his ships so his men could flood out
to take Lycian territory. Even today, on the undulating water here, where
whole shoals of fish skim the surface as they are hunted from the deep,
in some remote bays in the region, rough, ancient stone steps from the
period still lead from beaches up scrubby hillsides 800 feet to nowhere
– 2,400-year-old docking points. The Karians had long been a sea-faring
culture. The Father of History, Herodotus, himself either fully Karian

or Karian-Greek, and born in Halikarnassos, tells us that the Karians originally lived on islands and colonised the mainland.[1] Karians could indeed have been amongst the number of the elusive 'Sea Peoples' who dominated the Mediterranean at the end of the Bronze Age. Spend time on the Aegean and you appreciate its potency and relevance – it is the fastest, most efficient way to reach and benefit from the continents of Asia, Africa and Europe, and to appreciate the cultures and challenges of each island, each peninsula and each mainland coast within landfall.

As a result, the kingdom of the Karians had a cosmopolitan outlook; it offered access to Asia inland through the perilous pass-routes of the mountains of Anatolia, and hosted traders from North Africa and the Eastern Mediterranean on their way to the Aegean and the Black Sea. Karia looked south too. As wandering warriors, the Karians were first put on the Egyptian payroll by Pharaoh Psamtik II. (Incidentally, it was a gilded statue of a priest of Psamtik II that turned up as an antique in the Roman-period homes at Ephesus. Is it too fanciful to think this might be a family heirloom originally collected by a Karian soldier-for-hire?) Karian troops quickly gained a reputation for being ferocious fighters, alongside the Greek mercenaries who travelled with them. Karians typically spoke Greek, as well as their own Phoenician dialect, and we can imagine them amongst the reprobates who scored 'I was here' graffiti in Ancient Greek all over the legs of the vast sculpture of Pharaoh Ramesses II at Abu Simbel over 2,600 years ago in 593 CE.[2] The Karian people were amongst the founders of the shared Egyptian trading station of Naukratis on the banks of the Nile in northern Egypt. With a sea-mouth at the port-towns of Thonis-Heracleion and Canopus, 140 miles downriver from the Giza pyramids (marshy waters which today are skimmed by predatory pirates, and weather-worn fishermen in wooden boats bearing a speedwell-blue evil eye to ward off harm), the Karians regularly travelled to and from Egypt as merchants and as mercenaries.

Terrorists as well as traders and travellers, we get a sense of the anxious respect afforded to the Karians by their first description in the literary sources, where Homer beats out: '[they] came to the war all decked with gold, like a girl'[3]

The Karians were also in demand with the Persians (who, thanks to some initial double-dealing by one of Halikarnassos' leading strategists, were sufficiently revived to take back control of Egypt around Mausolos's lifetime) as allies, negotiators, goods-mules and battlefield soldiers. When Mausolos succeeded his father, he knew he was in a strong position – the young man had been made a satrap by the Persian Emperor Artaxerxes II; Mausolos knew that Persia needed him.

So Mausolos started his reign on the front foot. In a bold move, the young leader re-located his capital from the city of Milas – where he had constructed that exceptional tomb for his father overlooking the wide plains of Mylasa – to coastal Halikarnassos in c. 370 BCE. His ballsy, fresh, model city was now Greece's eastern seaboard and Persia's western edge. A neat grid system of roads – popularised by Hippodamus of nearby Miletus – marked Halikarnassos out as a hyper-modern cosmopolis. From the vantage of his fortified palace on a spit of land, Mausolos could admire his fleet down below. The historian-general Xenophon – he who erected that Ephesus-tribute shrine to the goddess Artemis near Olympia – was a contemporary eyewitness who described Mausolos's Karian fleet as boasting 100 vessels. These boats were paid for by Persia, the overlord of the day, and represented the western powerbase of the Achaemenid Persians – the imperial power whose first king was Cyrus the Great.[4] All Mausolos had to do was to pay the Persians 400 talents as a tribute, so although on paper a Persian satrap, he effectively had the pleasure of full rule of Karia. He starts to give himself the new, cultic title, King of the Karians.

It seems this man had a vision. Mausolos (who ruled from 377 to 353 BCE) was now king of a cosmopolitan people with an identity – king of the *koinon* or community and territory of the Karians. He subsidised strategic towns such as Amos, also still being uncovered in the pine-rich Bozburun peninsula (in ancient times, the Rhodian Pereia). His influence was felt right along the coast at the recently excavated, handsome settlement of Kaunos, inland from Marmaris, which Mausolos enlarged with huge terraces and walls. This thriving community exported salt, salted fish, pine resin, black mastic, figs and slaves. Kaunos's tumbled warehouses and marketplace are still visible in the undergrowth. Remember, the Karians were descendants of the sea-faring Phoenicians, a Bronze Age people originally based in the Levant, who operated almost like an Amazon delivery service for the ancient world. Mausolos, his father and the rest of his family had seawater running through their veins.

The port-location of Halikarnassos is a signifier of the international ambition of the dynasty of Hekatomnos, the Hekatomnids. The city's life-giving spring was secured behind a fortified arsenal with walls that embraced the coastline like an archer's bow. The double harbour here meant warships could surprise any attackers – and all this was surveyed by Mausolos's fortress-palace. On a spit of land, with generous reception rooms, hailed by the ancient architect Vitruvius in the first century BCE for its decorations, with bricks and imported marble from the island of Proconnesus 350 miles to the north in the Sea of Marmara, its walls were 'so finely burnished they are as translucent as glass to look at'.[5] Ashlar blocks from this great palace are still visible, as is the slipway to the private boats of a second, secret, royal harbour.[6]

But when you sail past this curving, comfortable stretch of the Anatolian coast, it does beg a punctuation mark. Generously shaped, like a theatre, the sweep is almost too gentle, too inviting. Elsewhere along the coast here rocks can rise from the sea like mini-mountain ranges, perhaps it felt like a good challenge to try to match them. Mausolos's brightly coloured death-tower would erupt like a firework on the landside horizon.

When I first visited the site of the Mausoleum in 1986, the entrance was through a small metal gate, which would be open if you were lucky, and led onto a grassy patch framed by masonry blocks. One elderly companion remembered being chased away by a local inhabitant here in the 1960s – who was using the plot to grow her aubergines while excavations continued around her.

Today, the footprint of the Wonder of Halikarnassos is still charmingly bucolic; a fig tree provides shade, a place to sit to listen to the call to prayer from the nearby mosque. Cars rumble and honk their way past – this is still just off the main east–west street in the modern town of Bodrum. Squares that once traded luxury goods between three continents now push fake Louis Vuittons for plagues of tourists and masks against modern pandemics. Those goods, borne across the Mediterranean and accompanied by a fly-by of curious cormorants or by super-yacht-beating streams of swift seagulls, would have been churned through the pounding seas round here, sometimes indigo blue, sometimes hazed to the horizon. Ancient traders would have steered by the stars at night, and by the sun during the day, until beached whales of islands, or the comfort of mainland coasts appeared on the horizon. Orphans of antiquity still dot modern-day Bodrum in all kinds of unexpected places: a slab from the temple of Aphrodite as a windowsill; carved masonry blocks, whitewashed and turned back to front as kitchen tables in grand private homes; a theatre overlooking a dual carriageway, and stunning city walls acting as windbreaks to back gardens. All hints at the glory days of Mausolos's new, notable centre of power.

Entrance to the well-kept site, now through a turnstile, is a slight let-down, given what must once have been a breath-taking arrival – through the original, giant, monumental entrance which once led to the Mauso-leum, a soaring, marble wedding-cake confection over 150 feet tall. This skyrocket of a construction would have dominated the eastern side of its six-acre precinct. Although most of the original Mausoleum has been stolen, re-used, or shipped off through time, including voraciously by the British in the nineteenth century, fragments of Mausolos's Wonder are still anticipated to be found, because the scale of the building works here between 361 and 351 BCE was simply enormous. Like his father before him, Mausolos would choose to be buried not outside the 4-mile stretch of the walls he raised to protect his new-build city, but within. With foun-dations that have appeared in the excavations to measure 130 by 130 feet, from the 200 fragments of friezes, 250 of sculpture, and column shafts, piecing together the Mausoleum is an extreme and precise exercise.[7] Some scraps (including an eroded stone panel representing an Amazon) have even ended up on the island of Rhodes, and are displayed like a foundling child in the archaeological museum there.

Initially all that appears to be left in situ of the Mausoleum structure is a rock-cut rectangle for its foundations, the impressive ceremonial staircase for Mausolos's body (now covered in weeds) and a few finely cut, fallen marble column drums. But then, like seeing ants in the grass, your eyes adjust, and clues start to emerge from all around. Although much has been stolen, cannibalised, or ground down for mortar, we are looking for the remains of a building described as being in five layers and established above an older, Bronze Age burial and an aqueduct which brought mountain-cold spring water from the hills behind the city (with a subterranean cult of water-nymphs close by). The Mausoleum had a rectangular podium or basement, then thirty-six colonnades in an en-closure very reminiscent of the Temple of Artemis at Ephesus. On top of this was a stepped pyramid, approached by twenty-four ornamental steps, a stairway towards heaven; then an apex or pedestal; and above everything a quadriga – a splendid four-horse chariot. Although many of the gems of this structure have disappeared, there are still clues in situ to the Mausoleum's astounding greatness: massive blocks; delicately carved tablets; thick columns, painstakingly designed with internal connecting systems; square and round post- and peg-holes to ensure the interlocking of each column drum in this notoriously geo-seismic region.

The Mausoleum was designed by the architect-sculptor Pytheos, possibly a court engineer, himself also inspired by the nearby Temple of Artemis. Indeed, we hear from Vitruvius that Pytheos co-wrote a treatise on the Mausoleum with the sculptor Satyros.[8] But the Mausoleum (and Pytheos' other work at nearby Priene, where there are also cornices of lion heads as spouts for rainwater, with lotus flowers and palmettes decorating the surfaces in between, and coffers on the ceiling boasting sculpture in low-relief) enjoys a new flourish of freedom. The remnants left on site show battles between the gods and giants, Athena, Zeus, Gaia, Hermes, Kybele, Aphrodite, Dionysos and Herakles – and new fragments are still being identified as the analysis of the site continues. All have an almost intimidating energy. The sculptors Scopas, Leochares, Bryaxis and Timotheus, we are told, were also brought in to raise Mausolos's Wonder. Although this list feels suspiciously like a roll-call of all the named artists operating at this time (Scopas, you will recall, decorated Artemis's columns at Ephesus and Leochares worked at Olympia), the probability is that at least some were directly involved. We should imagine the artists thrilling to the task, quietly competitive no doubt, aware this was one of those commissions, and creative chances, of a lifetime.[9]

It is possible to get up close to some of these works of art both on the ground in Bodrum and in the British Museum in London. In London the pumping-veined, ripple-soft-necked power of one surviving war horse from the quadriga – which we commoners were never meant to see, as it was raised so high – leaves us in no doubt of Mausolos's ego or the skill of the artisans he and his family employed. Segments of the wheels of the chariot have survived, and the horses' harnesses too; today Instagram influencers and bloggers try to get the best up-nostril view of the horses. Slabs of friezes which would have edged the first level of the towering tomb tell the story of the battle between Lapiths and Centaurs. A room-long display shows Amazonian women being felled or launching themselves into the attack. Originally painted red with a background of blue, details on the carvings were picked out in gold or bronze. Tiny specks of pigment still survive on the stone. And two other figures have been taken from the site – a couple, quite possibly Mausolos himself and his wife Artemisia. The lion-maned male figure certainly has a wonderfully imperious expression, and his cascading locks match those of the young man on the side of Hekatomnos' tomb, although identification as the royal couple has yet to be proved.[10]

Vitruvius adds the detail that again some of the blocks here were 'highly polished like glass'.[11] The full complement showed the king hunting, fighting, honouring the gods, receiving what seem to be foreign ambassadors. It is history and fantasy incarnate. In Turkey edges of the site are still littered with fragments and stelai – Amazons fight, bearded men with broken stonework moustaches smile enigmatically, muscles tense in stone; there are toppled columns here that expose those hollow shafts between each column drum which would have locked the architecture together with metal rods. And in the grounds of the nearby crusader castle of St Peter – built on the site of Mausolos's palace – ancient lions frown and curl their claws, the folds of their skin creasing under the haunches and stretching over their backbones with astonishing realism; panthers climb into giant jars, and bearded sphinxes – the signifiers of Eastern influence – glare with supernatural disdain. Originally there were over-life-size lions and tigers here too, decorating window ledges, and the entire storyboard of Amazonian history along the castle's walls. But these, the finest surviving sections of the original Mausoleum, were shipped out to Britain in 1877. Today the lions sit as often overlooked finials on the British Museum's staircase as you enter to the left-hand side. The artwork from the Hekatomnids' world is quite remarkable, sadly worthy of both praise and plunder. It's understandable that Karia had the reputation for sponsoring some of the finest marblework in all of Europe and Asia.

All over this Wonder, originally, would have been a riot of colour. The paint first used is still just visible on some of the carvings in situ, vermillion and ultramarine, today a tint of red and blue. Recent analysis has revealed the intensity of pigment used. As with the so-called Alexander Sarcophagus, currently in Istanbul's Archaeological Museum, figures were picked out, allowing the marble substructure to be visible. 3D statues were coloured top to toe. Analysis of statuary from the fifth and fourth centuries in museum collections shows that lips were painted with a pink lacquer made from madder pigment; cinnabar and iron-oxide tones could be added to plump out the lips; Egyptian blue gave skin a translucent feel (some sculptures even use raw alabaster for skin for the same reason); cheekbones and jawbones have white highlights – exactly as highlighter is used in make-up today.[12] Clothes could be a red ochre or mustard yellow; blue stripes have recently been identified on the Parthenon sculptures. Funerary monuments in particular favoured colour – there was a sense that the polychrome experience brought the dead back to some kind of life. Mausolos's tomb would have been a firework in the sky.

And why the Mausoleum's unique, pyramid-shaped apex, on top of a burial place that would be the equivalent of a fourteen-storey-high building today? There can be no doubt Egypt was one key influence.

For the Karians, with that outpost at Naucratis – a four-day sail south on the North African coast – and with form as Egyptian mercenaries, it makes sense that Egyptian inspiration should shout loud in the Mausoleum. There was regular and close interchange between the two cultures. Take, for instance, the finely carved tombstone of a Karian woman called

Tombstone of a Karian woman from Saqqara in Egypt, c. 540–530 BCE, showing the cross-cultural influences in play in Archaic (and Classical and Hellenistic) Karia.

Piabrm (a good Karian name, like her husband's – Usold), found in the great necropolis at Saqqara, where humans and animals alike are buried in miles of sand, and whose pyramids inspired the Great Pyramid at Giza. Piabrm, with her handsome double-chin and plump-pillow chest, is laid out and lamented as typically happened with Greek mourners. One participant, close to her, is cutting his forehead with a knife – a gesture particularly prominent in Karian mourning ritual. Above, the Egyptian god of learning, Thoth, makes his way towards the sacred Apis bull, who the Egyptian goddess Isis protects with outstretched wings.[13] We can see why the Mausoleum would show a jumble of funerary traditions (both bespoke and off the shelf), and why we must imagine that Mausolos was not, as he has been portrayed, barbaric, a non-Greek at the eastern limits of civilisation, but a man with an intimate knowledge of three continents, with a cornucopia of cultural precedent to draw from, with an eclectic understanding of diverse civilisations, and a sophisticated relationship with both Egyptians and Persians.

Mausolos clearly employed craftsmen who were electrified by the cultural pioneers of the past. The Mausoleum made close reference not only to the Great Pyramid and to Artemis's mighty colonnaded Temple at Ephesus (the Mausoleum at Halikarnassos had a similar arrangement and layout of 36 columns), but also to the sphinxes of Babylon. That star Scopas from the marble-rich island of Paros, a master at coaxing pathos and emotion out of stone, was described in the *Laterculi Alexandrini*[14] as one of the principal sculptors of both gods and men.* The Mausoleum probably fielded 400 sculptures. Don't forget, there was Bryaxis too, the artist favoured by kings; Leochares from Athens, who sculpted the fine figures of the Macedonian royals Philip, Alexander, Amyntas III, Olympias and Eurydice I in the Philippeion; Timotheus, whose sumptuous stone-work from the Sanctuary of Asclepius at Epidauros can still be seen in the National Archaeological Museum in Athens, slender goddesses whose stone-clothes rustle and swirl, and who would have once overlooked the dream and snake therapies in Greece's first health spa. And finally Praxiteles, renowned for his sculptures at Olympia and Ephesus, as well as for his Knidian Aphrodite. It is unlikely

---

* Indeed, in Pliny's opinion, Scopas' Venus was better than Praxiteles' more famous Knidian Aphrodite.

The giant, mystical bird-deity Bennu from Ancient Egypt. Tomb of Irinefer, c. 1290 BCE.

An ivory miniature of Khufu throned — the only surviving sculptural image of King Khufu.

The stunning main entrance to Babylon constructed for King Nebuchadnezzar II, The Gate of Ishtar, now in the Pergamon Museum in Berlin.

A wooded hill, possibly parkland in Nineveh, with irrigation canals fed from an aqueduct, North Palace, c. 645-635 BCE.

The city walls of Babylon surrounding the hanging gardens and the tower of Babel, as represented in a hand-coloured copperplate engraving from Friedrich Johann Bertuchs' *Bilderbuch fur Kinder* (Picture Book for Children), published in 1792.

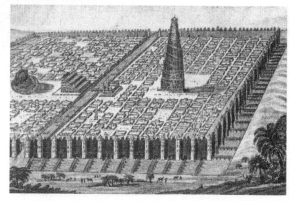

A detailed miniature of the ancient Greek female artist Timarete painting the goddess Artemis from *De Claris Mulieribus*, c. 1440 CE.

Terracotta amphora jar, c. 530 BCE, showing Amazons in combat with Herakles clothed in short tunics and Scythian hats.

One of the golden figurines excavated from the Temple of Artemis at Ephesus – a goddess, priestess or adorant.

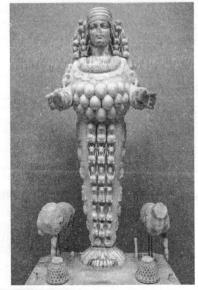

A Roman copy of the 'poly-mastic' Artemis of Ephesus of the Hadrianic period, known as 'Beautiful Artemis', from the second century CE.

The Statue of Zeus at Olympia reconstructed by A.-C. Quatremère de Quincy in 1814 (above) and a panorama view of the archaeological site of Olympia in Greece (below).

One of the many imagined representations of the Mausoleum of Halikarnassos, crucially missing the brightly coloured paint we know decorated the marble.

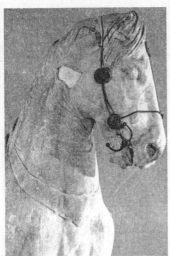

A lion statue and horse's head from the Mausoleum at Halikarnassos, c. 350 BCE, both currently in the British Museum. A four-horse chariot group was positioned on the top of the stepped pyramid which crowned the Mausoleum.

Mausolos' name carved in stone at Labraunda, photo taken by the author.

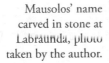

'Dutch Ships Entering the Port of the Island of Rhodes', c. 1818/30 by Japanese artist Utagawa Kunitora.

One of the men thought to be responsible for the design of the Colossus was Chares of Lindos, himself a student of the renowned sculptor Lysippus. A number of works by Lysippus survive, including this statue of an Hellenistic hero in bronze.

The Colossus of Rhodes, 1760, imagined by an unknown artist.

A 3D rendering of the Pharos Lighthouse at Alexandria.

The female Pharaoh Hatshepsut's Punt expedition – to collect precious minerals and trees – on the walls of her funerary temple at Deir-el-Bahri.

Two of the stained-glass panels commissioned for the Empire State Building in New York and installed in the north lobby in 1963 – the Great Pyramid and the Hanging Gardens of Babylon.

Modern 3D images of the Seven Ancient Wonders commissioned by the Australian Insurance company Budget Direct.

that *all* these superstars would have worked here together, in truth – but the achievement of the Mausoleum was so very great, the world wanted to remember that it had attracted the greatest artists of all time.

And Halikarnassos' favourite son Herodotus incarnates the kind of influence that would have been at play. Herodotus was fascinated by Egypt. He had travelled to North Africa to understand the works of men – the word Herodotus uses is *ergon*, a little closer to 'deed', which implies effort, intelligence, and application. His enthusiasm was contagious. Authoring his vast *Histories* – a lifetime's work, it seems – and exhilarated perhaps by the adrenaline of his connection with the underdog Karians, which had defeated, against the odds, the dominant superpower of the day, the Persians, Herodotus was writing with hope 'that human achievement may be spared the ravages of time'.[15] What could have been a triumphalist exercise in chauvinism was far from it. His *Histories* were remarkably inclusive. Herodotus asserted that great deeds were achieved by Greeks and non-Greeks alike. He tries to experience the world from within another's skin: so the Persian King of Kings, Xerxes, 'on whose empire the sun never set', and whose forces had attacked Herodotus' hometown, is allowed attributes of strength and valour.[16] Herodotus is shocked that another Persian emperor, Cambyses, mocks the religion of the Egyptians, reasoning, 'Everyone believes his own customs to be far and away the best . . . only a madman would think to jeer at such matters.'[17] Herodotus himself, described disparagingly as a *philo-barbaros* (a lover of barbarians) – an Anatolian with a Phoenician language and dialect – was an excellent example of the cosmopolitan make-up of the Karian seaboard settlements.*[18]

There was local influence in the tomb's design too. The tapering chamber design resembled that of Mausolos's father, Hekatomnos, and Lycian influence can be read in the high podium. Mid-nineteenth-century photographs of the site – with blocks tumbled from its roof – reveal how impressive the pyramid summit would have been. This building was exuberant and eclectic – although often lauded for its Greek influence, the

---

While Herodotus was a child, in his hometown a beautiful temple to Apollo had been raised on Halikarnassos's headland. Apollo's sister Artemis was also worshipped here. But Herodotus, probably a failed revolutionary, who may have tried to oust a pro-Persian, Greek dynast from Halikarnassos, ended up an exile on the nearby island of Samos, rather than living out his days in his hometown.

Mausoleum was in fact a very un-Greek pot-pourri. The palace of Darius I in Susa, modern-day Iran, was built by Karian stonemasons – who left graffiti as a kind of Karian tag. Many believe the Mausoleum of Cyrus the Great in Pasargadae – which would be much admired by Alexander on his momentous campaigns in the East[19] – was influenced by western Anatolian styles and craft.[20] Monumental and extravagant tombs were very much a Karian thing – more turning up in archaeological rescue digs every season. Karians were known for the wealth of their burials, and the weapons in them. When the sacred island of Delos was cleared of dead bodies as part of a ritual purification, over half were said to belong to Karians.[21] And the Karians' love of burying their dead in the centre of cities – hence the Mausoleum – was a funerary choice Alexander the Great would go on to emulate, with his grand plans for tombs for Hephaestion.[22]

While Egyptians turned the great mountains of the desert into a giant pyramid, this Karian king's tomb was turning the crags and heights of southern Turkey into its own mountain.

But Mausolos's Mausoleum was also shafting into the future. Resting on a blue limestone terrace, over 785 feet long, the structure was 145 feet high – that's about half the height of London's Big Ben – on a podium 105 by 125 feet wide. The bottom layer was made of white marble. Above that a section again of blueish limestone – the backdrop to around 120 sculpted human and animal figures, all progressing towards a seated Mausolos, in front of a door to his palace (or to the afterlife?) in the centre of the eastern side. Above the blue limestone, more white marble (some of the finest imported all the way from the Pentelic quarries near Athens) was decorated with a brutal battle scene. Amazons featured prominently once again, just as they were used to decorate the temples at Olympia and Ephesus.

Sections of this Amazon drama are still being newly identified. And it has been noticed that some of the carving on these panels is rather sub-standard – on slab 1,009, for example, one poor woman has her head twisted at an angle of 180 degrees.[23] Decorative pattern books were probably used for some off-the-shelf elements like these sky-scraper reliefs which were never intended to be seen with the naked eye. The marble for the Amazons came from the island of Kos, sometimes visible through the sea-mists across the water from Halikarnassos – only the interior green tufa stone was local. Above the Amazon frieze rose a colonnade.[24] The roof was a stepped pyramid, 23 feet high with 24 steps. Here there was a row of lions, possibly a double row, and then, almost certainly, Mausolos and his sister-wife Artemisia II, literally on a pedestal, controlling that quadriga – a thrashing, four-horse chariot.[25]

The whole structure was a frothing collision of North and South, East and West.

The new form of Ionic column with a distinctive bow-curve capital created for the Mausoleum of Halikarnassos.

An entirely new kind of capital was developed here, with catherine-wheel curls at either end and a bowing curve in the centre. Copy-cat columns in the style of those invented for the Mausoleum still stand at the nearby great temple of Apollo at Didyma. They are there too in the sanctuary of Zeus in Olympia, to honour Ptolemy II and his wife-sister Arsinoe – those columns restored and, since 2017, elegantly standing in the Olympic site. Similar columns can be found in the lush countryside around Ephesus, raised in the remote, romantic Belevi Mausoleum, high on a hill, surrounded by mountainsides of peaches and olives. Karian architects developed new ways of joining masonry blocks together with decorative dove-tail bronze clamps, and bronze central hooks to hoist delicate carvings and architraves into place without the danger of ropes rubbing out painstakingly made detail – all styles and tricks employed as far away as the Stoa of Attalos in Athens and in the streets of Alexandria in northern Egypt.[26] This is not the East 'waiting' for Greek galvanisation. It is a robust civilisation, cherry-picking ideas of interest from elsewhere, and pioneering their own, new, ingenious forms of art and design.

So, the daring, eccentric, uncompromising monumental edifice of the Mausoleum, protected by new walls and new gates, was erected to celebrate Mausolos's life, his death, and his sponsorship of the new hyper-modern city at Halikarnassos. This was a Wonder which embodied the human drive to be remembered and to be celebrated after death, because your life as lived was felt to be a resounding success.

The Mausoleum Wonder is therefore the summation of a particular time and place. This was a dynamic moment in Karia. First coming into focus in the Bronze Age, with Luwian-Hittite roots, speaking a language of Phoenician origin, holding their own against invading Mycenaeans, absorbed by the legendarily rich King Croesus of Lydia in the sixth century BCE (he whose gold decorated and adorned the Temple of Artemis at Ephesus), then liberated as a distinct state by the Persians, with sister satrapies of Ionia and Lydia – under Mausolos, Karia was on the move. Karian first-born boys were sent off east to be educated at the Persian court; they were saturated in Persian ways of being (and, interestingly, would also have experienced the extravagant royal rock-cut tombs at Naqs-i Rustam). Serving the interest of the Great King in Persia, inscriptions show us there was a harsh, strictly enforced imperial and local tax regime which meant serious cash for serious projects could be raised.[27] In the newly uncovered tomb at Uzunyuva in Milas that stunning, confident dynastic family portrait makes something very clear. With Mausolos and his sisters Ada and Artemis and his brothers Idrius and Pixadorus crowded around their dead father Hekatomnos, once Karia had become an independent satrapy, power was not going to be handed back to Persia but passed down through the Hekatomnid bloodline in this fledgling kingdom.

After the long Peloponnesian Wars on Greek territories that reached what is now Turkey – towards the start of which the belligerent Statue of Zeus at Olympia had been produced, and during which the archaic Temple of Artemis had been completed, a conflict which had dragged in Persia and much of Anatolia as allies of either Athens or Sparta – the slump and trauma of the war was followed by a spurt of energy. The

Persians, buoyed by their conquest of Egypt and their role as kingmaker to one Spartan or Athenian general or another, were invigorated.

And just as with the Egypto-mania following the discovery of Tutankhamun's tomb hot on the heels of World War I, and Parisian fashion after World War II, in the fourth century BCE a forced involvement in Greek affairs meant the rulers of the East were expressly interested in the fashions of the West. There was a rush of Greek-ness on what is today the Turkish coast, and in particular at Halikarnassos. The Greeks in turn were sick of being farmers who fought in the spring and watched their crops being burnt in late summer by other Greek fighters, who should have been brothers-in-arms. So in the fourth century warships turned into trading vessels, and merchants were back out on the seas. Communities in the Eastern Mediterranean were falling back in love with the world, during a brief window of peace in a century of almost total war. The world was ready for some good times.

This was Mausolos's moment.

So we have an impressive footprint of a gargantuan building, some stunning fragments, and many vivid descriptions of the Mausoleum. But Halikarnassos itself has been so cannibalised through time, to get a better sense of the spirit of Mausolos's pride and joy, it helps to head to the Latmos mountains. Because 5 miles inland from Halikarnassos, to the north, and just under half a mile above sea level, sheltering in amongst an evergreen forest, we can find evidence of Mausolos's and Artemisia's world, even Mausolos's name, in a delightful place called Labraunda.

Labraunda is, for the modern-day historian, a mountain-side wonder. A site built by Mausolos and his family which has escaped the systematic looting that the Mausoleum at Halikarnassos has endured down time. A sacred settlement, where the soul of Halikarnassos and the Hekatomnid dynasty was believed to sit. The temple of Zeus here – facing south-east so the king of the gods could watch the rising sun – was designed by the same architect as the Mausoleum, Pytheas of Priene. Pytheas was a pioneer, with a passion for the past. His work in this remote, honey-rich site paid homage not only to the archaic Temple of Artemis at Ephesus, but also to the great Temple of Hera at Samos – abandoned now too, where snakes wind through the grasses and the warm flags of the goddess's sacred way lead towards not a sanctuary but a car park. But in its

heyday the temple was graced with fine statues, and an extremely handsome giant altar. The new, flamboyant, multi-cultural Karian style would
come to influence the whole of Asia Minor. Labraunda gives us a sense
of Halikarnassos' edgily successful nature: a party-ish place, because up
here in the hills were shrines and sanctuaries, but also dining rooms, and
gathering places for honoured guests to enjoy evocative nocturnal rituals.

An elegant outer gateway or *propylon* marked the entrance to Labraunda's sanctuary. Weapons (and livestock) had to be left behind – a rule
that was broken at least once. An inscription in Mylas records that during
the wild rites in Labraunda, there was, one night, an attempt on King
Mausolos's life.[28] Unpopular because of the taxes the king had extracted
from his people, one has to wonder whether his steady erection of a
giant, show-off tomb was the tipping point for one Karian man with
a grudge. From this sky-bound vantage-point of Labraunda, Mausolos
could worship one of his favourite gods – Apollo, Artemis's twin brother.
Images of both Apollo and Zeus are punched on either side of the coins
that Mausolos minted. A recently discovered 121-line poem, also from
the Uzunyuva district of Mylasa, written in Greek, praises a great *anax*
or lord, either Mausolos or his father or grandfather, or perhaps a god
– either the potent Egyptian god Serapis, who was thought to have a
hotline to the underworld, or the Karian moon-god, Men, or a composite
god, Zenoposeidon. This *anax*, with the help of the goddess Artemis, res-
cues a man called Pytheas by moonlight. We should think of these heady
words being recited in the dark, beating out an association between the
king and supernatural, nocturnal powers. Mausolos's dynasty seemed to
have a special affection for the god Men, equated with Egyptian Serapis.
Imagine envoys coming here from Egypt, Assyria and Persia – different
cultures meeting in the soft light of these hills, decoding one another's
familiar-yet-strange beliefs. Not appropriation, but acceptance by two-
way assimilation.

Exploring this monument-crammed site, it is easy to envisage the
throng here. The splendid dining room, named by archaeologists Andron
B (one of the men-only spaces at Labraunda), boasts 24-and-a-half-foot-
high columns, a 36-by-32-and-a-half-foot room, and a clear inscription:
'Mausolos son of Hekatomnos, dedicated the Andron and everything
that is inside to Zeus Labraundos'. After the unknowable enigmas and
question marks of Giza, Babylon, Ephesus and Olympia, it is electrically

exciting to see the name of the creator of one of the Seven Wonders face to face. And what a place this wonder-builder sponsored. Along with twenty-two dining couches, there was wood decorated with bronze, topped with sphinxes at the corners – an incarnation of the Eastern nature of Labraunda and the Eastern aesthetic of the Karians. There was, too, an area for ritual cleansing. Wonderfully, we are told by the Roman author Aelian in his *On The Nature of Animals* (12.30) that the fish and eels who swam in the ponds up here were bejewelled, sporting golden earrings and necklaces. Just imagine that sparkling play of submerged, reflected light, magnified by the water. And the statue of Zeus here showed the great god not with a thunderbolt, nor supporting a victorious Nike, but holding a lotus-tipped sceptre. Lotus flowers have a narcotic effect. Labraunda must have seen some pretty heady behaviour. On one relief, now in the British Museum, Mausolos's younger brother and sister are shown flanking an outsize Zeus: the god looming between the prince and princess has a lotus flower to hand. One inscription suggests there was an altar to Mausolos here too – perhaps, with his territories laid out beneath him, sacred and secular, the great king was also worshipped as a divine hero?

Idrius – Mausolos's younger brother – was not to be outdone by his elder sibling. At Labraunda, Idrius built his own (east) stoa, 145 feet long, colonnaded, and his own andron (Andron A). He constructed a sacred way from Labraunda right down to the Karians' old capital below, Mylasa. And then the *pièce de résistance*, a necropolis that *is* a mountain. Built to support a huge superstructure, surveying the whole sacred site, Idrius's tomb was clearly intended to have the impact of his brother's Wonder. Unlike the Mausoleum, memory of this burial place has been lost, just as Idrius's name has largely been forgotten by history.

There are clues up on the slopes of Latmos mountain to the nature of the man who was buried in the Mausoleum, and the sensibilities of the dynasty he headed. That great nature goddess Kybele – ancestor of the Ephesian Artemis – was present here underneath a dramatic split rock, which dangles precariously from the upper reaches of the slopes of Mount Latmos, sheltering a spring. Terracotta figures of Kybele from the archaic period have also been discovered, and her form in the rock itself, where a stone-carved niche would have been thought to be a gateway between life and death, between one world and another. Meanwhile the god whom Mausolos worshipped here under the trees was Zeus of the Labrys – Zeus of the double-headed axe. This axe, it was said, had mystical origins – originally wrenched by Herakles from the hands of the Amazonian Queen Hippolyte while the super-hero was serving as a slave in the court of Queen Omphale. This was a scene imagined on the Amazon frieze around Mausolos's towering tomb. The labrys axe, we are told, ended up in the Lydian royal treasury at Sardis, Croesus' capital, and was then stolen by the rebel king of Mylasa, Arselis. The double-headed axe suggests a link to Minoan Crete, and a link too to a culture that valued its women.

This (atypical) pro-female trait of the Karians is a vital clue in the decoding of this particular Wonder. Because the female sponsor, co-creator and co-funder of this Wonder was Queen Artemisia II – Mausolos's wife *and* sister. The Karians did not just find inspiration in royal Egyptian architecture, but in the royals' bedroom habits. Mausolos's shrewd marriage to his sister was a double celebration, keeping dynastic control and influence in the family alarmingly tight.

Artemisia II came from good, sturdy stock. Her great-grandmother, Artemisia I, was a remarkable character. It was this Artemisia who escaped with the illegitimate children of the Persian Emperor Xerxes to seek safety in the sanctuary of her namesake goddess, Artemis, at Ephesus. Queen of Karia, half Cretan, half Karian, one of the very few female naval captains ever in world history, Artemisia I was a right-hand woman to the Persian emperor. As queen she led ships from Halikarnassos and also from the islands of Kos, Nisyros and Kalyndos. Advising against what would indeed turn out to be a disastrous naval engagement, she commanded a section of Xerxes' fleet at the Battle of Artemision and in the climactic Battle of Salamis at the end of Persia's wars with Greece. The Greeks were so appalled and riled by Karia's queen, they put a price of 10,000 drachmas on her head to bring her back alive, 'since it was thought intolerable that a woman should make an expedition against Athens'.[29] They also compared her in comedy to the ferocious Amazons.[30] In recognition of Artemisia's brilliance, we are told that Persia's mighty emperor gave the queen a full suit of fine Greek armour.[31] One of the precious gifts left at the entrance to the burial chamber within the Mausoleum in Halikarnassos, also now in the British Museum, is a beautiful alabaster jar with the words 'Xerxes the Great King' inscribed in Old Persian, Egyptian, Babylonian and Elamite (the language spoken in what is now western Iran and southern Iraq). Experts agree this was almost certainly a gift from the great Persian emperor to Artemisia I – an heirloom tenderly protected, then dedicated to another Artemisia, Artemisia II, and to her brother-husband in his outré burial place.

We know tantalisingly little about Artemisia II. But what we know is good. Artemisia was a keen botanist. The anti-malarial drug Artemisinin is named for her – after the herb *Artemisia annua* – and is still gathered daily for its medicinal use by the women of the nomad tribes of Arabia and Sinai, the Bedouin. (On the desert of the Hismā Plateau in northern Saudi Arabia I was recently offered some Artemisinin – known commonly as sweet wormwood or sweet sagewort by Bedouin women.) Artemisia was also a razor-sharp strategist and ferocious leader, as had been her namesake and great-grandmother. One reference to a 'Queen Artemisia' in the works of a Roman-period author from Bithynia (the northern edge of what is now Turkey, spreading from the Hellespont to the Black Sea), Polyaenus, erroneously attributed to the legendary naval captain, may well describe Mausolos's wife. In this account we hear that Artemisia, wanting to take a city in the Latmos mountain range, organised a vibrant procession of musicians, high priests, priestesses and eunuchs to worship at the shrine of the Mother of the Gods. The townsfolk travelled the seven stades out of the city to see this wondrous, clashing display. With their homes empty, Artemisia sent the soldiers in to take control. Thus, says our source, 'did Artemisia, by flutes and cymbals, possess herself of what she had in vain endeavoured to obtain by force of arms'.[32] Whether this was fact or a fanciful tale, it speaks of Artemisia's feisty reputation.

As a taste of her character, it is worth summarising another terrific story about Artemisia II relayed by the Roman author Vitruvius. He tells us that the men of Rhodes, 'outraged' that Karia should be left in the hands of a woman after Mausolos's death, set sail to attack the Karian capital. Artemisia hid her fleet in her secret, second harbour, and instructed the people of Halikarnassos to welcome the Rhodians in as liberating heroes. Tricked by the town's cheers, the Rhodians came on shore, leaving their boats unmanned on the water. As the Rhodians celebrated on land – no doubt drinking, raping, looting, the things conquering armies do – Artemisia gently pulled their boats deep out to sea. Stranded, the Rhodians were encircled by the Karians and slaughtered.

Now Artemisia loaded her own sailors onto the Rhodian ships. The fleet was decked with laurel as if in victory. Entering the harbour at Rhodes, Artemisia's men were able to spring onto the shore and slaughter the island's leading citizens. We think this tale is apocryphal, playing into a misogynistic fear of effective women, and siege narratives (Artemisia's cryptic fleet has shades of a Trojan horse), but what this story does recall is the historical reality of the interconnectivity of the littoral Wonder-sites, and the variegated nature of their protagonists.

It also tells us that stories of a shrinking violet, pining for her husband after his death, are less likely than the supposition that Artemisia – who ruled in her own right – built a tomb that she could be proud of. Artemisia ruled for between two to three years after her husband Mausolos's death; when she died in 351 BCE, under those friezes that commemorated Amazonian women, she was buried alongside him.

The Mausoleum was a monument to death, to blood and to sex. Stones decorated with priestesses whose diaphanous dresses clearly show their vulvas; clusters of grapes ready for Bacchic ritual; the skulls of bulls on fragments of masonry in the Mausoleum site, all hint at the morbid, meaning-rich rituals which took place here.

Because we know there was mass slaughter as Mausolos was buried. Leading down towards the burial chamber itself, the Mausoleum's monumental stairway is still accessible to archaeologists. Descending on these worn, elegant, 2,300-year-old stones gives a sense of the ceremonial impact of the royal funeral here. Now where there are thistles and but-terflies, there would have been streams of blood. A flock of sheep, five oxen, eight lambs, birds too, were all butchered above the steps. Hens' eggs were laid on the cuts of meat. Think of that moment – the sistra rhythmically chiming, a pounding of drums, skin, hooves, entrails, all taken by the butcher. Just as I witnessed in a blood-sacrifice ritual at the Kamakhya temple in Assam, the larger animals were hamstrung first, their throats were slit, then the animals were decapitated. All but their heads and feet were left for the king to eat in the afterlife. The carcasses of the sacrificial victims – whose remains have been carefully analysed by archaeologists – were delivered to the area at the bottom of the steps, just outside the relatively modest entrance to the tomb itself.

The door of the tomb was made of green andesite, smart-locked to prevent any re-opening. To access this portal, archaeologists had to move a vast tufa block, a plug rolled into place to seal the entrance. The walls of the burial chamber itself – when explored in the sixteenth century by crusader knights – appeared to be covered with carved coloured marble (more likely, in truth, painted stucco). The burial chamber was also sealed with white marble doors. Doors similar to this, with wooden features and bronze studs all carefully carved from stone, can be found in the tombs of Alexander the Great's family in northern Greece, dating to just a couple of decades later. Turned, ornamental marble nails are still on display in the charming little museum on Bodrum's Mausoleum site. Stones from the tomb moved to the courtyard of the crusader castle are scored ready to catch offerings of wine and blood. Carvings of serpents here are a reminder that the construction of Mausolos's Karian tomb was all about death and rebirth.*

Utterly painstaking work by excavators in the 1970s identified shards of alabaster from the royal sarcophagus and spangles of gold thread from a cloth which could well have been used to wrap Mausolos's cremated bones and ashes, and which would then have been placed in a gold larnax box. The remains of eight ribbed glass bottles have been found, beautiful things, influenced by Mesopotamia and Egypt, and tinged with a yellowish green. There were animal-shaped drinking cups from Assyria; an ivory-veneered box and furniture; semi-precious stones – glass and agate beads and gold jewellery; 933 pottery fragments, hinting at red-figure ware of the very finest quality (where delicate red figures are thrown into contrast by a black background), from a Greek city-state. There was even an ivory fragment showing the lower half of a seated figure, probably the decoration for an ornamental couch. Some archaeological detectives have followed the trail of the gold-wire fragments out of the tomb's interior to implicate the tomb robbers of ancient history.[33] Because there is no doubt that within a few years of interment, Mausolos's grand tomb was reopened and pillaged.

Mausolos died in 353 BCE, and seventeen years later so did another king – whose intact tomb was discovered in 1993. The burial of Philip II, Alexander the Great's father, is one of the most extraordinary survivors,

---

* Up until the 1930s in both Turkey and Greece, there were still sacrificial rites involving animals, at the time of and after burial, with the skull of the deceased being paraded from one home to another.

ever, in human history. The riches it contained are, simply, breath-taking. So to try to help imagine the splendour of Mausolos's long-looted final resting place, we need look no further than the burials of Philip and his family. Part of a sprawling necropolis in ancient Aigai in northern Greece, a two-hour drive from Thessaloniki – within tumulus tombs which have been peerlessly preserved in situ – one can find the ornate statement of wealth that mattered to the kings of the day. There was decorated armour with an exquisite, hectic energy – breastplates, greaves and shields; dainty ivory figures of Dionysos; golden crowns so delicate, when doors open the oak-leaves still tremble in the breeze; solid-gold boxes lined with soft cloth for the bones of a king. This is precisely the kind of wealth that Karians would have packed into Halikarnassos' Wonder.

So this is how we should try to imagine Mausolos's burial. Credited with conceiving of and constructing the entire Mausoleum Wonder, Artemisia II, who outlived her husband by two years, would certainly have been responsible for its completion, and for overseeing the burial rites of her brother-husband. History tells us that Artemisia arranged for literary works, plays, and poetry recitals to be performed at her Mausolos's funeral, all praising the dead, with prizes offered to the most mournful. The capacious sanctuary around the giant tomb itself would certainly have accommodated displays like these. The discovery of that incredible Karian poem translated in 2019 reveals the kind of verse that would have been recited. We also know from a first-hand witness that Artemisia organised public-speaking contests, with the prize being given in her dead brother-husband's memory – one winner, the historian Theopompus from Chios, he who also leaked Herostratus' name as an arsonist, eagerly wrote about the process. There is the enchanting possibility that all this took place in a walled sanctuary that contained gazelle and wild deer, to give the impression of a Persian paradise garden (or like the Artemision in Ephesus's deer park). By mounting these funerary games, Artemisia may have been trying to buttress the notion of Mausolos's heroic status – a man who occupied a space somewhere between the mortal and the divine.

And here's a thought. A curious story was told of Artemisia by Aulus Gellius, a Roman author, possibly of African origin, who wrote his work *Attic Nights* during long, cold winter evenings on the Greek mainland. Aulus Gellius reports that the queen was so bereaved, she drank a daily potion made out of Mausolos's bones and from the ash of his funeral pyre, and eventually pined to death.[34] For centuries this gruesome biographical detail has been both disputed and hailed as the ultimate example of uxorial loyalty – a kind of wish that this is how all women should behave. But remember, we know from bone evidence that generations later, gladiators in the region – whose games were originally conceived as part of funerary ritual – ate ground bone and ash. So either this is a muddled memory of the gladiatorial customs of Asia Minor, or, perhaps, Artemisia, from a long line of Amazonian fighting women, did indeed perform her own version of post-mortem cannibalism – not to slavishly honour her husband, but to steal his strength.

Coincidentally, in Halikarnassos, in 1873, a stele was discovered that depicts two women, bare-breasted, fighting. The names they have been given are 'Achillia' (a female Achilles) and 'Amazon'. These are female gladiators and their nominations are highly theatrical; the fact that both women have taken their helmets off and are facing one another suggests they have drawn equal in a contest during gladiatorial combat. The fighting women from this corner of the ancient world spawned the phenomenon of gladiatrices – a perverted, polluted version of the Amazons' historical truth, and a twisted evolution of the real, doughty female fighters, Artemisia II and her grandmother Artemisia I.[35]

The burial place of Artemisia herself in the chamber next door to her husband-brother is another story. Unlike poor Mausolos, Artemisia's burial was left undisturbed. The Wonder on the coast of southern Turkey might more accurately be called the Artemision of Halikarnassos. It was certainly a glorious tribute to a feisty Karian queen. Focusing for a moment on Mausolos's other sister, Ada, who may well have helped Artemisia complete the Mausoleum after Mausolos's death, also helps us to appreciate the robust role that women played in Karian culture.

Princess Ada re-entered the world after a chance discovery by a construction survey close to Halikarnassos in 1989. I remember passing the workers, looking hot but elated thanks to their remarkable reveal. Inside a simple stone sarcophagus was a woman of forty-four or so. She was buried with a gold *stephanos* or crown, a splendid myrtle wreath decorated with fruits and flowers, and with a gold-spangled dress and antelope head gold bracelets. Once again her crown of flowers is heart-achingly delicate. Ada was born around the time her family moved their capital to Halikarnassos. After Mausolos's death, Ada's husband-brother Idrius – he who would continue with the enhancement of Labraunda – took the reins of power. But when Idrius died Ada was chased out of town by her younger brother Pixadorus and ruled in exile from nearby Alinda in the Latmos mountains. She would have her revenge.

In 334 BCE, when Alexander the Great, aged just twenty-two, was on his blitzkrieg of the region, Princess Ada saw an opportunity for self-preservation and for retribution. The very year that the Macedonian general-king meddled in the making of Artemis's Temple Wonder at Ephesus, and with the Mausoleum freshly dominating the Halikarnassos skyline, as it had done for over a decade, Alexander attacked.

The Macedonian adventurer stole in from the hills of the north-east, where sections of Mausolos's original wall still stand and where a defensive ditch, almost certainly constructed by Alexander, is still clearly visible. The natural ring-shield of hills around the Karians' harbour provided a bird's-eye view for attackers (as the ancient theatre still does today). Mausolos's Myndos Gate and vast sections of the walls also still stand on the swanky, western side of town. At dawn, twenty-first-century locals use the gates as a shortcut on foot or moped. The watchtowers are perfectly placed to survey the main harbours of Bodrum town and auxiliary bays. We should imagine Halikarnassos' soldiers on taut alert scanning the horizon where today coasts are still laced with castles, while Alexander's men scrambled over hillsides themselves like turrets, stumbling on rocks and through scrub to take their prize. Ada seems to have been best pleased. Adopting Alexander, surrendering her powerbase of Alinda to him, the princess stood by his side during the fortnight-thunderstorm of attack. In return, she asked to be restored as Queen of Karia. Alexander obliged, and as thanks Ada sent the *ubermensch* gifts of sweets and cakes. Somewhat peevishly the boy-wonder replied that he marched only on a light breakfast – but he carried on with his siege of the city, and, despite the fact that the Persian pretenders had torched Halikarnassos on their retreat, he installed Ada as queen of the Karian lands.

Later authors compared Ada's might and influence to that of the legendary Queen Semiramis, she who was also credited with sponsoring the Gardens of Babylon.[36] Alexander was clear that Ada was a force to be reckoned with, a match even for his mother Olympias, about whom he hissed that she might well have charged him nine months' rent for the use of her womb.

And there is an interesting backstory to this relationship. While still in Macedonia as a teenager, Alexander was said to have entered secret negotiations to marry Ada's young niece, the daughter of Pixadorus – the dysfunctional brother-prince who would eventually wrest control from his older sister. Was the murder of Alexander's father, Philip II – at the wedding of Alexander's beloved sister Cleopatra – in part spurred by Alexander's defence of this Karian firebrand, who other Macedonians judged to be a barbarian? If Alexander was involved in the plot to murder his own father, might the parricide have been partly sparked by his bid for independence and self-determination? Until new evidence emerges, the details of the cause of Philip's brutal death will remain murky, but Alexander's appreciation of, and emotional interest in Halikarnassos shines clearly.

When Alexander eventually built his lover Hephaestion's tomb in Babylon, he wanted it grander than any other he had seen for any Macedonian. His architect Deinocrates (who would go on to help to build the city of Alexandria, home of the Pharos Lighthouse Wonder) constructed Hephaestion's giant burial place and demolished some of Babylon's walls to do so. Sources tell us this giant grave was 200 feet tall, decorated with finely carved friezes, just like the Mausoleum, and that it cost 10,000–12,000 talents (tens of millions of dollars) to build.[37] As the world-conqueror planned his lover's burial, Alexander must, surely, have had in mind the Mausoleum of Halikarnassos, that gaudy, towering tomb which he had stared down on, in 334 BCE, just fifteen years or so after it had been built, when it was still bright with novelty.

The Mausoleum was a single man's laudation – commemorating his re-founding of Halikarnassos, in a way that proved Karia's ownership of ideas of civilisation from Lycia, Persia, Greece and Egypt. It was, too, a statement about a remarkable, vigorous, incestuous dynasty of pioneering men, and powerful women who would be a role model for Ptolemaic Egypt, and then, in turn, for Rome. Artemisia and Ada set a bar of efficacy and notoriety for the Egyptian queens Arsinoe and Cleopatra, and eventually the Roman aristocrats Agrippina, Julia and Octavia. Asserting a magnificence in death, Mausolos and his sister-queen, with their four-horse chariot, were ready to race across the sky like the sun god Apollo to meet in the heavens. Five hundred years later, the scholar and scathing essayist Lucian would destroy Mausolos's pretension.

In an imagined dialogue with the philosopher Diogenes the Cynic in the underworld, Mausolos boasted he deserved the greatest honour because he was tall, handsome, a superb warrior and was commemorated with the biggest and most beautiful tomb known to man. Diogenes quietly pointed out that Mausolos's hairless, skinless, eyeless skull would now look the same as the Cynic's own, and that while the tomb might still give some pleasure to the locals, all it was for the dead king was a weight bearing down on his lifeless corpse.

In Book One of his sweeping *Histories*, Herodotus voices a salient observation through the mouth of that Lydian plutocrat who had helped to create the Wonder at Ephesus – Croesus, now deposed, as he addresses his new Persian master Cyrus: 'The first lesson you should acknowledge is that there is a cycle to human affairs, one that as it turns never permits the same people forever to enjoy good fortune.'*[38] Mausolos's Wonder reminds us both of the brilliance, and of the futility of human effort. Mausolos impacted the power-dynamics of the ancient world; he was buried in a Wonder of the World, but that could not prevent him dying prematurely, and two years before the wife who outlived him.

Halikarnassos, Ephesus and Sardis all stayed under Achaemenid rule.[39] With the help of Ada at Halikarnassos, Karia was taken by Alexander the Great and was then controlled by his successors. The Roman author and politician Cicero commented that by the first century BCE, Halikarnassos was much depleted, virtually empty. The Mausoleum was initially left as an idiosyncratic monument, a spectacle for locals and sightseers into late antiquity and the early Middle Ages, and was then slowly allowed to degenerate. In the sixth century CE an anonymous author, Pseudo-Nonnus, a cleric who probably lived in Syria or Palestine, commentating on Gregory Nazianzus of Cappadocia's descriptions of the Mausoleum (Gregory being particularly interested in the value and significance of the number seven, and both authors interested in other Christians' interest in Greek mythology), tells us that the burial was still an intimidating site.[40] Mausolos and Artemisia had at least secured the immortality they desired.

*

---

* Another son of Mausolos's city, Dionysius of Halikarnassos, would nail a similarly helpful axiom, at the time of the Roman Emperor Augustus: 'History is philosophy, teaching by example.'

Mausoleum of Halikarnassos, engraving from a drawing by Cesare Cesariano, from De Architectura libri dece traducti de latino in vulgare *by Lucius Vitruvius Pollio, 1521.*

The Mausoleum under construction, engraving by Antonio Tempesta (Florence, Italy, 1555-1630), published 1610.

Postage stamp from Mongolia depicting the Mausoleum of Halikarnassos c. 1990. This was one of a series that commemorated all Seven Wonders.

An engraved imagining of the Mausoleum by a representative of the English School, 1890s.

To understand the continuing story of the Mausoleum's fate, we first have to head out across the sea to the nearby island of Rhodes, and then to the hot, butter-stoned archipelago of Malta in the Western Mediterranean, halfway between Europe and Africa. Because our most eloquent eye-witnesses to the fate of this Wonder were, counter-intuitively, crusading knights.

On the site of Mausolos's palace, a small castle had been raised in the eleventh century CE by the Seljuks – the Turko-Persian colonisers who swept west, starting out in the Aral Sea, and who took vast swathes of the Byzantine Empire, their invasion one of the triggers for the First Crusade. We know the Mausoleum was still relatively intact a hundred years later because Eustathius of Thessalonika (that monk and Homeric scholar originally from Constantinople, who rose to the rank of bishop, and who was described in mediaeval sources as 'the most learned of men of the age') declared the site 'was, and is' a Wonder.[41]

The Mausoleum appears in the works of the Florentine humanist Boccaccio, who afforded Artemisia high praise in his work *On Famous Women*.[42] And from this time onwards we find the re-working of the Mausoleum as imagined by Western artists, a popular humanist activity. Indeed, the Mausoleum was conjured in guises ranging from obelisk thin, pagoda-like, to something a little resembling Noah's Ark. (A collection of these Mausoleum fantasies are displayed along the walls of the tiny museum at the Wonder-site in Bodrum.) A series of earthquakes took their toll, dislodging much of the tomb's superstructure, and by 1400 CE, the Mausoleum was largely in ruins, only sections of the base recognisable.[43] Rather than a gaudy assertion of the possibilities of the continuation of life, the Mausoleum was increasingly imagined (by this time, along with our other Seven Wonders) as an incarnation of decay.

> In vain do earthly Princes then, in vain
> Seek with Pyramides to Heaven aspired;
> Or huge Colosses built with costly pain;
> Or brasen Pillows, never to be fired,
> Or Shrines made of the Metal most desired,
> To make their Memories for ever live;
> For how can mortal Immortality give?

Such one Mausolos made, the World's great wonder,
But now no remnant doth thereof remain:
. . . All such vain Monuments of earthly Mass,
Devour'd of Time, in time to nought do pass.

But Fame with golden Wings aloft doth fly,
Above the reach of ruinous Decay,
And with brave Plumes doth beat the azure Sky.
Admir'd of base-born Men from far away:
Then whoso will with vertuous Deeds assay
To mount to Heaven, on Pegasus must ride,
And with sweet Poets Verse be glorifide.

EDMUND SPENSER, *The Ruins of Time*, 1591

Yet our eyewitnesses to the Mausoleum-in-distress were itinerant, crusading warrior-monks who had come to Halikarnassos thanks to a crisis.

The Order of the Hospitallers, or the Order of the Knights of St John, had started life, as their name suggests, as a monastic hospital order tending to the sick and wounded Christians, Muslims and Jews alike in Jerusalem before, during and after the First Crusade. Taking vows of chastity, these Knights became a formidable force, honed fighters and men hungry for science and learning. But success can generate jealousy and rightful retaliation. Expelled from the Holy Land in 1187, losing their multiple properties in Jerusalem, and elsewhere in the Levant, the Knights had been forced to become peripatetic. Hopping from Acre to Cyprus (their stocky Cypriot castle at Colossi still stands) and Rhodes (in 1309, having originally launched their attack in 1306), occupying Kos in 1314 and again in 1336, then on to Italy and Nice (and eventually Malta), these holy-warriors had moved some distance at this point from their role as healers of the casualties of the crusades.[44] Now they were the Mediterranean's policemen – scanning the horizon for Barbary pirates to attack, and conducting their own acts of piracy under the sign of the cross.

As part of the Knights Hospitallers' negotiations to keep a foothold in the region, at the end of the fourteenth century the military order negotiated the rights to land at Bodrum from the Ottoman Sultan Bayezid I, in exchange for Smyrna (modern-day Izmir) – mounting a publicity campaign in the West to raise the funds for their efforts. The stronghold was supplied with building materials and victuals from nearby Kos, one of the islands which the Knights already owned – whose seaside crusader castle still overlooks the coast. Kos, Rhodes and Halikarnassos are relatively near neighbours across the foaming seas; workaday rusting ferries and the super-yachts of the rich easily ply between the three in high season. And in 1402 the first black-cloaked crusader knights from Rhodes arrived in Halikarnassos, to begin the construction of St Peter's Castle – Petri Castellum – on the site of what had once been Mausolos and Artemisia's palace. The Latin name Petri (or Petrum) would eventually be transmuted into the Turkish Boudroum – Bodrum, as the town roundabout is now known.

Spirits and ambition apparently undimmed and intent on controlling Asia, the Knights set up castles here and also on Symi, Tilos, Nisyros, Kalymnos and Leros, with their Grandmaster stationed in intimidating luxury at Rhodes. Construction workers at St Peter's Castle were guaranteed, by Papal Bull no less, a place in heaven and absolution for their sins. As you might imagine, from 1409 the works came in a rush. The castle's walls – made partly of spolia from the Temple of Apollo which Herodotus had watched being built – were completed by 1437. Each 'langue' of the order had a watchtower – German, English, French, Italian – a signifier of the international nature of the Knights' order. The Knights' game was a highly strategic and manipulative one, playing off the Ottomans versus the Egyptian-based sultanate of the Mamluks, and setting Turkic princes against one another.

But earthquakes and man-made attack meant the castle of St Peter itself needed constant maintenance. The partially collapsed Mausoleum was just too convenient a quarry site, and between 1494 and 1522 vast swathes of its cut and decorated stone were cannibalised for use in the strengthening of Bodrum Castle against Ottoman attack. Those friezes of Amazons decorated its walls, those finely sculptured lions its window-ledges. Some sculpture was ground down for lime – as the great temple of Artemis on her birth-island of Delos had been – but some carefully selected pieces, including that section of the Amazonomachy and Centauromachy, and a running leopard, were brought in in 1505 and 1507 and preserved. An Eastern-style mini-*lamassu*, still in situ in the castle, is a reminder of the deeply rooted Asian influences in Mausolos's wedding-cake creation.

First, the remnants of Mausolos's and his successors' great constructions throughout ancient Halikarnassos were taken, and then, as needs grew more pressing and the immediate stone began to run out, hackers went to the tomb of the Mausoleum itself. Green volcanic interior blocks originally used to construct the inner burial chamber became sections of the castle's walls – you can still see them mortared in today. Far more was lost than was preserved. When the Hungarian cannon designer Urban had followed the money and sold his cannon-technology to the Ottomans, the Knights had a serious issue ahead of them. Those walls now needed to resist the terrible punch of gunpowder-propelled cannon balls which hurtled out at 655 feet per second. The stones of the Wonder were ground down again for lime, to cement blocks together, used to reinforce the castle's walls, fortifications needed to counter an escalating arms race. In 1522 the castle was surrendered to Ottoman Turks and on 1 January 1523 the Knights headed to their new home on Malta.[45]

But not before Commandeur de la Tourette, a Lyonnaise knight, on visiting the Mausoleum site in 1522, had supplied a detailed description of the tomb's interior.[46] The account was published in French by Claude Guichard in 1581. Working forensically, thanks to this curious traveller, we have vivid descriptions of walls of the tomb 13 feet high, richly painted. Once again some reliefs of an Amazonomachy or Centauromachy had somehow stayed in place. Life-size sculptures stood on a high plinth. De la Tourette witnessed a complexity of design that was a fitting reflection of the complexity of Mausolos's personal and public life.*[47]

In 1523 the Knights finally evacuated Rhodes, taking with them their archive and treasure, and their fascination for antiquities. Halikarnassos held out for a brief time, but that master of strategy, the Ottoman Suleiman the Magnificent, swiftly prevailed. Having attacked the Knights' headquarters in Rhodes with – it was said – 200,000 ships (impossible, surely!), one of the stipulations of the crusaders' defeat was that the castle of St Peter at Bodrum be handed over to Ottoman control.

---

* We should not underestimate the continuity of wonder, and our capacity for it – it is easy to imagine those Western crusader knights for whom that glittering sea, those hot winds, the golden-stone castles that rose out of golden rocks, must themselves have been a religious experience.

When the Knights moved to their new stronghold in Malta, their headquarters was secured by the gift, each year, of a peregrine falcon to Charles V on All Souls Day. The Grandmaster here, Jean Parisot de la Valette – who himself had spent a year as a slave of the Turks – cracked down on gambling, whoring, and duelling, and called in the great talents of the day – including the student of Michelangelo, Francesco Laparelli – to construct his new headquarters, Valetta. The Grandmaster occupies the self-same lodgings today. I last saw him coming home after a shopping trip in Rome, with two small Bulgari shopping bags. Artists like Caravaggio were also enticed in – men who would be inspired by the antiquity carefully looted by those vagabond knights. Many jewels of antiquity were collected up and displayed in the Knights' new Maltese home. And as boats came to Malta, or to Rhodes, to service the Levantine trade, the double harbour of Halikarnassos and its collapsed, crumbling Wonder became a backwater. But the memory of the Mausoleum lived on.

John Soane, an antiquity-loving son of a brick-maker who would go on to design the Bank of England, was an adoring fan of a number of the Seven Wonders. It is thanks to the neo-classicism of Soane's home in West London, a public library since 1931, where I learned to read as a child, that I developed a passion for the ancient world. On his travels through Europe, Soane acquired a miniature copy of the polymastic Artemis from the Temple at Ephesus, and a model of the Mausoleum of Halikarnassos 'restored' (that is, reimagined, just as we might create a CGI model today). Soane visited the Colosseum in Rome and styled an entire room in his country villa in Ealing with a Greek pot, the Cawdor Vase, as his muse. The Cawdor Vase depicted the race between Pelops and Oenomaus, that mythical event said to have inspired the Olympic Games. Soane even designed a mausoleum for his much-mourned personal friend James King who drowned on a boating trip to Greenwich. These homages to the ancient Wonders which Soane gathered in are still on display in London, and still draw visitors today.

But the Mausoleum site itself, although occasionally visited, was neglected for 300 years. In 1748–9 James Caulfeild, First Earl of Charlemont, had drawings made of the Amazon reliefs in St Peter's Castle – which had been there for over 200 years. A British expedition under C. T. Newton, Her Majesty's Acting Consul in Rhodes, excavated the area – a colonialist enterprise which explains why many of the sculptural reliefs, lions, and those twisting horses' heads, along with what could possibly be Mausolos and Artemisia themselves, have ended up in the British Museum in London. The scheme was set up by the British Ambassador, Stratford Canning, sending the Oriental Secretary, Charles Alison, out on a scouting mission to Bodrum in 1844 on his way to Syria, along with Henry Layard – who was also collecting the reliefs from Mesopotamia which depicted those luscious gardens in Nineveh, all to come into the 'protection of the British Museum'.[48]

Stratford Canning, triumphantly, callously tongue-in-cheek, informed the British Museum: 'The above mentioned gentleman has lately broken into a Turkish fortress, and carried off some dozen blocks of marble . . . It took me three years of patience and occasional exertions to get them . . . '

As the lions were being chipped away from St Peter's Castle, Bodrum's Ottoman castle commander seized them, wrapped them in sheepskin and loaded them onto a boat set for Istanbul, with the blessing of the War Ministry. Trumped by a permit granted by Sultan Abdülmecid, the Turks were powerless – even though the castle commander pointed out, 'your permit covers only lions. But these are tigers' (wild tigers roamed eastern Anatolia up until the 1970s; the Anatolian or Caspian tiger was declared extinct only in 2003).

In a curious coincidence, when Newton was taking the Halikarnassos sculptures back to Woolwich on board the HMS *Gorgon*, guns had to be dropped off at Malta – the cultural and military entrepot of the Mediterranean – to allow for more sculpture on the decks. There are reports of some cut-stone ancient masonry from Anatolia being off-loaded and used as building material by the British army. The log of Captain George William Towsey describes the life-threatening journey made under his command by HMS *Gorgon*, sent specifically to bring these antiquities to England. Twenty tons' worth in sixteen chests. The lions have since flanked that main staircase of the British Museum as incidental decorations.

Their arrival was heralded in London with great fanfare. Newton produced both a text-book and a picture-book of his Mausoleum project. Two feet tall, his large site maps within demonstrate who owned the land round about Mausolos' and Artemisia's resting place – Omar's Well, Ahmed Bey's fig tree, almond trees and cornfields are all carefully

labelled. There are lithographs, taken from photographs, of workers paus-
ing, amphorae of water by their sides to slake the thirst of excavation.
Those tigers and lions sit on sheepskins and rush matting, with turbaned
men at the ready, thick ropes coiled for the sculptures' removal. There
are also coloured plates – approximations of the original painting scheme
and Mausoleum design. Newton's account is the record of a dubious endeavour given latter-day authority.

Today there is still a pomegranate tree on the Mausoleum site – and
a spring said to make men infertile or effeminate still runs nearby. This
spring is where Ovid sets his poem of the creation of the Hermaphrodite
– a son of Aphrodite and Hermes who is lured into the fountain pool here
by a nymph, and blends with her to become a thing both male and female.
This nymph, Salmacis, then attempts to rape Hermaphrodite, who curses
the water that saw this shame[49] – a mythological event immortalised by
the band Genesis in their eight-minute-long work 'Fountain of Salmacis'.
The site of this spring was only identified in 1995 – in a swanky suburb
(with Beko retailers on smart streets and stonemasons selling whole rock-
walls of crystals) on the hillside of Kaplan Kalesi, west of the harbour of
Halikarnassos.

A thrilling sixty-line poem inscription was also uncovered, dating from
100 BCE and praising the literary stars associated with the city. One lumi-
nary being the philosopher Heracleitus of Ephesus, a close personal friend
of Callimachus of Alexandria – the Callimachus who wrote so memor-
ably about the Amazonian dances at Ephesus, and who catalogued the
Wonders in his compendium, *A Collection of Sights in Lands Throughout
the World*. Callimachus, Heracleitus, Mausolos, Hermaphroditus, Hospitaller Knights, ships' captains, John Soane – all reminders of the web
of connections that bound our Wonders, the life and lives around them,
and our unbroken connection to the past, to other lives in other times,
and to other experiences.

As the modern Greek poet George Seferis wrote, in verse set in Ephesus, about the past as a poem and about humanity's relationship to history: 'The poem is everywhere. Your voice sometimes travels beside it like
a Dolphin keeping company for a while.'[50]

In Istanbul, a somewhat underwhelming modern iteration of the Mausoleum exists in MiniTurk – a popular theme park for families which

reconstructs some of the greatest historical monuments of Anatolia. Children drag their heels and slide by, catching kittens, planning the ice cream they will beg for in the overlooking café. Here in MiniTurk too is the Temple of Artemis, where, erroneously, but imaginatively, a giant statue of the many-breasted Artemis glowers from within the miniature white Temple.

These are fairish approximations from the evidence we have. An attempt at reconstructing our next Wonder is, necessarily, more speculative. While the Mausoleum was picked at by aggressors and adventurers, who cared nothing for the hubristic memorial of one Karian man, an island less than a hundred miles due south was flexing its muscles. Shamed by Artemisia, a mere queen, in direct response to Mausolos's rule, the island of Rhodes would go on to raise the stakes, to claim dominance in the Mediterranean and to raise its own Wonder – the Colossus of Rhodes, the grandest of all Seven, a man-god designed to trump all who had gone before.[51]

CHAPTER 6

THE COLOSSUS OF RHODES

302/292 BCE

Why, man, he doth bestride the narrow world
Like a Colossus; and we petty men
Walk under his huge legs, and peep about . . .

SHAKESPEARE, *JULIUS CAESAR*, ACT I, SCENE 2,

135–7, CASSIUS DESCRIBING JULIUS CAESAR

*'The Colossus of Rhodes' engraving produced by Philips Galle after designs by
Maarten van Heemskerck in 1572.*

But that which is by far the most worthy of our admiration, is the colossal statue of the Sun, which stood formerly at Rhodes, and was the work of Chares the Lindian, a pupil of the above-named Lysippus; no less than seventy cubits in height. This statue fifty-six years after it was erected, was thrown down by an earthquake; but even as it lies, it excites our wonder and admiration.

PLINY THE ELDER, *NATURAL HISTORY*,
BOOK 34, CHAPTER 18.41

Pliny the Elder was that unfortunate Roman naval commander and author who was an eyewitness to the destruction of Pompeii, Herculaneum, and other communities around the Bay of Naples during the apocalyptic volcanic eruption of Mount Vesuvius in 79 CE. Trapped near Stabiae, as he tried to lead one of the world's first state-sponsored rescue-missions, Pliny was asphyxiated on a beach by the gas and ash of Vesuvius' explosion. New archaeology in the region is showing us, ever more shockingly, how dreadfully the victims died here. For the inhabitants of the city of Herculaneum, close to the ferocious heat of the pyroclastic flows, death was almost instant or would have taken just two breaths. In Pompeii and Stabiae – a little further from the blast – the end could have been as long as 15 minutes. This was a fiendish destruction which paradoxically also preserved whole towns in southern Italy – sparking, ironically, from the mid-eighteenth century onwards a fetishistic obsession with the ancient world. But before Pliny suffered this hideous death, the commander, who was also a keen philosopher, geographer and naturalist, had enjoyed writing about some of our Wonders – the Great Pyramid, the Hanging Gardens, the Temple of Artemis at Ephesus.[1]

And on a happier adventure, he too had visited the gargantuan sculpture guarding the harbour on Rhodes island, the Colossus at Rhodes. A staggering 108 feet (70 cubits) high, with a skeleton of iron and a skin of bronze, this was a Wonder that became legendary within weeks of its completion.[2] Toppled just sixty or so years (fifty, by some estimates; our sources conflict on the precise dating) after it had been built, by a massive earthquake that also brought down the city's walls and caused shipyards on the coastline here to subside by 3 feet, this extreme sculpture actually spent more time on the ground than it did erect. Pliny went on to describe how visitors would try to put their arms around the fallen giant's thumbs; just one of the Colossus' monster digits was bigger than most life-size statues. In Pliny's day the hollow guts of the sculpture were still visible, including the interior rocks and iron frame which gave it ballast. But none of this manufactured material was a match for nature's mettle, and it was an earthquake that sent the statue, buckling at the knees, crashing down in around 227 BCE.[3] These tumbled remains littered the ground until at least the seventh century CE, when the final remnants of the ample Colossus were melted down for scrap metal. How the mighty can fall.

But despite the impact the Colossus had on many eyewitnesses when it was first built 2,300 years ago, this Wonder has been misconceived through history more than any other. In particular, the fantasy that the giant figure straddled the entrance to the harbour at Rhodes. Forget the image you might have in your mind of the Colossus statue, legs akimbo, reaching over a stretch of 390 feet or so (physically impossible – apart from impractical), holding aloft a torch which doubled as a lighthouse. This 'foot-in-both-camps' giant was in fact a mediaeval invention, a mirage that imprisoned the popular imagination for 800 years. Our first extant mention of this straddling Colossus was delivered courtesy of an Italian pilgrim and lawyer, Niccolò di Martoni, in 1394/5 CE. But the Colossus did not, as the world had it from the late fourteenth century onwards, have his left leg planted in a church called St Nicholas', nor his right leg in the Church of St John of the Colossus. Even today, in the most popular video games, such as *God of War II*, the Colossus (who comes to life and runs amok) straddles Rhodes' harbour from one side to the other. Nonetheless, hold onto your awe, because whatever its exact style and orientation, the Colossus, from our extant evidence, was indeed the largest sculpture ever produced in antiquity. For this reason, throughout the mediaeval period, Rhodes itself was called *Colossensis* – 'of the Colossus'. Just as the tomb of Mausolos in Halikarnassos gave the world mausoleums, so the Colossus sculpture at Rhodes gave us colossal, colossi, Colosseum, and copper-bottomed our mammalian belief that size matters.

The Colossus, as the mediaeval imagination would have it, dominated one of the busiest harbours in the Mediterranean from 292 BCE onwards.[4] The harbour bit is true. From the seventh century BCE the island of Rhodes was bustling with trade, and from the fourth century, after the foundation of the city of Rhodes, had become an entrepôt for the grain supplies of the Eastern Med. In truth, we now think the giant third-century BCE statue stood not at sea-level, but high above on the acropolis, the highest point of the city of Rhodes. Here the hulking sculpture would have been visible from far-off shipping lanes and would also have surveyed the rising and setting of the sun which, at midsummer, crosses a horizon of sea uninterrupted by any land. Because, of course, this Colossus was not just an outsize experiment in art; the Colossus of Rhodes was, in fact, a sun god in the form of burnished bronze.

The Colossus was a representation not of an Olympian deity, nor of a quasi-divine hero, but of Helios, the pre-Olympian Titanic god of the sun. The cult of Helios was honoured by others in Greece: the Athenian philosopher Socrates, for example (we are told by Plato), would have his daily mindfulness-moment with the sun god each morning. Helios turns up in grand shrines at Corinth; his altar could be found at rivers near Mycenae; in what is now Armenia; and in atmospheric Apollonia in Illyria (modern-day Albania), where fire-rituals utilised local oil deposits – even today the air here is tart with the smell of bitumen and nodding-donkey oil wells suddenly appear in otherwise idyllic countryside. In Illyria the god was also said to own a sacred flock of sheep. Helios can, too, be found on modest little late-Roman mosaics on remote Greek islands such as Astypalaia (where Alexander's helmsman Onesicritus wrote his history of Alexander the Great's campaigns), and indeed, driving his chariot on the pedestal of the throne of Zeus at Olympia. Spend any time in the Eastern Mediterranean, and it is impossible not to appreciate that closeness to the sun – the fireball that renders whole seas red, which can pierce through fine marbles and turn a hillside into a cornucopia of colour. This was, too, we must not forget, a world where there was little clock-time, only lives beaten out to the rhythm of the dawn and noon and eventide. Rhodes happens to sit in a band of territory that enjoys over 3,000 hours of sunshine per year. And what could be more central to life than sun-worship? We know now that our greatest star did indeed create life on earth; we are, truly, children of the sun. And Rhodes was the centre of mighty Helios's cult.

The horror of the sun behaving abnormally was burned into epic poetry, myth, and drama. Descriptions of the sun moving backwards across the sky, setting too soon in the day or travelling dangerously close to the earth and scorching Gaia herself were the stuff of nightmares.[5]

And as you might imagine, this was a god with a pyretic temper. When the companions of Homer's warrior-hero Odysseus dared to eat Helios's sacred cattle on their return from the Trojan War, the gods conferred, and drowned them all, leaving only Odysseus to continue his Odyssey home.[6] But on Rhodes, Helios was adored.

Here on Rhodes, from at least the time when the Classical Temple of Artemis at Ephesus and Artemisia's tomb were being raised, Helios was a central cult, honoured in the packed Helaia festival which took place every five years. The Helian games involved running races and performances, a number of which were hosted in the stadium and the theatre of Rhodes' acropolis, all now in sun-bleached fields, found and excavated in the twentieth century, but then damaged by artillery fire during World War II.[7] This festival was an extreme and excessive affair: men (and women, it seems)[8] came from far and wide to participate. There was a famous competition of the *kithara* (the lute-like instrument which we encountered in Ephesus); a four-horse chariot was sacrificed to the sea; and premier offerings were given to Helios – the giant Colossus sculpture being one such dedicated to the great god of fire. But Rhodes' Colossus, a gift to Helios, was not as you would normally see the deity depicted – not in a flaming chariot, drawing the sun across the sky. Rhodes' independent, upstanding Colossus was a formidable defender of a land and its people – which makes great sense when you consider the peculiar, intriguing, and very particular story of this Wonder's creation.

The Colossus was both hyper-modern, and a symbol harking back to the time before times; the protagonist of a protean political age, and a prehistoric generator of life. Helios was believed to have been there at the beginning of god-time, before the creation of man. He had missed out on the fundamental division of the world – of the sky to Zeus, the sea to Poseidon, the underworld to Hades (the earth, Gaia – a divine being originally credited with the creation of all these things – was later, as society itself became more patriarchal, said to belong to all three) – and therefore Helios insisted instead on being awarded the island of Rhodes which was in myth both a dowry and a bride. The island itself – said to be a submerged gift of the sun to the earth, raised up by Helios out of the waters and claimed by him – took its name from the nymph Rhodos with whom Helios had seven children. One of them, Phaethon, would then drive Helios through the sky in his golden phaeton or chariot.[9]

This giant Rhodian god was thus a memory of the old order of deities. The Greek gods were typically believed to have been born on earth or in the sea: even the sun god Apollo, twin brother of Artemis, was birthed on the sacred island of Delos or in that Ortygian glade close to Ephesus. (Around the time the Colossus was built, Apollo was increasingly conflated with Helios, a melding we very first hear of in a fragment of a lost play, *Phaethon*, by the Athenian dramatist Euripides.) But Helios, the original Apollo in many ways, was born in the air from the union of his Titan father Hyperion and his Titaness mother Theia, along with his sisters Selene the moon goddess, and Eos the goddess of the dawn. Whereas the Zeus at Olympia thundered, his luxuriant beard the signifier of a mature man in Greek culture, Rhodes' Wonder, the un-bearded, tousled, soft-lipped Helios, had the dangerous energy of a young, unpredictable man poised to do great things.

So in honour of man's ability to match the vastness of nature, and to survive in the world not just by conflict, but diplomacy, an enormous sculpture was erected by the rulers of Rhodes at the beginning of the Hellenistic Age.

Our best estimates are that this statue would have been 98–114 feet tall and must have left some evidence of its manufacture in the island itself. How on earth did the Rhodians complete such a titanic project? Pliny tells us in his *Natural History* that there were hundreds of bronze workshops in the town close to the Colossus, which continued to produce giant works even after the Colossus had fallen.[10] Ongoing archaeological discoveries brilliantly buttress the historical sources. Rescue digs in Rhodes have come across a number of foundries, some of an industrial scale, from the Hellenistic period. So today on the Hill of Agios Stefanos, in cellars that are 2,300 years old, there are giant pits 11-and-a-half feet wide and 11-and-a-half feet deep, with descending steps. In these dark spaces that taste of time, there is evidence too of crucibles and access for giant bellows' nozzles. With run-off channels installed, these discoveries point to the use of the lost wax method, capable of forming complex shapes from molten metal. First a life-size model with a substructure of wood and clay would have been made and skinned with finely decorated wax. Then clay moulds were produced and heated violently, until the wax was eventually melted out and replaced by a bronze shell. (Debate rages amongst modern-day sculptors and academics as to exactly how monumental bronze sculptures of the time were produced. Some think they were cast from life; with the Colossus, clearly, that was not an option.)

More recent discoveries on the Greek mainland, on the southern slopes of the Acropolis in Athens, have revealed a casting pit 40 feet long. Here, fragments of a clay mould still exist – in this case a *peplos* or dress for a goddess figure was being produced.[11] Evidence from Olympia too shows that smelting of bronze alloys did not happen in a shaft furnace, but in transportable crucibles mounted on an iron frame. The enslaved and the free would have worked together. In Homer's poetry we are told that the craftsman-god Hephaestus wiped himself down in the furious heat of the furnace with a sponge. Sponges can be harvested off the coast of Rhodes and other neighbouring islands, so we might well imagine them being used in great quantities here.[12] The scale of production for the Colossus would have been immense, and lasting over many months, it would have polluted the bright Rhodian landscape with smuts and smoke stains.

A number of men were quickly attached to the design and creation of this memorable statue, including the local sculptor Chares of nearby Lindos (himself the pupil of the bronze maestro of the Mediterranean, Lysippus), and also the Telchines, legendary inventors of smithing.

Lysippus was himself a bit of an ancient wonder, an artist who had a reputation for a fluid, naturalistic style. He had also built other colossi in Sicily and had become the personal sculptor to Alexander the Great, no less. That upward gaze, lips parted; that leonine hair, at once both female and male and typical of Alexander, is all Lysippus's. This inspired artist was capturing (and promoting) a new kind of energy; a personal, wild-haired Alexander-brand that travelled across the reach of Alexander's conquests. As Asclepiades wrote:

> Lysippus modelled Alexander's daring and his whole form.
> How great is the power of this bronze! The brazen king
> seems to be gazing at Zeus and about to say:
> 'I set Earth under my feet; thyself, Zeus, possess Olympus'.[13]

Works attributed to Lysippus include the famous four horses of St Mark's, now visible as replicas above the San Marco Piazza in Venice (the originals are inside the basilica, which also boasts those golden mosaics featuring the pyramids of Giza), but originally produced for the people of

Chios as a quadriga (a four-horse chariot), then taken to Constantinople by Byzantine emperors, only to be looted back to Italy as horse-head decapitations after the Fourth Crusade of 1204. Lysippus's work is also apparent in 'Eros Stringing his Bow', which survives as a charming Roman-copy marble in the generous corridors of the Capitoline Museum in Rome. And then there is the so-called Getty Bronze, a youthful Olympic victor reaching up to his olive-wreath crown (rescued from the seabed in the 1960s, spending a while under the bed of an art dealer in Mount Street, London, and now overlooking the sub-tropical gardens of the Getty Museum in Malibu, California), which also gives us a taste of his verve. In 2010 a handsome bronze seized from an illegal trader, currently being studied in the storerooms of Thessaloniki Museum, was also identified as Lysippus's work. So we have strong hints of the confident, sensuous style that would have been passed down to Lysippus's pupils, such as Chares. We might imagine these next-generation, undergrowth artists trying to outdo their famous teacher, imitating and developing his style, on a gargantuan scale.

Another of Lysippus's pupils was Bryaxis. As well as being a contributor to Mausolos' and Artemisia's Mausoleum at Halikarnassos, by the time Pliny the Elder was writing, Bryaxis was credited with building at least five (relatively modest) colossi on Rhodes itself.

Lysippus was the artist allowed to capture the all-conquering hero in 3D (although perhaps, one suspects, not over-emphasising the diminutive stature of his sponsor).* Alexander was often shown with a spear, like Achilles, images of whom from the late fourth century BCE onwards were increasingly being modelled to look like Alexander; and with a neck tilting slightly to the left. Given the time and the context of its making, it would be strange if the Colossus had not had more than a hint of Alexander about him. And what of that gargantuan scale? Well, Rhodes had close ties to Egypt, and the inspiration for the Colossus almost certainly came from North Africa, where giant statues were highly favoured. A similar experience of saturated vastness is still possible to attain in the Ramesseum in Luxor, just at the edge of the Valley of the Kings. Here the fallen giant head and part of the torso of Ramesses II (Ramesses the Great)

---

* Alexander the Great, you will recall, also chose the decorator of Ephesus, Apelles, to paint his portrait in the guise of the Olympian Zeus in Artemis's Temple.

– inspiring the opening lines of Shelley's oft-quoted poem 'Ozymandias' (itself sparked by the work of the ancient Greek author Diodorus Siculus), 'Look on my Works, ye Mighty, and despair!' – has a rare appeal.[14] It is at once enormously vulnerable and hugely imposing. Even though only half the size of the Colossus, the sheer mass in the Ramesseum is impossible to forget. Think too of the Memnon, colossal sculptures (on which was scratched the name of the astrologer Balbillus from Alexandria and Ephesus), ranging towards the banks of the Nile, and the giant kings and queens outside Abu Simbel (graffitied on by Karian mercenaries). Indeed, the oldest extant metal statue in the world, dating back over 4,300 years, came from Egypt: a metal incarnation of the Pharaoh Pepi I.[15] Recently restored, still glaring out at intimidated tourists with limestone and obsidian eyes from its glass cage in the Egyptian Cairo Museum (inside this bronze core was a smaller bronze sculpture – possibly representing Pepi's son Merenere), we can understand better the divine humanity that these figures were expected to incarnate.

The creation of the Colossus was said to have taken twelve years. Cast in sections, working from the feet up, which were planted on a marble plinth, itself around 60 feet in diameter and 10–15 feet high, the resources used were enormous, far more than could be supplied locally. This perhaps explains the many years the statue took to complete. There have been suggestions that the feet up to the ankles were made of stone and clad in bronze, in order to root the colossal body, the legs and body rising like a human column (legs set apart would have been structurally impossible). The curved plates of bronze, cast in situ, rising at a rate of around 6-and-a-half to 8 feet a year, accessed by an external mound of earth (a little like the system some suggest was used for the Great Pyramid), could have been joined by rivets or T-clamps.[16] And the name? *Kolossos* is a Greek word – with unknown, pre-Greek, possibly Asiatic origins – originally meaning simply an ordinary statue. Monumental statues – think of that seated Ramesses II afront his temple at Abu Simbel in southern Egypt, or the Zeus at Olympia – are often around 30–40 feet tall. This Colossus, three times that height, was unparalleled.

So, let's try to determine where exactly this monster towered? Arriving at Rhodes by boat today, past the tree-covered, rocky promontories all about, is the start of the detective story. Ferries from other Greek islands and the Turkish mainland still pull in at Rhodes' old, commercial harbour.

Immediately one starts to think: did the giant in fact stand between this and the old military anchorage next door? A focal point between the two, as ships drew in across a wide sea, straddling the harbour visually but not physically? This is certainly a possibility: the waters become choppier as one approaches the coast, so it would have been excellent to have a blaring beacon such as the Colossus to steer to. Or should we lift our eyes further up to the skyline horizon? The heights of Rhodes island appear to rise up out of the water. Today, the island's Castle of the Knights Hospitaller dominates the summit of the old town. At the very top of the Street of Knights, leading up to the castle, an old Ottoman schoolhouse is being renovated. This schoolhouse stood on the site of the Great Mosque of Rhodes, itself on top of the Church of St John of the Collachio, which dates back to at least the fourteenth century. Excavations of a series of crypts and underground passageways linking to the Ducal Palace next door have recently proven that the site has been used since the Hellenistic Age. Some of the limestone blocks identified here could well have belonged to the base of the statue. By the same token, could this enigmatic Wonder's foundations indeed be traced within the Castle of the Knights of St John? Outsize foundation blocks have recently been identified in the dank dungeons here. The palace itself has a magnitude, housing ancient mosaics looted and brought in from Kos in a fascistic exercise of the 1930s, an attempt to appropriate the power of antiquity. Was this where the Wonder of Rhodes originally stood?

Or did the Colossus loom over the limestone plateau at the island's highest point, Monte Smith (named for the British Napoleonic-era General Sydney Smith and bombed in World War II)? Here, today shaded by ramithia trees, there are flat plains, perfect for dancing, wrestling and parading in the Helaia. The remains of a temple of Artemis and a temple of Apollo dominate the site now. Given that we know this was where the Helian festival and games took place, does it not make sense that the cult statue of the god Helios would have stood here too – just as Zeus was to be observed in his temple surveying the tracks of the Olympic Games? With views out across both the Aegean and the Mediterranean, the elemental deity would certainly have had a purview of a territory that drew many from Asia and Europe in through the sea-mists so common here, from the compact little Hellenistic settlement of Amos, now almost lost in trees on the Gulf of Marmaris, to the big power-players of the day – Ephesus, Athens, Olympia and Alexandria. A beautiful stadium still stands, where the games of Helios would have been sweated out. Victors were crowned with leaves of the white poplar, which shimmer in the breeze with the radiance of the sun. And a handsome, life-size head of Helios from the period – looking the spitting image of Alexander – sits, blindly, in a cool room in Rhodes' old museum. The holes for this god's solar rays are still clearly visible. One can imagine Rhodes' scandent Colossus as the summation of many Alexander-like mini-sun-god sculptures here.

The life and exploits of Alexander the Great were a critical factor in the statue's generation. We are fortunate that the Colossus was conceived, because this Wonder carries both hard history and human psychology; it is persuasive proof of the fact that as a species we choose to create our way out of a crisis.

The conception and creation of the statue arose from a dangerously divisive situation. The city of Rhodes, on the island of Rhodes, had been established only in 408 BCE, as the federal capital of what had originally been three distinct city-states on the island: Lindos in the east, Kamiros to the west, Ialysos to the north-east. The new-build city quickly boasted over 60,000 inhabitants. But within a hundred years, by the end of the fourth century BCE, Alexander the Great's ferocious ambition had burnt through the region, passed, and left a scorched earth behind. After Alexander died in 323 BCE, there was an unseemly play for power.

During the capture of the nearby island of Cyprus by one of Alexander's generals, Antigonus the One-Eyed – inheritor not just of Alexander's grand army of 60,000 men, but crucially of his treasure chest of over 25,000 talents of gold – the soldier asked the Rhodians to demonstrate their allegiance. Unwisely, in hindsight, they rebuffed Antigonus who, unsurprisingly riled, trained his sights on the islanders. Antigonus commanded incredible firepower, but the Rhodians held their resolve and stayed true to another one-time companion of Alexander, Ptolemy I, whose own territorial base was Alexandria in north Egypt. The Rhodians' choice was, on the face of it, the right one. Not only did Ptolemy I seem to be Alexander's favourite, he forcibly took charge of Alexander's body to bury, but he had also been given control of the rich, fertile lands of Egypt: Kemet, the Black Land, as it was known to the ancients. Rhodes was keeping a beady eye on the grain supplies that came via the Nile out of Alexandria, and those luxury goods and raw materials which had given Egypt such appeal for the last 2,500 years.

Antigonus's son, Demetrius I, known as Demetrius Poliorcetes (Demetrius the Besieger), who had also laid waste to Babylon in 310 BCE, was sent to instil the realisation, in no uncertain terms, in the Rhodians that theirs was the wrong choice. This was a history-making moment we will return to.

Rhodes had long been the unwelcome focus of other interests from the classical period onwards: occupied by the Persians, fought over by the Athenians and the Spartans, ravaged by the bully-boy Athenian aristocrat Alcibiades (that unlikely companion of the philosopher Socrates who had won such plaudits at Olympia), and then harassed by the Karians (who would go on to raise the Mausoleum at Halikarnassos). In 377 BCE, together with Thebes, Chios, Methymna, Mytilene and Byzantium, Rhodes was a founding member of the Second Athenian League against the threats of that Karian patriarch Hekatomnos, father of Mausolos and founder of the Mausolean dynasty. But just twenty years later, the Rhodians broke away from Athens with the promise of support from King Mausolos, who then turned nasty, fostering an anti-democratic coup, installing his own man Agesilochus. Mausolos's widow Artemisia II, as you will recall, became infamous for her duplicitous naval attack on the island. Not even the pleadings of the ancient world's greatest orator, Demosthenes, could relieve the Rhodians of these unwanted interventions.

Rhodes had become a victim of its own success, because the Rhodians had something that everyone wanted – an unparalleled maritime record, and therefore the potential to offer mastery of the sea.

Rhodes was an island that was not insular, that had long looked out. No fewer than five harbours made an enviable maritime hub.[17] With easy access to three continents, it could control lawful trade, and deal with the pirates who were a stubborn cancer in antiquity, particularly in the Mediterranean. Here, coves easily concealed boats which then sprang out like scorpions to attack their prey. Ships were frequently scuppered, crews killed or taken hostage, cargo ransacked. Pirates could act as lone wolves, or they were, more typically, encountered as organised crime cartels. The piratical Arabian Nabataean civilisation, for example – neglected by history – was as famous for its trading nous, delivering luxuries like frankincense from southern Arabia (modern-day Yemen, Oman and Saudi Arabia) and bitumen for caulking from the Dead Sea, as it was for springing attacks on trading ships in the Red Sea and beyond. When we think of the logistics of creating five of the Seven Wonders across those Mediterranean seas, we should never have to the fore of our minds the formal navies of great civilisations, but instead the jagging attack of endemic piracy.

But the ancients had a plan. At this time, a series of customs and agreements defined by the people of Rhodes, loosely gathered in the *Lex Rhodia*, set a standard for maritime behaviour. This prototype Law of the Sea then migrated into the Roman system of justice and on into the law-giving campaign of one of the emperors of Constantinople, of the New Rome – Justinian I and his Justinianic code. Justinian's *Corpus Juris Civilis* enshrined Western jurisprudence. And the *Nomos Rhodion Nautikos*, developed in Constantinople around 700 CE, was an accepted thumb-rule of maritime behaviour well into the thirteenth century CE. As the Roman Emperor Antoninus Pius declared, 'I rule the earth, Rhodes' law rules the sea.'[18]

Rhodes has not forgotten its particular contribution to history in this regard. Just off the Street of the Knights where hot tourists range up and down, seeking out culture and shady tavernas, the island still hosts diplomats from across the world to debate matters of the sea and international trade under the auspices of the Aegean Institute of Maritime Law.

The katabatic winds and squalls in the straits which separated Rhodes from the Anatolian mainland, as well as seabed trenches, appropriately named Pliny and Strabo, made sailing conditions here unpredictable. The historian Appian describes a blazing conflict between Mithridates VI, Rome's Black Sea-based enemy who besieged the sanctuary at Ephesus, and the Rhodians. When Mithridates' fleet was blown off course, 'the Rhodians promptly sailed out to meet them, fell upon them while they were still scattered and suffering from the effects of the tempest, captured some, rammed others, and burned more – and took about four hundred prisoners'.[19] It is little surprise that wrecks litter this part of the world. One, discovered at Serçe Limani, just across the water off mainland Turkey, and being investigated by the Institute of Nautical Archaeology at Texas A&M University, dates to exactly the time of the construction of the Colossus, c. 280–270 BCE. The cargo of this Hellenistic merchant-ship included resin-lined, grape-seed-filled wine amphorae, all kept safe in a lead-lined hull. There's even a lead pipe which might be our first evidence of a bilge-pipe. This chance find has yielded wonderfully precise evidence for the experience of being a sailor at the time. The Colossus statue was being raised to glare out across the strategic, busy Aegean Sea.

The lead hull of the Serçe Limani wreck had trapped snares of fabric – both wool and hemp have been found in other ships, used to help plug any gaps in the boats' sides. A single wooden toggle is all that is left from a system in the Serçe Limani boat designed to stop the sail-cloths flapping, and a single marble ring, lowered into the water to help disentangle fouled nets and mooring cables. But the seabed was – still is – littered with amphorae, a cargo of at least 600 containers, transport-ready. There are amphora-stamps from the island of Thasos, and resin lining, suggesting that some of the cargo was the highly prized Thasian wine from the northern Aegean island. There is fine-glazed black ware, which probably originated in Athens or Alexandria, and chubby perfumed-oil pots, perhaps from the Nile Delta. Just these contents alone demonstrate the spider-web of connection Rhodes enjoyed across Greece and Egypt.[20]

The Rhodians' reputation as ferocious warrior-seamen endured. The Greek captain-for-hire Mentor, in command of Karian mercenaries, helped Persia to re-conquer Egypt in the 340s, while Mentor's brother Memnon fought against Alexander the Great's father, the Macedonian King Philip II. (There is a chance that the Belevi Mausoleum near Ephesus, very like the Mausoleum of Halikarnassos in design, was built as a tomb for Mentor and Memnon or for Antigonus the One-Eyed.) Mentor's first, Persian wife would go on to become Alexander's mistress and mother of one of his sons. But when Alexander defeated Persia, the Rhodians would find themselves on the wrong side of history. The island forcibly capitulated to Alexander the Great, surrendering with a delegation of ten ships at Tyre (on the western seaboard of modern-day Lebanon) in 332 BCE, where Alexander had proved his ruthlessness by crucifying many hundreds of Tyre's inhabitants after a seven-month siege when the island city refused to come over to his camp; a public bolt-shot of revenge. Rhodes' future looked set; part of the new world-order as dictated by Alexander the Great's appetite.

But then Alexander died. Immediately the Rhodians expelled the

Macedonian garrison from their city, and set their sights on liberty, self-rule and self-determination. The islanders capitalised on their not-so-secret weapon, their navy, and their shipyards were patrolled by security to prevent industrial espionage or sabotage. As the seamen garnered an ever-growing reputation for their stylish smash-and-grab tactics, the fly-weights of sea-contest, so the economic reputation of the island grew. Rhodes became a little like the Switzerland of the Eastern Mediterranean – Rhodian businessmen turning up in all kinds of deals, their assets stored on the island. The appreciation of the Eastern Mediterranean business network was shown by the universality and number of the dedications to Rhodes after it was devastated by that earthquake in 228 BCE which would tumble their Wonder. Terracotta amphorae-handles, stamped with the Rhodians' symbol, have made their way across Europe, Western Asia and North Africa, demonstrating that the Rhodians at this time dominated the grain trade out of Alexandria, from Cyprus and even across the Black Sea.[21] Centuries later, the Rhodians would still be described as 'richer than any other Greek people'.[22]

Inevitably, such a valuable asset was unlikely to escape notice. After the death of Alexander, as we know, the megalomaniac conqueror's generals, in particular Antigonus, Seleucus and Ptolemy, were battling it out for control of the now vast Macedonian empire. Initially, with Cyprus under his belt and tasting a winning streak, Antigonus asked simply for Rhodian ships made of Syrian timber, wanting to harness Rhodian maritime assets in his scrap of acrid rivalry with Ptolemy I in Egypt. The Rhodians complied, and then thought again. They did not really want a fight. When Antigonus attacked their merchants travelling the swell-ripped seas between the island and Egypt, they, quite justifiably, fought back. When Antigonus's son Demetrius the Besieger rocked up at their coastline, they agreed to parlay. But then Demetrius made impossible demands, ordering the surrender of 100 hostages and access for the Antigonid fleet to occupy Rhodes' double-harbour and ports around the island. The Rhodians locked their gates, and a storm was unleashed. The siege of Rhodes was about to begin.

Demetrius gathered a huge force of 200 ships, 170 supply vessels, a rag-bag of pirates and opportunists, all waiting to plunder the treasure trove that was Rhodes. I have walked through shipyards from the same period, recently excavated at Kition in nearby Cyprus. Imagining the worlds and generations-worth of experience these shipyards serviced and moved – with the warships being pulled up and down stone slipways, just like these, their sails beginning to belly on the sea – has real resonance. Later sources described an infantry force of 40,000, together with cavalry, being assembled, not to mention the scavenging siege-chasers who could smell easy pickings. The attackers swiftly managed to get ashore and build a camp south of the city of Rhodes, just out of missile-reach. For the Rhodians, holed up inside their tight fortress citadel, the arrival of these besiegers must have been a sickening sight.

Accounts of how the Rhodians reacted give a brilliant insight into the reality of ancient life. They swiftly made provision for the children of the fallen, expelled foreigners they could not trust to fight and promised slaves-turned-soldiers their freedom and enfranchisement. But as the islanders raised their harbour walls, Demetrius' men were also raising four-storey-high floating siege-machines – carried on cargo ships and protected by a floating boom to prevent ramming. Cretan archers acted as snipers, while Rhodians tried to protect their moles and walls against fire-bombs, and to harry their attackers with fire-ships. Then Demetrius turned his laser-focus to the land. A pyramid-like siege engine – this time 9 storeys, 150 feet high, 60 feet wide, weighing in at 360,000 pounds, with artillery emplacements, battering rams 180 feet long, bridges and a towering attack platform, itself flanked by moveable tents protecting more battering rams 100 feet long – was produced to buttress the work of sappers and mines. With stone walls at its base and catapults on upper levels, clad in iron and hides, and with water tanks in place to douse any fires, this was a beast of a war-machine. In a harbour and hinterland now chirpy with international visitors happily quaffing wine and buying hand-embroidered tea-towels, it is hard to imagine the terror and deprivation of blockade. The aggressions continued for a year.

Despite all this, offered the chance to destroy statues of Antigonus and Demetrius, the Rhodians, nobly, refused – remembering that these men had at one time been their allies. Ptolemy I sent food supplies across the water from Egypt. The outnumbered Rhodians refused to give up, or to give in. As the siege dragged on, where today men sell fresh fish, and pilgrim-tourists mourn the loss of Jewish lives following the pogroms here during World War II, Rhodians would have starved, and Demetrius' men would have become food for the fishes as bodies floated in the water. But the Mediterranean world did not want this kind of zero-sum attrition, and envoy after envoy was sent to sue for peace. The attenuating maw of conflict was all too familiar. Eventually a deal was agreed; the original 100 hostages were to be surrendered, but Rhodes was to remain independent and ungarrisoned, allied with Antigonus except in a circumstance where Ptolemy I might be attacked. Aggression had sharpened into diplomacy.

The siege had lasted a whole year. Despite its stalemate, it had earned Demetrius that second name 'Besieger', and Ptolemy the epithet *Soter* or 'Saviour'. The latter was fostered by an appreciation of something new and important: the horror of belligerence fed by greed and affront, and the plangent possibilities of rationale, of parlay, of ways to resolve disputes that did not simply end in bloodshed. The world was buzzing with stories of the Rhodians' impressive handling of the affair. In 306 BCE we see the first international approach from a fledgling state in the Greek world, a people who would re-shape antiquity – the Romans. It would later be an intense Roman interest in Rhodes that would help to keep the story of the Colossus bright in the collective imagination.

This great siege at Rhodes set a standard for wartime diplomacy and directly catalysed the generation of the most anthropomorphic of all the Seven Wonders. Because what happened next was the antithesis of all the terrible scenes of cultural destruction that litter the pages of history: the smashing of Byzantine icons by the Frankish thugs of the Fourth Crusade; the burning of books on *Kristallnacht* in Berlin; the decimation of the Buddhas of Bamiyan in Afghanistan. For now trauma was physically turned into triumph.

Having seen, day in, day out, the terrible Helepolis, the siege-breaker machine, advance, the beleaguered Rhodians were allowed to use battle and siege spoil – sold off as armament scrap – to fund their brilliantly preposterous project. At the cost of 300 talents (one talent was loosely the equivalent of 24 kilograms of silver), that brazen sun god rose from the ashes. The colossal Helios was a statement of hope. A Wonder that incorporated the wonderful powers of arbitration, compassion, and simple common sense.

Built 'as a house is built on top of itself', the statue was also, in some ways, an incarnation of the psychological make-up of Rhodes. An island that stands out by its sheer size from the many thousands of others in the

Mediterranean, one of the most substantial next to Crete. It is also an island with a ferocious sense of itself politically, which pursued a clever policy of what has been called 'studied neutrality'[23] – a strategy that reaped tangible rewards, politically, economically and culturally. As well as those archaeological discoveries of casting pits, and Pliny's account, numerous inscriptions from the island refer to small, family-run bronze-casting and artisanal workshops, so we should imagine the creation of the Colossus as a binding, island-wide effort.[24] A work of creation that would come to define Rhodes. Because the Colossus of Rhodes would not be alone. From Pliny the Elder we hear that by the time he visited in the first century CE, there were 3,000 bronze statues on the island, and a crop of around 100 colossi.

We are, truly, the stories that we tell about ourselves. Furthermore, as neuroscientists tell us, our memories are a narrative we invent to buttress our identity. So it should perhaps be no surprise that an epigram – composed almost certainly in the second century BCE, a hundred years or so after the Colossus was built – was later presumed to be the very inscription which decorated the feet of the Colossus sculpture, describing the Rhodians as descendants of Hercules, and Rhodes as 'master of land and sea'. By the time the epigram was written, the Rhodians had found their feet once more. They had shaken off Demetrius the Besieger, and were positioning themselves as the favourites of the rising power in the region – those Italian interveners who had tried to encourage a diplomatic solution to the Rhodian siege, the Romans. The Rhodians needed to believe they were masters of all they surveyed, and even if their great Colossus had been felled by Mother Nature, they could imagine that this monster bore witness to their greatness before they truly became great. Societies on their uppers always want to assert they have enjoyed previous Ages of Gold.

And whereas an understanding of the past came predominantly, up until the Hellenistic Age, from collective, face-to-face experiences (with a few notable exceptions, such as the writings of Herodotus, Xenophon or Thucydides), by the time the Colossus had fallen, a tradition of global historiography was developing, of pasts being written and widely shared. So the Colossus was more easily grouted into history as part of a triumphalist narrative. The Rhodian historian Zeno – drawing on official documents in archives, and on public display commemorating this event – dramatises the siege splendidly. It is our great loss that, maddeningly, his history of Rhodes, written in the third century BCE, survives only in fragments. The Colossus rose in the Mediterranean-wide imagination at exactly the same time as those writers in Alexandria were raising the reputation of works of human achievement into Wonder-lists. It was astonishing, and it was built in the right place at the right time to become the stuff of legends.

A romantic idea entered the canon – that, because during the siege of Rhodes even the enslaved had fought on the battlements to defend their masters' island, Demetrius was left so impressed by Rhodian valour that he bequeathed his siege-engines to the islanders as a tribute to their physical and moral fibre. Parts of this machinery were then melted down to build the Colossus, an emblem of arbitration.

Whatever the literal truth of that story, the Rhodians were not planning to let bygones be bygones, to let anyone forget what they had been through. A recent archaeological discovery has revealed that 1,000 sling-shot bullets from the attacking cavalry of Macedonian veterans and allies had been triumphantly seized and piled up, to prove that the undefeatable had indeed been defeated;[25] and a festival was mounted to praise Ptolemy I, who had helped the Rhodians break siege. Inquiring of the Oracle of Zeus Ammon at Siwah – which, recall, was a version of the Olympian Zeus – whether Ptolemy could be honoured as a god,* an affirmative response led to a shrine being built to Ptolemy in the old city of Rhodes, and a cult of their saviour upheld in Rhodes island and more broadly in the League of the Cycladic Islands.[26] Rhodes was on top once more, a mercantile centre in a hyper-charged Eastern Mediterranean world, and so the colossal Wonder was raised; unique, unforgettable, and a child of the civilising power of mediation. But it was a totem that would be felled by the power of the earth within half a century.

It is hard to imagine the horror when this Wonder toppled. Earthquakes are desperately distressing psychologically as well as physically. They play into our fear of helplessness. In this earth-struck land, as well as walls in the city crashing down, killing and maiming, to hear that bronze behemoth split and shatter, to see that beautiful, sunlit, hopeful face bruised and bent on the ground – while some of the islanders who

---

* A not-so-subtle imitation of his predecessor Alexander, who, according to Arrian (*Anabasis* 3.3–5), had himself declared a son of a god by Ammon in the Libyan desert.

helped to raise it must still have been alive – must have felt like a ghastly omen.

Ptolemy III (the grandson and son of Ptolemies I and II, who would build our final Wonder, the Pharos Lighthouse at Alexandria) offered to raise the statue from the dead. There was an offer too from that new power-monger on the block, Rome. Rather conveniently, might one suggest, the Rhodians retorted that an oracle had advised against the Colossus' rehabilitation. Leaving it as compelling, nostalgic scrap was certainly the cheaper option. A re-erection might result in appropriation, a claim somehow that the history, narrative and brilliance of the statue belonged to whomever could afford to pay for its resurrection. Even if these Wonders are in some ways timeless, they are also very much of their times.

So, the fallen Colossus joined Rhodes' other attractions for travellers and pilgrims. Rhodes was increasingly becoming a destination not just for traders and raiders, but for culture tourists. The fabulous Lindian Chronicle – a huge, inscribed stone stele, reused in the floor paving of Rhodes' Byzantine church of St Stephen – describes the dedications and gifts left by ardent pilgrims in the city's temple to Athena on the island, including arms and armour allegedly from the Trojan War and gifts from none other than Herakles. There were natural attractions too: cool, spring-fed valleys, populated by giant moths that seem happier resting disguised as leaves. There are still whole villages dedicated to honey-production in the south of Rhodes, roadsides thick with mountain tea. And as well as travelling to see the floored Colossus, tourists also visited the so-called tomb of Helen of Troy (on Rhodes today a rainbow is still called by some 'Helen's noose', since one alternative version of her myth says the shamed Spartan queen hanged herself from a tree on the island).[27] More feasibly, in one temple, the jewellery of Artaxerxes II of Persia was on display as well as the linen corselet of Pharaoh Amasis of Egypt. The travellers took away stories and brought wealth. The Colossus of Rhodes became a firm fixture not just in the Hellenistic Greek, but also in the Roman, psyche and soon in the minds of those in the expanding Roman domains. In c. 200 BCE, operating on the principle that my enemy's enemy is my friend, the Rhodians cosied up with the Romans, and their outsize icon became another expression of culture and identity which now belonged to Rome.

However, it was a new golden age for Rhodes that would tarnish. By 167 BCE, when the Rhodians seemed to be drifting away from Rome once more, they were punished by the emerging superpower which, spitefully, made the island of Delos (the sacred birthplace of Apollo and his twin sister)[28] a free port.* Substantial amounts of Rhodes' business were snatched by the Delians. New excavations on evocative Delos show the luxury goods imported, the cash and the bling pull of the island. Now, rather than on Rhodes with its formerly coveted villas, it was on Delos that merchants built expensive homes boasting the latest fashions: marble decorations from Sicily, architecture from Italy, grotto features from Alexandria – all currently being excavated.

Even so, the great and the good of the Eastern Mediterranean world continued to flock to Rhodes. The much-travelled Greek geographer from Anatolia, Strabo, ebulliently declared, 'I am unable to speak of any other city as equal to it, or even as almost equal to it, much less superior to it.'[29] Julius Caesar, Cicero, and the future Emperor Nero all came here to perfect their speechwriting and debating skills. Many practised their art by praising the Colossus project. The satirist Lucian compared historians to the sculptors of the Seven Wonders, and said putting style over substance was the equivalent of putting the head of the Colossus on the body of a person of restricted growth. This island and its stories were the basis for performative communication.[30] Rhodes might have lost its independence and pole position politically. But the idea of its statue did not lose its power or pull. And partly thanks to its preposterously confident creation, Rhodes acquired the reputation as a pioneering cultural hub, an island of the arts.

The Colossus became both a goal and a prototype. Rhodes' sculpture sparked a trend for giant statues – for example, at the Roman port of Ostia, at Patras in the Peloponnese and at Caesarea in Palestine. These colossal wannabes must surely have been a little like pale imitations of ground-breaking cultural giants; imagine perhaps the lacklustre sequels of *Star Trek* or the *Indiana Jones* franchise or the faux Eiffel Tower and Statue of Liberty in Las Vegas. The Colossus might have fallen, but

---

* Not only that, but Delos acquired the abominable accolade of being one of Europe and North Africa's main slave-trading centres; we are told that 10,000 enslaved people a day would be penned, bought and sold here.

still the cultures that followed, especially Roman, simply could not get enough of it.

Nero (that confirmed Hellenophile) commissioned a giant Colossus-homage statue of himself at the end of the Appian Way and at the entrance to his Domus Aurea, his Golden House Palace in Rome. His was a project where everything was outsized. Descending into the remains of the Domus Aurea today, the ceilings and arches, now 40 feet underground, rear 100 feet above one's head. The work was undertaken by the artist Zenodorus, who, it was said, had designed and constructed the world's biggest-ever sculpture in Roman-occupied Gaul (on land owned by the Arverni tribe, near modern-day Puy de Dôme) – an enormous figure of the messenger and money god Mercury. Zenodorus's Mercury, dominating the surrounding countryside, took ten years to build, around 50 CE; his creator was clearly a leader in his field. Pliny the Elder, again an eyewitness, described the artistry of Zenodorus's clay models while working on the Nero Colossus commission in Rome, and the delicacy of its wooden frame: 'Zenodorus was counted inferior to none of the artists of old in his knowledge of modelling and chasing . . .'[31]

But Nero's sculpture was, even so, just a bit shorter than the Colossus, intended to rise a mere 98 feet. Originally given the face of the psychotic emperor, when Nero fell from grace, Rome's own colossus was firmly restyled as the god of the sun. The giant artwork was finally fully erected in 75 CE, the date suggesting delays and complications in its construction. The comparison with Rhodes' masterpiece must have been full-square in the minds of Nero's eventual successor Vespasian, not only because the emperor gave this man-god a crown of solar rays, each at least 22 feet long, and called him Sol, but because, as is witnessed by Martial's epigram, Rome's folly became a cultural meme: 'Don't let yourself be detained by that giant mass, that wondrous Colossus, built to distract from the labours on Rhodes.'[32]

But then the imitation-Wonder became, like Rhodes' original, a casualty of personality politics. In 126–8 CE the Emperor Hadrian, wanting Rome's Sol-Colossus spot for his own temple dedicated to the goddess Roma (the first time Rome was worshipped independently as a goddess) and to Venus Felix (Venus of fertility and prosperity), used twenty-four elephants to move the upright sculpture to just outside the Flavian

Amphitheatre, which would come to be known as the Colosseum in the middle ages*[33] – as described in *The Wonders of Rome*, a pilgrim guide written around 1000 CE. The remains of Hadrian's new temple are now incorporated into the church and monastery of S. Francesca Romana (originally S. Maria Nova, possibly built as early as the eighth century BCE, nestling right next to the Roman Forum). While the Hadrianic base for Rome's colossus, measuring 58 by 48 feet, was cut down and covered over in 1933 during the fascistic re-modelling of Rome's city centre, the brick ramp used for the statue's movement has recently been identified within the east side of the Temple of Venus. The precise location of the statue is marked today by a tree, under whose branches tourists shade. Hadrian had planned to give the sun, Sol, a matching moon colossa, Luna, but never got round to it – a measure of the enormity of these construction tasks. The Emperor Commodus removed the Roman colossus' head, replacing it with his own, styled as Hercules: a move which was then reversed. But the colossus would live on: the Flavian Amphitheatre it had once overlooked would come to be re-named the Colosseum. And there are glimpses still of the colossus' presence. Today, at the perimeter of the Colosseum, the base of the giant remains. The marble cladding has been lost, but a faint footprint and gentle humps are just about visible, ignored by tourists who pose with Albanians in Roman centurion dress, and shade themselves from the sun with parasols made in Taiwan.

Rome's colossus was last described as standing in 394 CE. The record of its destruction is lost in what some have mis-named 'The Dark Ages' following the fall of Rome in the fifth century CE, although the English Father of History, Bede, is wrongly credited (in what is in fact a copycat work by a misty figure, the Pseudo-Bede) as hailing the Roman giant in a poem in a collection of his works composed in the eleventh century CE: 'As long as the Colossus stands, Rome will stand, when the Colossus falls, Rome will also fall, when Rome falls, so falls the world.'[34]

And the original, fallen Rhodian Colossus continued to haunt imaginations. Just as Alexander's face had been the model for sun gods – Helios, Apollo, Sol, Mithras – so Alexander the Great increasingly came

---

* In the mediaeval period the Colosseum was believed to be a temple of the sun (the Latin 'to worship' is *colo, colere*).

to be worshipped as a deity in Hellenistic cities: Pergamum, Emesa, Ephesus and Alexandria. When in turn Alexander's Hellenistic world was Romanised, Alexander was worshipped in the Roman East too. And as the first Orthodox Christian Roman emperor, Constantine the Great, re-dedicated the city of Byzantium as Constantinople, making it his new headquarters for the Eastern Roman Empire, on the top of his 160-foot, porphyry 'Column of Constantine' there stood a towering bronze figure. With a solar crown and a relaxed pose, more than a little like that of the Colossus, this totemic monument was a mash-up of Helios, Sol, Sol Invictus, Apollo, Alexander and Jesus, the newly adored son of God. Those loose curls and that lion's mane which Alexander and Rhodes' Colossus used to sport offered themselves conveniently to the tousled locks of Jesus the potent, radical, boyish revolutionary – while in time, once the Statue of Zeus from Olympia had been imported to Constantinople too six decades later, a glaring, bearded king of the gods would come to be the role-model for a god who was no longer really a boy.

The afterlife of the statue, in the collective imagination, became the stuff of legends.

The fake news quickly started to circulate: In romantic versions of Rhodes' Colossus story, it was not just the proceeds of the sale of weapons in 304 BCE, but the arsenal of the besiegers itself that was melted down to build the statue. And as the ancient world gave way to the mediaeval, it was said that in 653 CE, following the occupation of Rhodes by the Arabs, with the help of 900 camels, a Jewish scrap-metal merchant from Edessa carted off the Colossus' remains. This apocryphal, anti-Islamic, anti-semitic tale was recorded by the Byzantine Emperor Constantine VII (Constantine Porphyrogenitus). The Colossus had clearly caught Constantine VII's fancy and his mind's eye.

Standing in the spine of the Hippodrome, in what was then Constantinople and is now known as Istanbul, is a stone obelisk. This monument was raised to match the Ancient Egyptian obelisk already in place, originally carved to honour the Egyptian Pharaoh Thutmose III, at the Hippodrome's southern end. Tourists eating the candyfloss readily sold here, or distracted by bird-seed sellers encouraging the pigeons to be fed, often pay less attention to the obelisk of the New Rome than they do to that of Ancient Egypt; but it is worth persevering. Restored by Constantine

VII (although rather beaten up in the later history of the city, when it was used as a climbing-wall by Ottoman Janissary soldiers), holes are still visible on the stone, readied to take the rivets to hold a splendid new bronze skin in place. It was proudly commemorated thus by Constantine:

> This four-sided wonder of the heavens, now destroyed by age, Emperor Constantine, father of Romanus, the glory of command, renovates to a better standard than the old spectacle. For the Colossus was an object of wonder in Rhodes, and this bronze [structure] is an object of wonder here.

As it still is. Walking through Istanbul's Hippodrome today, in just one hour I spent there on a hot July afternoon, travellers from Yemen, Canada, Bulgaria, Kuwait, the UK and Spain all came, all drawn to the towering stone, where, just beneath street-level, the Colossus' name, illegible to many, is immortalised in mediaeval Greek.

The human world seems irresistibly attracted to size, and it never wanted to forget Rhodes' giant Wonder.

Even right at the western edge of the Mediterranean, where the sea meets the Atlantic Ocean in the Strait of Gibraltar, in the dappled light of the modest Napoleonic cemetery in Gibraltar town, there is reference to the Colossus. A number of sailors were lost on HMS *Colossus* in 1805 at the Battle of Trafalgar – their memories marked with the neoclassical headstones which had become so fashionable at this time. The loss of the ship, named for an ancient statue (the Royal Navy has had six craft named *Colossus*), amongst cacti and palms and unlikely Union Jack flags, was also lamented.

When the Suez Canal was nearing completion in 1869 – a gargantuan project which would revolutionise global trade – a French artist with a passion for Egypt (both its modern life and its ancient art), Frederic Auguste Bartholdi, suggested the erection of a giant sculpture to mark the auspicious occasion. Bartholdi's design of a young Egyptian woman, dressed in the clothes of a labourer, inspired in part by the monumental sculptures of Ramesses the Great at Abu Simbel and at the Ramesseum, was named *Egypt carrying the Light to Asia*; it was turned down by the Egyptian authorities only because of its cost and complexity. But Bartholdi was not deterred. He repurposed his plan. A fund-raising scheme was organised, and in 1886 the Statue of Liberty – or to give it its correct, original name, *Liberty Enlightening the World* – was unveiled.

> Not like the brazen giant of Greek fame,
> With conquering limbs astride from land to land;
> Here at our sea-washed, sunset gates shall stand
> A mighty woman with a torch, whose flame
> Is the imprisoned lightning, and her name
> Mother of Exiles. From her beacon-hand
> Glows world-wide welcome; her mild eyes command
> The air-bridged harbor that twin cities frame.
> 'Keep, ancient lands, your storied pomp!' cries she
> With silent lips. 'Give me your tired, your poor,
> Your huddled masses yearning to breathe free,
> The wretched refuse of your teeming shore.
> Send these, the homeless, tempest-tost to me,
> I lift my lamp beside the golden door!'

'THE NEW COLOSSUS', A POEM WRITTEN BY
EMMA LAZARUS IN 1883 TO RAISE FUNDS FOR THE
PEDESTAL OF THE PROPOSED STATUE OF LIBERTY

The Statue of Liberty, dedicated to commemorate the French and American Revolutions, and directly inspired by the idea of the Colossus, soars 53 feet higher than the ancient original. A false judgement has been made about the fact that the Statue of Liberty looks forwards, and the Colossus looked back; it is a trite evaluation to the effect that the ancients understood only the past, whereas America looked ahead to a brighter future. Actually for the ancients, time never quite worked in such a binary way. For them the past was a version of the present, an inspiration and an instruction. Even the future could be found in time behind – a perception of the power of the past that neuroscientists have now proved. We cannot have a future idea unless we access a memory of some kind; one of the reasons we still remember these ancient Wonders today.

Although the mediaeval period, with its own maritime obsessions, wanted the Colossus to straddle the harbour at Rhodes, ironically it might be a mediaeval and early modern castle that hides the Colossus' truth. Here in the old town, with its Jewish quarter, and squat military lookouts, and bomb damage from the two world wars of the twentieth century, young archaeologists are beginning to dig, to try to find remnants of Rhodes' stupendous Wonder. The stronghold of the Knights Hospitaller – that self-same knightly order who would go on to cannibalise the Mausoleum of Halikarnassos in Turkey, or indeed the Church of St John of the Collachio or the Ducal Palace – may yield its secrets soon.

The Colossus has continued to inspire, from Salvador Dali to the insurance company Budget Direct – a Wonder that has been much re-imagined. It is there in the 1961 movie, *The Colossus of Rhodes*; it is present as the Titan of Bravos, enthralling in *Game of Thrones*; and at the time of writing, it is in *Assassin's Creed* (along with the other six Wonders); and, as mentioned, in *God of War* where, as the player, you have the chance to fight the giant statue itself.

Whereas the Great Pyramid was an incursion into the natural world, but aimed to be a part of it, the Colossus was built and was perceived as proof incarnate of man's dominance over Gaia, the earth. A perceptive description of the Colossus project comes from Philo of Byzantium, who chose to employ a hyperbolic tone: 'the artist used so much bronze for the work there was almost a shortage of metals, for all the earth's mines were exploited in carrying out the project . . . for in the world a second Sun stood to face the first'.[35] As with all works of this nature, and particularly of this scale, the monuments came at a price. With these Wonders of civilisation, the process of mass industrialisation was beginning. Ice cores from Greenland show a rise in pollution levels from the Bronze Age onwards, which soar in the Hellenistic Age and the Roman Empire, only to drop when impacted by natural disasters such as the Antonine Plague.[36] To build a statue 100 feet tall, celebrating one of the greatest stars in the cosmos, sets in train a plundering of the earth's resources which now threatens life on earth itself.

And the monumentality of the statue would also be put to sinister use.[37] In 1935, when Adolf Hitler asked his architect Speer to conceive of a site suitable for the Nazi party gathering at Nuremberg, one of his creative resources, his mood-board if you like, was the Seven Wonders. Hitler believed that great cultures expressed themselves through monumental art. Speer developed a 'Theory of the Value of Ruins', asserting that ancient aesthetics and construction methods would deliver a time saturated power for the new imperator who had designs on world domination. However, the Third Reich's life would prove to be shorter even than that of the Colossus of Rhodes.[38] Walking through Nuremberg now, morally so laden with historical despoliation, with its abandoned cars, half-hearted street vendors and drug-dealers, is a cold reminder of where the extremes of human design can lead.

The Colossus might be the direct result of a peace agreement, but the hyper-confident scale of the work, the sheer amount of bronze and energy it used to create one giant divine-man, was symptomatic of a new epoch

Cartoon by Edward Linley Sambourne, published in London's Punch Magazine, *showing Cecil Rhodes as a modern day Colossus, towering across the continent of Africa with outstretched arms.*

in world history, when human ambition would declare war on the resources of earth, sea and sky.

Rhodes, visible from modern-day Turkey, ancient Anatolia, is just a few
hours of sailing from the wondrous Temple of Artemis at Ephesus and
the Mausoleum of Halikarnassos, four days from the Statue of Zeus at
Olympia, three from the Great Pyramid at Giza, and a day from Alexandria – a sea-passage whose length was much debated by ancient authors:
4,000 stades, thinks Strabo in his *Geography*; 5,000 according to others;
3,750, says Eratosthenes the Alexandrian mathematician.[39] It is no surprise that Pausanias, tourist and tour-guide, who wrote with such passion
about all ancient Wonders, came from the Anatolian seaboard. In this
part of the world, it is the land that is dark – the sea is flame-yellow at
sunset, and diamond-bright just after dawns that glow and burn. Islands
lie colossally like basking whales. But then these stepping-stones run
out, and, heading for Africa, the next stop south from Rhodes becomes
Egypt. And despite the difficulty of the journey, ships arriving in this
new continent would soon be guided in by Egypt's 'second sun' – a remarkable lighthouse called the Pharos, which led to the extraordinary
port city of Alexandria. Alexandria was home to a truly lucent Wonder,
a monument which makes its first appearance in a definitive, extant list
of Seven Wonders only in the fifth century CE, but which helps us to
compute and comprehend all the others that have gone before.

CHAPTER 7

✦

THE PHAROS LIGHTHOUSE AT ALEXANDRIA

C. 297 BCE

The most remarkable and extraordinary structure upon which it rested; it was like a mountain, almost reaching the clouds, in the middle of the sea. Below the building flowed the waters; it seemed to be as it were suspended above their surface, while at the top of this mountain rose a second sun to be a guide for ships.

THE ADVENTURES OF LEUCIPPE AND CLITOPHON 5.6, ACHILLES TATIUS,
RESIDENT OF ALEXANDRIA, SECOND CENTURY CE

'*The Lighthouse of Alexandria*' *engraving produced by Philips Galle after designs by Maarten van Heemskerck in 1572.*

Our final Wonder constitutes the ultimate gift of a man with unparalleled power. Alexander the Great, whose own narrative touches each and every Wonder, was unstoppable. He did not just blaze through our past and his present; he colonised the world's future. And in the land that he had taken from the Persians, which the Persians (aided by the Karians) had taken from the native Egyptians, Alexander initiated a culture that would sustain a Wonder which shone out across two millennia. A refulgent expression of intellectual brilliance and of our desire to match the radiance of the gods, and a celebration of man's control of an element perceived for millennia to be sublime – fire.

Alexander wished he possessed a Homer to record his life story in epic poetry; if only he had just taken the time to dictate his experiences to one of the many scribes who we know accompanied his campaigns. Because this young Macedonian man was one of the few individuals who witnessed Egypt's Great Pyramid, Babylon's Hanging Gardens and walls, Ephesus' mighty Temple of Artemis, Olympia's Statue of Zeus, and the Mausoleum of Halikarnassos first hand. The fallout from his blistering reign sparked the raising of the Colossus at Rhodes. The scholars who gathered in one of the cities he founded, Alexandria on the northern Egyptian coast, watched over by the beam of our final Wonder, conceived and compiled the Seven Wonder lists which have entranced the world for two millennia.

And what a Wonder the Pharos Lighthouse at Alexandria was – a symbol of light and learning, a symbol of salvation. Unlike Rhodes' short-lived Colossus, Alexandria's towering Wonder survived for over 1,500 years; in fact, some of its monumental stones are still visible today under the waters of the southern Mediterranean, built into the walls of the Renaissance fort, Al Qait-Bey. They can also be made out, if only just, in the arc of Alexandria's great harbour.

Beaten in height only by the Great Pyramid, Alexandria's Lighthouse was the second-tallest structure in the world, an engineering triumph. The Pharos spun up 400 feet into the sky over the linchpin port of Alexandria. It played with a sequence of geometrical shapes: oblong, circular, and square. Built of marble and local limestone, from around 297 BCE across a period of fifteen years, decorated with pink granite which had been carried downstream along the Nile from the pitted reaches of the Aswan desert (many blocks 36 feet long and weighing in at 75 tonnes), the Pharos was topped with a 50-foot-high statue of a Greek god – almost certainly Zeus Soter, Zeus the Saviour.[1]

The Pharos was a Wonder in a place of huge significance, a place that really mattered. Alexandria was, and is, promise incarnate. This double-port, in the early third century BCE, had become the gateway to Africa, and the mouth from which at least 135,000 tons a year of grain would later be gorged from the 'bread-basket of Rome' to feed the budding Roman Empire.* The port of Alexandria was where trade from Southern Arabia, East Africa and the Red Sea penetrated a Europe-oriented market. Three hundred giant galleys could dock here. But Alexandria was, also, an exceptionally perilous port to enter, with fierce winds blowing onto its lee-shore, and submerged rocks breaking up the sea and ships with equal certainty. A poignant poem by the Latin elegiac poet Propertius (composing at the time of Emperor Augustus) mourns a young man drowned by 'the waves that have no gods', on the way to Pharos.[2] On the harbour's eastern edge, man-made debris provided further hazards.

Arriving at Egypt by sea had, for centuries, been both a delight, and a danger. It is described in Homer's *Odyssey* as a journey inspiring powerful poetry and representing a 'long and painful way'.[3] Ancient mariners tried to help one another out, sharing pointers and tips, a kind of ancient Sat Nav service: 'From Calameum to the Old Woman's Knee is eight miles. The promontory is rough and on the top there is a rock, and a tree grows on the beach. There is a harbour and water laps right up to the tree. Be careful of the south wind.'[4] And although Alexandria promised so much in terms of culture and opportunity, it also afforded appalling conditions for the sailor – a featureless coastline, hidden sandbanks, temperamental surf. Even today, there are constant rebuilding programmes to try to calm the waters here and shore up the coastline; concrete creations, being installed for the last five years I've visited, prod the sea like giant sea-urchins and tumble out to the foundations of the Lighthouse itself.

So, as a practical guide to safe-harbour, the Pharos would become a brand for Alexandria, and a beacon of hope, in every sense. It was also wonderful in many ways.

---

* Sicily is also commonly called the 'bread-basket of Rome'; both were necessary to feed the enormous population across the empire.

The beneficent beam of the Pharos was generated by a furnace during the night, and by day, the rays of the sun reflected from mirrors of what was almost certainly beaten copper. Later authors became rather carried away when describing the reach of this shaft of artificial light, some asserting it could penetrate all the way to Constantinople itself (at a distance of close on 700 miles, completely impossible). The flame was also imagined as a kind of massive torch – similar to that held by the Statue of Liberty in New York or by our modern Olympians. Indeed, on one first-century CE glass beaker from Begram (just north of Kabul in Afghanistan, the seat of the ancient Kushan Empire) depicting the Lighthouse, Zeus appears to hold either a giant torch or a giant thunderbolt. It is exciting to think how dramatic, how aesthetically striking, such an arrangement would have been – but surely it was impossible in engineering terms for such a sculpture-mounted beacon to be functional.

On this beaker (temporarily looted, but at the time of writing kept safe in the Kabul Museum), the sea behind the Lighthouse is peppered with craft, as it still is today; a handsome sailing boat, a rowing boat and a modest merchant's barque are carefully moulded into the surface. Even if it weren't for the other evidence we have – the ancient stone anchors littering the seabed, the evocative lines of literary description – holding this rare, delicate, prized possession, one can immediately imagine the energy of a harbour filled, those rocking ships that were vessels of civilisation in every sense.

Today, a jolly causeway that runs a quarter of a mile out to sea makes it easy to visit the original site of Alexandria's Wonder.

The Pharos Lighthouse took its name from the island it was built on, Pharos. Pharos first surfaces on record in Homer's epic poem the *Odyssey*, when the King of Sparta, Menelaus – who, we are told, was stranded on the island briefly on his way back from the Trojan War by the sea god Proteus – describes it to Odysseus's son Telemachus as 'an island in the surging sea in front of Egypt's river', with good anchorage, where men launch their 'shapely ships' when they have drawn supplies of fresh 'black water'.⁵ Pharos is the jumping-off point for a Homeric, Egyptian adventure, in which Menelaus travels up the 'heaven-fed' waters of the Nile, and makes offerings to the gods.⁶ As a result, King Menelaus and Queen Helen enjoy gorgeous gifts back in their palace in Sparta, sent to them by Egyptian royals: silver baths for Menelaus, a silver and gold basket on wheels for Helen, a golden distaff – all of which were thought to be just fairy-tale fantasies, until a wheeled golden basket and a golden spindle from the Bronze Age (the age that inspired the story of the Trojan War) were actually discovered in an archaeological dig.[7]

Pharos's connection with Helen continues: in one version of her myth it was said that this much-desired Greek royal sat out the Trojan War itself on the island of Pharos in the court of King Proteus while a mere *eidolon*, a phantom of the 'world's desire', was fought over on the Trojan plains.[8] In other mythic inventions, Helen dawdled and dandled on Pharos, playing with seals and with her runaway lover Paris, and then made what must have been a rather testy homeward-bound trip with her husband Menelaus to Sparta after ten long years of siege, cruelty, tragedy and loss.[9]

A thousand years or so after the setting of Homer's epic myth, in the age of Alexander and the Ptolemaic age that followed his death, this crescent of coastline in North Africa was the object of a confident and clever regeneration programme.

The story went that, on arriving in Egypt in around 332/1 BCE, Alexander the Great was drawn to Pharos itself by Homer in a dream.[10] The king-adventurer spotted an opportunity: without any chalk to hand, Alexander ordered his soldiers to lay out the divisions for his namesake-city with flour. Birds swooped to steal the grain – a bad omen? No, the soothsayers soothed, just proof that Alexandria would be rich in the fruits of the earth.[11] Those at the time knew that the megalomaniac's ambition was even greater; they understood that Alexander, neurons firing from hours spent in the company of his tutor, the pioneering philosopher Aristotle, would surely want his to be a city that nourished minds.[12]

Another tradition, the Alexander Romance (set down from the third century CE, and later, largely fanciful, but transmitting some references to actual, historical facts), gave an Egyptian god the credit for the idea of the transformation of Pharos. In the Romance, we hear that Alexander had travelled down the Nile from Memphis to Canopus, on his way to Siwah, via the modest fishing village of Rhacotis. Recalling this fertile delta at the edge of the Mediterranean Sea, it was said that when Alexander embraced the potency of the great god Ammon in that other green-filled space to the south – the Siwah Oasis, rimmed by the intense heat of the desert – the god told the Macedonian conqueror first that

Alexander was 'of his seed', and then that he would found a city on 'the island of Proteus'.[13]

The great god Ammon had form with this kind of proclamation. Sheltering from the desert sun close to the Valley of the Kings at Deir El Bahri (the mortuary temple of the female Pharaoh Hatshepsut), painted wall carvings, still bright with their original colours, tell the same story: how Ammon had given his seed to Hatshepsut's mother and then inspired the female pharaoh to mount an expedition to the enigmatic land of Punt – probably Ethiopia or Yemen, or a southern trading station on the Red Sea, quite possibly that harbour complex of Wadi al-Jarf built to serve the construction of the Great Pyramid.

The Alexander Romance continues with the story, relating that the Macedonian king proceeded to seek out Pharos, via Taposiris.* But in truth, Alexander could possibly not even have made it to the putative site of Alexandria; instead, he just ordered his men to build the city, and then allowed those men to pick up the slack of the project, and the bill. Deinocrates was the engineer he left in charge, a technician from Rhodes who had also constructed Hephaestion's funeral pyre in Babylon, and who had helped to supervise the re-building of the Temple of Artemis at Ephesus. Alexandria was officially founded on 7 April 331 BCE, around four months after the Macedonian king had been declared to be a god.[14] But even if he never set foot in it, of all the cities named Alexandria (or Alexandrio, as they were first called) around the world – over thirty at the last count – this one, the Pharos Lighthouse's hometown, was claimed to be Alexander's favourite.

Alexandria was known officially as 'Alexandria by Egypt', a separate entity from Egypt proper. This brand-new metropolis was, consciously, a centre of Hellenism – a city built to spread a culture, to forge a new identity. With its Lighthouse and its library, its museum and its futuristic layout, Alexandria was the talk of the known world. It became the place to be, because it became the place to be seen. Was it Alexander who proposed a causeway linking the coastal ridge to Pharos Island, thereby creating two harbours, one commercial, one military (the western,

---

* A trading city on the shores of Lake Mareotis – home, some have said, of the burial of Cleopatra VII (the tomb under consideration almost certainly is not the burial of the last great Pharaoh of Egypt, but the grave here is marked, interestingly, by a tower that resembles a lighthouse).

man-made harbour confidently titled 'Happy Returns')? Certainly, this meant that, whichever the direction of the prevailing wind, a harbour would be available. Or did this happen as a result of natural silting? Did Alexander generate the hyper-modern, experimental vision for Alexandria according to which districts were named simply, and rationally, Alpha, Beta, Gamma, Delta, Epsilon? It was a fresh-start, multi-ethnic city, with Egyptians living in Rhakotis, Greeks and Macedonians in Brucheum, a Jewish community (whose language was Aramaic or Hebrew) in the Delta district in a quarter bordering the royal area of Regia, and mercenaries operating across the settlement, all the way from Gaul.[15] Did the great, driven leader stipulate that the Nile be joined to the harbour by a canal?

These all could have been ideas in Alexander's brilliant, fevered brain, but, although it carried Alexander's name, Alexandria was in truth masterminded by one of the all-conquering king's most loyal boyhood companions, Ptolemy I. We have already met Ptolemy – a trigger for the siege of Rhodes, resulting in the construction of the Colossus. Growing up together in Pella in northern Greece, at the acutely ambitious court of Philip II, Ptolemy and Alexander had been the closest of companions. Witnessing the recent archaeological excavation of the water-channel at Pella from the communal baths of the mess room there, watching that splashing drainage system, pulled out of the earth, it is easy to imagine the bond between Ptolemy and Alexander, where the companions sweated and played and bathed as teenagers, and the twelve years of blood-soaked campaigning ahead of them.

On Alexander's death, Ptolemy I had asked for the province of Egypt to be bequeathed as his domain, and to be the caretaker of Alexander the Great's body. The plan would certainly have been to make Egyptian Alexandria the centre of the cult of Alexander the man-god – with the Lighthouse its guiding light and beacon. (Of course, the whereabouts of Alexander's body today and exactly where it ended up after his death in Babylon are, at the time of writing, still a mystery.) The Pharos had a double purpose: both practical – its role as a lighthouse – and ideological, as an emblem of association with Alexander and his one-world vision. The Lighthouse was certainly like the brilliant tip of a lit lamp, whose blue-heat centre was the Ptolemaic palace, with residential and commercial districts round about. The illumination for a museum-city, a microcosm of universal culture. An African city that faced Europe.

The initial construction of the Pharos was possibly the year of Ptolemy I's death (although Eusebius, Bishop of Caesarea, a later source, suggested 283/2 BCE), around four decades after Alexander had died. A work, then, imagined and fund-raised for by Ptolemy I (to the tune of 800 silver talents – at least $19 million), but finished off by his son and successor, Ptolemy II.

What a sight this must have been, both in its creation and its completion. At the eastern entrance to Alexandria's harbour the base of the Lighthouse stretched for a massive 1,115 by 1,115 feet and was protected by breakwaters on three sides, with corner turrets supporting the four-storey building. Entrance was by a ramp which continued inside. The ground floor was well lit, with room for a permanent garrison, a station for animals and their supplies, and a central hoist to lift food, fuel and other sundries within the tower. With a smaller rectangular base 105 feet wide, this raised ground floor reached a height of around 245 feet. Open windows on the building were designed to allow the whirling winds here to pass through without dragging the whole structure over. An octagonal storey (the eight sides representing the eight wind directions) with spiral staircases 195 feet high, was then topped by an elegant, pillared circular level, 98 feet high, which in turn carried the lighting mechanism up another 50 feet. To prevent earthquake damage, the masonry blocks were probably held together with a combination of wooden buffers and molten lead. (A number of blocks on the bottom of the bay are broken, showing they have fallen from a great height. Earthquakes would eventually undo this Wonder.)

Standing across the bay from the Lighthouse's foundation, imagining it ranging 460 feet into the sky, the audacity of its creation is heart-stopping. This building was well over three times the size of the Colossus – the world's first skyscraper. Its footprint is similar to that of the Tower of London. The light was designed to shine out across 300 stades – 37 or so miles. One ancient source, the Jewish-Roman historian Josephus, confirmed that the Pharos could be seen at that distance.[16] Not so much a Lighthouse, then, as a citadel of light.

Walking around the Lighthouse's perimeter today, the ghostly impression of its scale is still staggering. The Hellenistic Pharos foundations now support that Ottoman-period fort, bombarded and then extensively re-worked by the British in 1882. The air here at the end of the mole – the link to the mainland – still seethes with the wind that whips straight off the sea; one can imagine the miracle of the skyscraper stones, known more properly as the 'Tower of the Isle of Pharos', standing against such might. Today, the light in the harbour at night is predominantly spilled by illuminated helium balloons and the candyfloss carts which hawkers push to the families who come in their thousands to sit on one of their favourite beaches. Pearls of street-lights fringe the entire bay; 2,300 years ago the ancient Alexandrians also had oil-powered street-lighting, but, despite this impressive, high-tech, ancient illumination, the Lighthouse's beam would have been supreme. This was a Wonder that pierced a potent portion of the ancient experience – the night.[17]

Our travelling Wonder-companion Pliny the Elder noted that the Pharos's watchfire was so bright, it was in danger of being mistaken for a star, 'the appearance of fire from a distance being similar'.[18] A poet from the Bay of Naples, Statius, compared its light to that of the moon.[19] In fact the 'star' was a huge bonfire, either atop the pinnacle statue or beside it, fuelled possibly by naphtha (an ancient form of petrol) and papyrus combined, supplied by pack-animals winding their way up two by two on ramps outside the tower's edge. The giant statue – variously identified as Zeus, Soter, or Poseidon, or as Ptolemy or his wife, or even the sun god Helios (although since Alexander considered himself to be descended from Zeus, the Olympian Father of the Gods seems most likely) – was also described as being able to trace the course of the sun.[20]

Not only was the Lighthouse there for the sake of ships, it also served as a telecommunications tower. The Pharos' flashing heliography was translatable. Flaming towers and beacons were an essential feature of the ancient world. In Homer's epic poem the *Odyssey*, composed in the Iron Age and often describing the Bronze Age, and in Aeschylus's play *Agamemnon*, we hear of the news of the victory at Troy travelling back to Greece as one beacon communicated with the next.[21] Spreading information fast over vast distances, there was a level of sophistication in the lighthouse messages which is lost on us today: a pyretic morse-code that allowed for inter-continental information to be shared. It has been estimated that fire-dispatches could travel up to 500 miles in under an hour.

Archaeology buttresses the literary sources: on Crete a line of Bronze Age communication has recently been identified running through the central spine of the island. Fire-beacons or *soroi* made of baked clay, the ashes from ancient communications still visible, have been discovered.

Satisfyingly, a number of *soroi* inhabit vantage points still used for communication today – Ederis Soros, for example, on the northern coast of Crete, was employed by Allied forces in the second half of the twentieth century to host their satellite dishes, and by mobile network providers in the twenty-first.[22]

The Lighthouse at Alexandria would have been freighted with expectation in antiquity. Not just a welcome to a city, but a siren-system, capable of a visual clarion call of triumph or distress.*

Today, there is still an edgy energy to the Lighthouse's location. Local boys ride their horses up and down the mole, hoping to catch business from tourists, stubborn tea-makers brew their chai come rain or storm. It was not for nothing that the goddess Isis Pharia, Isis of the Pharos, was worshipped at Alexandria; an Egyptian divine mother reaching out to steady the masts of boats on coins or holding wind-filled sails.[23] Alexandria and its eastern harbour stretches along the coastline ahead; behind the Lighthouse foundations lies the seething possibility of the Middle Sea, the Great Green, as Egyptians called it. And it is here, in the sea, where the Lighthouse's secrets are being revealed.

In 1994, on the seabed stretching out beneath the Pharos, through the gauze and swirl of the water, divers reached 85 feet below the surface to submerged treasure: columns sculpted to look like papyrus plants, massive stone blocks, twenty-five sphinxes. This was all incredible enough, but then there was more: a Ptolemaic queen in the form of Isis, originally 40 feet high; and someone who seemed to be a matching pharaoh, both stone humans carved in pink granite from Aswan. Was this a giant statue group of Ptolemy II and his sister-wife Arsinoe – sculptures which had decorated the front of the Lighthouse? Here was a Greek king dressed as an Egyptian pharaoh – a fusion of Eastern and Western power. Six bases in total almost certainly supported a king and queen each – giants greeting (or intimidating) boats as they sailed into the Great Harbour, and an Alexandrian fleet which, by the time of the Battle of Actium, numbered close on 500 ships. In truth, this was an archaeological wonderland. The finds stretched out over an area of 5 acres. Over 3,000 architectural blocks have been recovered, hundreds of columns or column fragments,

---

* Sirens, incidentally, are named after the Siren women-bird-monsters of ancient myth.

including chunks of grey-veined Proconnesian marble imported from quarries on the Marmara Island (originally Proconnesus Island) in the Sea of Marmara south of what was then Byzantion, and is now Istanbul – a building material that was also used in the construction of the Mausoleum of Halikarnassos and the Temple of Artemis at Ephesus.

Then there were objects a thousand years older than the construction of the Lighthouse: papyrus-decorated columns of the Pharaoh Ramesses II, aka Ramesses the Great, re-purposed for Alexandrian mansions; the remains of three obelisks belonging to Pharaoh Seti I, the ruler whose paint-spangled tomb is the largest and most impressive in the Valley of the Kings, and dues to Tuthmose III, whose obelisk still stands in Istanbul opposite the monument commemorating the Colossus of Rhodes. Sphinxes too – their inscriptions showing they originally came from Egypt's first city named in Greek, Heliopolis, the city that worshipped the sun and that flourished even before Khufu dreamt up his Great Pyramid.

And crucially, for our investigation, there were also architectural remnants which have been identified by the original underwater archaeologists as belonging to the Pharos structure: a 38-foot-high red granite block, the fragment of a door frame, weighing in at 70 tons, another door frame 16 feet high,[24] flagstones and lintels. The same red granite that was used to protect Khufu's body in his Great Pyramid, and to line the Great King's tomb.

If you know where to look you can find these Wonder-remnants above ground too, built into the structures of the modern fort. Limestone blocks from the Pharos Lighthouse frame windows; ancient granite treads sit at the entrance to doorways, casually stepped over by hundreds of thousands of tourists that visit each year. Giant planks of stone have been abandoned to become stone benches, ideally placed to sit on to watch the sun set over the western edge of the city, over the entrance to the western harbour known in antiquity as the Gate of the Moon. And as you enter the keep of the castle itself, pause for a moment, because the doorway of Fort Qait-Bey is nothing less than the Pharos's own red granite, shipped down the Nile all the way from Aswan, described as a defining feature of the original Lighthouse. The significance of this coloured stone, you will recall, is often missed. Because red granite is a magical rock. A soft, dull, charcoaled pink in most lights, but in its original location out in the desert, when the sunlight strikes at certain angles at particular times of day, especially in contrast to sand or sandstone, the 'red' granite appears to turn a psychedelic lilac-purple. It is little surprise that this protean stone turns up both in Alexander's pride and joy, and in Khufu's great tomb. The ancients must have believed red granite brought with it some kind of sorcerer's power.

The construction of the Pharos Lighthouse Wonder tells us a great deal about the ambitions of the early Hellenistic Age, and the geopolitics of this formative epoch of antiquity. Ptolemy I was one of those five closest companions of Alexander, who were expelled from the Macedonian court by Alexander's jealous father, Philip II. Ptolemy was raised, probably as a page, in the deep-wooded hills at Pella, north of Mount Olympus. Trained to hunt wild boar (only young men who had trapped and killed a boar without a net were allowed to recline to eat in the King of Macedon's palace) and lions, his loyalty to his liege would have been ferocious. Like Alexander, Ptolemy I may well have been taught directly by Aristotle; at the very least he would have been exposed to the philosopher's ideas. Ptolemy seems to have been both questioning and practical; a man who could deal with the abstract and the actual.

After he died, Alexander the Great's body had been transported from Babylon in a massive gold hearse – a moving temple, pulled by sixty-four mules. Ptolemy I intercepted the cortege in Damascus in modern-day Syria, and brought the body first to Memphis in Egypt, and then almost certainly to Alexandria. A symbolic gesture – proof that Ptolemy's turf was the true successor to Alexander's searing ambition. Adventurers, archaeologists and charlatans alike still search for Alexander's tomb in the dank, subterranean Hellenistic city which lies beneath Alexandria's beautiful, crumbling, concrete modern streets.[25] It is yet to be discovered.

Ptolemy II, aged just twenty-two, inherited a remarkable city from his father Ptolemy I, who died aged about eighty-two – and extraordinary expectations. Alexandria was in truth the legacy of his father's vision and his endurance. Ptolemy I ruled for close on forty years, the only one of Alexander the Great's immediate successors to die of natural causes. It was Ptolemy I who had joined Pharos Island to the shore, creating the Heptadromion – the 7-stade causeway and a bold demonstration of Greek urban planning, mirroring a causeway that Alexander built as he besieged the city of Tyre. The causeway is now that mole, which today is occupied by the tenacious Greek yacht club, mobile phone and lamp shops, and stalls selling shells from the sea. It was Ptolemy I who helped to conceive the vision of the experiment in urban living that was Alexandria.

Partly to legitimise his claim to power (he was not Ptolemy I's oldest son), Ptolemy II tactfully deified his parents as *theoi soteres* – saviour gods. Ptolemy II then went on to rule Alexandria and the province of Egypt from 283 to 246 BCE. But his reign was very different from his father's. Whereas Ptolemy Senior was a campaigning military officer, Junior preferred diplomacy to direct action, and established his credentials as a culture and pleasure and party king early in his reign. Ptolemy II mounted elaborate parades through the city – featuring ostriches, elephants, zebras, big cats, buffaloes and a rhinoceros. He enjoyed killing elephants too, hunting them down for sport.

There was a playfulness, an exuberance, to Ptolemaic Alexandria. While Olympia had its Olympic Games, Ephesus its Artemisia, Rhodes its Helaia, here in Alexandria the greatest festival was the Ptolemeiaea – the most enormous fiesta in honour of the Ptolemies. Greece's festivals had been predominantly about *agwn/agon* (contest) and mystic ritual. The Ptolemeiaea was a very public display of pleasure and imagination. Alexandria was a centre of automata – there was nothing the Alexandrians loved more than an automated snail the size of a small car, machines that vended water, giant phalluses tipped with spurting stars. The gods Dionysos and Aphrodite were avidly worshipped in Alexandria. An 80-foot-high image of the god of wine was once paraded through the streets on the backs of 100 elephants. Tritons – half men, half fish – those constant reminders that the Mediterranean brought wealth and opportunity to the women and men who fringed its shores, decorated the Pharos Lighthouse; it is quite possible that these sculptures, depicted blowing their horns, were not just for show, but also mechanical, making a fabulous sound, a form of ancient robotics – used both to entertain and to act as an early warning system in times of trouble. A recent suggestion, very appealing, is that the great god Zeus Soter also acted like a giant bronze weathervane, one of the first in the world, moving to point the direction of winds with not a thunderbolt, or a torch, but the giant ship's rudder which he held in one hand.[26]

So who paid for all of this? The geographer Strabo – who came to Alexandria in around 25 BCE – tells us that the whole monumental project was an offering from one Sostratus of Knidos, a successful entrepreneur and mariner (mind you, the essayist Lucian of Samosata in his *Hippias* 2 says Sostratus helped Ptolemy I capture the Egyptian city of Memphis, so is this second Sostratus perhaps a grandson of Sostratus Senior, part of a Knidian dynasty?), and was dedicated with a showy inscription on behalf of mariners to the Divine Royal Saviours, Ptolemy I and his Queen Berenice. Some reported that the dedication extended to Castor and Pollux, the Dioscuri (Helen of Troy's twin brothers and heroes who were thought to roam the oceans in the form of St Elmo's Fire and keep sailors safe at night). The dedication seems to have been displayed beneath over-life-size sculptures. There are candidates for these Pharos sculptures at the bottom of the sea which could be gods, or the pharaonic couple. Given the fluid nature of identification and association between divine heroes and humans, most likely these Pharos sculptures were an alchemy of both royal rulers and mythological beings.[27]

Still visible in the tenth century CE, the dedication on the eastern side of the Pharos (the key entry point for sailors) was described by the Arab historian al-Mas'udi as being made of lead letters about one and a half feet (a cubit) wide. And thrillingly, sections of marble, with indentations in the stone and holes ready to take metal letters, are now being pulled up from the seabed around the Lighthouse. During my last visit, a number were lying inland in desalination tanks in the city, waiting to be examined.

The subject of the dedication is a thrilling conundrum: because, it was whispered, the Lighthouse held a secret. The story went that Sostratus in fact had left a hidden message, inscribed on the Lighthouse (or on its surmounting statue) and then covered in plaster – an inscription that was less cravenly obsequious to those in power, and more personal: 'Sostratus the Knidian friend of the sovereigns dedicated this for the sake of the safety of those who sail the seas'.[28] A Sostratus was indeed a friend of the sovereigns; he was Ptolemy II's ambassador to the sacred island of Delos – a high-status and high-net-worth position. He would have been rich, influential, well connected. We know that this Sostratus also left dedications at the oracle site of Delphi on mainland Greece. The Sostratus of Knidos must have understood the value of a guiding light, especially into two busy ports, because his hometown on the south-west coast of what is now Turkey also has a double harbour. On the Anatolian coast where the volcanic buckling has left the coastline a marble-cake of layers, the Knidian harbours are natural. Knidos (the city famous for commissioning Praxiteles' lovely nude sculpture of Aphrodite) is a settlement that tumbles down the coastal cliffs; the story that Knidian Sostratus not only sponsored the Lighthouse Wonder, but also designed Knidos's own hanging roof-gardens, makes some sense.[29]

Whoever built it, paid for it, or claimed it, the Pharos Lighthouse, hymned by one eye-witness poet as 'cutting the breadth and depth of heaven', was a pride of Alexandria, and quickly became an emblem for the city – as it still is today: images of the Lighthouse adorn many public institutions in the region, from primary school playgrounds to the crest of Alexandria University. Its image is even painted in bright colours on concrete apartment walls on the city's outskirts. The Lighthouse was replicated on coins and as lamps, where an olive-oil or mutton-fat light would have blazed through peepholes, a miniature version of the massive Wonder. So the Pharos was a logo, a successful brand; and, additionally, a midwife to ideas.

Alexandria, the city that levied incoming boats of their papyrus scrolls tightly written with philosophies, plays, tax accounts, histories and treatises, realised its founder's dream: that knowledge itself could be power.[*30] Ptolemy II wrote to kings and leaders across the Hellenistic world asking them to send works of literature, poetry, science, medicine and engineering. Thinkers who flourished in the Lighthouse's city included Euclid (who developed geometry, and whose work *The Elements* was still being used as a school textbook in the 1960s), Eratosthenes (who measured the circumference of the earth), Archimedes (who revolutionised engineering), then Galen (who did the same for medicine) and Claudius Ptolemy (the great geographer). Euclid was active when the Pharos Lighthouse was being built. Fascinated by the works of Pythagoras, that visionary thinker from the pine-rich island of Samos, the mathematician proved Pythagoras's theorem (which had in fact already been employed by the Babylonians 500 years before) and urged other pioneers around him to apply it. A steam-engine was invented by Heron of Alexandria.[31] And it was here that the earth would be divided into the climate zones we still use

---

* i.e. 2,000 years before the Book of Proverbs phrase, 'A wise man is strong; yea, a man of knowledge increaseth strength' was popularised by Francis Bacon and Thomas Hobbes.

today. All this is the kind of intellectual resource the Lighthouse-builders had access to. Given that Pharaoh Ptolemy could send out demands for every book in the world to be delivered to his capital, just think what magnitude of tower he could raise. Philo talks about the great value of kings supporting (for that euphemism, read 'funding') the research here – much of it military. Ground-breaking military developments often result in innovations in civil society. We should think perhaps of a city with the reputation of Tokyo in the seventies or Boston in the noughties. A city attracting attention.

> The city in general has grown so much in later times that many reckon it to be the first city in the civilised world, and it is certainly far ahead of all the rest in elegance and extent and riches and luxury.[32]
>
> DIODORUS SICULUS, WRITING C. 60 BCE

From the effective inception of Roman imperial ambition, when Rome first started to flex her international muscles in North Africa in the early third century BCE, and at a time when the Wonder-lists were starting to be drawn up in Alexander's city, the legendary general Scipio Africanus, while taking on Hannibal and his Carthaginian Empire, also visited Alexandria.[33] A renowned Hellenophile, Scipio's most desired destination was the Pharos. He was 'particularly interested in the features of the lighthouse'.[34]

In Latin, the same verb is often used to describe the Lighthouse as that used to describe the Great Pyramid, and indeed other giants of the landscape – mountains, hills, trees: *extollere*, to raise up.[35] Roman authors knew what they were doing with this linguistic choice – hinting that these kinds of erections represented man wanting to play god, a pastime that is thrilling because it excites and delivers a frisson of fear.

In fact, the Romans seem to have been somewhat intimidated by Alexandria and its towering Pharos, realising the Lighthouse was not just a passive protector, but a crucial component of the city's armoury.

> . . . it is impossible for a ship to gain entrance to the harbour against the wishes of those who hold Pharus.[36]

This was Caesar's immediate fear, and while the enemy were occupied

with the fighting he landed soldiers, seized the lighthouse, and stationed a garrison there. By these means he secured the safe delivery to
him by ship of food and reinforcements (for he sent a summons to all
the nearby provinces to provide the latter).[37]

Pliny tells us in his *Natural History* that any flame that burns constantly – such as the flame of the small Roman lighthouse of Ostia, or the
resplendent light of Alexandria – is a danger, in that they can be mistaken
for stars.[38] In some descriptions of the Pharos by leading Roman authors
such as Lucan,* the Lighthouse takes on an animated, almost sinister
form.[39] It is described as a 'mountain' – dangerous, massive, threatening.
Although the Pharos promised salvation – 'the mountain thanked for
its nocturnal light' – that monstrous, elevated, artificial beam, in the
Roman mind, acquired a sulphurous tinge – more akin to the spewing of
volcanoes, or the ravaging lick and billow of street fires which destroyed
so many treasures in the ancient world.[40]

And of course the Pharos was particularly mistrusted by the Romans,
because, come the first century BCE, it belonged to a woman. Alexandria
was becoming a centrifugal force for the play of power between Rome
and Egypt's last great Ptolemaic pharaoh, Queen Cleopatra VII.

It is tantalising to try to imagine the relationship that Queen Cleopatra might have had with this Wonder. Highly intelligent, a woman
who spoke at least nine languages and was famed as a mathematician, she
must have been delighted with her city's giant, record-busting torch. She
was almost certainly involved in the repair of the Lighthouse after the
Alexandrian War of 48/47 BCE. One later source, Ammianus Marcellinus,
claims Cleopatra actually built the Pharos, but he must be mistakenly
referring to restoration work, for instance of the aqueduct that supplied
water to Pharos Island. Interestingly, the very first mention we have of
Cleopatra in Arabic sources comes courtesy of one Ibn 'Abd al-Hakam
who, in the mid-ninth century CE, is under the impression that 'Queen
Qulpatra' was responsible for the Pharos's building.[41] The mind-blowing
Lighthouse, a work of staggering stature, was understandably associated
with the reign of an exceptional, stand-out woman.

When the Romans overran Egypt and Cleopatra was first brought

---

* In an account of the Roman civil war, written during Nero's reign.

to Rome with her father as a child and as a beseeching client, control of the Pharos would be paraded as an exemplar of the imperial power's dominant reach. During Julius Caesar's triumph in the capital, a model of the Lighthouse, complete with a replica flame, was dragged through Rome's streets, around the Palatine Hill, past the Circus Maximus, and on so as to be shamed in front of the temple of triumphant Jupiter.[42] With the defeat of Cleopatra and Mark Antony many miles away across the Adriatic in the Battle of Actium, the Lighthouse would be lost to the Ptolemies, whose drive had raised Egypt's second Wonder.

From Rome's perspective, Alexandria, and indeed the province of Egypt, were considered so crucial and such a potential tinderbox that both were apportioned as part of the emperor's personal belongings. And during the reign of Domitian (from 81 CE), through to Commodus (192 CE), with the single exception of Nerva (96–8 CE), the Lighthouse appears on the reverse of a number of silver drachma coins minted in Alexandria; we can clearly see its ramp, the Tritons, the surmounting god, and on some the goddess Isis Pharia, wafting in to protect her Lighthouse-child.[43]

As the Roman Empire expanded, the Lighthouse continued to capture the imagination. In Lucian of Samosata's brilliant sci-fi parody, *Icaromenippus*, written in the second century CE, the eponymous hero Menippus flies to the moon, and can recognise the earth down below only because he can spot two of the Seven Wonders – the Colossus of Rhodes and the Pharos Lighthouse. In the Christian author Epiphanius of Salamis's *Weights and Measures*, compiled in c. 300 CE, we read that '. . . the tower of Pharas, the first Wonder . . . It is held together by glass and lead, and is 600 yards high'.[44] Alexandria's Wonder was coming to mean something as a political statement and as a project prototype.*

And in what was the Roman province of Arabia Petraea, in the city of Jerash in Jordan, the Pharos can still be seen in mosaic form in the floors

---

* In 404 CE Synesius, the Platonic-lover-correspondent of the Alexandrian philosopher-mathematician, Hypatia, jauntily describes a journey by boat from Alexandria to his hometown of Cyrene. Ten years before he had talked of a naked-flame Lighthouse alerting of danger close to the island of Paros – which still today has whipping winds – the scourge of fishermen, the delight of wind-surfers. And watchtowers – many still standing on the islands of the Cyclades, in particular Siphnos – would all have had their own forms of bright-light alerts and smoke-screens. One can imagine the Alexandrian with an interest in lighthouses baked into his worldview.

of the Church of St John the Baptist (531 CE) and the Church of Saints Peter and Paul (535–50 CE), portrayed as being almost a third of the size of the walled city of Alexandria itself. At dusk in Jerash, where Artemis was worshipped so ardently, goats nonchalantly pick their way through the ruins while young Syrian men, refugees from the war just across the border, help to clear stones that have tumbled from the latest earth tremor in the region – the force that would eventually fell the Lighthouse too. In 539 CE local mosaic-makers added the Lighthouse into a panel of fifty images in a church built by Bishop Makarios in the Calansho Desert in Central Libya. Here the Pharos is shown crowned by a statue of Helios – a confusion perhaps with Rhodes' own colossal Wonder? Or could it be that the Lighthouse's crowning glory was indeed the sun god, a portrait of Alexander the Great in sublime form . . .

The Gallo-Roman historian, Gregory of Tours (who also compiled a list of the Seven Wonders which included Noah's Ark, Solomon's Temple and the Colosseum), described the Pharos as still being fully functioning in the sixth century CE. The Lighthouse is even described by a twelfth-century Chinese administrator of maritime trade, Zhao Rukuo, from Quanzhou in southern China, in his *A Description of Barbarian Nations: Records of Foreign People*:

> The country of O-kön-t'o [Alexandria] belongs to Wu-ssï-li [Egypt]. According to tradition, in olden times a stranger, Tsu-ko-ni [Alexander the Great] by name, built on the shore of the sea a great tower under which the earth was dug out and two rooms were made, well connected and very well secreted. In one vault was grain, in the other were arms. The tower was two hundred chang high. Four horses abreast could ascend to two-thirds of its height. In the centre of the building was a great well connecting with the big river . . . On the summit there was a wondrous great mirror; if war-ships of other countries made a sudden attack, the mirror detected them beforehand, and the troops were ready in time for duty.[45]

A stunning (but under-used) catalogue of evidence for the structure of the Lighthouse comes from the numerous Arabic authors who studied the building first-hand. Valuing technology, invention and engineering – not to mention the mind-opening nature of travel and travel-writing

– the many Christian and Muslim pilgrim eyewitnesses who journeyed to Alexandria specifically to experience this Wonder supply detailed descriptions of the Lighthouse's form and function. Al-Masudi in 944 CE (AH 333) reported jewels on the seabed around the Lighthouse, 'thrown in by Alexander the Great' (a reference presumably to the remnants of the ancient city lying visibly on the bottom of the sea). A decade later we hear of Christian families enjoying picnics in the Pharos's grounds (just as families still do here on festival days today). Abu Hamid al-Gharnati, travelling from Al-Andalus on Hajj, visiting in 1110 CE (AH 503/4) and again in 1117, wrote of the Lighthouse's mirror acting as a kind of death ray, spotting enemy ships on the horizon and then blasting them from its 'Chinese Iron' (steel) surface (*kharsini* in Arabic – and quite possibly a later addition from Chinese technology). For others, the Pharos had talismanic, almost magical properties, with treasure being buried in its core or under the rocks below, and the mirror able to reflect an image of Constantinople itself (unlikely, given the Queen of Cities lay at a distance of 600 nautical miles). Interestingly, when Al-Idrisi visited in 1154 CE (AH 548/9), he described windows ranging up an internal staircase, and made the point that the fire both illuminated by night, and vulcanised the Lighthouse by day – spewing smoke high into the air.

One of the greatest wonders that we saw in this city was the lighthouse which Great and Glorious God had erected by the hands of those who were forced to such labour as 'a sign to those who take warning from examining the fate of others' [Quran: 15:75] and as a guide to voyagers, for without it they could not find the true course to Alexandria. It can be seen for more than seventy miles, and is of great antiquity. It is most strongly built in all directions and competes with the skies in height. Description of it falls short, the eyes fail to comprehend it, and words are inadequate, so vast is the spectacle.[46]

But one of the most vivid and relational descriptions comes from Abu'l Hajjaj Youssef Ibn Mohammed el-Balawi el-Andaloussi, another pilgrim to Mecca from Al-Andalus, whose account is the most detailed of any from the ancient or mediaeval worlds. In 1166 CE (AH 561) el-Balawi explored the Pharos with a group of companions. His excitement is palpable, pouring from the ink on the page. Having made it across the causeway with dry feet, we hear how one of el-Balawi's companions, scrambling under one of the arches that supported the 600-foot-long ramp, 'stretched out his arms but was still unable to reach the sides . . .' Then documenting each chamber and cranny together, the researcher-adventurers thoroughly measured the space, dropping down stone-weighted strings to record heights between stages. You sense the author's frustration when he is unable to read his own writing at one point: 'the figure which I had written down in my original notes is not very clear . . .' But fortunately there is one entry that reassures: 'I had written details in ink, which had not smudged.' Gathering precise octagon, stairwell and parapet measurements, he finally climbs to the summit, now '. . . a mosque built with four doors and a cupola. It is 5.49m high and 36.60m in diameter . . .'[47] The explorers conquered sixty-seven rooms in total, apart from one, which, frustratingly, led straight into the sea. As for all visitors, the possibility of getting lost in the 300-plus interior spaces was very real. Even today, in the much-reduced fort, it is possible to mislay your sense of direction in the labyrinth of chambers and stairs.

At around the same time that el-Belawi was physically exploring the Lighthouse, it was being immortalised in Venice. Make your way through the serenaders and seagulls of St Mark's Square. Crane your neck and look up into the ceiling of Capella Zen (Zeno's Chapel in St Mark's Basilica), and the Lighthouse soars into the sky on a field of gold-glass. Dating to c. 1200, the crowning statue and mirror have gone, but a small mosque, with a visible minaret (some argue that the Pharos was inspiration for the architectural form of the minaret,[48] though Syrian church towers seem more plausible), crowns the tower instead. It is in this same mosaic that the other Wonder of Egypt – the great pyramids on the Giza Plateau, with fantasy, peek-a-boo windows – are also commemorated. There is a possibility that the word 'minaret' derives from *Menara* – a constantly burning flame. This too is disputed, but the word for 'lighthouse' in Spanish, Portuguese and Italian – *faro*, *farol*, *faro* – definitely owes everything to the Pharos. So the Lighthouse of Alexandria, even if we do not realise it, is a creation baked into languages spoken across the majority of the globe. It was a Wonder that was a physical presence in, and a cultural influence on, the mediaeval (and modern) world.

Lighthouse of Alexandria from Kitāb al-Bulhān, *note the minaret, c. 1330–1450 CE.*

The Pharos of Ptolemy King of Egypt, imagined c. eighteenth-century.

The Lighthouse on Pharos island, Alexandria, Egypt, after a fanciful nineteenth-century illustration, looking a little like a Hawksmoor spire.

Another nineteenth-century imaginary depiction of the Lighthouse, this time resembling the Tower of Babel.

But then a hammer blow fell. In the seas off the North African coast the frequent earth tremors ripple the waters with one minor tsunami after another; nights can be disturbed with the thunder-thud of earthquakes. Since 320 CE at least twenty-seven serious earth movements had shaken the Pharos, with one particularly devastating convulsion in 956 CE. For the Lighthouse the mortal strike of Mother Earth came courtesy of an earthquake on 8 August 1303 CE – whose tremors also impacted the Great Pyramid at Giza, juddering some of its casing stones to the ground.

In 1326, even though one of the Pharos's faces was badly damaged, the author-adventurer Abu Abd Allah Mohammed Ibn Battuta could still reach the door via a ramp, noticing the position inside for the Lighthouse keeper, and many chambers. Ibn Battuta notes that one El-Malik an-Nasir had tried to build a replacement, smaller lighthouse alongside the original, like the shoots of a dying tree, 'but was prevented by death from completing the work'.[19] Twenty years later, even this entrance was unapproachable, and whatever remained was razed or cannibalised by the Mamluk sultan, Ashraf Qait Bey, who started out life as a Circassian, was captured as a slave by Ottoman forces, was freed and then went on to patronise architectural projects in Cairo, Mecca, Medina, Jerusalem, Gaza, Damascus and Rosetta. In 1477, Qait Bey built a stocky fortress on the Lighthouse's giant footprint, a version of which stands to this day, although its minaret and walls were bombed by the British in 1882. Today, walk around Alexandria's bay and the absence left by the Lighthouse is still appreciable. Where there are now scudding clouds and seagulls, there was once a skyscraper, double the height of the cranes trying to rebuild modern Alexandria's harbour walls to hold back the sea.

And just as Queen Cleopatra (the first Ptolemaic pharaoh to learn and appreciate Egyptian) and Hypatia, the martyred pagan philosopher and mathematician, must some nights have looked at the Lighthouse to imagine, and writers such as Gustave Flaubert, Jean Cocteau and E. M. Forster wandered the city trying to envisage it still there, the Pharos has left a mark in our minds, like a sun-spot that glows from within half-closed eyes.

In the texts of the poet Callimachus's *Aetia*, compiled in Alexandria in around 250 BCE, we hear of the origins of *thaumasia* and *mirabilia* – wonders, rituals, miracles, beliefs; a kind of catalogue for Hellenistic and Roman writers of charming and curious Greek idiosyncrasies. The

Wonders, including the Pharos Lighthouse, were all examples of *philotimia* – literally a love of honour, wanting to be known for your works. And too of a very particular relationship with *eros* – the Greek word meaning passionate desire or ambition. Callimachus, an immigrant to Alexandria, who personalised poetry in a way that would go on to influence Western literature, was on to something: the hopeful fact that we, as a species, can draw great comfort, delight, and inspiration from another's *erga* – efforts or deeds or achievements. And as the beacon of a city that valued knowledge above gold, we should imagine the Lighthouse as the herald of an age where, finally, the pen really could be mightier than the sword.

Alexander the Great was, there is no doubt, driven by *pothos* – a yearning to expand, to do, and be, more.

We can imagine Alexander crossing seas pleated like old skin, breathing in new landscapes as a smoker breathes in the vape of strangers, or a grounded landloper moves closer to hear the snatched fragments of a foreign language. Think of the places where Alexander had intervened: Samos with its slopes covered in pines; rocky, windy Chios; Lesbos with its salt-lakes and lagoons where Alexander's tutor Aristotle had thoughtfully studied the biome, and where the minters of Mytilene had coinstruck Alexander with the horns of Ammon. The scrub-flat coastline that leads into Troy – where Alexander made sacrifice to the Trojan heroes, and to Achilles, stark-naked like an Olympic hero. The bright coasts of the Levant, modern-day Lebanon, the glittering curve of coast from which Alexander sent frankincense to the altars of Macedon; an Eastern Mediterranean world all now ruled by Macedonians. We should think of Alexander, too, in Tyre, where he besieged an island, built a causeway to connect it to Asia, and crucified lines of men. He was there in the coasts and mountains of Anatolia where he besieged again; in Persia, Afghanistan and India where the irrepressible conqueror slaughtered and desired and sweated to Dionysos' tune. In sand-stormed Egypt where he allowed the Greek world to be told he was the son of a god. Babylon where he died so young. In that short, blazing life Alexander had married a Bactrian, two Persians, and then appropriated aspects of Persian culture to style himself a new kind of king. He had made his way to Alexandria, after he had had himself crowned Egyptian pharaoh at Memphis. The

Hellenistic Age is known as the age that spread Hellenism – Greek-ness; more correctly, and interestingly, it was an age that spread a northern Greek unorthodoxy, and an unglazed Greek culture with a very porous surface.

In some senses, the wonder of the Seven Wonders was a unifying romance for the Hellenistic Age. Sites all visited by Alexander, stitched together by sailor-plied, sea-sick pitching sea and the thread of his ravening ambition; catalogued in Alexander's dream city, the greatest and largest cosmopolis in the ancient world. The Wonders inhabit a time that sees the culmination of the age of word of mouth: when men recorded mighty works on papyrus instead, but still kept the memory of each Wonder alive by the stories they shared of each – antiquity's oxygen of publicity. The Wonders are the last great works to populate not primarily the page, but our imaginations.

Alexander the Great inhabited and promoted a world where writing was the future. The Greek phonetic alphabet, added to the Phoenician writing system, was sponsoring the common reader. Alexander might have yearned for a poet like Homer to immortalise his life in oral, epic poetry, but instead one of his followers, Callisthenes, a relative of Aristotle, wrote a mealy-mouthed, somewhat pedestrian and critical account which has survived only as the ghost of an idea in others' writings. As a counterbalance, the Alexander Romance, added to throughout late antiquity and into early mediaeval times, styles Alexander as the last of the great Egyptian pharaohs and as a flawed superhero. Papyrus fragments discovered in the sands of Egypt show that schoolchildren were given work-tasks to try to compose speeches 'in the style of' Alexander.

Lucian uses Alexandria's Lighthouse, and Sostratus's hermetic inscription (revealed after its official gypsum covering praising the pharaoh had fallen away), as an allegory for the writing of history itself: 'even he had no regard for the immediate moment, or his own, brief lifetime: he looked to our day and eternity, as long as the tower shall stand and his skill abide. History should be written in this spirit, with truthfulness and an eye to future expectations rather than with adulation and a view to the pleasure of present praise.'[50]

The Pharos, the youngest of the ancient Wonders, channelled an idea that the oldest, the Giza Pyramid, also represented – that what matters to us, strange mammals that we are, is immortal fame. It is odd, is it not, that we should care so passionately not just about our legacies, but about the opinion of those, yet to be born, whom we will never know or meet? The Seven Wonders are an expression of hope, because they are projects whose plans are measured out in centuries. They are built in the belief that there will be a future.

There is still boat-building on Egypt's northern coastline, along the sea close to Rashid – Rosetta in Greek, home of the famous Rosetta Stone. The waterfront here is busy, as workers fire bricks to raise their homes, and use mattock wood to fashion the flat-bottomed boats that make their way along the Nile. As they work, barges transporting stone from the south power past into the Mediterranean, and ships bringing goods from Europe nudge their way into the tributaries of the Nile. Everywhere there is a wide horizon, the green of the land round Egypt's river-artery, and then the iris of the sea.

Ships delivering food and luxuries from Alexandria to our other Wonder destinations – Ephesus, Halikarnassos, Rhodes, even east to Babylon and west to Olympia – would generally head out in an anti-clockwise direction around the Mediterranean, the Middle Sea. And one day, one ship would take with it news of Alexandria's freshly minted and lambent, looming Lighthouse Wonder. Up towards Cyprus and the Levant this ship would have travelled, passing the wide mouth of the River Nile, bringing with it sand from the feet of the Great Pyramid. And like the first great Wonder – the Pyramid at Giza – the last, the Pharos, was built on a limestone outcrop surrounded by sand, but was fed by a great river that brought sub-Saharan Africa together with the great oceans of the world.

Now, the Mediterranean rim of the Pharos is spiked with those giant concrete-urchins, each 6-and-a-half feet tall, delivered here to hold back the sea, rising at a rate of 1 foot in 30 years; seawater heated by the equivalent of four Hiroshima bombs per second, the fall-out of civilisation eating itself, of us having ideas that seem wonderful in the moment and at the time of their conception.

The Pharos Lighthouse lit a land of knowledge. Now it is only knowledge that will ensure we can survive, to create new wonders.

CONCLUSION

✤

The greatest touchstone of any work is Time, who reveals even a man's heart beneath his breast.

SIMONIDES, SIXTH CENTURY BCE, L.G., II, 403

We all search for meaning. For stories with plots. For events with a pattern. We love the idea of Seven Wonders because it is a grouping that gives cohesion to history. And whereas our Seven Ancient Wonders have often been understood as a disparate collection, in truth they all relate to one another geographically, physically and culturally. Wonders serve a rich triple purpose. They were constructed partly to feed our need for wondrous tales – to experience and talk about the biggest, the best, the tallest, the most strange, the most bold. They encourage a saturation in the now, by submitting to a present, pure sensation of wonder. They remind us of our overwhelming desire to collaborate and to create beyond the possibilities of the individual.

Creativity has been described as our ability to project ideas onto the world. Ideas and symbols are passed down from one generation to another. This symbolic cultural heritage shapes, psychologically and physiologically, how we interact with society and the planet; it actively impacts how we live. Symbolic inheritance is a phenomenon only recently identified by anthropologists. Simply put, not only do physical creations like the Seven Ancient Wonders shape the world that made them, they shape generations to come. Because symbolic inheritance is biologically passed, at a molecular level, from one generation to another. Ideas of these Wonders are written into our genes.[1]

The Seven Wonders are all burning expressions of will and hope. They were made by men, and sometimes women, who forced success out of highly challenging environments. They are all powerful because of what they can accomplish beyond the point of creation: a machine to travel to the afterlife; an attempt to replicate nature; nature's power understood; divine power honed, made achievable by mortals; mortality commemorated; diplomacy celebrated; the light of the world given human form, light given to humans. Because the point of a Wonder is its relevance to the here and now, *and* the there and then. The Wonders connected their creators to their ancestors and to other cultures, and in their making, crafted an immortality for their works and for themselves.

Alexander the Great had a transporting belief in possibilities. Riding out through his territories, the young king would have seen Mount Olympus, the tallest mountain in Greece, and a home to gods. He would have known that he was born from hallowed earth, from the centre of sublime power. He seems to have convinced himself that he was indeed the son of Zeus. It was said in the notebooks that were supposedly left after his death that he had simply wanted to 'better the best'.[2] He came from a corner of the world where the moon can rise as red as the sun. When he visited Babylon, he dreamt of raising his own pyramid higher than Khufu's Great Pyramid of Giza. It was from this fevered moment that the Seven Wonders list was compiled. And just as the Hellenistic Greeks traced their ancestry back to gods and heroes, so it was appropriate to list, alongside their contemporary Wonders (the Mausoleum of Halikarnassos, the Colossus of Rhodes, the Lighthouse of Alexandria), the titans that went before this age: Giza's Pyramids, Babylon's Gardens, Ephesus' Temple and the Zeus at Olympia.

Culture, and understanding culture, is physically passed on as carbon molecules in the cosmos. We swim every moment of every day in a cultural ocean that also lapped the feet of our earliest ancestors. It is why we can feel connected to and can learn from communities of the deep past; women and men of all degrees learning how to live in the world, as a human-dominated world was working out how to live with itself. It is also why the Greek word for the past, *apotuxo*, 'to have happened before', is perhaps a more helpful nomination of previous times than the incursion of the Middle English word of c. 1300, *passen*, 'to go by', or the modern English *past*, 'to have gone by'. Things that have happened before can happen again.

It is therefore little surprise that the Ottoman rulers – within whose domain all the Seven Wonders were contained – described themselves as the Caesars who had taken Alexander the Great's place; no surprise that a statue of Alexander the Great welcomes international visitors into Istanbul's airport – the biggest international nexus in the world – and to an on-site airport museum with artefacts that range from prehistory onwards, including Mausolos as the satrap of Karia, leonine and bearded on a coin. We treasure totems of the past because we need them.

The museum at Alexandria (sometimes called the Mouseion) takes its name from the Muses – those Greek goddesses who inspired art, culture and history, and who were the daughters of memory (the goddess Mnemosyne) and power (the king of the gods, Zeus). 'Muse' in turn derives from a Proto-Indo-European root, *men* – which also gives us the words men, mankind, memory and mind. Being human and remembering are one and the same thing; physiologically we are creatures of memory. Remembering the past and imagining all kinds of futures occupies the human mind's waking hours. Not only is it true to say that I think, and therefore I am part of the community of mankind, but it is true that we are nothing if we do not remember, if we do not use our minds to create wonderful things that are relevant to past, present and future.

Perhaps we create wonders to prove something; and we write about them to understand many things.

As the torch of conquest is forced into a territory, embers scatter far and wide. So it was with Alexander's conquests, and so it was with the acquisition of knowledge in Alexandria. Alexandria, and Hellenistic culture's fetishisation of wisdom – the search for information and for meaning – was the very thing that sparked the creation, in the first place, of lists of Seven Wonders.* An accretion of knowledge from east and west, from south and north, was the very thing that made them.

Hunting for the truth of these Seven Wonders of the Ancient World

---

* Our understanding of the context of the Egyptian world of the oldest Wonder was certainly generated by an Alexander-influenced outlook. It was almost certainly the historian and high priest Manetho on the Nile Delta who wrote a *History of Egypt* and ranked the Egyptian pharaohs into their various dynasties, who popularised the Greek version of the Egyptian Khufu, Cheops, with the result that for many the burial place of Khufu is still known as the Cheops Pyramid. Thank you for the torch analogy.

and their creators – the Great Pyramids, the Hanging Gardens of Babylon, the Temple of Artemis at Ephesus, the Statue of Zeus at Olympia, the Mausoleum of Halikarnassos, the Colossus of Rhodes and the Lighthouse of Alexandria – has taught me much, including an axiomatic truth that powerful civilisations leave behind great monuments; great civilisations leave behind powerful ideas.

Just as the number seven is indivisible, each seventh being equal to the others, none of its factors greater than the others, so each of the Seven Wonders tells us something equally important about the human journey. And the final Wonder, the Pharos, a saviour of knowledge, reminds us that wisdom is our ultimate salvation.

POSTSCRIPT

✤

THE GREAT LIBRARY OF ALEXANDRIA

The Lighthouse in Alexander's city not only emitted light, but welcomed it in, in the form of knowledge that would then be stored in Alexandria's great library. This aggressive acquisition of insight famously began in Alexandria when port officials confiscated scrolls 'from the ships' as docking tax.[1] Athenians lent originals for copying, and Alexandrians, dishonourably, kept the originals and sent back the facsimiles. Stealing, perhaps, the idea of the library from Aristotle and the Lyceum in Athens, the Alexandrian library project incarnates a tenacious trope of humankind, that we seek similarity and novelty, the known and the unknown, with equal zeal.

The first librarian of Alexandria was a poet called Zenodotus from the city of Ephesus. He had the job of cataloguing and ordering the works of Homer (it was probably Zenodotus who organised Homer's *Iliad* into twenty-four books), and Zenodotus and Callimachus introduced the system of alphabetical listing to libraries.[2] The commentary, the glossary and the index were also innovations here – Alexandria's librarians encouraged the Hellenistic world's list aesthetic.*

Of course, Alexandria's library was not the first in the ancient world; the idea of a library seems to go back to Uruk in Mesopotamia, in what is now Iraq, and to the birth of writing itself, at least 5,400 years ago. Uruk, another major city of the great goddess Inanna, held in its temples tens of thousands of tablets – lives turned into lines on baked clay. These

---

* Here the notion of the specialness of seven was also perpetuated; another librarian at Alexandria, Demetrius of Phaleron, asserted in 297 BCE that the priests of Egypt would praise their gods via seven Greek vowels. The library of Alexandria protected truth and untruths alike.

tablets turn up in Syria too, in Ebla, dating back c. 4,600 years, originally stacked on wooden shelves; and in central Iraq, where one recent excavation in Sippar revealed tablets still in situ.³ And in Sennacherib's library in Nineveh, possibly shaded by the Hanging Gardens, in his 'Palace Without Rival', the texts of vanquished adversaries were gathered in like war trophies. So, humans wrote things down – and then some of those things were curated, held onto as the physical creation of shared memory.

But Greece had for most of its history been an oral culture. Socrates was allergic to the written word. It was primarily Aristotle, Alexander the Great's boyhood tutor, who sponsored a belief in the superiority of writing over agonistic oral debate. In Alexandria scholars competed to collect, translate, interpret and evolve. To publish knowledge in a new, ecumenical form: the *byblos*, the papyrus book – originally a scroll.

It was in Alexandria's library that the first extant Seven Wonders list was compiled. But then Alexandria's library was destroyed. Its beauty was chipped away at by greed, covetous, deracinating aggression and ennui. In 48 BCE in the Alexandrian War, as Julius Caesar's troops set fire to Egyptian ships in the dock, the flames spread first to boats and then to warehouses. Sources do not tell us that the library itself was damaged, but warehouses at the quay were – the feeder system for the great library itself, where manuscripts were impounded or collected.⁴ It was said that 40,000 papyri had been destroyed. As has been remarked, libraries became not just an asset, but a liability.⁵

But the Roman general Mark Antony, Cleopatra's husband, a decade on reportedly imported 200,000 new scrolls – an estimate of the entire contents – from the library at Pergamum in Asia Minor as a gift to Cleopatra. The town's name gives us the word parchment via the late Latin *pergamena charta*. This anecdote of excessive generosity was almost certainly exaggerated or even invented, a tale used to discredit both the rogue Roman and his 'Egyptian whore'.⁶ It is entirely plausible, though, that manuscripts at this time were considered both diplomatic and love gifts.

Not all volumes could have been destroyed in the Lighthouse's city. The pagan philosopher and mathematician Hypatia derived huge inspiration from Alexandria's library in the fifth century CE. It was said that, when Arabs arrived two hundred years later in 642 CE, the invading Amr Al petitioned Caliph Omar for advice on how to deal with the contents of the library. Our source, Bar-Hebraeus, tells us Caliph Omar responded, 'If what is written in them agrees with the Book of God, they are not required; if it disagrees, destroy them.' And, we are told, Arab forces allegedly did so. But our source is a Christian, writing in the thirteenth century, when the 'barbarity' of Islam had to be proved. Caliph Omar's criterion of works complying with the Qu'ran would be unlikely, given early Islam's voracious devouring of knowledge and reason, particularly at this time.[7] The truth is more prosaic. The truth is that the decline of the library was more a whimper than a bang. Complacency is the enemy of culture; the enemy of wonder and wondering.

> Look on my Works, ye Mighty, and despair!
> Nothing beside remains. Round the decay
> Of that colossal Wreck, boundless and bare
> The lone and level sands stretch far away.
>
> 'OZYMANDIAS' II–14, BY PERCY BYSSHE SHELLEY,
> PUBLISHED IN 1818, FOUR YEARS BEFORE SHELLEY
> DROWNED IN THE BAY OF POETS

A NOTE ON OTHER WONDERS

✤

In Book Two of his great *Histories*, Herodotus describes Egypt as 'a land which boasts an inordinate number of wonders, and possesses more monuments surpassing description than any other in the world. Reason enough then, to describe it at some length.'[1] We can easily understand why Egyptian Wonders are two sevenths of the list – but why *only* two? Herodotus also talks of the 'wonders' on the island of Samos where he was almost certainly exiled as a failed revolutionary – the water-tunnel through a mountain designed by Eupalinos (using Pythagorean principles, Pythagoras being another child of the island); the great temple-complex of Hera.[2] Both the Samian wonders survive – Eupalinos's newly restored 3.7-mile tunnel is simply astounding. Other authors added other structures such as the Temple of Solomon, the Colosseum, the Great Wall of China. As I write this sentence, gargantuan ancient structures are being uncovered in Crete, Saudi Arabia, Armenia and China *et alia*. We should consider the exciting certainty that many more Wonders than those listed have been created by human hand, and that while most have been lost, new ancient Wonders could still be waiting to be discovered. The Wonder-catalogue of the world never diminishes; it only expands.

ACKNOWLEDGEMENTS

❖

Philosophy begins with wondering.

ARISTOTLE, *METAPHYSICS* 982B

I am nothing without the people I love, and without people who, by wondering, are wisdom-lovers.

Thank you, as ever, to Prof. Paul Cartledge – for the illumination, the luminous inspiration, and for reading many drafts of this new Byblos-Laterculus. Thank you, Julian Alexander and Sarah Stamp, for always bearing with me. Thank you to Maddy Price for waiting so long for the book, she birthed a child; to Ed Lake for being this volume's godfather; to Chris Howard-Woods for your wisdom and advice; and to Alan Samson for conceiving this project, over lunches and laughter.

Thank you too to Prof. Armand D'Angour, Dr Konstantinos Anto-nopoulos, Prof. Michael Cosmopoulos, Prof. Alexander Evers, Sven Kasser, Dr Irving Finkel, Prof. Simon Hornblower, Prof. Salima Ikram, Prof. Robin Lane Fox, Prof. Antony Makrinos and Dr Daniel Potter (and again to PC), for reading individual chapters and for saving me from infelicities, and from myself.

Junior Collins, Hannah Critchlow, Mohamad Hawash, Omer Karaçan, Namak Khorsan, Mohammad al-Kindi, Shula Subramaniam, Imogen Stead, Laura Aitken-Burke, Marike Littlefair, Chloe Tye, Tabitha Chamberlayne, Freya Doggett, Celia Riddiough and Artemis Aperigi have all been stellar in their practical and editorial support.

Zaur Cabryli, Carena Dimech, Sahir Erozan, Spiro and Milly Flam-buriari, Charlotte and James Heneage, Annabelle and dear departed Nikos Louvros, Dr Andreas Pittas, Ceylan Şensoy, Ruth Sessions, Justin

Stead and, most exquisitely, Ömer Koç allowed me to immerse myself in the Eastern Mediterranean, North Africa, the Near East or Central Asia on the dedicated trail of the truth of these Wonders and the people who made them.

Dr Daniel Antoine, Sven Becker, Anthony Beevor, Prof. Trevor Bryce, Prof. Kara Cooney, Savaş Elmas, Aysa Ergir, Dr Stefanos Geroulanos, Prof. Angie Hobbs, Robin Hurlestone, Prof. Chris Jackson, Prof. Angeliki Kottaridi, Prof. Sabine Ladstätter, Prof. Mark Lehner, Prof. Joe McConnell, Prof. Alfonso Moreno, Prof. Armand Leroi, Dr Sarah Parcak, Magdy Rashdy, Dr Sahar Saalem, Konstantinos Skourlis, Dr Costas Synolakis, Prof. Pierre Taillet and Dr Joyce Tyldesley have all been exceptionally kind in the sharing of their research and sagacity and answers to many random queries. Jo Roberts-Miller and Simon Fox came in at the final furlong and made everything possible.

I thank each and every scholar, archaeologist, artist, writer or wisdom-lover who has gone before me and has generated the works, data and digs I have immersed myself in for the last decade while researching and writing this book. I have travelled with you – I am the dust on your feet.

The earth has been kind in giving up its resources to make these Wonders. My mother sometimes gave up a daughter, my daughters a mother, my best friend Jane a best friend, and my husband a wife to make this book. Wondering can be a cruel mistress, yet it is too charismatic and compelling. We are fortunate to meet and mingle with wonder in this world, all power to the wonder-makers of the past and future.

BIBLIOGRAPHY

❖

Abadal, J. et al. (2021), *Time and History in the Ancient Near East: Proceedings of the 56th Rencontre Assyriologique Internationale, Barcelona, July 26th–30th, 2010*. University Park, PA: Penn State University Press.

Abdelnaby, A.E. & Elnashai, A.S. (2013), 'Integrity assessment of the Pharos of Alexandria during the AD 1303 earthquake', *Engineering failure analysis* 33: 119–38.

Akurgal, E. (2015), *Ancient Civilizations and ruins of Turkey*. Ankara: Phoenix Yayinevi-Unal Sevindik.

Alexander, M.W. & Violet, W. (2014), 'The Marketing of People: Slave Trade in the Ancient Near East', *Journal of Business and Behavioral Sciences* 26(2): 138.

Algaze, G. (2018), 'Entropic Cities: The Paradox of Urbanism in Ancient Mesopotamia', *Current anthropology* 59(1): 23–54.

Allen, J.P. & Der Manuelian, P. (2005), *The Ancient Egyptian Pyramid Texts*. Atlanta: Society of Biblical Literature.

Amin, M.A. (1970), 'Ancient Trade and Trade Routes between Egypt and the Sudan, 4000 to 700 B.C.', *Sudan Notes and Records* 51: 23–30.

Andreou, E. & Andreou, I. (2010), *Elis: The City of the Olympic Games*. Athens: Archaeological Receipts Fund.

Anthony, D.W. (2007), *The Horse, the Wheel, and Language: How Bronze-Age Riders from the Eurasian Steppes Shaped the Modern World*. Princeton, NJ; Oxford: Princeton University Press.

Antikas, T.G. (2004), *Olympica Hippica. Horses, Men and Women in the Ancient Olympics*. Athens: Evandros.

Appian, trans White, H. (1899), *The Roman History of Appian*. Lond. &c.

Arnold, I.R. (1936), 'Festivals of Rhodes', *American Journal of Archaeology* 40(4): 432–6.

Arnold, I.R. (1972), 'Festivals of Ephesus', *American Journal of Archaeology* 76(1): 17–22.

Ashley, M. (1980), *The Seven Wonders of the World*. London: Fontana.

Ashmole, B. & Yalouris, N. (1967), *Olympia: the sculptures of the temple of Zeus.* London: Phaidon.

Ashmole, B. (1972), *Architect and sculptor in classical Greece.* New York: New York University Press.

Assmann, J. (2003), *The mind of Egypt: history and meaning in the time of the Pharaohs.* Cambridge, MA; London: Harvard University Press.

Athenaeus, trans. Olson, S.D. (2010), *Athenaeus of Naucratis, The Learned Banqueters.* Cambridge, MA: Harvard University Press.

Azize, J. (2002), 'Wrestling as a Symbol for Maintaining the Order of Nature in Ancient Mesopotamia', *Journal of ancient Near Eastern religions* 2(1): 1–26.

Bachvarova, M.R. (2016), *From Hittite to Homer: the Anatolian background of ancient Greek epic.* Cambridge: Cambridge University Press.

Baitinger, H. & Völling, T. (2006), *Werkzeug Und Gerät Aus Olympia.* Berlin: Walter De Gruyter.

Baitinger, H. (2019), 'Commemoration of War in Archaic and Classical Greece. Battlefields, Tombs and Sanctuaries', 131–47 in Giangiulio, M., Franchi, E. & Proietti, G. (eds), *Commemorating War and War Dead.* Stuttgart: Franz Steiner Verlag.

Baker, H.D. (2001), 'Degrees of freedom: Slavery in midfirst millennium BC Babylonia', *World archaeology* 33(1): 18–26.

Bammer, A. & Muss, U. (2007), 'Eine frühes Quellheiligtum am Ayasolukhügel in Ephesos', *Anatolia antiqua. Eski Anadolu* 15(1): 95–101.

Bammer, A. (1990), 'A Peripteros of the Geometric Period in the Artemision of Ephesus', *Anatolian Studies* 40: 137–60.

Bar Hebraeus, trans. Wilmshurst, D. (2016), *The Ecclesiastical Chronicle.* Piscataway, NJ: Gorgias Press.

Barker, G. (2000), 'Farmers, Herders and Miners in the Wadi Faynan, Southern Jordan: a 10,000-year Landscape Archaeology', 63–85 in Barker, G. & Gilbertson, D. (eds), *The Archaeology of Arid Lands.* London: Routledge.

Barringer, J.M. & Hurwit, J.M. (2005), *Periklean Athens and Its Legacy: Problems and Perspectives.* Austin: University of Texas Press.

Barringer, J.M. (2005), 'The Temple of Zeus at Olympia, Heroes, and Athletes', *Hesperia* 74(2): 211–41.

Barringer, J.M. (2021), *Olympia: a Cultural History.* Princeton, NJ; Oxford: Princeton University Press.

Bartlett, C. (2014), 'The Design of The Great Pyramid of Khufu', *Nexus network journal* 16(2): 299–311.

Bashir, M.S. & Emberling, G. (2021), 'Trade in Ancient Nubia: Routes, Goods, and Structures', 995–1014 in Emberling, G. & Williams, B.B. (eds), *The Oxford Handbook of Ancient Nubia.* Oxford: Oxford University Press.

Bassett, S.G. (2000), '"Excellent Offerings": The Lausos Collection in Constantinople', *The Art bulletin (New York, N.Y.)* 82(1): 6–25.

Bawany, H. (2012), 'A Bridge between Traditions: The Virgin Mary in Christianity and Islam', *Verbum* 9(2): 35–43.

Bean, G.E., Cook, J.M. & W.H.P. (1955), 'The Halicarnassus Peninsula', *Annual of the British School at Athens* 50(50): 85–171.

Beckwith, C. (2015), *Greek Buddha: Pyrrho's Encounter with Early Buddhism in Central Asia*. Princeton, NJ: Princeton University Press.

Behrens-Abouseif, D. (2006), 'The Islamic History of the Lighthouse of Alexandria', *Muqarnas* 23(1): 1–14.

Bernal, M. (1987), *Black Athena: The Afroasiatic Roots of Classical Civilization Volume I: The Fabrication of Ancient Greece 1785–1985*. London: Vintage.

Bernal, M. (1996), *Black Athena: The Afroasiatic Roots of Classical Civilization Volume II: The Archaeological and Documentary Evidence*. New Brunswick, NJ: Rutgers University Press.

Berthold, R.M. (2009), *Rhodes in the Hellenistic Age*. Ithaca, NY: Cornell University Press.

Bianchi, R.S. (1993), 'Hunting Alexander's Tomb', *Archaeology* 46(4): 54–5.

Bigwood, J. (2017), 'Ctesias' Description of Babylon', *American Journal of Ancient History* 3(1): 32–52.

Bing, P. (1998), 'Between Literature and the Monuments', 21–43 in Harder, A., Regtuit, R.F. & Wakker, G.C. (eds), *Genre in Hellenistic poetry*. Groningen: Egbert Forsten.

Blok, J.H. & Krul, J. (2017), 'Debt and Its Aftermath: The Near Eastern Background to Solon's Seisachtheia', *Hesperia* 86(4): 607–43.

Bloom, J.M. (1990), 'Cresswell and the Origins of the Minaret', *Muqarnas* 8(1): 55–8.

Boardman, J. (2002), *The Archaeology of Nostalgia: How the Greeks Recreated their Mythical Past*. London: Thames & Hudson.

Bodi, D. (2021), '"Let the Sleeping Dogs Lie" or the Taboo (NÍG.GIG=ikkibu) of the Sacredness of Sleep as Order and Noise at Night ("tapage nocturne") as Disorder in Some Ancient Near Eastern Texts', 19–36 in De Graef, K. & Goddeeris, A. (eds), *Law and (Dis)order in the Ancient Near East: Proceedings of the 59th Rencontre Assyriologique Internationale Held at Ghent, Belgium, 15–19 July 2013*. Eisenbrauns, Penn State University Press.

Bogaard, A. et al. (2018), 'From Traditional Farming in Morocco to Early Urban Agroecology in Northern Mesopotamia: Combining Present-day Arable Weed Surveys and Crop Isotope Analysis to Reconstruct Past Agrosystems in (Semi-)arid Regions', *Environmental archaeology : the journal of human palaeoecology* 23(4): 303–22.

Borger, R. (1974), 'Die Beschwörungsserie Bit Meseri Und Die Himmelfahrt Henochs', *Journal of Near Eastern Studies* 33(2): 183–96.

Borowitz, A. (2005), *Terrorism for self-glorification: the herostratos syndrome*. Kent, OH: Kent State University Press.

Boutsikas, E. (2020), *The Cosmos in Ancient Greek Religious Experience: Sacred Space, Memory, and Cognition*. Cambridge: Cambridge University Press.

Bowe, P. (2015), 'A Deliberation on the Hanging Gardens of Mesopotamia', *Garden History* 43(2): 151–67.

Bremen, R.V. (2007), 'Networks of Rhodians in Karia', *Mediterranean historical review* 22(1): 113–32.

Brennan, S. & Thomas, D. (eds) (2021), *The Landmark Xenophon's Anabasis*. New York, NY: Pantheon Books.

Brereton, G. (2018), *I am Ashurbanipal: king of the world, king of Assyria*. London: Thames & Hudson.

Brier, B., Morabito, M.G. & Greene, S. (2020), 'The Khufu I Boat: An Empirical Investigation into Its Use', *Journal of the American Research Center in Egypt* 56(1): 83–99.

Brown, A.R. (2021), 'Antiquarian knights in Mediterranean island landscapes: the Hospitaller Order of St John and crusading among the ruins of classical antiquity, from medieval Rhodes to early modern Malta', *Journal of medieval history* 47(3): 413–32.

Burleigh, N. (2008), *Mirage: Napoleon's Scientists and the Unveiling of Egypt*. New York, NY: Harper.

Caesar, J., trans. Carter, J. (2008), *Oxford World's Classics: Julius Caesar: The Civil War: with the Anonymous Alexandrian, African, and Spanish Wars*. Oxford: Oxford University Press.

Campion, N. (2012), *Astrology and Cosmology in the World's Religions*. New York, NY: New York University Press.

Canter, H.V. (1930), 'The Venerable Bede and the Colosseum', *Transactions and proceedings of the American Philological Association* 61: 150–64.

Carnarvon, F. (2007), *Carnarvon & Carter: The Story of the Two Englishmen who discovered the Tomb of Tutankhamun*. Newbury: Highclere Enterprises.

Carnarvon, F. (2009), *Egypt at Highclere: The Discovery of Tutankhamun*. Newbury: Highclere Enterprises.

Carr, J.C. (2016), *The Knights Hospitaller: A Military History of the Knights of St John*. Barnsley: Pen & Sword Military.

Carrington, H. (2006), *The Seven Wonders of The World Ancient, Medieval and Modern*. USA: Kessinger Legacy Reprints.

Carroll, M. (2003), *Earthly Paradises: Ancient Gardens in History and Archaeology*. London: British Museum.

Cartledge, P. (2018), *Democracy: A Life*. Oxford: Oxford University Press.

Casson, L. (1994), *Travel in the ancient world*. Baltimore, MD; London: Johns Hopkins University Press.

Ceccarelli, M. (ed.) (2004), *International Symposium on History of Machines and Mechanisms: proceedings HMM 2004*. Dordrecht; Boston, MA: Kluwer Academic.

Chariton, trans. Goold, G.P. (1995), *Chariton: Callirhoe*. Cambridge, MA; London: Harvard University Press.

Charles River Editors (2013), *The Seven Wonders of the Ancient World*. CreateSpace.

Charney, N. (2018), *The Museum of Lost Art*. London: Phaidon.

Chau, Ju-kua, trans. Hirth, F. & Rockhill, W.W. (1966), *Chau Ju-Kua: His Work on the Chinese and Arab Trade in the Twelfth and Thirteenth Centuries, Entitled Chu-fan-chi*. Amsterdam: Oriental.

Chioti, L. (2021), 'The Herulian Invasion in Athens (A.D. 267): The Archaeological Evidence', 319–39 in Fachard, S. & Harris, E. (eds), *The Destruction of Cities in the Ancient Greek World: Integrating the Archaeological and Literary Evidence*. Cambridge: Cambridge University Press.

Christiansen, T. et al. (2020), 'Insights into the Composition of Ancient Egyptian Red and Black Inks on Papyri Achieved by Synchrotron-based Microanalyses', *Proceedings of the National Academy of Sciences* 117(45): 27825.

Chugg, A. (2002), 'The Sarcophagus of Alexander the Great?', *Greece and Rome* 49(1): 8–26.

Cioffi, R.L. (2016), *Travel in the Roman World*. Oxford Handbooks Online.

Clayton, P.A. & Price, M.J. (1989), *The seven wonders of the ancient world*. London: Routledge.

Cole, S.G. (1998), 'Domesticating Artemis', 24–41 in Blundell, S. & Williamson, M. (eds), *The sacred and the feminine in ancient Greece*. London: Routledge.

Cole, S.G. (2004), *Landscapes, gender, and ritual space: the ancient Greek experience*. Berkeley, CA: University of California Press.

Collon, D. (2003), 'Dance in Ancient Mesopotamia', *Near Eastern archaeology* 66(3): 96–102.

Connelly, J.B. (2007), *Portrait of a priestess: women and ritual in ancient Greece*. Princeton, NJ; Woodstock: Princeton University Press.

Cook, B.F. (2005), *Relief sculpture of the mausoleum at Halicarnassus*. Oxford: Oxford University Press.

Cook, J. (2013), *Ice Age Art: the Arrival of the Modern Mind*. London: British Museum Press.

Cooney, K. (2020), *When Women Ruled the World: Six Queens of Egypt*. Washington, DC: National Geographic.

Cooper, K. (2013), *Band of Angels: the Forgotten World of Early Christian Women*. London: Atlantic Books.

Copley et al. (2001), 'Detection of palm fruit lipids in archaeological pottery from Qasr Ibrim, Egyptian Nubia', *Proceedings of the Royal Society. B, Biological sciences* 268(1467): 593–7.

Cordova, C.E. (2007), 'The Degradation of the Ancient Near Eastern Environment', 125–41 in Snell, D.C., *A Companion to the Ancient Near East*. Oxford: Blackwell.

Crane, T. (1974), 'The Apotheosis of Classical Architecture', *The Classical outlook* 52(1): 5–6.

Critchlow, H. (2022), *Joined-Up Thinking*. London: Hodder & Stoughton.

Crowther, N. (2001), 'Visiting the Olympic Games in Ancient Greece: Travel and Conditions for Athletes and Spectators', *International journal of the history of sport* 18(4): 37–52.

Curlee, L. (2002), *Seven Wonders of the Ancient World*. New York, NY: Atheneum Books for Young Readers.

Dalley, S. (2013), *The mystery of the Hanging Garden of Babylon: an elusive world wonder traced*. Oxford: Oxford University Press.

Da Riva, R. (2013), 'Neo-Babylonian Monuments at Shir Es-Sanam and Wadi Es-Saba (North Lebanon)', *Wiener Zeitschrift Für Die Kunde Des Morgenlandes* 103: 87–100.

Daim, F. & Ladstatter, S. (eds) (2011), *Bizans Doneminde Ephesos*. Istanbul: Ege Yayinlari.

Dale, T.E.A. (2000), 'Stolen property: St Mark's first Venetian tomb and the politics of communal memory', 53–104 in Pendergast, C.S. & Del Alamo, E.V., *Memory and the Medieval Tomb*. London: Routledge.

Dalley, S. & Oleson, J.P. (2003), 'Sennacherib, Archimedes, and the Water Screw: The Context of Invention in the Ancient World', *Technology and Culture* 44(1): 1–26.

Dalley, S. (1993), 'Ancient Mesopotamian Gardens and the Identification of the Hanging Gardens of Babylon Resolved', *Garden History* 21(1): 1–13.

Dalley, S. (2008), 'Babylon as a name for other cities including Nineveh', 25–33 in Biggs, R.D., Myers, J. & Roth, M.T. (eds), *Proceedings of the 51st Rencontre Assyriologique Internationale: held at the Oriental Institute of the University of Chicago, July 18–22, 2005*. Chicago, IL: Oriental Institute of the University of Chicago.

Darke, D. (2020), *Stealing from the Saracens: How Islamic architecture shaped Europe*. London: Hurst & Company.

Davison, C.C. (2009), *Pheidias: The Sculptures & Ancient Sources*. London: Institute of Classical Studies, School of Advanced Study, University of London.

De Grummond, N.T. & Ridgway, B.S. (eds) (2000), *From Pergamon to Sperlonga: sculpture and context*. Berkeley, CA; London: University of California Press.

De Haan, H.J. (2010), *The large Egyptian pyramids: modelling a complex engineering project*. Oxford: Archaeopress.

De Meyer, M. (2011), 'Inlaid eyes on Old Kingdom coffins: a history of misidentification', *The Journal of Egyptian Archaeology* 97: 201–3.

De Nie, G. (1985), 'The spring, the seed and the tree: Gregory of Tours on the wonders of nature', *Journal of Medieval History* 11(2): 89–135.

Democritus, ed. and trans. Olson, S. D. (2010), *Athenaeus: The Learned Banqueters*, Volume VI: Books 12-13.594b. Loeb Classical Library 327. Cambridge, MA: Harvard University Press.

Depuydt, L. (1997), 'The Time of Death of Alexander the Great: 11 June 323 B.C. (–322), ca. 4:00–5:00 PM', *Die Welt des Orients* 28: 117–35.

Diels, H. (1904), *Laterculi Alexandrini aus einem Papyrus ptolemäischer Zeit.* Berlin: G. Reimer.

Dillery, J. (1999), 'The First Egyptian Narrative History: Manetho and Greek Historiography', *Zeitschrift für Papyrologie und Epigraphik* 127: 93–116.

Diodorus Siculus, trans. Oldfather, C.H. (1933), *Diodorus of Sicily in Twelve Volumes.* London: W. Heinemann; Cambridge, MA: Harvard University Press.

Dodson, A. (2003), *The Pyramids of Ancient Egypt.* London: New Holland.

DuBois, P. (1991), *Centaurs and Amazons: Women and the Pre-History of the Great Chain of Being.* Ann Arbor, MI: University of Michigan Press.

Dunand, F. & Adler, W. (2013), 'Traditional Religion in Ptolemaic and Roman Egypt', 165–88 in Salzman, M. (ed.), *The Cambridge History of Religions in the Ancient World.* Cambridge: Cambridge University Press.

Durrell, L. (2000), *Reflections on a Marine Venus : A Companion to the Landscape of Rhodes.* London: Faber.

Eckstein, F. (1988), 'Trompeter in Olympia', 52–64 in Wissemann, M. (ed.), *Roma renascens. Beiträge zur Spätantike und Rezeptionsgeschichte. Ilona Opelt von ihren Freunden und Schülern zum 9.7.1988 in Verehrung gewidmet.* Frankfurt: Peter Lang.

Eggermont, P.H.L. & Hoftijzer, J. (1962), *The moral edicts of King Aśoka: included: the Greco-Aramaic inscription of Kandahar and further inscriptions of the Maurian Period.* Leiden: E. J. Brill.

El Daly, O., (2008), *Egyptology: The Missing Millennium. Ancient Egypt in Medieval Arabic Writings.* Oxford: Routledge.

Elsner, J. & Rutherford, I. (eds) (2007), *Pilgrimage in Graeco-Roman & early Christian antiquity: seeing the gods.* Oxford: Oxford University Press.

Emery, W.B. (1970), 'Preliminary Report on the Excavations at North Saqqara, 1968–9', *Journal of Egyptian Archaeology* 56: 5.

Empereur, J.-Y. (1998), *Alexandria rediscovered.* London: British Museum Press.

Erdemgil, S. et al. (1986), *Ephesus Museum.* Istanbul: DO-GU.

Evren, A. et al. (2015), *Ephesus.* Ismir: Dilam.

Fales, F.M. & Fabbro, R.D. (2014), 'Back to Sennacherib's Aqueduct at Jerwan: A Reassessment of the Textual Evidence', *Iraq* 76: 65–98.

Faulkner, N. (2012), *A visitor's guide to the ancient Olympics.* New Haven, CT; London: Yale University Press.

Fedak, J. (2016), *Monumental Tombs of the Hellenistic Age: A Study of Selected Tombs from the Pre-Classical to the Early Imperial Era.* Toronto: University of Toronto Press.

Feldt, L. (2016), 'Religion, Nature, and Ambiguous Space in Ancient Mesopotamia: The Mountain Wilderness in Old Babylonian Religious Narratives', *Numen* 63(4): 347–82.

Fletcher, J. (2008), *Cleopatra the Great: The Woman Behind The Legend*. London: Hodder & Stoughton.

Flower, M. (1997), *Theopompus of Chios: History and rhetoric in the fourth century B.C.* Oxford: Clarendon Press.

Fonte, G.C.A. (2007), *Building the Great Pyramid in one year: an engineer's report*. New York, NY: Algora Pub.

Fortson, B.W. (2010), *Indo-European Language and Culture: an Introduction*. Malden, MA; Oxford: Wiley-Blackwell.

Foss, C. (1979), *Ephesus after antiquity: a late antique, Byzantine and Turkish city*. Cambridge: Cambridge University Press.

Fox, M. (2001), 'Dionysius, Lucian, and the Prejudice against Rhetoric in History', *The Journal of Roman studies* 91: 76–93.

Frahm, E. (1997), *Einleitung in die Sanherib-Inschriften*. Wien: Institut für Orientalistik der Universität.

Frahm, E. (2003), 'New sources for Sennacherib's first campaign', *ISIMU* 6: 129–64.

Frahm, E. (2008), 'The Great City: Nineveh in the Age of Sennacherib', *Journal of the Canadian Society for Mesopotamian Studies* 3: 13–20.

Fraser, P.M. (1972), *Ptolemaic Alexandria*. Oxford: Clarendon Press.

Friedman, R. et al. (2018), 'Natural mummies from Predynastic Egypt reveal the world's earliest figural tattoos', *Journal of Archaeological Science* 92: 116–25.

Frothingham, A.L. & Marquand, A. (1896), 'Archæological News', *The American Journal of Archaeology and of the History of the Fine Arts* 11(1): 62–144.

Fuentes, A. (2017), *The creative spark: how imagination made humans exceptional*. New York, NY: Dutton.

Gabbay, U. (2003), 'Dance in Textual Sources from Ancient Mesopotamia', *Near Eastern archaeology* 66(3): 103–5.

Gabra, G. (2003), 'The Revolts of the Bashmuric Copts in the Eighth and Ninth Centuries', 111–19 in Beltz, W. (ed.), *Die koptische Kirche in den ersten drei islamischen Jahrhunderten*. Halle (Saale): Institut für Orientalistik, Martin-Luther-Universität.

Gabrielsen, V. (1999), *Hellenistic Rhodes: politics, culture, and society*. Aarhus: Aarhus University Press.

Galán, J.M. (2000), 'The Ancient Egyptian Sed-Festival and the Exemption from Corvee', *Journal of Near Eastern Studies* 59(4): 255–64.

Galen, trans. Kühn (1828), *Opera omnia, Volume 17, Part 1*. Berlin: C. Cnobloch.

Galli, M. (2007), 'Pilgrimage as Elite Habitus: Educated Pilgrims in Sacred Landscape During the Second Sophistic', 253–90 in Elsner, J. & Rutherford, I. (eds), *Pilgrimage in Graeco-Roman & early Christian antiquity: seeing the gods*. Oxford: Oxford University Press.

Gantz, T. (1996), *Early Greek myth: a guide to literary and artistic sources*. Baltimore, MD; London: Johns Hopkins University Press.

García Romero, F. (2013), 'Sports tourism in Ancient Greece', *Journal of tourism history* 5(2): 146–60.

Garland, R. (2010), *The Eye of the Beholder: Deformity and Disability in the Graeco-Roman World*. London: Bloomsbury Publishing.

Garland, R. (2014), *Wandering Greeks: The Ancient Greek Diaspora from the Age of Homer to the Death of Alexander the Great*. Princeton, NJ: Princeton University Press.

George, A.R. (2013), 'The poem of Erra and Ishum: A Babylonian Poet's View of War', 39–71 in Kennedy, H., *Warfare and Poetry in the Middle East*. London: I.B. Tauris.

Georgius, trans. Bekker, I. (1838), *Georgius Cedrenus, Ioannis Scylitzae ope.* Bonnae: E. Weber.

Geroulanos, S. (1994), *Trauma: Wund-Entstehung und Wund-Pflege im antiken Griechenland*. Mainz: Zabern.

Gibson, B. & Harrison, T. (eds) (2013), *Polybius and his world: essays in memory of F.W. Walbank*. Oxford: Oxford University Press.

Goddio, F. & Masson-Berghoff, A. (2016), *The BP exhibition: sunken cities: Egypt's lost worlds*. London: Thames & Hudson.

Goldhill, S. (2005), *Love, Sex & Tragedy: Why Classics Matters*. London: John Murray.

Goldhill, S. et al. (2006), *Wonders of the World*. London: The Folio Society.

Graf, F. (2002), 'Pedestals of the Gods', *Zeitschrift Für Papyrologie Und Epigraphik* 141: 137–8.

Graham, D.W. (2006), *Explaining the Cosmos: the Ionian Tradition of Scientific Philosophy*. Princeton, NJ; Oxford: Princeton University Press.

Graves, R. (2012), *The Greek Myths*. London: Penguin Books.

Greaves, J., ed. Butler, J.A. (2018), *John Greaves, Pyramidographia and Other Writings, with Birch's Life of John Greaves*. Newcastle upon Tyne: Cambridge Scholars.

Green, B.A.N. (2015), *Building the Khufu Pyramid – Shedding New Light*. UK: Bernard A.N. Green.

Greenbaum, D. (2016), *The Daimon in Hellenistic astrology: Origins and influence*. Leiden; Boston, MA.

Griffiths, J.G. (1966), 'Hecataeus and Herodotus on "A Gift of the River"', *Journal of Near Eastern Studies* 25(1): 57–61.

Gumus, M.D. (2020), *Ancient Ephesus with reconstructions and aerial photographs*. Izmir: Dilam.

Gurtner, D. (2006), 'The Veil of the Temple in History and Legend', *Journal of the Evangelical Theological Society* 49(1): 97–114.

Hagen, J. & Ostergren, R. (2006), 'Spectacle, architecture and place at the Nuremberg Party Rallies: projecting a Nazi vision of past, present and future', *Cultural geographies* 13(2): 157–81.

Hagen, J. (2008), 'Parades, public space, and propaganda: the Nazi culture parades in Munich', *Geografiska annaler. Series B, Human geography* 90(4): 349–67.

Hall, E. & Wyles, R. (2008), *New directions in ancient pantomime.* Oxford; New York: Oxford University Press.

Halton, C. & Svärd, S. (2018), *Women's writing of ancient Mesopotamia: an anthology of the earliest female authors.* Cambridge: Cambridge University Press.

Handler, S. (1971), 'Architecture on the Roman Coins of Alexandria', *American Journal of Archaeology* 75(1): 57–74.

Harder, A., Wakker, G.C. & Regtuit, R.F. (eds) (1998), *Genre in Hellenistic Poetry.* Groningen: Egbert Forsten.

Harifi, S. (2021), 'Giza Pyramids Construction: an ancient-inspired metaheuristic algorithm for optimization', *Evolutionary intelligence* 14(4): 1743–61.

Harissis, H.V. (2009), *Apiculture in the prehistoric Aegean: Minoan and Mycenaean symbols revisited.* Oxford: John and Erica Hedges Ltd.

Harrington, N. (2012), *Living with the Dead: Ancestor Worship and Mortuary Ritual in Ancient Egypt.* Oxford: Oxbow.

Harris, W.V. & Ruffini, G. (2004), *Ancient Alexandria between Egypt and Greece.* Leiden: Brill.

Hassan, S. (1949), *The sphinx: Its history in the light of recent excavations.* Cairo: Government Press.

Hawass, Z. (2005), *Tutankhamun and the Golden Age of the Pharaohs.* Washington, DC: National Geographic Society.

Hawass, Z. (2006), *Mountains of the pharaohs: The untold story of the pyramid builders.* Cairo: American University in Cairo Press.

Hawass, Z. & Saleem, S.N. (2018), *Scanning the Pharaohs: CT Imaging of the New Kingdom Royal Mummies.* Cairo; New York, NY: The American University in Cairo Press.

Haynes, N. (2022), *Stone Blind: Medusa's Story.* London: Mantle.

Heckel, W. & Yardley, J. (2004), *Alexander the Great: Historical texts in translation.* Malden, MA; Oxford: Blackwell Publishing.

Heidel, A. (1953), 'The Octagonal Sennacherib Prism in the Iraq Museum', *Sumer* 9(2): 117.

Hemeda, S. & Sonbol, A. (2020), 'Sustainability problems of the Giza pyramids', *Heritage science* 8(1): 1–28.

Henderson, J. (2009), *Longus, Daphnis and Chloe; Xenophon of Ephesus, Anthia and Habrocomes.* Cambridge, MA; London: Harvard University Press.

Henry, O. & Belgin-Henry, A. (eds) (2020), *The Carians: from seafarers to city builders.* Istanbul: Yapı Kredi Yayınları.

Heraclides, trans. Wehrli, F. (1953), *Herakleides Pontikos.* Stuttgart: Schwabe & Schule Des Aristoteles.

Hero, trans. Schmidt, W. (1899), *Heronis Alexandrini Opera Quae Supersunt Omnia.* Stutgardiae: In Aedibus B.G. Teubneri.

Herodotus, trans. Godley, A.D. (1926), *Herodotus: The Histories.* Cambridge, MA: Harvard University Press; London: Heinemann.

Herodotus, trans. Holland, T. (2013), *The Histories.* London: Penguin Classics.

Herodotus, trans. Waterfield, R. (2008), *Herodotus, The Histories.* Oxford: Oxford University Press.

Holmes, B. (2012), *Gender: Antiquity and its Legacy.* Oxford: Oxford University Press.

Homer, trans. Fagles, R. (1991), *Homer, The Iliad.* London: Penguin Books.

Homer, trans. Fagles, R. (2006), *The Odyssey.* New York: Penguin Books.

Homer, trans. Lattimore, R. (1951), *The Iliad.* Chicago: University of Chicago Press.

Homer, trans. Murray, A.T. (1924), *The Iliad.* Cambridge, MA: Harvard University Press; London: Heinemann.

Homer, trans. Rieu, E.V. (1946), *The Odyssey.* Harmondsworth, Middlesex: Penguin.

Homer, trans. Wilson, Emily (2018), *The Odyssey.* New York: W.W. Norton and Company.

Hopkins, K. & Beard, M. (2005), *The Colosseum.* London: Profile.

Hornblower, S. (1982), *Mausolus.* Oxford: Clarendon Press.

Howell, A. et al. (2015), 'Late Holocene uplift of Rhodes, Greece: evidence for a large tsunamigenic earthquake and the implications for the tectonics of the eastern Hellenic Trench System', *Geophysical journal international* 203(1): 459–74.

Hughes, B. (2005), *Helen of Troy: Goddess, princess, whore.* London: Jonathan Cape.

Hughes, B. (2010), *The Hemlock Cup: Socrates, Athens, and the search for the good life.* London: Jonathan Cape.

Hughes, B. (2019), *Venus and Aphrodite.* London: Weidenfeld & Nicolson.

Ibn Faḍl Allāh Al-ʿUmarī, Aḥmad Ibn Yaḥyá & Krawulsky, D. (1986), *Masālik Al-abṣār Fī Mamālik Al-amṣār: Dawlat Al-Mamālīk Al-ūlá.* Bayrūt: Al-Markaz Al-Islāmī Lil-Buḥūth.

Ibn Jubayr, trans. Broadhurst, R.J.C. (1952), *The travels of Ibn Jubayr: being the chronicle of a mediaeval Spanish Moor concerning his journey to the Egypt of Saladin, the holy cities of Arabia, Baghdad the city of the caliphs, the Latin kingdom of Jerusalem, and the Norman kingdom of Sicily.* London: Jonathan Cape.

Ighnāṭyūs Afrām I & Moosa, M. (2003), *The Scattered Pearls: A History of Syriac Literature and Sciences.* Piscataway, NJ: Gorgias Press.

Ignatiadou, D. (2004), 'The finds from the tomb chamber of Maussolos: Glass vessels' in Zahle, J. & Kjeldsen, K. *The Maussolleion at Halikarnassos: Reports of the Danish Archaeological Expedition to Bodrum vol. 6: Subterranean and pre-Maussolan structures on the site of the Maussolleion.* Jutland: Aarhus University Press.

Ionescu, C. (2022), *She Who Hunts: Artemis: The Goddess Who Changed the World*. Tellwell Talent.

Isayev, E. (2017), 'Between hospitality and asylum: A historical perspective on displaced agency', *International review of the Red Cross* 99(904): 75–98.

Jenkins, I. & Waywell, G.B. (eds) (1997), *Sculptors and Sculpture of Caria and the Dodecanese*. London: British Museum Press.

Jenkins, I. et al. (2015), *Defining beauty: the body in ancient Greek art*. London: The British Museum.

Jeppesen, K. & Zahle, J. (1973), 'The Site of the Mausoleum at Halicarnassus Reexcavated', *American journal of archaeology* 77(3): 336–8.

Jeppesen, K. & Zahle, J. (1975), 'Investigations on the Site of the Mausoleum 1970/1973', *American journal of archaeology* 79(1): 67–79.

Johnson, W.A. (1994), 'Oral Performance and the Composition of Herodotus' "Histories"', *Greek, Roman and Byzantine Studies* 35(3): 229–54.

Jones, K.R. (2014), 'Alcaeus of Messene, Philip V and the Colossos of Rhodes: a Re-examination of Anth. Pal. 6.171', *Classical Quarterly* 64(1): 136–51.

Jordan, P. (2002), *The seven wonders of the Ancient World*. Harlow: Longman.

Kaltsas, N. (2009), *Olympia*. Athens: Archaeological Receipts Fund.

Kantzia C. & Zimmer, G. (1989), 'Rhodische Kolosse. Eine Hellenistische Bronzegusswerkstatt', *Archäologischer Anzeiger*: 488–523.

Kanz, F. & Karl, G. (2009), 'Dying in the Arena: the Osseous Evidence from Ephesian Gladiators', 211–20 in Wilmott, T., *Roman amphitheatres and Spectacula: a 21st-century perspective: papers from an international conference held at Chester, 16th–18th February, 2007*. Oxford: Archaeopress.

Kappel, D. (2013), 'Soldiers and Savants: an Enlightened Despot Discovers Egypt', *Seton Hall University Dissertations and Theses* (ETDs): 1869.

Kawae, Y. (2011), 'Geomorphological Aspects at the Giza Plateau in Egypt during the Age of Pyramid Building', *Journal of Geography*: 864–8.

Kawae, Y. et al. (2013), '3D Reconstruction of the "Cave" of the Great Pyramid from Video Footage', *The Eurographics Association*: 227–30.

Kebric, R.B. (2019a), 'The Colossus of Rhodes: Some Observations about Its Location', *Athens Journal of History* 5(2): 83–114.

Kebric, R.B. (2019b), 'The Colossus of Rhodes: Its Height and Pedestal', *Athens Journal of Humanities & Arts* 6(4): 259–98.

Keesling, C.M. (2017), *Early Greek portraiture: monuments and histories*. Cambridge: Cambridge University Press.

Kemp, B.J. (2006), *Ancient Egypt: Anatomy of a Civilization*. London; New York, NY: Routledge.

Kennedy, R.F. et al. (2013), *Race and ethnicity in the classical world: an anthology of primary sources in translation*. Indianapolis: Hackett Publishing Company, Inc.

Ker, J. & Wessels, A. (eds) (2020), *The Values of Nighttime in Classical Antiquity:*

Between Dusk and Dawn. Leiden: Brill.

Kerényi, C. & Holme, C. (2015), *Archetypal Images in Greek Religion: 5. Zeus and Hera: Archetypal Image of Father, Husband, and Wife*. Princeton, NJ: Princeton University Press.

Kholod, M.M. (2016), 'The Cults of Alexander the Great in the Greek Cities of Asia Minor', *Klio* 98(2): 495–525.

Kılıç, M. (2014), 'The Cults of Nemeseis and Tyche at Smyrna', *Belleten* 78: 833–58.

Kingsley, P. (1995), *Ancient Philosophy, Mystery, and Magic: Empedocles and Pythagorean Tradition*. Oxford: Clarendon Press.

Köcher, F. (1959), 'Ein spätbabylonischer Hymnus auf den Tempel Ezida in Borsippa', *Zeitschrift für Assyriologie und Vorderasiatische Archäologie* 53 (Jahresband): 236–40.

Kofisa (2005), *Caria: Through The Eyes of European Travellers*. Maslak: MAS Matabaacilik.

Kollia, E.I. & Antonopoulos, K. (eds) (2017), *The Work of The Ephorate of Antiquities of Ilia in the years 2015–2017*. Ancient Olympia: Ministry of Culture and Sport.

Kottaridi, A. & Walker, S. (eds) (2011), *Heracles to Alexander the Great: Treasures from the Royal Capital of Macedon, a Hellenic Kingdom in the Age of Democracy. A collaboration between the Ashmolean Museum, University of Oxford and the Hellenic Ministry of Culture and Tourism, 17th Ephorate of Prehistoric and Classical Antiquities*. Oxford: Ashmolean Museum.

Koursi, M. (ed.) (2003), *The Olympic Games In Ancient Greece*. Athens: Ekdotike Athenon.

Kowalzig, B. (2007), *Singing for the Gods: Performances of Myth and Ritual in Archaic and Classical Greece*. Oxford: Oxford University Press.

Kraay, C. (1976), *Archaic and classical Greek coins*. London: Methuen.

Kraft, J.C. et al. (2007), 'The geographies of ancient Ephesus and the Artemision in Anatolia', *Geoarchaeology* 22(1): 121–49.

Krinitzsky, E.L. (2005), 'Earthquakes and soil liquefaction in flood stories of the ancient Near East', *Engineering geology* 76(3): 295–311.

Kriwaczek, P. (2012), *Babylon: Mesopotamia and the Birth of Civilization*. London: Atlantic.

Kuhrt, A. (1995), *The Ancient Near East c. 3000–330 B.C.* London: Routledge.

Ladstatter, S. (2014), *Terrace House 2 in Ephesos: an archaeological guide*. Istanbul: Homer Kitabevi.

Langgut, D., Finkelstein, I. & Litt, T. (2013), 'Climate and the Late Bronze Collapse: New Evidence from the Southern Levant', *Tel Aviv* 40(2): 149–75.

Lapatin, K.D.S. (2001), *Chryselephantine statuary in the ancient Mediterranean world*. Oxford: Oxford University Press.

Laugier, E.J. et al. (2021), 'Reconstructing Agro-pastoral Practice in the Mesopotamian-Zagros Borderlands: Insights from Phytolith and FTIR Analysis of a Dung-rich Deposit', *Journal of archaeological science, reports* 38: 103–6.

Leach, H.M. (1982), 'On the Origins of Kitchen Gardening in the Ancient Near East', *Garden history* 10(1): 1–16.

Ledger, M.L. et al. (2018), 'Intestinal Parasites from Public and Private Latrines and the Harbour Canal in Roman Period Ephesus, Turkey (1st c. BCE to 6th c. CE)', *Journal of archaeological science, reports* 21: 289–97.

Lee, J. & Sattin, A. (2018), *Egypt*. Fort Mill, SC: Lonely Planet.

Lehner, M. (1997), *The Complete Pyramids*. London: Thames & Hudson.

Lehner, M. E. (2020), 'Lake Khufu: On the Waterfront at Giza – Modeling Water Transport Infrastructure in Dynasty IV', 191–292 in Bárta, M. & Janák, J. (eds), *Profane Landscapes, Sacred Spaces*. Sheffield: Equinox Publishing Ltd.

Lehner, M. & Tallet, P. (2022), *The Red Sea Scrolls: How Ancient Papyri Reveal the Secrets of the Pyramids*, London: Thames & Hudson.

Leichty, E. (2011), *The royal inscriptions of Esarhaddon, king of Assyria (680–669 BC)*. Winona Lake, IN: Eisenbrauns.

Leick, G. (2002), *Mesopotamia: The Invention of The City*. Penguin Books: London.

Leloux, K. (2018), 'The Campaign of Croesus Against Ephesus: Historical & Archaeological Considerations', *Polemos (Zagreb)* 21(42): 47–64.

Lenzen, H.J. (1959), 'The Greek Theatre in Babylon', *Sumer* 15(1): 39.

Lesko, L.H. & Brown University (1986), *Egyptological studies in honor of Richard A. Parker: presented on the occasion of his 78th birthday, December 10, 1983*. Hanover, NH: published for Brown University by University Press of New England.

Lethaby, W.R. (1913), 'The Sculptures of the Later Temple of Artemis at Ephesus', *The Journal of Hellenic Studies* 33: 87–96.

Lethaby, W.R. (1914), 'Further Notes on the Sculpture of the Later Temple of Artemis at Ephesus', *The Journal of Hellenic Studies* 34: 76–88.

Lethaby, W.R. (1916), 'Another Note on the Sculpture of the Later Temple of Artemis at Ephesus', *The Journal of Hellenic Studies* 36: 25–35.

Lethaby, W.R. (1917), 'The Earlier Temple of Artemis at Ephesus', *The Journal of Hellenic Studies* 37: 1–16.

Leyra, I.P. (2014), 'The Order of the Seven Greatest Islands in the "Laterculi Alexandrini" ("P.Berol." 13044r)', *Zeitschrift für Papyrologie und Epigraphik* 192: 85–8.

Lidonnici, L.R. (1992), 'The images of Artemis Ephesia and Greco-Roman worship: a reconsideration', *Harvard Theological Review* 85(4): 389–411.

Lightbody, D. (2016), 'Biography of a Great Pyramid Casing Stone', *Journal of Ancient Egyptian Architecture* 1: 39–56.

Liritzis, I., Westra, A. & Miao, C. (2019), 'Disaster Geoarchaeology and Natural Cataclysms in World Cultural Evolution: An Overview', *Journal of coastal research* 35(6): 1307–30.

Lowe, D. (2016), 'Twisting In The Wind: Monumental Weathervancs In Classical Antiquity', *The Cambridge Classical Journal* 62: 147–69.

Lucian, trans. Harmon, A. M. (1936), *The Passing of Peregrinus. The Runaways. Toxaris or Friendship. The Dance. Lexiphanes. The Eunuch. Astrology. The Mistaken Critic. The Parliament of the Gods. The Tyrannicide. Disowned*. Loeb Classical Library 302. Cambridge, MA: Harvard University Press.

Luiselli, M.M. (2014), 'Personal Piety in Ancient Egypt', *Religion compass* 8(4): 105–16.

Lummus, D. (2017), 'Placing Petrarch's Legacy: The Politics of Petrarch's Tomb and Boccaccio's Last Letter', *Renaissance quarterly* 70(2): 435–73.

Lundbom, J.R. (2017), 'Builders of Ancient Babylon: Nabopolassar and Nebuchadnezzar II', *Interpretation (Richmond)* 71(2): 154–66.

Lykesas, G. et al. (2017), 'The Presence of Dance in Female Deities of the Greek Antiquity', *Mediterranean journal of social sciences* 8(2): 161–70.

Macdonald, S. (2006a), 'Undesirable Heritage: Fascist Material Culture and Historical Consciousness in Nuremberg', *International journal of heritage studies* 12(1): 9–28.

Macdonald, S. (2006b), 'Words in Stone?: Agency and Identity in a Nazi Landscape', *Journal of material culture* 11(1–2): 105–26.

Magli, G. (2018), 'From symbols to written landscapes. The role of astronomy in ancient Egyptian architecture', *Lebenswelt (Milano)* 11: 125–33.

Maglio, E. (2013), 'Knowledge and preservation of ancient Rhodes. From a typological analysis of urban fabric to a practical project for urban heritage', 1233–40 in Bombardieri, L. et al. (eds), *SOMA 2012: identity and connectivity: proceedings of the 16th Symposium on Mediterranean Archaeology, Florence, Italy, 1–3 March 2012*. Oxford: Archaeopress.

Malamidou, D. (2006), 'Les nécropoles d'Amphipolis: nouvelles données archéologiques et anthropologiques', 199–208 in Guimier-Sorbets, A.M., Hatzopoulos, M.B. & Morizot, Y. (eds), *Rois, cités, nécropoles: institutions, rites et monuments en Macédoine. Actes des Colloques de Nanterre et d'Athènes, janvier 2004*. Athènes: Centre de recherche de l'antiquité grecque et romaine.

Malleson, C. (2016), 'Informal intercropping of legumes with cereals? A reassessment of clover abundance in ancient Egyptian cereal processing by-product assemblages: archaeobotanical investigations at Khentkawes town, Giza (2300–2100 BC)', *Vegetation History and Archaeobotany* 25(5): 431–42.

Mallwitz, A., Schiering, W. & Deutsches Archäologisches Institut (1964), *Die Werkstatt des Pheidias in Olympia*. Berlin: De Gruyter.

Manley, B. (2012), *Egyptian Hieroglyphs for Complete Beginners*. London: Thames & Hudson.

Manning, S. (1875), *The Land of the Pharaohs: Egypt & Sinai Illustrated by Pen and pencil*. London: Religious Tract Society.

Maqrīzī, Aḥmad Ibn ʿAlī, trans. Bouriant, U. (1895), *Description Topographique Et Historique De L'Égypte*. Paris: E. Leroux.

Marzahn, J. (1995), *The Ishtar Gate: The Processional Way, The New Year Festival of Babylon*. Mainz: Verlag Philipp von Zabern.

Matheson, S., & Pollitt, J. (1994), *An obsession with fortune: Tyche in Greek and Roman art*. New Haven, CT: Yale University Art Gallery.

Mayor, A. (2000), *The first fossil hunters: Paleontology in Greek and Roman times*. Princeton, NJ; Oxford: Princeton University Press.

Mayor, A. (2014), *The Amazons: Lives and Legends of Warrior Women across the Ancient World*. Princeton, NJ: Princeton University Press.

McCall, H. (2008), *Mesopotamian Myths*. London: British Museum.

McConnell, J.R. et al. (2018), 'Lead Pollution Recorded in Greenland Ice Indicates European Emissions Tracked Plagues, Wars, and Imperial Expansion during Antiquity', *Proceedings of the National Academy of Sciences* 115(22): 5726–31.

McCoskey, D. (2012), *Race: Antiquity and its legacy*. London; New York, NY: Bloomsbury Academic.

McKenzie, J. (2007), *The Architecture of Alexandria and Egypt, c. 300 B.C. to A.D. 700*. New Haven, CT; London: Yale University Press.

McNeely, I.F. & Wolverton, L. (2008), *Reinventing Knowledge: From Alexandria to the Internet*. New York, NY; London: W. W. Norton.

McWilliam, J. (2011), *Statue of Zeus at Olympia: New Approaches*. Newcastle upon Tyne: Cambridge Scholars Publishing.

Melcher, M. et al. (2009), 'Investigation of ancient gold objects from Artemision at Ephesus using portable μ-XRF: Studies of Objects: Manufacturing Skills and Alloy Selection', *Archéosciences* 33: 169–75.

Melville, S.C. (2014), 'Women in Neo-Assyrian texts', 228–40 in Chavalas, M.W. (ed.), *Women in the Ancient Near East: A Sourcebook*. London: Routledge.

Merkelbach, R. & Stauber, J. (1996), 'Die Orakel des Apollon von Klaros', *Epigraphica Anatolia* 27: 1–54.

Metropolitan Museum of Art (1999), *Egyptian Art in the Age of the Pyramids*. New York, NY: Metropolitan Museum of Art.

Minetti, A.E. & Ardigó, L.P. (2002), 'Halteres used in ancient Olympic long jump', *Nature (London)* 420(6912): 141–2.

Miszczak, I. (2020), *The Secrets of Ephesus: TAN Travel Guide*. Fairfield: Aslan.

Mo, G.B. (2017), 'Collecting uncollectables: Joachim Du Bellay', *Culture unbound* 9(1): 23–35.

Moller, V. (2019), *The map of knowledge: how classical ideas were lost and found : a history in seven cities*. London: Picador.

Monnier, F. & Lightbody, D. (2019), *The Great Pyramid, 2590 BC onward: Owner's workshop manual*. Yeovil: Haynes.

Monroe, M.W. (2019), 'Mesopotamian Astrology', *Religion compass* 13(6): e12318.

Moreno, A. (2009), '"The Attic Neighbour": The Cleruchy in the Athenian Empire', 211–21 in Ma, J., Papazarkadas, N. & Parker, R. (eds), *Interpreting the Athenian Empire*. London: Duckworth.

Morgan, L. (2011), 'Enlivening the Body: Color and Stone Statues in Old Kingdom Egypt', *Source: Notes in the History of Art* 30(3): 4–11.

Munn, M.H. (2006), *The Mother of the Gods, Athens, and the Tyranny of Asia: a Study of Sovereignty in Ancient Religion*. Berkeley, CA; London: University of California Press.

Muss, U. (2007), 'Late Bronze Age and Early Iron Age Terracottas: Their Significance for an Early Cult Place in the Artemision at Ephesus', 167–94 in Sagona, A.G. & Çilingiroğlu, A. (eds), *Anatolian Iron Ages 6: the proceedings of the Sixth Anatolian Iron Ages Colloquium held at Eskisehir, 16–20 August 2004*. Leuven; Dudley, MA: Peeters.

National Geographic (2018), *History, March/April*.

Naunton, C. (2018), *Searching for the Lost Tombs of Egypt*. London: Thames & Hudson.

Nawotka, K. (2003), 'Freedom of Greek Cities in Asia Minor in the Age of Alexander the Great', *Klio – Beiträge zur Alten Geschichte* 85(1): 15–41.

Newton, C.T. & Pullan, R.P. (1862), *A History of Discoveries at Halicarnassus, Cnidus and Branchidae, Volume 2, Part 1*. London: Day & Son.

Ní Mheallaigh, K. (2020), *The Moon in the Greek and Roman Imagination. Myth, Literature, Science and Philosophy*. Cambridge: Cambridge University Press.

Nicholson, H. (2001), *The Knights Hospitaller*. Woodbridge: Boydell Press.

Nordquist, G. (1996), 'The Salpinx in Greek Cult', *Scripta Instituti Donneriani Aboensis* 16: 241–56.

Nur, A. & Cline, E.H. (2000), 'Poseidon's Horses: Plate Tectonics and Earthquake Storms in the Late Bronze Age Aegean and Eastern Mediterranean', *Journal of archaeological science* 27(1): 43–63.

Nuzzolo, M. & Krejčí, J. (2017), 'Heliopolis and the Solar Cult in the Third Millennium BC', *Ägypten Und Levante* 27: 357–80.

Oates, J. (1979), *Babylon*. London: Thames & Hudson.

Oliver, I.C. (2017), *The Audiences of Herodotus: the Influence of Performance on the Histories*. ProQuest Dissertations Publishing.

Palagia, O. (2019a), *Ancient Greek and Roman Art and Architecture. Volume 1. Handbook of Greek Sculpture*. Berlin; Boston, MA; De Gruyter.

Palagia, O. (ed.) (2019b), *Handbook of Greek Sculpture*. De Gruyter.

Panagiotaki, M., Panagiotakis, N. & Sarris, A. (2020), 'Introduction: Lightning – fire – kiln – beacon', 1–10 in Panagiotaki, M., Tomazos, I. & Papadimitrakopoulos, F., *Cutting-edge technologies in ancient Greece: materials science applied to trace ancient technologies in the Aegean world*. Oxford: Oxbow.

Parker, R.A. (1974), 'Ancient Egyptian Astronomy', *Philosophical Transactions of the Royal Society of London. Series A, Mathematical and Physical Sciences (1934–1990)*, 276(1257): 51–65.

Parry, D. (2004), *Engineering the pyramids*. Stroud: Sutton.

Parys, L. (2017), *Le récit du Papyrus Westcar: Texte, traduction, interprétation*. Bruxelles: Editions Safran.

Pasinli, A. (2012), *Istanbul Archaeological Museums*. Istanbul: Mumhane Caddesi Mangir Sokak.

Pausanias, trans. Jones, W.H.S. (1876), *Description of Greece*. London: W. Heinemann; Cambridge, MA: Harvard University Press.

Pedersen, P. (2017), 'The Totenmahl Tradition in Classical Asia Minor and the Maussolleion at Halikarnassos' in Mortensen, E. & Poulson, B., *Cityscapes and monuments of western Asia Minor: Memories and identities*. Oxford: Oxbow Books.

Pedersen, P. (2015), 'On the Planning of the Maussolleion at Halikarnassos', *Hamburger Beiträge zur Archäologie und Kulturgeschichte des antiken Mittelmeerraumes 3 Antike. Architektur. Geschichte. Festschrift für Inge Nielsen zum 65. Geburtstag*: 153–66.

Peled, I. (2013), 'Eunuchs in Hatti and Assyria: A Reassessment', 785–98 in Feliu, L. et al. (eds), *Time and History in the Ancient Near East: Proceedings of the 56th Rencontre Assyriologique Internationale at Barcelona, 26-30 July 2010*. Winona Lake, IN: Eisenbrauns.

Penrose, W.D. (2015), 'The Discourse of Disability in Ancient Greece', *The Classical world* 108(4): 499–523.

Penrose, W.D. (2016), *Postcolonial Amazons: Female Masculinity and Courage in Ancient Greek and Sanskrit Literature*. Oxford: Oxford University Press.

Perrottet, T. (2003), *Pagan Holiday: On the Trail of Ancient Roman Tourists*. New York, NY: Random House Trade Paperbacks.

Phillips, C. (2007), *Socrates in Love: Philosophy for a Passionate Heart*. New York, NY; London: W.W. Norton.

Pliny the Elder, trans. Rackham, H. (1938), *Natural History*. Cambridge, MA: Harvard University Press; London: Heinemann.

Plutarch, trans. Scott-Kilvert, I. (1965), *Plutarch: The Makers of Rome: Nine Lives*. Penguin.

Pollard, J. & Reid, H. (2006), *The rise and fall of Alexandria: birthplace of the modern mind*. New York, NY; London: Viking.

Pollitt, J.J. (2000), 'The Phantom of a Rhodian School of Sculpture', 92–110 in De Grummond, N.T. & Ridgway, B.S. (eds), *From Pergamon to Sperlonga: Sculpture and Context*. Berkeley, CA; London: University of California Press.

Poole, S.L. (1959), *Lord Stratford Canning in Türkiye Anıları*. Ankara: Yurt.

Popović, M. (2007), *Reading the human body : Physiognomics and astrology in the Dead Sea Scrolls and Hellenistic-early Roman period Judaism*. Leiden: Brill.

Portman, I. (2008), *The Temple of Dendara: The House of Hathor*. Cairo: The Palm Press.

Potts, D.T. (2001), 'Before the Emirates: an Archaeological and Historical Account of Developments in the Region ca 5000 BC to 676 AD', 28–69 in Al Abed, I. & Hellyer, P. (eds), *The United Arab Emirates: A New Perspective*. London: Trident Press.

Potts, D.T. (2000), 'Alexandria: the umbilicus of the ancient world' in MacLeod, R.M. (ed.), *The Library of Alexandria: Centre of learning in the ancient world*. London: I.B. Tauris.

Price, S. (1999), *Religions of the Ancient Greeks (Key Themes in Ancient History)* Cambridge, MA: Cambridge University Press.

Pulak, C. et al. (1987), 'The Hellenistic Shipwreck at Serçe Limanı, Turkey: Preliminary Report', *American journal of archaeology* 91(1): 31–57.

Quatman, G.B. (2019), *House of Our Lady (Meryem Ana Evi), The Story of the Virgin Mary's Last Years*. Lima: The American Society of Ephesus.

Quirke, S. (2001), *The cult of Ra: Sun-worship in ancient Egypt*. London: Thames & Hudson.

Radner, K. (2012), 'The seal of Tašmetum-šarrat, Sennacherib's queen, and its impressions', 687–98 in Lanfranchi, G.B. et al. (eds), *Leggo! Studies Presented to Frederick Mario Fales on the Occasion of His 65th Birthday*. Wiesbaden: Harrassowitz.

Raign, K.R. (2019), 'Finding Our Missing Pieces – Women Technical Writers in Ancient Mesopotamia', *Journal of technical writing and communication* 49(3): 338–64.

Ramage, A., Craddock, P.T. & Cowell, M. (1999), *King Croesus' Gold: Excavations at Sardis and the History of Gold Refining*. London: British Museum.

Rawlinson, H. (2014), with F.A. Wood (originals 1850, 1860), *A commentary on the cuneiform inscriptions of Babylonia and Assyria: Including readings of the inscription on the Nimrud obelisk, and a brief notice of the ancient kings of Nineveh and Babylon* (Cambridge library collection). Cambridge.

Rawson, P. (2018), 'The Conceptual Basis of Archaic Greek Sculpture', 17–31 in Gosebruch, M. (ed.), *Festschrift Kurt Badt zum siebzigsten Geburtstage: Beiträge aus Kunst- und Geistesgeschichte*. De Gruyter.

Reade, J. (1978), 'Studies in Assyrian Geography: Sennacherib and the Waters of Nineveh', *Revue D'assyriologie Et D'archéologie Orientale* 72(1): 47–72.

Reade, J. (2000), 'Alexander the Great and the Hanging Gardens of Babylon', *Iraq* 62: 195–217.

Reinberger, K.L. et al. (2021), 'Isotopic evidence for geographic heterogeneity in Ancient Greek military forces', *PloS One* 16(5): E0248803.

Reiner, E. (1995), *Astral magic in Babylonia*. Philadelphia: American Philosophical Society.

Retallack, G.J. (2008), 'Rocks, views, soils and plants at the temples of ancient Greece', *Antiquity* 82(317): 19–657.

Richter, G. (1966), 'The Pheidian Zeus at Olympia', *Hesperia* 35(2): 166–70.

Ridgway, B.S. (1971), 'The Setting of Greek Sculpture', *Hesperia* 40(3): 336–56.

Ristvet, L. (2014), 'Between ritual and theatre: Political performance in Seleucid Babylonia', *World Archaeology* 46(2): 256–69.

Roberts, P. et al. (2018), 'Fossil herbivore stable isotopes reveal middle Pleistocene hominin palaeoenvironment in "Green Arabia"', *Nat Ecol Evol* 2(12): 1871–8.

Robinson, A. (2012), *Cracking the Egyptian Code: The Revolutionary Life of Jean-Francois Champollion*. London: Thames & Hudson.

Robinson, E.S.G. (1951), 'The Coins from the Ephesian Artemision Reconsidered', *The Journal of Hellenic Studies* 71: 156–67.

Rogers, G.M. (2013), *The Mysteries of Artemis of Ephesos: Cult, Polis, and Change in the Graeco-Roman World*. New Haven, CT: Yale University Press.

Rohde, D., Olson, S. & Chang, J. (2004), 'Modelling the recent common ancestry of all living humans', *Nature* 431: 562–6.

Romano, D.G. (1985), 'Boycotts, Bribes and Fines', *Expedition* 27(2): 10.

Romer, J. & Romer, E. (1995), *The seven wonders of the world: a history of the modern imagination*. London: Seven Dials.

Rose, H.J., Dietrich, B.C. & Peatfield, A.A.D. (2016), 'Rhodes, cults and myths', *Oxford Research Encyclopedia of Classics*.

Rose, M.L. (2003), *The Staff of Oedipus: Transforming Disability in Ancient Greece*. Ann Arbor, MI: University of Michigan Press.

Roth, M. (1989), *Babylonian marriage agreements: 7th–3rd centuries B.C.* Kevelaer: Neukirchen-Vluyn: Butzon & Bercker; Neukirchener Verlag.

Russell, J.M. (1997), 'Sennacherib's Palace Without Rival Revisited: Excavations at Nineveh and in the British Museum Archives', 300 in Parpola, S. & Whiting, R.M. (eds), *Assyria 1995: Proceedings of the 10th anniversary symposium of the Neo-Assyrian Text Corpus Project, Helsinki, September 7–11, 1995*. Helsinki: The Neo-Assyrian Text Corpus Project.

Russell, J.M. (2021), *The Writing on the Wall: Studies in the Architectural Context of Late Assyrian Palace Inscriptions*. University Park, PA: Penn State University Press.

Salama, A. et al. (2018), 'Paleotsunami deposits along the coast of Egypt correlate with historical earthquake records of eastern Mediterranean', *Natural hazards and earth system sciences* 18(8): 2203–19.

Salzman, M.R. (ed.) (2013), *The Cambridge History of Religions in the Ancient World*. Cambridge: Cambridge University Press.

Sarhosis, V. et al. (2016), 'On the stability of colonnade structural systems under static and dynamic loading conditions', *Bulletin of earthquake engineering* 14(4): 1131–52.

Scarre, C. (1999), *The seventy wonders of the ancient world: The great monuments and how they were built*. London: Thames & Hudson.

Schiering, W. (1991), *Die Werkstatt des Pheidias in Olympia Teil 2, Werkstattfunde*. Berlin: De Gruyter.

Schindel, N. & Ladstätter, S. (2016), 'Ephesus 2016', *The Numismatic Chronicle* 176: 390–98.

Schmid, S.G. (2013), 'The Twisted Amazon: A Small Mistake with a Big Effect at the Maussolleion of Halikarnassos', 303–20 in Katsonopoulou, D. & Stewart, A. (eds), *Proceedings of the Third International Conference on the Archaeology of Paros and the Cyclades*. Athens: Dictynna.

Schneider, T. (2002), *Lexikon den Pharaonen*. Patmos-Albatros.

Schneider, T. (2013), 'Ägyptologen im Dritten Reich: Biographische Notizen anhand der sogenannten "Steindorff-Liste"', 120–247 in Schneider, T. & Raulwing, P., *Egyptology from the First World War to the Third Reich: Ideology, Scholarship, and Individual Biographies*. Leiden: Brill.

Schowalter, D. et al. (2019), *Religion in Ephesos Reconsidered: Archaeology of Spaces, Structures, and Objects*. Boston, MA: Brill.

Scobie, A. (1990), *Hitler's state architecture: the impact of classical antiquity*. University Park, PA: Penn State University Press.

Sebillotte Cuchet, V. (2015), 'The Warrior Queens of Caria (Fifth to Fourth Centuries BCE). Archeology, History, and Historiography', 228–46 in Fabre-Serris, J. & Keith, A., *Women & War in Antiquity*. Baltimore, MD: Johns Hopkins University Press.

Sennacherib, & Luckenbill, D.D. (1924), *The annals of Sennacherib*. Chicago, IL: University of Chicago Press.

Serdar, Y. (2016), 'Men, Women, Eunuchs, Etc.: Visualities of Gendered Identities in Kassite Babylonian Seals (ca. 1470–1155 B.C.)', *Bulletin of the American Schools of Oriental Research* 376(376): 121–50.

Shaked, S. (1969), 'Notes on the New Aśoka Inscription from Kandahar', *Journal of the Royal Asiatic Society of Great Britain & Ireland* 101(2): 118–22.

Shalev, Z. (2002), 'Measurer of All Things: John Greaves (1602-1652), the Great Pyramid, and Early Modern Metrology', *Journal of the history of ideas* 63(4): 555–75.

Shaw, I. & Nicholson, P. (2002), *Dictionary of Ancient Egypt*. London: British Museum.

Shaw, I. (ed.) (2000), *The Oxford History of Ancient Egypt*. Oxford: Oxford University Press.

Shorter, A. (1937), *The Egyptian gods: A handbook*. London: Kegan Paul, Trench, Trubner & Co.

Shutler, Paul M.E. (2009), 'The problem of the pyramid or Egyptian mathematics from a postmodern perspective', *International journal of mathematical education in science and technology* 40(3): 341–52.

Siddall, L.R. (2014), 'Sammu-ramāt: Regent or Queen Mother?', *La Famille Dans Le Proche-Orient Ancien: Réalités, Symbolismes Et Images*. Penn State University Press, 497–504.

Siewert, P. & Taeuber, H. (eds) (2013), *Neue Inschriften von Olympia: die ab 1896 veröffentlichten Texte*. Vienna: Holzhausen.

Sinn, U. (2004), *Das antike Olympia. Götter, Spiel und Kunst*. Munich: C. H. Beck.

Sissa, G. (1990), *Greek virginity*. Cambridge, MA; London: Harvard University Press.

Smith, W. (1849), *Dictionary of Greek and Roman biography and mythology*. London: Walton.

Sneed, D. (2020), 'The Architecture of Access: Ramps at Ancient Greek Healing Sanctuaries', *Antiquity* 94(376): 1015–29.

Sokolowski, F. (1965), 'A New Testimony on the Cult of Artemis of Ephesus', *The Harvard theological review* 58(4): 427–31.

Souyoudzoglou-Haywood, C. & Papoulia, C. (eds) (2022), *Archaeology of the Ionian Sea: Landscapes, Seascapes and the circulation of people, goods and ideas from the palaeolithic to the end of the bronze age*. Oxford: Oxbow.

Speake, J. (ed.) (2015), *Oxford Dictionary of Proverbs*. Oxford: Oxford University Press.

Spier, J., Potts, T. & Cole, S.E. (eds) (2018), *Beyond the Nile: Egypt and the Classical World*. Los Angeles: Getty.

Spivey, N.J. (2004), *The Ancient Olympics*. Oxford: Oxford University Press.

Spivey, N.J. (2013), *Greek sculpture*. Cambridge: Cambridge University Press.

Spyridakis, S. (1969), 'The Itanian Cult of Tyche Protogeneia', *Historia: Zeitschrift Für Alte Geschichte* 18(1): 42–8.

Stark, F. (2010), *Ionia: A Quest*. London: Tauris Parke.

Steele, J. (1992), *Hellenistic Architecture in Asia Minor*. London: Academy Editions.

Stewart, A.F. (2015), 'Scopas, Parian sculptor and architect, active c. 370–330 BCE'. Oxford Classical Dictionary, Oxford University Press.

Stiros, S.C. & Blackman, D.J. (2014), 'Seismic coastal uplift and subsidence in Rhodes Island, Aegean Arc: Evidence from an uplifted ancient harbour', *Tectonophysics* 611: 114–20.

Stiros, S.C. (2020), 'Monumental articulated ancient Greek and Roman columns and temples and earthquakes: archaeological, historical, and engineering approaches', *Journal of seismology* 24(4): 853–81.

Stock, F. et al. (2013), 'In Search of the Harbours: New Evidence of Late Roman and Byzantine Harbours of Ephesus', *Quaternary international* 312: 57–69.

Stock, F. et al. (2016), 'Human Impact on Holocene Sediment Dynamics in the Eastern Mediterranean – the Example of the Roman Harbour of Ephesus', *Earth Surface Processes and Landforms* 41(7): 980–96.

Stock, F. et al. (2019), 'Late Holocene Coastline and Landscape Changes to the West of Ephesus, Turkey', *Quaternary international* 501: 349–63.

Stol, M. (2016), *Women in the Ancient Near East*. Boston, MA; Berlin: De Gruyter.

Stoneman, R. (2011), *The ancient oracles: making the gods speak*. New Haven, CT: Yale University Press.

Strabo, trans. Jones, H.L. (1929), *The Geography of Strabo*. London: Heinemann; Cambridge, MA: Harvard University Press.

Stronach, D. (1978), *Pasargadae: A report on the excavations conducted by the British Institute of Persian Studies from 1961 to 1963*. Oxford: Clarendon Press.

Tacitus, trans. Moore, C.H. & Jackson, J. (eds) (1931), *Tacitus' Histories Books 4–5; Annals Books 1–3*. Cambridge, MA: Harvard University Press.

Taita, J. (2015), 'The Great Hecatomb to Zeus Olympios: Some Observations on IvO No. 14', 112–39 in Patay-Horváth, A. (ed.), *New approaches to the Temple of Zeus at Olympia: proceedings of the first Olympia-Seminar 8th-10th May 2014*. Newcastle upon Tyne: Cambridge Scholars Publishing.

Tallet, P. (2013), 'Research Report: The Wadi el-Jarf Site: A Harbor of Khufu on the Red Sea', *Journal of Ancient Egyptian Interconnections* 5(1).

Taylor, J. (1859), *The Great Pyramid: Why was it built? & who built it?* London: Longman, Green, Longman, and Roberts.

Thommen, L. (2012), *An environmental history of ancient Greece and Rome*. Cambridge: Cambridge University Press.

Thucydides, trans. Warner, R. (1972), *History of the Peloponnesian War*. Harmondsworth: Penguin.

Toksoz, C. (1986), *Les Sites Antiques de L'Anatolie Occidentale: Priene, Milet, Didymes, Aphrodisias*. Istanbul: Hankur Matbaacilik.

Trethewey, K.R. (2018), *Ancient Lighthouses: and Other Lighted Aids to Navigation*. Torpoint, Cornwall: Jazz-Fusion Books.

Tyldesley, J. (2006), *Chronicle of the Queens of Egypt: From Early Dynastic Times to the Death of Cleopatra*. London: Thames & Hudson.

Tyldesley, J. (2008), *Cleopatra Last Queen of Egypt*. London: Profile.

Tyldesley, J. (2010), *Myths & Legends of Ancient Egypt*. London: Allen Lane.

Uphill, E. (1965), 'The Egyptian Sed-Festival Rites', *Journal of Near Eastern Studies* 24(4): 365–83.

Valk, J. (2020), 'Crime and Punishment: Deportation in the Levant in the Age of Assyrian Hegemony', *Bulletin of the American Schools of Oriental Research* 384: 77–103.

Van Andel, T.H. & Runnels, C.N. (1995), 'The earliest farmers in Europe', *Antiquity* 69(264): 481–500.

Van De Mieroop, M. (2004), 'A Tale of Two Cities: Nineveh and Babylon', *Iraq* 66: 1–5.

Verderame, L. (2018), 'Slavery in Third-Millennium Mesopotamia', *Journal of global slavery* 3(1–2): 13–40.

Vikatou, O. (2006), *Olympia: The Archaeological Site and the Museums*. Athens: Ekdotike Athenon.

Vogel, S.C. & Barsoum, M.W. (2016), 'D-99 Can Neutron Diffraction Contribute to Elucidating How the Great Pyramids of Giza Were Built?', *Powder diffraction* 22(2): 185.

Vorderstrasse, T. (2012), 'Descriptions of the Pharos of Alexandria in Islamic and Chinese Sources: Collective Memory and Textual Transmission', 457–81 in Cobb, P. (ed.), *The Lineaments of Islam: Studies in Honor of Fred McGraw Donner*. Leiden: Brill.

Vout, C. (2018), *Classical Art: A Life History from Antiquity to the Present*. Princeton, NJ: Princeton University Press.

Wallace, R.W. (2016), 'Redating Croesus: Herodotean Chronologies, and the Dates of the Earliest Coinages', *The Journal of Hellenic Studies* 136: 168–81.

Walpole, R. (1817), *Memoirs Relating to European and Asiatic Turkey*. England: Longman, Hurst, Rees, Orme and Brown.

Wankel, H. et al. (1979), *Die Inschriften von Ephesos*. Bonn: Habelt.

Wee, J.Z. (2014), 'Lugalbanda Under the Night Sky: Scenes of Celestial Healing in Ancient Mesopotamia', *Journal of Near Eastern studies* 73(1): 23–42.

Weitzmann, K. (1951), *Greek mythology in Byzantine art*. Princeton, NJ: Princeton University Press.

Wheatley, P. & Dunn, C. (2020), 'The Great Siege of Rhodes', 179–202 in *Demetrius the Besieger*. Oxford: Oxford University Press.

Wiemer, H.-U. (2013), 'Zeno of Rhodes and the Rhodian View of the Past', 279–306 in Gibson, B. & Harrison, T. (eds), *Polybius and his world: essays in memory of F.W. Walbank*. Oxford: Oxford University Press.

Wilkinson, J. & Egeria (2015), *Egeria's Travels*. Oxford: Aris & Phillips.

Wilkinson, R.H. (2003), *The Complete Gods and Goddesses of Ancient Egypt*. London: Thames & Hudson.

Wilkinson, T. (2010), *The rise and fall of ancient Egypt: the history of a civilisation from 3000 BC to Cleopatra*. London: Bloomsbury.

Wilkinson, T. (2019), *Lives of the Ancient Egyptians*. London: Thames & Hudson.

Williamson, G. (2007), 'Mucianus and a Touch of the Miraculous: Pilgrimage and Tourism in Roman Asia Minor', 220–52 in Elsner, J. & Rutherford, I. (eds), *Pilgrimage in Graeco-Roman & early Christian antiquity: seeing the gods*. Oxford: Oxford University Press.

Winkler, E.-M. & Wilfing, H. (1991), *Anthropologische Untersuchungen an den Skelettresten der Kampagnen 1966–69, 1975–80, 1985*. Wien: Oesterreichischen Akademie der Wissenschaft.

Wiseman, D.J. (1983), 'Mesopotamian Gardens', *Anatolian studies* 33: 137–44.

Wolkstein, D. & Kramer, S. N. (1983), *Innanna: Queen of Heaven and Earth: Her Stories and Hymns from Sumer*. London: Harper Perennial.

Worthington, I. (2014), *By The Spear: Philip II, Alexander the Great, and the Rise and Fall of the Macedonian Empire*. Oxford: Oxford University Press.

Worthington, I. (2016), *Ptolemy I: King and Pharaoh of Egypt*. Oxford: Oxford University Press.

Yalçın, S. (2016), 'Men, Women, Eunuchs, Etc.: Visualities of Gendered Identities in Kassite Babylonian Seals (ca. 1470–1155 B.C.)', *Bulletin of the American Schools of Oriental Research 376*: 121–50.

Yiannakis, T. (1997), '"With wreaths from the groves they crowned the victors": a description of the Rhodian games', *International journal of the history of sport* 14(2): 200–206.

Yildiz, Y. (2007), *Bodrum Museum of Underwater Archeology and Caria*. Ismir: Toprak.

Yilmaz, Y. (2014), *Ancient Cities of Turkey*. Istanbul: YEM Yayinlari.

Yilmaz, Y. (2015), *Tears of Anatolia: Our Historical Artifacts that were taken abroad*. Istanbul: NEVA Basim.

Yoshimura, S. & Kurokochi, H. (2013), 'Research Report: Brief Report of the Project of the Second Boat of King Khufu', *Journal of Ancient Egyptian Interconnections* 5(1): 85–9.

Yoshimura, S. (2006), *Sakuji Yoshimura's Excavating in Egypt for 40 Years: Waseda University Expedition 1966–2006 – Project in celebration of the 125th Anniversary of Waseda University*. Tokyo: Waseda University, 134–7.

Zabrana, L. (2019), 'The Artemision in the Roman Era: New Results of Research within the Sanctuary of Artemis', 158–70 in Schowalter, D. et al. (eds), *Religion in Ephesos Reconsidered: Archaeology of Spaces, Structures, and Objects*. Leiden; Boston: Brill.

Zafiropoulou, D. (ed.) (2005), *Rhodes: From the 4th c. AD to its capture by the Ottoman Turks (1522): Palace of the Grand Master*. Athens: Archaeological Receipts Fund.

Zientek, L. (2017), 'The Pharos of Alexandria: A Man-Made "Mountain" in Lucan's Bellum Clulle', *Illinois Classical Studies* 42(1): 141–61.

Zimmer, G. (2020), 'Rhodian bronze casting workshops in the light of new finds', 47–54 in Panagiotaki, M. et al. (eds), *Cutting-edge technologies in ancient Greece: materials science applied to trace ancient technologies in the Aegean world*. Oxford: Oxbow Books.

NOTES

PREFACE

1 Abdelnaby & Elnashai (2013), 119–38.

2 Scarre (1999) comprises a catalogue of the seventy wonders, but this only contains those of the ancient world; many more modern monuments have been informally dubbed as 'wonders'. UNESCO's World Heritage List could be considered a modern version of a wonders-list. The list, which as of 29 November 2022 contains 1,154 properties, can be easily explored at https://whc.unesco.org/en/list/

3 'Seven Wonders of the World', *New World Encyclopedia*, retrieved 8 April 2022 from https://www.newworldencyclopedia.org/entry/Seven_Wonders_of_the_World

4 It is unclear whether Herysfyt was a separate divine entity, or whether it was simply another name for Herishef. Much like the two Antipaters, they have been confused and combined by the fog of time, and by the association with Herakles.

5 Brodersen, K. (2016), 'Seven Wonders of the ancient world', *Oxford Classical Dictionary*, retrieved 21 September 2022 from https://doi.org/10.1093/acrefore/9780199381135.013.5878

6 Diels (1904), 2. See also www.trismegistos.org/text/65645

7 The conflict after Alexander's death is typically referred to as the Wars of the Diadochi, but this term seems to simplify the prolonged period of complex and petty fighting which actually occurred.

8 The 'palace' complex at Ai Khanoum and its resemblance to typical Macedonian palace floorplans is an excellent example of the spread of Greek culture during this period.

9 Inscriptions in Eggermont & Hoftijzer (1962). For a summary of the significance of the inscription, see Shaked (1969), 118–22.

10 Hall (2008), 296. Ristvet (2014), 256–69. Susa had a theatrical connection with Ancient Greece, forming the setting for Aeschylus's *Persians*, first

performed in Athens in 472 BCE. In Babylon, there is clear archaeological evidence for a Greek-style theatre, which was attended by the Greek-speaking population in the city. For more information on the Greek quarter in Babylon, specifically the theatre, see Lenzen (1959), 39.

11　This expression, *non sufficit orbis*, was first attributed to Alexander the Great by the Roman poet Juvenal in his Satires X.168. However, it has become widely recognised in modern times, used by Ian Fleming for James Bond's family motto; the translation of the motto was used as the title of the 1999 film *The World Is Not Enough*.

12　Plutarch, *Alexander* VIII.2.

13　Plutarch, *Alexander* II.1 tells us that Alexander was a descendant of Heracles on his father's side, and of Aeacus on his mother's side. Both these figures were connected to Perseus: Heracles' mother Alcmene was a great-granddaughter of Perseus, while Aeacus was Perseus' sibling. There was a legacy of Macedonian kings claiming descent from Zeus, Heracles, Perseus and Dionysos. Herodotus, *Histories* VIII.137–9, has an account of the Macedonian royal family tree, tracing it back to Perdiccas, great-great-grandson of Heracles.

14　Coins from the reign of Alexander the Great which combine the head of Athena on the obverse and the club of Heracles on the reverse are rather rare; the two examples collected by the American Numismatic Society were minted in modern-day Cyprus and Turkey. Further information on these coins can be found at http://numismatics.org/pella/id/price.3127?lang=en and http://numismatics.org/pella/id/price.1361?lang=en (both retrieved 17 December 2022). In contrast, the British Museum's collection yields a silver stater with the head of Athena on the obverse and Heracles fighting a lion on the reverse, the online entry for which can be found at https://www.britishmuseum.org/collection/object/C_1934-0312-3 (retrieved 17 December 2022).

15　An interesting perspective on this can be found in Popovic (2007), passim, or in Greenbaum (2016), passim; alternatively, Oll, M. (2011), 'Hellenistic astrology as a case study of "cultural translation"', cultural translation, is a helpful way of thinking about why astrology spread in popularity across the Hellenistic world. University of Birmingham MPhil thesis, retrieved 9 January 2023 from http://etheses.bham.ac.uk/id/eprint/1603

16　Spyridakis (1969), 42–8, proposes a good explanation of why Tyche appealed during the turbulent beginnings of the Hellenistic period. See Matheson (1994) for more information on the worship of Tyche in the Greek world, particularly in Athens where she was worshipped as Agathe Tyche ('Good Fortune'). Tyche appeared on Seleucid coinage in the second century BCE, as evidenced at http://numismatics.org/sco/id/sc.1.1614 (retrieved 17 December 2022). Pausanias visited many temples to Tyche, mentioning the one at Smyrna and its statue of Tyche in his *Description of Greece* IV.30.6. More information on the cult of Tyche at Smyrna can be found in Kılıç (2014), 833–58.

17 Beckwith (2015), passim.

18 Heron of Alexandria invented a steam engine in the first century CE in his *Pneumatics* 50; Vitruvius, *On Architecture* I.6.2, also wrote about this invention. The 'first computer' is the Antikythera mechanism, discovered in the 1900s from a shipwreck. Euclid, who lived in Alexandria, is commonly named the 'father of geometry', while Eratosthenes of Cyrene is credited with creating the system of longitude and latitude.

19 Plutarch, *Alexander* LXIV.8.

20 Plutarch, *Alexander* LXIV.7.

21 Antipater's poetry is preserved in *The Greek Anthology* at *Anth. Pal.* IX.58.

22 Diodorus Siculus, *Library of History* II.11.5.

23 Pseudo-Hyginus, *Fabulae* CCXXIII. It is interesting to note that the two *Fabulae* which precede this wonders-list are also lists of seven – 221 is a list of seven wise men, while 222 was a list of seven lyric poets.

24 None of the three authors wrote lists comparable to Antipater's poem, but they certainly mention the Wonders. Strabo in *Geography* XIV mentions the Colossus of Rhodes (XIV.2.5) and the Mausoleum of Halikarnassos (XIV.2.16), while *Geography* XVII mentions the Pharos Lighthouse (XVII.1.6) and the Great Pyramid (XVII.1.33). Josephus in his *Antiquities*, and Quintus Curtius Rufus in his mostly lost *Histories of Alexander the Great* also write about some of the monuments, but any mention of one of the Wonders is secondary to the purpose of these authors.

25 *Anth. Pal.* IX. 58. There is a chance that these lines were composed by the earlier Antipater of Sidon, but copying and re-copying of the text down time has muddled the two authors and their works.

26 *Add MS 19391*, ff 12v–13v. The digitised manuscript can be accessed through the British Library at https://www.bl.uk/manuscripts/FullDisplay.aspx?index=0&ref=Add_MS_19391 (retrieved 21 November 2022). The digitisation project is an exciting development in academia, and the quality is excellent – although the mediaeval script can be challenging to read.

27 Plutarch, *Alexander* VII.1–2.

28 *Anth. Pal.* IX.58: the list attributed to Antipater. Gregory of Tours wrote about the Pharos in his *Historia Francorum*; for more information on Gregory of Tours, see de Nie (1985), 89–135. Retrieved 19 December 2022 from https://doi.org/10.1016/0304-4181(85)90016-8

29 The first use of *historie* can be found in Herodotus, *Histories* I.1, as he introduces his monumental work.

30 Dalley (1993), 9.

31 Philo of Byzantium includes the walls in his list of Seven Wonders, which was found in the ninth-century CE Heidelberg 398 manuscript.

32 Percy Bysshe Shelley, 'Ozymandias', 11.

33 Qu'ran XL.67. These seven stages of life begin at conception, with birth as the third stage of life.

34 Philo of Alexandria, *Legum Allegoria* I.15, specifically refers this notion to the Pythagoreans; curiously, Philo's work *De Opificio Mundi* 100 completely contradicts this, saying that Pythagoreans actually associated the number seven more closely with Zeus and that 'other philosophers' thought that the number seven was equal to Athena Parthenos.

35 George in Kennedy (2013), 39–71.

36 Borger (1974), 183–96.

37 Critchlow (2022), passim.

38 Rohde et al. (2004), 562–6.

39 The Swiss genealogy centre iGENEA is responsible for this research – they identified the gene haplogroup R1b1a2, to which belong the child Pharaoh Tutankhamun and c. 50 per cent of all men in Western Europe.

40 UNESCO World Heritage List, retrieved 16 December 2022 from https://whc.unesco.org/en/list/

41 For any particularly keen fans of the HBO show, there are numerous websites vociferously debating exactly which landmarks in the series correspond to the Seven Ancient Wonders. The most obvious is the counterpart to the Colossus of Rhodes, which in the George R.R. Martin universe is cunningly named the Titan of Bravos.

42 Tacitus, *Annals* III.61, trans. Moore & Jackson (1931).

43 Christiansen et al. (2020), 27825, retrieved 10 April 2023 from https://doi.org/10.1073/pnas.2004534117

44 Both the *Laterculi Alexandrini* and Antipater (*Anth. Pal.* IX.48) list the pyramids (plural), rather than just the Great Pyramid of Khufu.

CHAPTER I: THE GREAT PYRAMID AT GIZA

1 See entry in Speake (2015).

2 One can chart a summation of pyramid tomb-building and of glorification of the dead in Egypt, catalysed by the unification of Upper and Lower Egypt over 5,000 years ago in 3100 BCE.

3 This figure is approximate – visitor numbers have been in a state of flux for the past few years due to the pandemic, but a recent study by the Egyptian Observatory of the Egyptian Center for Thought and Studies seems to support this number. For a summary of the study, see 'Study: 12.9 million tourists visit Egypt annually', *Egypt Today* (2022), retrieved 9 January 2023 from https://www.egypttoday.com/Article/6/118549/Study-12-9-million-tourists-visit-Egypt-annually

4   Handwerk, B., 'Pyramids at Giza', retrieved 17 December 2022 from https://www.nationalgeographic.com/history/article/giza-pyramids

5   Such displays of the power of the state could be found everywhere, the Heb Sed festival, when the pharaoh had to physically run around structures representing the country as a celebration of his continued rule. See Uphill (1965), 365–83; Galán (2000), 255–64; Kemp (2006), 105–10 and Parry (2004), passim.

6   Both the *Laterculi Alexandrini* and Antipater (*Anth. Pal.* IX.58).

7   Hassan (1949), 36. The stele depicts a sphinx, two pyramids and two scribes.

8   Burleigh (2008), passim; Kappel (2013), retrieved 9 January 2023 from https://scholarship.shu.edu/dissertations/1869/; Schneider in Schneider & Raulwing (2012), 120–247.

9   Although the palace has held the Guinness World Record for Heaviest Building since 1984.

10 Gabra (2003), 112.

11 Tales from Syrian literature can be explored in Ighnatyus Afram (trans. Moosa) (2003).

12 Idrīsī, *Anwār*, 60–62.

13 Versions of the myth can be found in Wilkinson (2003).

14 See entry for Ra in Shorter (1937).

15 Nuzzolo & Krejčí (2017), 357–80.

16 Quirke (2001), passim.

17 Potts in Al Abed & Hellyer (2001), 28–69.

18 On the mathematical proportions of Khufu's Pyramid, see Bartlett (2014), 299–311; de Haan (2010); and Harifi (2021), 1743–61.

19 'The Great Pyramid' (1885), *Scientific American* 53(5) 66, retrieved 17 December 2022 from http://jstor.org/stable/26088484

20 Sirius was Isis' star, so was associated with Osiris; the Hall of Judgement, where Osiris and Isis sat, was the crucial point in the Egyptian afterlife where a heart was weighed to judge how good or bad that person's life had been.

21 This wall surrounding the Giza complex is known as 'The Wall of the Crow'. For more information see AERA's article 'The Wall of the Crow', retrieved 10 April 2023 from https://aeraweb.org/wall-of-the-crow//

22 This belief can be found throughout the Pyramid Texts, trans. Allen (2005).

23 Retrieved 19 December 2022 from https://www.egyptianmuseumcairo.com/egyptian-museum-cairo/artefacts/statuette-of-khufu/

24 Parys (2017), passim.

25 Tallet (2013), 76–84.

26 Kuper, R. & Förster, F. (2003), 'Khufu's "mefat" expeditions into the Libyan Desert', *Egyptian Archaeology* 23, the biannual magazine from the Egypt Exploration Society, 25–8, retrieved 19 January 2023 from https://www.ees.ac.uk/egyptian-archaeology-magazine

27 Yoshimura (2006), 134–7.

28 Wilkinson (2010), 51.

29 Pyramid Texts of Unas, 267, 365.

30 Winkler & Wilfing (1991), passim.

31 Enmarch, R. (2018), 'New texts from an old site: discoveries from the September 2018 season at the Hatnub alabaster quarries', retrieved 19 December 2022 from https://www.liverpool.ac.uk/archaeology-classics-and-egyptology/blog/2018/hatnub/

32 Metropolitan Museum of Art (1999) 41, 52ff.

33 Lightbody (2016), 39–56.

34 Antipater of Sidon, *Anth. Pal.* IX.58.

35 There are a variety of estimations surrounding the weight of the Great Pyramid and its materials, but J. Romer (2007) in *The Great Pyramid: Ancient Egypt Revisited*, 157, suggests 6 million tonnes.

36 Although the Egyptian Greek priest Manetho, who wrote the *Aegyptiaca*, declared that Khufu's reign was 63 years, historians such as Schneider (2002), 100–104, have asserted otherwise. On the building of the pyramids, see Hawass (2006), passim.

37 For summary see Monnier & Lightbody (2019), 140–59.

38 This discovery was exposed by Dr Viktor Ivanovich in 2001, for a documentary series, *The Secret KGB Files*. The discovery of an electro-magnetic force has, rather frustratingly, led to further conspiracy theories which refer to aliens.

39 Liljas, A., 'Old age in ancient Egypt', retrieved 18 December 2022 from https://blogs.ucl.ac.uk/researchers-in-museums/2015/03/02/old-age-in-ancient-egypt/#:~:text=. Cf. Winkler & Wilfing (1991).

40 Abdelnaby & Elnashai (2013), 119–38 and Hemeda & Sonbol (2020), 1–28.

41 Schiødt, S. (2021), 'Medical Science in Ancient Egypt. A translation and interpretation of Papyrus Louvre-Carlsberg (PLouvre E 32847 + PCarlsbery 917)'; University of Copenhagen, 'Ancient Egyptian manual reveals new details about mummification', retrieved 18 December 2022 from https://news.ku.dk/all_news/2021/02/ancient-egyptian-manual-reveals-new-details-about-mummification/. See also Rageot, M. et al (2023) 'Biomolecular analyses enable new insights into ancient Egyptian embalming' Nature, 614, 287–293, retrieved 10 April 2023 from https://doi.org/10.1038/s41586-022-05663-4

42 BM EA32751, retrieved 19 January 2023 from http://www.britishmuseum.org/collection/object/Y_EA32751

43 Friedman et al. (2018), 116–25, retrieved 19 January 2023 from https://doi.org/10.1016/j.jas.2018.02.002

44 Author's translation.

45 Metropolitan Museum of Art (1999), 252–3; Morgan (2011), 4–11.

46 Kawae et al. (2013), 227–30; Kawae (2011), 864–8.

47 See Parker (1974), 51–65; Campion (2012), 82–93; Magli (2018), 125–33.

48 Thank you to Mark Lehner for first drawing my attention to this idea.

49 Iron, to the Egyptians, was a metal associated with royalty – hence finding it in the Pyramid. Filings linked to creation as well as destruction have been found elsewhere in Egypt; take, for example, the Sphinx at Gebel el-Silsila, where iron filings were found as a result of the work of ancient chisels. For more, see Pappas, S. (2019), 'The Ram-Headed Sphinx of Gebel el-Silsila', retrieved 19 December 2022 from https://www.livescience.com/64869-photos-ram-headed-sphinx.html

50 BM EA67818, retrieved 19 January 2023 from https://www.britishmuseum.org/collection/object/Y_EA67818. The piece of cedar is part of the special collection owned by the University of Aberdeen.

51 A wide variety of Egyptian tablets have been used to indicate that the Egyptians devised our modern, 365-day calendar – items such as the Palermo Stone, which recorded a list of kings, have proven helpful to determine dating for reigns of individuals such as Khufu.

52 Amin (1970), 23–30.

53 Griffiths (1966), 57–61.

54 There is evidence for such fertility in the Nile Valley – see Copley et al. (2001), 538–42 for a case study on palm fruit from Qasr Ibrim. Retrieved 9 January 2023 from https://doi.org/10.1098/rspb.2000.1394

55 A summary of the Khufu boat project can be found here: https://english.ahram.org.eg/News/416631.aspx, retrieved 19 December 2022. See also Yoshimura & Kurokochi (2013), 85–9, retrieved 9 January 2023 from https://doi.org/10.2458/azu_jaei_v05i1_yoshimur

56 Brier, Morabito & Greene (2020), 83–99.

57 See Bashir & Emberling in Emberling & Beyer Williams (eds) (2021), 995–1014.

58 Luiselli (2014), 105–16.

59 Herodotus, *Histories* II.148.

60 Herodotus, *Histories* II.124.

61 Herodotus, *Histories* II.126.

62 Herodotus, *Histories* II.125. The ancient equivalent of £5 million was 1,600 silver talents – a huge sum when we consider that a talent was roughly a month's wage.

63 Strabo, *Geography* XVII.1.33.

64 Pliny the Elder, *The Natural History* XXXVI.17.

65 *Itinerarium Egeriae*, trans. Wilkinson (2015).

66 Dale in Pendergast & Del Alamo (2000), 53–104.

67 Darke (2020), 234.

68 Violet Moller (2019), 'Power And Curiosity: How The Abbasid Caliph Al-Mamun Pushed The Boundaries Of Scientific Knowledge', retrieved 18

December 2022 from https://cvhf.org.uk/history-hub/writing/power-and-curiosity-how-the-abbasid-caliph-al-mamun-pushed-the-boundaries-of-scientific-knowledge/

69 Okasha El-Daly, *Egyptology: The Missing Millennium* (2005) UCL Press, 47 and 87.

70 Al-Maqrizi, *Description topograpique et historique de l'Égypte*, trans. Bouriant (1895).

71 The Greeks in turn called the Egyptian god Thoth Hermes.

72 Ogier VIII, Seigneur d'Anglure, wrote about the construction of mediaeval Cairo in *The Holy Jerusalem Voyage*. Though it is highly likely that the limestone from Khufu's Pyramid was used for the Alabaster Mosque, there is little conclusive evidence to support this. See also Lightbody (2016), 39–56.

73 See Butler's 2018 edit of John Greaves' writings for further detail; see also Shalev (2002), 555–75.

74 Newton's autographed manuscript notes have been auctioned off at Sotheby's, but pictures of the manuscripts can be viewed online.

75 Nathaniel Davison's journals were collated in Walpole (1817).

76 Taylor (1859).

77 Isaiah XL:8 (KJV), retrieved 15 December 2022 from https://www.biblegateway.com/passage/?search=Isaiah+40&version=KJV

78 Pyramid Texts of Unas 267.

79 The plateau Akhet Khufu.

CHAPTER 2: THE HANGING GARDENS OF BABYLON

1 Plutarch, *Alexander* V.1.

2 Plutarch, *Alexander* V.1

3 Herodotus, *Histories* I.179.

4 *Anth. Pal.* IX.58.

5 Dalley (1993), 7.

6 The walls of Babylon were on the original list compiled by Antipater of Sidon (*Anth. Pal.* IX.58), displacing Alexandria's Lighthouse in the list of seven.

7 Plutarch, *Alexander* LXXII.2.

8 Herodotus, *Histories* I.179.

9 Most notably, the second book of Diodorus Siculus' *Library of History* used material taken from Ctesias' *Persika*.

10 Cleitarchus' *History of Alexander* is not an extant work, but Strabo drew on his writings frequently, something he often mentions. The information on the mechanics of the Hanging Gardens can be found in Strabo, *Geography* XVI.5.

11 Diodorus Siculus, *Library of History* II.10.

12 Strabo, *Geography* XVI.1.5.

13 Strabo, *Geography* XV.1.18–20.

14 Plutarch, *Alexander* LXIV.

15 Josephus, *Against Apion* I.139, 141 & *Jewish Antiquities* X.224, 226.

16 The words of Berossus were summarised by Josephus in his *Against Apion*.

17 Josephus, *Against Apion* I.19.

18 Ctesias' *Persika* was quoted by Plutarch in his *Regum et imperatorum apophthegmata*.

19 Barker (2000), in Barker & Gilbertson, 63–85.

20 Köcher (1959), 236–40; Wiseman (1983), 138.

21 Langgut, Finklestein & Litt (2013), 149–75; Bogaard et al. (2018), 303–22; Laugier et al. (2021), 38.

22 Genesis I:28 (ESV), retrieved 15 December 2022 from https://www.biblegateway.com/passage/?search=Genesis+1&version=ESV

23 Roberts et al. (2018), 1871–8.

24 Epic of Gilgamesh, Tablet IV details the journey to the Forest of Cedar.

25 Daniel Robert Bertoni (2014), 'The Cultivation and Conceptualization of Exotic Plants in the Greek and Roman Worlds', doctoral dissertation, particularly section 3.2, retrieved 16 December 2022 from http://nrs.harvard.edu/urn-3:HUL.InstRepos:12269841

26 Plants, People, Planet, 'Persia & Islam', retrieved 18 December 2022 from https://plantspeopleplanet.org.au/01/k1/k2/k10/. Cf. Arrian, *Anabasis* VI.29, where Persian kings such as Cyrus loved nature so much that his tomb was surrounded by gardens.

27 With particular thanks to Stephanie Dalley and her fascinating 2013 monograph *Mystery of The Hanging Garden of Babylon – An Elusive World Wonder Traced*.

28 Frahm (2003), 129–64.

29 2 Kings XXIV–XXV contains the story of Nebuchadnezzar capturing Judah, sacking Jerusalem, and taking the Jewish people into exile in Babylon. Throughout the Old Testament, Nebuchadnezzar is mentioned numerous times – if you wish to track his presence, he can be found in 1 Chronicles VI, 2 Chronicles XXXVI, Ezra I–VI, Nehemiah VII, Esther II, Jeremiah XXI–LII, Ezekiel XXVI–XXX and Daniel I–V. Though Nebuchadnezzar is not mentioned by name in the New Testament, the deportation to Babylon is mentioned in Matthew I.

30 Brisa Neo-Babylonian Inscription at Wadi El-Sharbin, see Da Riva (2013), 87–100.

31 Russell (1997), 300.

32 Col. vi, lines 15–27.

33 Heidel (1953), 117; col. vi, lines 39–65.

34 Diodorus Siculus, *Library of History* II.10.3.

35 BM 118802, retrieved 18 December 2022 from https://www.britishmuseum.
    org/collection/object/W_1851-0902-509

36 Philo of Byzantium, *On the Seven Wonders of the World* I.

37 Philo himself wrote a vivid description of this irrigation system.

38 Frothingham & Marquand (1896), 115.

39 Depuydt (1997), 117–35.

40 Frahm (2008), 13–20.

41 BM 129397, retrieved 9 January 2023 from https://www.britishmuseum.org/
    collection/object/W_1938-0520-1

42 These actions are recounted on the Prism of Sennacherib, BM 91032, re-
    trieved 9 January 2023 from https://www.britishmuseum.org/collection/
    object/W_1855-1003-1

43 Fales & del Fabbro (2014), 73.

44 Luckenbill (1924), 17; Frahm (2008), 14; Reade (1978), 47–72.

45 Dalley (2013), *The Mystery of the Hanging Garden of Babylon*. Reproduced
    with permission of The Licensor through PLSclear.

46 BM 91032, retrieved 18 December 2022 from https://www.britishmuseum.
    org/collection/object/W_1855-1003-1

47 From a stone tablet of Sargon II. For further detail see Dalley (2013). Re-
    produced with permission of The Licensor through PLSclear. Also 43. Bowe
    (2015), 165 remarks that the reference to Amanus might have been a generic
    rather than specific term.

48 Col. vii, lines 7–52.

49 Prism of Sennacherib, trans. Dalley (2013). Reproduced with permission of
    The Licensor through PLSclear.

50 Trans. Radner (2012), 692. For more on the inscription see Russell (2021),
    276–7.

51 Fales & del Fabbro (2014), 65–98.

52 Van De Mieroop (2004), 1–5.

53 BM 124874, retrieved 18 December 2022 from https://www.britishmuseum.
    org/collection/object/W_1856-0909-48_8

54 Brereton (2018), passim.

55 Diodorus Siculus, *Library of History* II.10.

56 BM 46226, retrieved 18 December 2022 from https://www.britishmuseum.
    org/collection/object/W_1881-0706-688

57 *Epic of Gilgamesh*, Tablet IV describes the expedition to the salt-cedar
    forest.

58 Diodorus Siculus, *Library of History* II.10.5, trans. Oldfather (1933).

59 This is a common Persian proverb.

60 Wee (2014), 23–42; Monroe (2019); Bodi (2021), 19–36.

61 Quoted in Campion (2012), 124–34.

62 See Rawlinson (2014), passim.

63   'The Lady of the Evening' can be found in Wolkstein, D. & Kramer, S. N. (1983).

64   BM 124798, a relief wall panel from the time of Sennacherib, depicting servants carrying birds, hares and dried locusts. Retrieved 28 September 2023 https://www.britishmuseum.org/collection/object/W_1851-0902-11

65   Peled (2013), 785–98; Yalçin (2016), 121–50.

66   Sennacherib's cylinder (cylinder no. 103000), col. v, lines 52–56.

67   The Met's collection contains a cuneiform tablet that details the proxy contract for the purchase of a slave in the Egibi archive. It is a good indicator of harsh attitudes towards slavery during this period, retrieved 30 October 2023 from https://www.metmuseum.org/art/collection/search/321533

68   The deportation to Babylon and the destruction of the temple in Jerusalem is told in 2 Kings XXIV–XXV. Nebuchadnezzar sending Daniel into the lions' den can be found in Daniel VI.

69   Psalm CXXXVII (ESV), retrieved 15 December 2022 from https://www.biblegateway.com/passage/?search=Psalms+137&version=ESV

70   BM 124920, retrieved 18 December 2022 from https://www.britishmuseum.org/collection/object/W_1856-0909-53

71   Roth (1989), No.9; Kuhrt (1995), 610.

72   Stol (2016); Raign (2019), 338–64.

73   Dalley (1993), 3.

74   Halton & Svärd (2018), 150.

75   Dalley (2013), 36.

76   See Melville (2014), 228–40; Dalley (2013).

77   Siddall (2014), 497–504.

78   Chariton, trans. Goold, G.P. (1995) was one of the first novels.

79   Leichty (2011), 199, 207.

80   *Epic of Gilgamesh*, Tablet I.9–22.

81   'Tower of Babel Stele' published in Andrew George, *Cuneiform Royal Inscriptions and Related Texts in the Schøyen Collection*, Cornell University Studies in Assyriology and Sumerology, vol. 17, Manuscripts in the Schøyen Collection, Cuneiform texts VI. CDL Press, Bethesda, MD, 2011, text 76, pp. 153-169, pls. LVIII-LXVII.

82   Aristotle, *Politics* III.1.12. The British Museum in London alone has 41 objects which come from Babylon's Ishtar Gate: these can be explored at https://www.britishmuseum.org/collection/term/x32759 (retrieved 19 December 2022).

83   Nebuchadnezzar inscription on walls of Babylon, lines 54–60.

84   Herodotus, *Histories* I.178. For Ctesias' opinion on Babylon's walls, see Bigwood (2017), 32–52. Cleitarchus' *History of Alexander* is now lost, but it was paraphrased in Diodorus Siculus, *Library of History* II.7.3–5.

85   Judith I:1 (GNT), retrieved 15 December 2022 from https://

www.biblegateway.com/passage/?search=Judith%20I&version=GNT

86   Azize (2002), 1–26; Campion (2012), 124–34; Feldt (2016), 347–82; Lund-bom (2017), 154–66.

87   *Homeric Hymn XXX to Gaia*. Evelyn-White (1914) translates this line as 'Through you, O queen, men are blessed in their children and blessed in their harvests, and to you it belongs to give means of life to mortal men and to take it away', while West (2003) writes, 'From you they become fertile in children and in crops, mistress, and it depends on you to give livelihood or take it away from mortal men'. The destructive, ructious aspect of Gaia is also alluded to in Hesiod, *Theogony* 158–66, where Gaia shares her evil plan to castrate Ouranos with her sons; it appears, too, in Hesiod, *Works and Days* 121, 140, 156, where different Ages of Man are covered by the earth – destroyed by their creator. Previous translations of Homeric Hymn XXX perhaps do not sufficiently convey the vengeful side of Gaia, which has been attempted in the author's translation. We must remember that the audience of the Homeric Hymns lived in much closer proximity to nature, and were no stranger to Gaia's destructive outbursts, which we now call natural disasters. The idea that Gaia would be willing to take life away from humans was not foreign to an ancient audience. Indeed, many of them may have lost family members to an earthquake or landslide, a rumbling of Gaia. Let us also not forget what Gaia meant to the Greeks – she was not just the goddess of the earth, but the earth itself. Humans were building lives on the earth; they were, quite literally, weighing on her, so they were a natural burden. This burden, which weighed on Gaia, could force her to take drastic action – the flood story in Ovid's Metamorphoses I shows us how the ancient Greeks and Romans understood this outburst of Gaia's latent rage.

88   Van De Mieroop (2004), 1–5, Dalley (2008), 25–33.

89   Genesis XI.1–9 (NIV), retrieved 17 December 2022 from https://www.biblegateway.com/passage/?search=genesis+11&version=NIV

90   New evidence from the tomb of an unknown soldier in Amphipolis, northern Greece, shows the monogram of Hephaestion – this was a man who was meant to be remembered across the Empire.

91   Plutarch, *Alexander*, LXXIII–end.

92   Tacitus described Nero's Golden House as such in his *Annals* XV.42.1.

93   Dr Robert Koldewey's dig at Babylon which began in 1899 was threatened by the British Expeditionary Force shelling Baghdad.

94   Boardman (2002), 186.

95   Cylinders of Nabonidus.

96   The story of the Tower of Babel appears in Genesis XI.1–9, while the Whore of Babylon appears in Revelation XVII.

97   Quintus Curtius Rufus, *History of Alexander* I.5.1.31–35.

CHAPTER 3: THE TEMPLE OF ARTEMIS AT EPHESUS

1   Antipater of Sidon, *Anth. Pal.* IX.58.
2   Damnatio memoriae; see entry in Smith (1849).
3   Theopompus' account of the leak can be found in his *Philippica*; see also Flower (1997) and Borowitz (2005).
4   Plutarch, *Alexander* III.3.
5   Plutarch, *Alexander* III.4.
6   Valerius Maximus, *Facta et Dicta Memorabilia* VIII.14.5.
7   Chaucer, *House of Fame* III.1843–1845.
8   Miguel de Cervantes (1615), *Don Quixote* Part II.8.
9   Colley Cibber (1699), *Richard III* Act III.1.
10 Jean Paul Sartre (1939), *Erostratus*.
11 Speech of 6 October 1939, retrieved 17 December 2022 from https://hitler.org/speeches/10-06-39.html
12 Herodotus, *Histories* II.73 mentions the phoenix as a real bird which he has not seen but is sacred to the Egyptians; he does not mention the regeneration of the phoenix, or its link to ashes, which presumably was a later invention.
13 The British Museum alone holds 1,319 objects from the Temple of Artemis. A list can be explored at https://www.britishmuseum.org/collection/term/x31276 (retrieved 17 December 2022).
14 ISAISC Editorial Board (2020), 'Australian Archaeologists Discover the Course of Achaemenid Royal Road near Persepolis', retrieved 19 December 2022 from https://isaisc.com/the-discovery-of-the-ancient-royal-road-near-persepolis/
15 Bammer & Muss (2007), 95–101; Muss (2007), 167–94; Bachvarova (2016), passim.
16 Gantz (1996), 26–7.
17 Clayton & Price (1989), 160–65.
18 Ovid, *Metamorphoses* III.155–6.
19 Kraft et al. (2007), 121–49.
20 Homer, *Odyssey* VI.162–7.
21 Lidonnici (1992), 389–411.
22 Pliny the Elder, *The Natural History* XXXVI.97.
23 Pliny the Elder, *The Natural History* XXXVI.97.
24 Pliny The Elder, *The Natural History* XXXVI.21.
25 Livy, *History of Rome* I.48.
26 Croesus minted coins in electrum, gold and silver: there are no examples yet of an image of Artemis on a gold or silver coin, but during excavations at the site at the beginning of the twentieth century, a hoard of electrum coins were discovered as offerings left to Artemis, so there is a good chance

that there was coinage which depicted the goddess. For more on the coins retrieved from the site, see Robinson (1951), 156–67; Kraay (1976), 20–26.

27 Ramage & Craddock (1999), passim.

28 Herodotus, *Histories* I.26.

29 Leloux (2018), 47–64. See also Lethaby (1917), 1–16.

30 Nicolaus of Damascus FrGH901, F65.3; Ael VH 3.26.

31 Melcher et al. (2009), 169–75.

32 Bammer (1990), 137–60; Wallace (2016), 168–81; Leloux (2018), 47–64.

33 Pliny the Elder, *The Natural History* XXXVI.21.

34 Herodotus, *Histories* III.60.

35 For an expansion of this idea, see Haynes (2022).

36 Herodotus, *Histories* I.87.

37 Herodotus, *Histories* I.214.

38 This myth became the plot of Euripides' *Iphigenia in Tauris.*

39 Pausanias, *Descriptions of Greece* VII.5.4–9 mentions wooden images of gods as well as temples being considered wonders even after destruction by fire.

40 An example of the animal figurines found at the sanctuary of Artemis at Ephesus is the bronze figure of a duck on display at the British Museum (1907,1201.258), retrieved 10 April 2023 from https://www.britishmuseum.org/collection/object/G_1907-1201-258.

41 For more information on the amber found at Ephesus, see A. Naso (2013) 'Amber for Artemis: Preliminary Report on the Amber Finds from the Sanctuary of Artemis at Ephesos', *Jahreshefte Des Österreichischen Archäologischen Institutes In Wien*, 82, 259-278.

42 Harissis (2009), passim.

43 Zabrana (2019), 158–70. In Pseudo-Apollodorus, *Bibliotheca* III.33, Dionysos was said to have visited Kybele in Phrygia, where she purified him and taught him the rite of initiation into the mysteries. Strabo tells the myth in *Geography* X.3.13, which mentions that Euripides depicted the two deities together in his *Bacchae*. The Silver Age poet Nonnus in his *Dionysiaca* gives a slightly different version, which presents Dionysus being cared for in Nysa by Kybele and nymphs.

44 Moreno in Ma et al. (2009), 211–21.

45 Cole (1998), 24–41.

46 Mayor (2014), 310–12.

47 Garland (2014), passim; Isayev (2017), 75–98.

48 Callimachus, *Hymn to Artemis* 237–9.

49 The fetishisation of Amazons in drama is most potently captured by Euripides in his tragedy *The Bacchae*; for the appearance of Amazons on vase paintings, see Mayor (2014), 152.

50 Autocartes Tympanistai fr. 1 – referenced in Aelian, *On the Nature of Animals* XII.9.

51 Claimed by Pindar fr. 174, disputed by Pausanias VII.2.7.

52 As dramatised by Euripides in his *Iphigeneia in Tauris* and *Iphigeneia in Aulis*.

53 The story of Polyxena's sacrifice was dramatised by Euripides in his *Hecuba*.

54 For the story of Orion, see Graves (2012), 132–6. The story of Artemis and Actaeon can be found in Ovid, *Metamorphoses* III.131–250.

55 Collon (2003), 96–102; Gabbay (2003); 103–5; Lykesas et al. (2017), 161–70.

56 Homer, *Iliad* V.53.

57 Wankel (1979), 1a.2.

58 Pliny the Elder, *The Natural History* XXXIV.53.

59 Pausanias, *Descriptions of Greece* IV.31.8, trans. Jones (1918).

60 Strabo, *Geography* XIV.1.23.

61 Ovid, *Metamorphoses* I.688–711.

62 Homer, *Iliad* XVI.179–86.

63 Sissa (1990), passim.

64 Penrose (2016), 100.

65 Pausanias, *Description of Greece*; Pliny the Elder, *The Natural World* XXXVIII.21; Lethaby (1913), 87–96; Lethaby (1916) 25–35.

66 Acts XIX:35 (ESV), retrieved 15 December 2022 from https://www.biblegateway.com/passage/?search=Acts+19&version=ESV

67 Melcher, Schreiner, Bühler, Pülz & Muss (2009), 'Investigation of ancient gold objects from Artemision at Ephesus using portable μ-XRF', retrieved 18 December 2022 from https://doi.org/10.4000/archeosciences.2172

68 Elinor Bevan (1985), 'Representations of animals in sanctuaries of Artemis and of other Olympian deities', retrieved 18 December 2022 from http://hdl.handle.net/1842/6862

69 Athenaeus, *The Learned Banqueters*, Vol VI: Books 12–13.594b. Olson, S. D. (2010) p. 73.

70 See Arnold (1972), 17–22 for distinctions between the two.

71 Stoneman (2011), 137.

72 Thucydides, *The Peloponnesian War* III.104.3.

73 Henderson (2009), *Longus, Daphnis and Chloe; Xenophon of Ephesus, Anthia and Habrocomes*, p.219.

74 Reinberger et al. (2021).

75 Plutarch, *Alexander* III.3.

76 Xenophon, *Ephesiaca* I.3.1, trans. Henderson (2009).

77 Arrian, *Anabasis* I.17.10–12. Cf. Nawotka (2003), 15–41; Garland (2014), 262–3; Kholod (2016), 495–525.

78 Price, S. (1999). *Religions of the Ancient Greeks (Key Themes in Ancient History)*, p. 181.

79 Zabrana (2019), 158–70.

80 Plutarch, *Antony* XXV–XXVI.

81 Plutarch, *Antony* XXIV.
82 Strabo, *Geography* XIV.1.23.
83 Strabo, *Geography* XIV.1.20. It is no coincidence that Marcus Terrentius Varro, a one-time supporter of Pompey and his campaigns, wrote, 'Seven works to be marvelled at in the world'.
84 Karya Naz Balkiz (2021), 'Turkey's gladiator graves tell a different story about the ancient warriors', retrieved 18 December 2022 from https://www. trtworld.com/magazine/turkey-s-gladiator-graves-tell-a-different-story-about-the-ancient-warriors-50717. See also Monika Kupper & Huw Jones (2007), 'Gladiators' graveyard discovered', retrieved 18 December 2022 from http://news.bbc.co.uk/1/hi/sci/tech/6614479.stm. For further information see Kanz & Karl (2009), 211–20.
85 Tacitus, *Annals* III.61.
86 *British Muslim Magazine*, 'The House of Maryam Ephesus, Turkey', retrieved 18 December 2022 from https://www.britishmuslim-magazine. com/2017/06/the-house-of-maryam-ephesus-turkey/. See also *Turkish Archaeological News* (2019), 'House of the Virgin Mary in Ephesus', retrieved 18 December 2022 from https://turkisharchaeonews.net/object/house-virgin-mary-ephesus. See also Abu Huzaifa, 'Maqam of Maryam', retrieved 18 December 2022 from https://www.islamiclandmarks.com/palestine-jerusalem/maqam-of-maryam-as. See also Bawany (2012), 35–43.
87 Foss (1979), passim.
88 Huneberc's Hodoeporicon – see https://sourcebooks.fordham.edu/basis/ willibald.asp, retrieved 19 December 2022.
89 Yilmaz (2015), 192–220.
90 Acts XIX:28 (ESV), retrieved 15 December 2022 from https:// www.biblegateway.com/passage/?search=Acts+19&version=ESV
91 Merkelbach & Stauber (1996), no.11; Graf, F. (2002), 'Pedestals of the Gods', *Zeitschrift Fur Papyrologie Und Epigraphik* 141: 137–8.

CHAPTER 4: THE STATUE OF ZEUS AT OLYMPIA

1 Hesiod, Pindar *Paean* XII. *Homeric Hymn 3 to Apollo* also mentions the account of Leto's rape and the birth of her children, but Artemis does not feature.
2 Karim Arafat (2016), 'Zeus in art', *Oxford Classical Dictionary*, tells us that Zeus did not assume a type until the early archaic period; retrieved 18 December 2022 from https://doi.org/10.1093/acrefore/9780199381135.013.6950. See also Kerényi (2015), 24–30, who asserts that Zeus, along with Hera and other gods, are mentioned in texts as early as 1300 BCE. The idea of a fixed twelve-god pantheon is not attested in Greek culture before 522 BCE,

when an altar of the twelve gods was set up in the agora at Athens by the archon Peisistratos, son of Hippias, and grandson of Peisistratos the tyrant; this account can be found in Thucydides, *History of The Peloponnesian War* VI.54.6–7.

3 Thucydides, *History of The Peloponnesian War* V.49–50; Romano (1985), 15–16.

4 Crowther (2001), 42.

5 Casson (1994), passim.

6 Georgios Kedrenos Historiarum Compendium I, in Bekker & Scylitzes (eds) (1838), 564. See also a discussion of these fossils in Mayor (2000), 99.

7 Pausanias, *Description of Greece* VI.4.8.

8 The Work of the Ephorate of Antiquities of Ilia 2015–2017, Ministry of Culture and Sport, General Directorate of Antiquities and Cultural Heritage, Ephorate of Antiquities of Ilia, 2017/18.

9 Thommen (2012), 30ff.

10 Lysias, *Olympic Oration* XXXIII.2.

11 Pindar, *Olympian* III.11–15.

12 Pindar, *Olympian* III.11–15.

13 Thommen (2012), 37–41.

14 Visit to the festival of the Yoni, Kamakhya Temple, Assam, India, 2011.

15 Pausanias, *Description of Greece* V.14.2.

16 Van Andel & Runnels (1995), 481–500; Retallack (2008), 642.

17 Pausanias, *Description of Greece* V.10.3.

18 A good eyewitness account for technicalities of the altar in the hecatomb ritual is Pausanias V.13.8–11. See also Taita (2015), 112–39.

19 Barringer et al. (2005), passim.

20 Ashmole & Yalouris (1967) contains an excellent description of the sculptural decoration on the Temple of Zeus at Olympia, along with high-quality photographs which show clearly the intensity of emotion on these sculptural friezes.

21 Faulkner (2012), 50ff.

22 Pausanias, *Description of Greece* V.11.1.

23 Homer, *Iliad* I.528–30.

24 For an understanding of Greek statuary, see Spivey (2013), passim; Rawson (2018), 17–31; Vout (2018), chapter 2; Palagia (2019b).

25 Keesling (2017), 98–9, 198–9.

26 An identification aided by a passage from Pausanias, *Description of Greece* V.15.1, which specified that Pheidias' workshop was just outside the sanctuary of Zeus.

27 See Sinn (2004), 225–7.

28 The cup is displayed in the Olympia Archaeological Museum, No. 3653.

29 Pausanias, *Description of Greece* V.10.2.

30 Mallwitz & Schiering (1964); Schiering (1991), passim; Davison (2009), 344–7; Palagia (2019b), 349–51.

31 Herodotus, *Histories* I.1, trans. Waterfield (2008).

32 Thucydides, *History of the Peloponnesian War* I.22.4 does not conclusively prove that Thucydides witnessed Herodotus' work being read to a crowd, but his rigorous explanation of his methods seems to imply that he had a good understanding of Herodotus' work and had possibly experienced a public reading of it.

33 Homer, *Iliad* XXIII.272–86.

34 Heraclides Ponticus, *On Oracles* F.130–41, trans. Wehrli (1953).

35 Homer, *Iliad* I.458–66.

36 See Baitinger in Giangiulio, Franchi & Proietti (eds) (2019), 131–45.

37 Homer, *Iliad* XXIII is the epitome of ancient Greek funerary games, held to commemorate the death of Patroclus. Virgil, *Aeneid* V is also a description of funeral games for Anchises – this seems to have been an intentional echo of Homer, and does not necessarily mean that funeral games were a tradition replicated in Rome.

38 The Open University, 'Day Three: Sacrifices (Hecatomb) and feast' in 'The Ancient Olympics: bridging past and present', retrieved 18 December 2022 from https://www.open.edu/openlearn/history-the-arts/the-ancient-olympics-bridging-past-and-present/content-section-7

39 The Stoic philosopher Empedocles is said to have offered a bull made of dough and decorated with herbs; see Antikas (2004) and Kingsley (1995), who explains the link between Empedocles and Pythagorean customs.

40 Barringer (2021), 29.

41 Baitinger & Volling (2007), 66.

42 Homer, *Iliad* I.467–73, trans. Fagles (1991). (N.B.: the line numbers are different in Fagles' verse translation – the line reference in his translation is I.557–63.)

43 Nordquist (1996), 241–56. See also Eckstein in Wissemann (ed.) (1988), 52–64.

44 Lucian, *Herodotus*, or *Aetion* 1; cf. Johnson (1994), 240–42 and Ian Cody Oliver (2017), thesis entitled 'The Audiences of Herodotus: the Influence of Performance on the Histories', 136–48, retrieved 19 January 2023 from https://scholar.colorado.edu/concern/graduate_thesis_or_dissertations/1v53jx019

45 Homer, *Odyssey* XIV.5–10.

46 Plutarch, *Alcibiades* XI.2, trans. Scott-Kilvert (1965).

47 Lucian, *The Passing of Peregrinus*, trans. Harmon, A. M. (1936).

48 Pliny, *The Natural History* XXXIV.16 and Lucian, *Pro Eikonibus* XI.

49 Penn Museum, 'The Women: Were the Ancient Olympics just for Men?', retrieved 18 December 2022 from https://www.penn.museum/sites/olympics/olympicsexism.shtml

50 Pausanias, *Description of Greece* V.6.20.

51 For a fascinating overview of the life story of the Olympia site, see Barringer (2021).

52 Pausanias, *Description of Greece* V.16.2.

53 Hugh M. Lee (2004), 'Stadia and Starting Gates', retrieved 18 December 2022 from https://archive.archaeology.org/online/features/olympics/stadia.html. See also Steve Haake (2016), 'Sports engineering is 2,300 years old', retrieved 18 December 2022 from https://engineeringsport.co.uk/2016/06/28/sports-engineering-is-2500-years-old/. See also Minetti & Ardigó (2002), 141–2. Pausanias, *Description of Greece* V.16.2 mentions that a robe was woven.

54 Pausanias, *Description of Greece* V.16.6.

55 Pausanias, *Descripiton of Greece* V.16.3.

56 Sneed (2020), 1015–29.

57 Pliny the Elder, *Natural History* 7.37.1.

58 Sneed (2020), 1018.

59 Geroulanos (1994), passim.

60 Rose (2003), passim; Penrose (2015), 499–523.

61 See Siewert & Taeubur (2013), 118–19, no. 69 (Olympia inv. 848).

62 Garland (2010), particularly ch 4.

63 McCoskey (2012); for further information on the topic of race and diversity in the ancient world, see Kennedy, Roy & Goldman (2013).

64 Thucydides, *History of the Peloponnesian War* II.47–55.

65 Thucydides, *History of the Peloponnesian War* II.49–52.

66 Thucydides, *History of the Peloponnesian War* II.65.3–6; Hughes (2010), 199–200. See also Hughes (2010), 154–8 for further detail on the plague of 430–428 BCE.

67 A Hellenistic Greek bronze statuette of an African man. Held in the Metropolitan Museum of Art, accession number 18.145.10. Retrieved 28 September 2023 https://www.metmuseum.org/art/collection/search/250673.

68 1 Maccabees I:41–59 has an account of Antiochus IV's imposition of pagan religion on the Jewish people. 1 Maccabees I:54 (GNT) vividly describes the Statue of Olympian Zeus as 'The Awful Horror'. Retrieved 15 December 2022 from https://www.biblegateway.com/passage/?search=1+Maccabees+1&version=GNT

69 1 Maccabees 23–24, Josephus, *Antiquities of the Jews* XII 5.2, Pausanias, *Descripiton of Greece* V.12.4 and C. Clermont Ganneau (1878) *The Veil of the Temple of Jerusalem at Olympia*, Palestine Exploration Quarterly, 10:2, 79-81, DOI: 10.1179/peq.1878.10.2.79.

70 Pausanias, *Description of Greece* V.11.

71 Suetonius, *Life of Caligula* 57.

72 Suetonius, *Life of Nero* 23–5.

73 Lucian, *Timon 4*.

74 Publius Herennius Dexippus, an Athenian historian, whose works 'Chronicle' and 'Scythian History' have only survived in fragments. Further info in Chioti (2021), 319–39.

75 Universität Mainz (2011), 'Olympia hypothesis: Tsunamis buried the cult site on the Peloponnese', retrieved 18 December 2022 from https://www.sciencedaily.com/releases/2011/07/110710204240.htm.

76 Bassett (2000), 6–25; Davison (2009), 349–51.

77 An account of the fire can be found in Bury, J.B. (1923). Bill Thayer (ed.). *History of the Later Roman Empire from the Death of Theodosius I to the Death of Justinian*, 393–394.

78 John of Damascus, *De Imaginibus Oratio* III.387.

CHAPTER 5: THE MAUSOLEUM OF HALIKARNASSOS

1 Herodotus, *Histories* I.171.

2 Goddio & Masson-Berghoff (2016), 37–9.

3 Homer, *Iliad* II.872, trans. Murray (1924).

4 Xenophon, *Agesilaus* II.26.

5 Vitruvius, *On Architecture* II.8.10.

6 Vitruvius, *On Architecture* II.8.10.

7 Bean et al. (1955), 85–171.

8 Vitruvius, *De Architectura* VII. Preface. 12.

9 Hornblower (1982), 225–34; 240–44.

10 Ashmole (1972), 157 is close to confidently identifying the statue as Mausolos, noting that the portrait features bear a resemblance to his coinage on Kos.

11 Vitruvius, *On Architecture* II.8.

12 Jenkins et al. (2015), 30–38.

13 BM EA67235, retrieved 18 December 2022 from https://www.britishmuseum.org/collection/object/Y_EA67235. For further information about this stele, see Emery (1970), 5.

14 *Laterculi Alexandrini* VII.3ff.

15 Herodotus, *Histories* I.1, trans. Holland (2014).

16 One shining example of Herodotus choosing to depict Xerxes favourably is his report of the king being mistaken for Zeus by a local man, which can be read in *Histories* VII.56.

17 Herodotus, *Histories* III.38, trans. Holland (2014).

18 The word *philobarbaros* was first used as an insult against Herodotus by Plutarch in *De Herodoti malignitate* 857a.

19 Alexander's visit to this tomb, and the inscription on the tomb, are recorded

by Arrian in *Anabasis* VI.29.5–8; Plutarch in *Alexander* LXIX.3; and Strabo in *Geography* XV.3.7.

20   Stronach (1978), passim.

21   Thucydides, *History of the Peloponnesian War* I.8.1.

22   Bianchi (1993), 54–5; Pausanias, *Description of Greece*.

23   Schmid (2013), 303–20.

24   Henry & Belgin-Henry (2020), 308–9, 353; Pedersen (2015), 153–66.

25   Jeppesen & Zahle (1973), 336–8; Jeppesen & Zahle (1975), 67–79.

26   Henry & Belgin-Henry (eds) (2020), passim.

27   The Bisitun inscription is a good example of what the Persian king expected to receive from his subjects; Herodotus, *Histories* III.89 also has an interesting account of the satrapies in the Achaemenid Empire and explains the taxation system in Persia.

28   Mylasa 114, Packard Humanities Institute Greek inscriptions database, retrieved 10 April 2023 from https://inscriptions.packhum.org/text/261043?bookid=512&location=1682

29   Herodotus, *Histories* VIII.93.

30   Aristophanes, *Lysistrata* 671–9.

31   Polyaenus, *Strategems* VIII.53.2.

32   Polyaenus, *Strategems* VIII.53.4.

33   Ignatiadou (2013), 183.

34   Aulus Gellius XVIII.3.

35   BM 1847,0424.19, retrieved 18 December 2022 from https://www.british museum.org/collection/object/G_1847-0424-19

36   Arrian, *Anabasis* I.23.7–8.

37   Plutarch, *Alexander* LXXII.5; Diodorus Siculus, *Library of History* XVII.115.5.

38   Herodotus, *Histories* I.207, trans. Holland (2014).

39   Weitzmann (1951), passim.

40   Lummus (2017), 464–5; Mo (2017), 23–35.

41   Bishop Eustathius is the last known commentator on the Mausoleum as a 'wonder of the world', in his commentary on the *Iliad* in the twelfth century. See Newton & Pullan (1862), 73. And pioneering work by Antony Makrinos.

42   Boccaccio, *De Mulieribus Claris* LV.

43   Brown (2021), 413–32.

44   Carr (2016), 99–100.

45   Romer (1995), 94.

46   Newton & Pullan (1862), 74–9.

47   DuBois (1991), passim.

48   Poole (1959), 133.

49   Ovid, *Metamorphoses* IV.285–388.

50   George Seferis, 'Memory II' (1969), op.cit: 373.

51 Bremen (2007), 113–32; Berthold (2009), 76–97.

CHAPTER 6: THE COLOSSUS OF RHODES

1 Pliny the Elder, *Natural History* XXXVI.16, XXXVI.20 and XXXVI.21 for the historian's description of the Great Pyramids, Hanging Gardens of Babylon and Temple of Artemis at Ephesus respectively.

2 The ancient accounts of the Colossus' size differ. Strabo in *Geography* XIV.2.5, when referring to a poem by an unknown author (presumably third century BCE), gives a height of 70 cubits, or 32.3 metres, echoed by Pliny in the *Natural History* XXXIV.18 and Philo of Byzantium (c. fourth–fifth centuries CE) in *On the Seven Wonders* IV. Pseudo-Hyginus in *Fabulae* 223 says it is 90 feet high, or 26.6 metres, while Pseudo-Bede in *On the Seven Wonders* puts it at 136 Roman feet, or 40.2 metres.

3 Stiros & Blackman (2014), 114–20; Howell et al. (2015), 459–74.

4 Maglio (2013), 1233–40; Stiros & Blackman (2014), 114–20; Kebric (2019a), 83–114.

5 Ovid, *Metamorphoses* I.746–II.400 tells the story of Phaethon, son of Helios, who takes a turn in his father's chariot, but loses control, travels too close to earth, and sets the world on fire.

6 Homer, *Odyssey* XII.352–425.

7 Arnold (1936), 432–6; Yiannakis (1997), 200–206.

8 *Ath. Mitt* XXV.107.

9 Although according to Ovid, *Metamorphoses* I.754–74, the nymph who mothered Phaethon was called Clymene – this was also her name in Euripides' lost tragedy *Phaethon* and in the Silver Age poet Nonnus' work *Dionysiaca*.

10 Pliny the Elder, *The Natural History* XXXIV.42.

11 Zimmer in Panagiotaki, Tomazos & Papadimitrakopoulos (eds) (2020), 47–53.

12 Homer, *Iliad* XVIII.414–15.

13 Archelaus or Asclepiades 120, in W.R. Paton (1918), *The Greek Anthology, Volume V: Book 16: Epigrams of the Planudean Anthology Not in the Palatine Manuscript*, 227.

14 Percy Bysshe Shelley, 'Ozymandias' 11.

15 Discovered in 1897 at Hierakonopolis, the 'City of the Falcon God' south of Luxor, Pepi's burial complex, including an early pyramid, at Saqqara was *men-nefer* – which would give its name to the living city opposite, Memphis.

16 Ceccarelli (2004), passim.

17 Stiros & Blackman (2014), 114–20; Kebric (2019a) 83–114.

18 Saumasius, *De modo usurarum liber* 200.

19 Appian, *The Mithridatic Wars* IV.26, trans. White (1899).

20 Pulak et al. (1987), 31–57.

21 Berthold (2009), 56.

22 Dio Chrysostom 31.100.

23 Berthold (2009).

24 Pollitt (2000), 104.

25 Kantzia (1989), 488–523.

26 Diodorus Siculus, *Library of History* XX.100.3–4.

27 Pausanias, *Description of Greece* III.19.10; Smith (1849), 'Helen' entry.

28 Hesiod, *Theogony* 918; Hesiod, *Works and Days* 770; *Homeric Hymn 27 to Artemis*.

29 Strabo, *Geography* XIV.2.5, trans. Leonard Jones (1929).

30 Lucian, *The Way to Write History* 23; 51. Translation by Fowler, H.W. and F.G (1905), *The Works of Lucian of Samosata*, retrieved 10 April 2023 from http://lucianofsamosata.info/wiki/doku.php?id=home:texts_and_library: essays:the-way-to-write-history. See Fox (2001), 76–93.

31 Pliny the Elder, *The Natural History* XXXIV.45–7.

32 Martial, *The Epigrams* I.70.7–8.

33 Albertson (2001), 'Zenodorus's "Colossus of Nero"', 95–118, retrieved 19 December 2022 from https://doi.org/10.2307/4238781

34 Bede's 'Collecteana' (i.e. collected works), but there is serious, sustained doubt as to whether he wrote it himself. See Canter (1930), 150–64.

35 Philo of Byzantium, *On the Seven Wonders of the World* IV.1, trans. Blackwood in Ashley (1980).

36 McConnell (2018), 5726–31.

37 Crane (1974), 5–6.

38 Scobie (1990), passim; Hagen & Ostergren (2006), 157–81; Macdonald (2006a), 9–28; Macdonald (2006b), 105–26; Hagen (2008), 349–67.

39 Strabo, *Geography* II.5.7.

CHAPTER 7: THE PHAROS LIGHTHOUSE AT ALEXANDRIA

1 Fraser (1972), 18–20; Bing (1998), 21–9, *contra* Handler (1971), 60.

2 Propertius III.7.34.

3 Homer, *Odyssey* IV.382–93, trans. Fagles (2006). (N.B: the Fagles edition has different line numbers – in the Fagles translation, this section occurs at lines 428–44.)

4 Anon., *Stadiasmus of the Great Sea*, 18.

5 Homer, *Odyssey* IV.354–9.

6 Homer, *Odyssey* IV.580, trans. Rieu (1946).

7 Hughes (2005), 232. On the culture of gift-giving between royalty in the ancient world, see Hughes (2005), 120–30.

8 This is the version of the myth as set out in the opening soliloquy of Euripides' *Helen* 1–60. This version is rather different from other accounts, as Helen in the tragedy is steadfastly loyal to Menelaus and excited by the prospect of returning to Sparta with him.

9 Stesichorus wrote about Helen in Egypt, depicting her as enjoying her time there, whereas Euripides portrays it as a solitary time of misery. Stesichorus' work does not survive, but it was summarised by Dio Chrysostom in *Orations* XI.40–42. Even Herodotus has an account of Helen in Egypt in *Histories* II.112–20, although his account is not rooted in myth – he writes that Helen and Paris were kept in Proteus' palace in Memphis, not on Pharos.

10 Plutarch, *Alexander* XXVI.3–6.

11 Plutarch, *Alexander* XXVI.8–10.

12 Plutarch, *Alexander* VII–VIII.

13 Pseudo-Callisthenes, *Alexander Romance* I.30.

14 Arrian, *Anabasis* III.3–4.

15 Josephus, *The Jewish War* II.18.8; Strabo, *Geography* XVII.1.6.

16 Josephus, *The Jewish War* IV.10.5. See also McKenzie (2007), 41–5.

17 Boutsikas (2020), passim; Ker & Wessels (2020), passim.

18 Pliny, *The Natural History* XXXVI.83.

19 Statius, *Silvae* III.5.101. For a first-century CE mention of the Pharos, see Josephus, *The Jewish War* IV.10.5.

20 Lowe (2016), 147–69; Trethewey (2018), 19.

21 Aeschylus, *Agamemnon* 7–10. Homer's *Odyssey* doesn't specifically mention that the news from Troy was conveyed by flaming beacons, but Odysseus in Book VII hears a story sung by a bard about the Trojan War, while he is a visitor at Alcinous' court, which both implies how quickly news could be spread in the ancient world and how long Odysseus has been travelling.

22 Panagiotaki *et al.* in Panagiotaki, Tomazos & Papadimitrakopoulos (eds) (2020), 3–6.

23 Handler (1971), 59–61; Dunand & Adler (2013), 178–80.

24 Empereur, *Alexandria Rediscovered* (1998), 67–87.

25 Alexander was said to have been buried in the middle of Alexandria; plenty of scholars have conjectured where this might have been, a question made more difficult by the archaeology of Alexandria. There is a so-called Sarcophagus Tomb of Alexander, found near Sidon, which could have belonged to the Phoenecian Abdalonymus of Sidon, or Mazaeus, a Persian whom Alexander had appointed to govern Babylon. The tomb decoration pays vivid tribute to Alexander – shown with his trademark lion's mane headdress. Archaeologists and historians have been desperate to find some object which could give us material clues about what happened when the dynast died, which could support the literary accounts of his majestic posthumous travels from Babylon to Memphis and Alexandria. See Chugg (2002), 8–26.

26 Lowe (2016), 147–69.

27 Strabo, *Geography* XVII.1.6.
28 Trethewey (2018), chapter 5.
29 Jordan (2002), 42.
30 Proverbs XXIV.5 (KJV), retrieved 18 December 2022 from https://www. biblegateway.com/passage/?search=proverbs+24&version=KJV
31 Hero, *Pneumatika* II.XI, trans. Schmidt (1899).
32 Diodorus Siculus, *Library of History* XVII.52.5.
33 Diodorus Siculus, *Library of History* XXXIII.28B.1.
34 Diodorus Siculus, *Library of History* XXXIII.28B.2.
35 Pseudo-Seneca; see Zientek (2017), 147.
36 Caesar, *The Civil War* III.112, trans. Carter (2008), 138.
37 Caesar, *The Civil War* III.112, trans. Carter (2008), 138.
38 Pliny, *The Natural History* XXXVI.18.
39 Lucan, *Pharsalia* VIII–X.
40 Lucan, *Pharsalia* VIII.463.
41 Futuh, 40–41; McKenzie (2007), 75–8.
42 Florus, *Epitome of Roman History* II.13.88; Appian, Civil Wars II.101.
43 https://ancientcoinage.org/lighthouses-of-alexandria.html has a good selection of these coins, which are part of Mark Staal's collection. Retrieved 19 December 2022.
44 Epiphanius of Salamis, *Weights and Measures* XI.53c.
45 Chau Ju-kua, *On the Chinese and Arab Trade in the twelfth and thirteenth centuries*, trans. Hirth & Rockhill (1966).
46 *The Travels of Ibn Jubayr*, trans. Broadhurst (1952), 32–3. Okasha El Daly's work in this field is superb.
47 Clayton & Price (1989), 153–5.
48 Bloom (1990), 56; Vorderstrasse (2012), 466.
49 Ibn Faḍl Allāh al-ʿUmārī, Masālik al-abṣār fī mamālik al-amṣār, trans. Krawulsky (1986), 156ff.
50 Lucian, *How to Write History* LXII.64.

CONCLUSION

1 Fuentes (2017), introduction.
2 Heckel & Yardley (2004).

POSTSCRIPT: THE GREAT LIBRARY AT ALEXANDRIA

1 This practice is described by Galen in his *Hippocratis Epidemiorum et Galeni in illum Commentarius I* (XVII.2), trans. Kühn (1828).

2 Lockwood, J. F. et al. (2016), 'Zenodotus, of Ephesus, b. c. 325 BCE', *Oxford Classical Dictionary*, retrieved 9 January 2023 from https://doi.org/10.1093/acrefore/9780199381135.013.6941
3 Examples from Potts (2000), chapter 2.
4 Ammianus Marcellinus, XXII.11.
5 Pollard & Reid (2006), 164.
6 Plutarch, *Antony* LVIII.5.
7 See Bar-Hebraeus, trans. Wilmshurst (2016).

A NOTE ON OTHER WONDERS

1 Herodotus, *Histories* II.35, trans. Holland and Cartledge (2014).
2 Herodotus, *Histories* III.60. Where the author has chosen the word 'wonders', Holland (2014) writes 'wonder-works'; the Loeb edition (Godley, 1926) avoids wondering and chooses 'greatest works' instead.

INDEX

✛

Page numbers in *italic* refer to images